The Archaeology of Israelite Society
in Iron Age II

The Archaeology of Israelite Society
in Iron Age II

Avraham Faust

Translated by
Ruth Ludlum

Winona Lake, Indiana
Eisenbrauns
2012

Library of Congress Cataloging-in-Publication Data

Faust, Avi.
 [Hevrah ha-Yisre'elit bi-tekufat ha-melukhah. English]
 The archaeology of Israelite society in Iron Age II / Avraham Faust ; translated
 by Ruth Ludlum.
     p. cm.
 Includes bibliographical references and indexes.
 ISBN 978-1-57506-179-5 (hardback : alk. paper)
 1. Jews—History—To 586 B.C. 2. Palestine—Antiquities. 3. Palestine—
Social conditions. 4. Excavations (Archaeology)—Palestine. 5. Bible. O.T.—
Historiography. 6. Iron age—Palestine. I. Title.
 DS121.55.F3813 2012
 933'.03—dc23

                                                      2012016150

In memory of my grandfather
Josef Zvi Wallersteiner
who loved the land and the book

Contents

List of Illustrations

Maps

Graphs

Figures

Photographs

Preface and Acknowledgments

Most archaeologists in the world consider the study of ancient societies to be a major theme of archaeological inquiry. Issues such as political organization, social stratification, community organization, and family structure constitute central questions in archaeological research, and scholars take an interest in studies in these areas even if they are unrelated to the specific case studies in which they specialize. However, these research questions are remote from the topics with which most Near Eastern archaeologists must deal. In the archaeology of the land of Israel and most of the neighboring areas, archaeological research has developed as a "handmaiden" to the study of the written sources. The first archaeological work in the region was initiated in order to illustrate and understand the written sources, particularly the Bible; thus the archaeology of the land of Israel focused on questions of political/biblical history.

Furthermore, even when archaeological research ceased attempting to illustrate or "prove" the veracity of the texts and adopted a more critical approach, the questions on the agenda continued to stem from the texts. Thus, for instance, in the past decade there have been lively debates regarding the historicity and very existence of the United Monarchy; the very research question stems from the written sources rather than from the archaeological evidence, regardless of scholars' attitude toward it. As a result, the gap between the archaeology of the land of Israel and other archaeologies has deepened, and archaeologists working in Israel (excepting those studying the prehistoric era) rarely publish in general archaeology journals.

It should be stressed that the land of Israel—where there have been hundreds of planned excavations, thousands of salvage excavations and most of the country has been thoroughly surveyed—is undoubtedly a region that has been studied archaeologically much more vigorously than most other areas of the world. Thus, the archaeology of Israel could make a greater contribution to the issues that archaeologists in other regions are concerned with, since in many cases the various studies are based on poorer sets of data than we have today in Israel. However, the extensive information we possess has hardly been used to help with questions of an anthropological nature, which is a missed opportunity. In other words: the archaeological database in Israel, perhaps the richest in the world, has paradoxically not been exploited to discuss the questions that interest most of the archaeologists around the world.

This book is an attempt to use the rich archaeological information at our disposal to learn about the structure of society in the land of Israel during the period of the Monarchy, or Iron Age II. Although the study of Israelite society in this period has attracted many scholars, most of them are biblical scholars and historians, they relied mainly on the Bible to reconstruct the nature of Israelite society, and they used the archaeological findings, at most, to illuminate the conclusions arising from the biblical texts. After more than a century of archaeological study in the land of Israel, this approach can be said to have exhausted itself. It is very difficult to innovate from the study of the written sources themselves, and it seems that research based on the archaeological findings has greater innovative potential, which is why this study differs from its predecessors. In this book, archaeological findings have usually served as a framework for the discussion, while the written sources usually only helped complete and illuminate the picture.

I should stress that I do not claim that studying the written sources is without value, since research dealing with a historical period that ignores the written sources is extremely problematic; however, it is worth reversing the current intellectual process by beginning the research into these issues on the basis of archaeological information, and then integrating (critically, of course) the written evidence into the discussion. Most of the debates in this book are written in this spirit, which may even shed new light on the written sources.[1] I hope that the research direction presented here will contribute to the understanding of Israelite society, significantly change many of the preconceptions regarding various aspects of this society that were based on the written sources, and even raise new issues that would not have been discussed at all without the emphasis on the archaeological findings.

The land of Israel is one of the world's most intensively studied regions, and Iron Age II is one of the periods that has been excavated and studied more than most. Our knowledge about this period is so extensive that it is impossible to deal with all the types of finds from the period in one book. In most chapters of this book, therefore, the emphasis is on architectural finds at various levels (town planning, public buildings, and private structures), and the smaller finds receive only partial discussion, both because they are less important for some of the central questions discussed in this work and because of space limitations. Thus, the current book only opens the discussion of the study of Israelite society and does not attempt to conclude it. We may hope that it raises interest and helps turn the archaeological research of ancient Israel toward social and anthropological topics that have yet to be exploited.

This book is an expanded and updated version of my Ph.D. dissertation (written in the Martin [Szusz] Department of Land of Israel Studies and Archaeology at Bar-Ilan University, under Profs. Shlomo Bunimovitz and Ze'ev Safrai), which was subsequently published by Yad Ben-Zvi (in Hebrew, under the title *Israelite Society in the Period of the Monarchy: An Archaeological Perspective*). The Ph.D. dissertation was written in the late 1990s and was later updated and edited when it was prepared for publication in Hebrew. The present monograph was extensively updated again, and several discussions were added and expanded. (I hope that

---

1. Note that some of the discussions of texts in this book are partial and not exhaustive and are intended for demonstrative purposes.

the numerous updates and additions have not made it more difficult to read.) Nevertheless, the basic structure of the book and of the various chapters was maintained, although it is likely that were I to start writing it today, I would have chosen a somewhat different structure, encompassing additional issues.[2]

In the course of the preparation of the present monograph for publication, I attempted to substitute the Hebrew references (used in the original book) with English equivalents, whenever possible. In a number of cases, however, I discovered that the English translations of the Hebrew works were not always identical (for various reasons). In those cases, therefore, I referred to both versions (in most places I referred to the English version, but when the Hebrew version contained data not included in the English publication, I referred to it). Both versions are included, of course, in the bibliography.

Finally, it is my pleasant duty to thank the many people who have helped in the writing and completion of this book, including my Ph.D. advisers Shlomo Bunimovitz and Ze'ev Safrai, who devoted their time and contributed their thoughts and advice to my work and even guided me to the research I am doing today. I also received advice and criticism from these professors: Hanan Eshel, Aharon Demsky, Shimon Dar, Shmuel Vargon, Israel Finkelstein, Amihai Mazar, Israel Eph'al, and particularly Joshua Schwartz. Prof. Jack Silver assisted greatly in processing the data relating to social stratification (especially in chap. 6). Over many years of collecting material for the study, I received information from Profs. Itzhak Beit-Arieh, Adam Zertal, Moshe Kochavi, Dr. David Amit, and from Shimon Riklin. Many useful comments on the text were also offered by Noam Mizrahi, who edited the Hebrew manuscript. Thanks are also due to Yair Sapir, Pirchia Eyal, and Anat Eisner for their help in the preparation of the maps, figures, and bibliography, and to Ruth Ludlam, who translated this manuscript from Hebrew.

Some of the ideas expressed here I developed when I was a visiting graduate student at Keble College and the Institute of Archaeology, Oxford University (1997–98). I received much advice, which significantly influenced the shaping of the study, from Dr. Roger Moorey. I also received important comments from Prof. Barry Cunliffe, Dr. Andrew Sherratt, Dr. Susan Sherratt, and Prof. Peter Riviere. The Ph.D. dissertation was written with the assistance of a Rottenschtreich Grant provided by the Planning and Budgeting Committee of the Council for Higher Education; and grants from the Krauthammer Chair in Archaeology; the Strauss Fund; the Moskovitz Fund at the Martin (Szusz) Department of Land of Israel Studies and Archaeology at Bar-Ilan University; and a research grant from the Memorial Foundation for Jewish Culture. The translation and update of this

---

2. This is also the reason that various issues did not receive proper treatment in this monograph and why chaps. 1 and 2, which summarize previous scholarship, are not fully up-to-date and do not reflect today's approaches (especially chap. 1), which differ from the approaches that were prevalent a decade ago. Nonetheless, because these chapters only summarize past research, I believe this deficiency will not reflect on the importance of the book in general. Finally, I hope that the many additions and updates will not inhibit the flow of the text.

work were assisted by the Kuschitsky Fund of the Martin (Szusz) Department of Land of Israel Studies and Archaeology, and the Ingeborg Rennert Center for Jerusalem Studies, both at Bar-Ilan University.

I owe special thanks to my wife, Iris, who took upon herself many tasks, thus helping me devote most of my time to research; and to my children, Kama, Marvah, and Yannai.

Abbreviations

General

H.	Hurvat
Kh.	Khirbet
m	meter(s)

Reference Works

AA	*American Anthropologists*
AAn	*American Antiquity*
AASOR	Annual of the American Schools of Oriental Research
ABD	Freedman, D. N. (ed.). *The Anchor Bible Dictionary*. 6 vols. Garden City, NY: Doubleday, 1992
ABS	*The American Behavioral Scientist*
ADAJ	*Annual of the Department of Antiquities of Jordan*
AJOS	*American Journal of Sociology*
BA	*Biblical Archaeologist*
BAR	British Archaeological Reports
BAR	*Biblical Archaeology Review*
BASOR	*Bulletin of the American Schools of Oriental Research*
BR	*Bible Review*
BHS	Biblia Hebraica Stuttgartensia
BZAW	Beihefte zur Zeitschrift für die Alttestamentliche Wissenschaft
EncMiq	Sukenik, E. L., et al. (eds.). *Encyclopedia Miqrait*. 9 vols. Jerusalem: Bialik, 1950–89. [Hebrew]
ErIsr	*Eretz-Israel*
IEJ	*Israel Exploration Journal*
HUCA	*Hebrew Union College Annual*
JAOS	*Journal of the American Oriental Society*
JAA	*Journal of Anthropological Archaeology*
JAR	*Journal of Archaeological Research*
JEA	*Journal of Egyptian Archaeology*
JFA	*Journal of Field Archaeology*
JJS	*Journal of Jewish Studies*
JNES	*Journal of Near Eastern Studies*
JSOT	*Journal for the Study of the Old Testament*
JSOTSup	Journal for the Study of the Old Testament: Supplement Series
NEA	*Near Eastern Archaeology*
NEAEHL	Stern, E. (ed.). *The New Encyclopedia of Archaeological Excavations in the Holy Land*. 5 vols. Jerusalem: Israel Exploration Society and Carta / New York: Simon & Schuster, 1993–2008
OTL	Old Testament Library
PEQ	*Palestine Exploration Quarterly*

RB	*Revue Biblique*
SBLSP	Society of Biblical Literature: Seminar Papers
SJOT	*Scandinavian Journal of the Old Testament*
TDOT	Botterweck, G. J., and Ringgren, H. (eds.). *Theological Dictionary of the Old Testament*. Grand Rapids: Eerdmans, 1974–
VT	*Vetus Testamentum*
ZAW	*Zeitschrift für die Alttestamentliche Wissenschaft*
ZDPV	*Zeitschrift des deutschen PalŠstina-Vereins*

Introduction

The Place of this Book in Research

Various aspects of Israelite society have been discussed in many studies in the recent and distant past. Many of these studies are comprehensive and relate to almost all aspects of society, while others examine a particular subject in detail. Most of these studies were written by biblical scholars or historians, relying mainly on information from the Bible and additional textual sources and sometimes also on sociological studies. A significant proportion of these studies did not use the archaeological evidence, or made very little use of it, usually as an illustration to accompany the text. Thus, for instance, the differences between the buildings in Tirzah (Tell el-Farʿah, North) were stressed to demonstrate the social differences that the eighth-century B.C.E. prophets were denouncing (for example, de Vaux 1992: 1301). In contrast to the wealth of historical studies, archaeological research in the land of Israel has rarely dealt with social issues at all or with Israelite society in particular (Geva 1989: 11–12; Dever 1995: 416; Faust and Maeir 1999).

Referring to several important introductory books written recently about the archaeology of the land of Israel, William Dever wrote: "(Y)et, however adequate these may be as introductions to the basic data, none makes any attempt to organize the data in terms of social structure, even though there are many suggestive possibilities. This is a serious deficiency in Syro-Palestinian and biblical archaeology, when one considers that the general field of archaeology has been moving toward social archaeology for 20 years or more" (Dever 1995: 416). Lack of discussion of social questions has characterized the archaeology of the land of Israel for some time, even though around the world these questions constitute an important component of archaeological research (see, for instance, Renfrew 1984; 1994; Gibbon 1984; Blanton 1994; Dark 1995; Renfrew and Bahn 2004; Trigger 2006, and many other studies). An example of the accepted approach to the study of Israelite society can be seen in the introduction of Hanoch Reviv's book about society in the kingdoms of Israel and Judah (Reviv 1993: 2):

> The main written source of information for our study is the Bible. This source is lacking, because referring to society, in the widest sense of the term, was granted marginal importance by the authors [. . . who] showed more interest in the political aspect [. . .] of the actions of prominent people, in religion and worship and in stressing God's role in history. The selective method used in the Bible, the bias [. . .] revealed in the writings has reduced the *realia* and [the value of the] information in its descriptions. So we can understand the reader's need for additional sources, to complement and compare, such as relevant archaeological findings. It is well known that the *realia* arising from the material culture may contribute indirectly, if not directly, to the clarification of various issues in the lives of the ancients. The archaeological findings

1

may be of great assistance if they are properly inserted into the appropriate historical and chronological system. However, despite the increasing tendency of scholars to turn to a social interpretation of the findings [. . .] the possibilities entailed in the archaeological findings are still restricted to a limited number of aspects in the social processes in Israel and the ancient Near East.

Most of the studies about Israelite society were indeed written from a textual perspective. However, the historical sources on which these studies are based raise various problems. They should not be viewed as a full and objective documentation of reality but as a very partial documentation reflecting the viewpoint of a small minority—the literate elite. The sources almost never refer to the majority of the population, which resided in the rural sector, or even to the lower classes, who were the majority in the urban settlements. The extensive editing of the Bible, which is the main written source we possess on Israelite society, only aggravates the problem. Thus, it is difficult to reconstruct the structure and history of Israelite society based solely on the written sources. The purpose of this book is to fill in the blanks and to analyze the structure of society in the kingdoms of Israel and Judah from an archaeological viewpoint. We shall analyze the various archaeological finds that we now possess and examine them, applying models and theories from the field of social and cognitive archaeology, using the tools of various social-science disciplines (anthropology, sociology, economics, geography, etc.).

In contrast to previous studies, archaeological evidence constitutes the main source of information for this work, while the information that can be obtained from the Bible (that can usually be interpreted in more than one way) will be presented, in most cases, as an additional and complementary tool. At the same time, this additional information sometimes helps us choose between alternate interpretations of the archaeological finds, and in some cases enables the understanding of cognitive and other phenomena. The written sources, problematic though they may be, are very important for the understanding of Israelite society and, as we shall see in the book's various chapters, their very existence allows us to make the discussion more precise and to reach answers that could not have been obtained using the archaeological evidence alone. It is clear that ignoring the historical sources due to the difficulties they pose would be like throwing the baby out with the bathwater; instead, this study will use them cautiously. It appears to me that the combination of archaeological research and the historical sources should be achieved in the spirit of the New Biblical Archaeology approach promoted by William Dever in recent years (Dever 1993a; see also T. W. Davis 1993; 2004; Bunimovitz 1995; 2001; Bunimovitz and Faust 2010; Faust 2006b).

This monograph is one of the first attempts at a large-scale study of Israelite society mainly from the archaeological evidence. However, not only society in general is studied here for the first time from this direction. Many of the specific questions arising from this topic also receive here their first archaeological examination. The question of social stratification in the period under discussion has so far received only a few random references, usually without any systematic study, and the same is true of the question of community organization. The differences between Israel and Judah will be reexamined while we refresh the research questions. The attempt to use archaeological findings to understand the cognitive aspects in this period is also quite new.

The rural settlements, an issue so far ignored in both historical and archaeological research (see, for example, Chaney 1986: 60; London 1989), receive full attention here. Since most of the population of Israel and Judah probably lived in this settlement sector, any attempt to investigate Israelite society without discussing it is doomed to failure. Despite all this, most previous studies have ignored this sector (which is why Ahlström termed Syro-Palestinian archaeology "tell minded": Ahlström 1982a: 25; see also London 1989, who wrote about the "urban bias" of Near Eastern archaeology). Even though hardly any research has been devoted to this type of settlement, the many surveys conducted in the past few years, particularly the salvage excavations accompanying various development projects, have provided a great deal of information about this settlement sector, and this enables us to learn about Israelite society as a whole.

We may hope that some of the discussions offered here make a methodological contribution, the benefits of which will exceed the boundaries of the discussion of Israelite society. The method of examining social stratification is based on previous studies, but it contains innovations and may help other studies dealing with different periods and regions. Similar benefits could arise from the discussion of the principles behind the relations of small finds to social stratification and other debates, such as the importance of the study of villages for identifying ethnic groups. However, it should be stressed that since the discussions in this book are preliminary in nature, some of the conclusions are temporary, and only further studies and an accumulation of additional information will enable them to be proved or disproved.

The Period under Discussion

This study deals with the period of the Monarchy, particularly with the eighth–seventh centuries B.C.E.[1] The reason for this is the nature of the material we currently possess. This period is one of the best-documented periods in the entire biblical era from almost all aspects of research: archaeology, epigraphy, and history. From the archaeological viewpoint, the levels from these centuries are in many cases the upper levels on the biblical tells, and therefore many of the excavations in the country reveal levels from this period. Due to the nature of archaeological excavations, a wider area of the upper levels will always be uncovered compared with the area of the levels below. The intensity of settlement in Iron Age II, particularly in the eighth century (and in parts of Judah also the seventh century), also contributes to our knowledge, since this was a period of demographic peak: a large proportion of the *tells* were settled, usually over extensive areas. The form of destruction of these

---

1. While the previous stages of the period of the Monarchy will be mentioned in the book and discussed, mainly in chapter 9, we shall not digress in this book into a detailed discussion of the processes that accompanied the transition from Iron Age I to Iron Age II or of the beginning of the period of the Monarchy.

levels also contributes to the archaeological knowledge of the period. Since in many cases the settlements were destroyed in war (probably during the campaigns of the kings of Assyria and Babylon), the findings remained *in situ*, which helps reconstruct the nature of human activity relatively accurately. Moreover, since the period raised great interest in the archaeology of the land of Israel (with its historical orientation), the excavators often focused on tells that had extensive settlement particularly in this period. Many settlements were widely exposed (Tell Beit Mirsim, Tel Beth-Shemesh, Megiddo, Beth Shean, and others), although some were excavated and published in a very unsatisfactory manner, which restricts our ability to use their data. The demographic and settlement growth that characterized the period led to the appearance of many more rural and agricultural settlements compared with most other periods, and settlements of this type have been excavated in salvage excavations.

From an epigraphic viewpoint, the sources from this period are also more plentiful than those from earlier periods. Presumably this results from the large number of excavations and findings from this period. But it does also appear that in this period literacy became more established and widespread than in the past, and as a result there is an increase in written findings, such as the Samaria ostraca, the Lachish letters, the Arad letters, and so on.

From the viewpoint of historical sources, no other period is documented in the Bible in such detail (at least before the Babylonian Exile). Most of the books of the Prophets and a significant proportion of the historical books describe this period. These books and some other biblical books were written during the period under discussion and thus contain a vast amount of information, albeit problematic, about it. In this period there are also more external historical sources (from Assyria, Babylon, etc.), but their relevance to this study is relatively marginal, and their main contribution is in reconstructing political and military history.

The Book's Structure

This book discusses the kingdoms of Israel and Judah in terms of complete social systems and also examines various aspects within them. The first two chapters present the conclusions of previous research on these issues, and the innovation there is only in the collation of the material and its organized and comprehensive presentation. The first chapter summarizes the extensive historical research and presents the basic components of Israelite society and the processes it underwent, while the second chapter summarizes the archaeological research, which is more limited in its extent.

The third chapter analyzes the archaeological findings from the cities and towns of the period. After proposing a definition of the urban sector, I present a short discussion of the research methodology and the main topics behind this study, such as the way to measure inequality in the archaeological record. The main substance of this chapter is analyzing the archaeological findings in each settlement in terms of the various social characteristics (public-royal components, social stratification, family size, economic organization, and so on). A comparison of the evidence from different cities enables us to try and learn about the general social features of each of the kingdoms, about common traits of all the settlements discussed, and about differences among different stages within the Iron Age.

The fourth chapter examines the rural sector. Here too, the discussion opens with a definition of the rural sector and its characteristics and continues with an analysis of the findings in each settlement, with an attempt to discover its degree of social stratification and the community organization. Next, several features that distinguish Israel compared with Judah are examined, and the eighth century B.C.E. is compared with the seventh. We also examine features common to the entire rural sector, such as family structure, community organization, and social stratification. The chapter notes the differences between the rural and the urban sectors and several methodological issues related to identifying community organization and family structure in the archaeological record.

The analysis in chaps. 3 and 4 applies mainly to the intermediate level (the "meso" level), meaning the individual settlement (on the various levels of analysis, see T. E. Levy [ed.] 1995: xiii–xiv; Clarke 1977: 11–15), and only afterward is there a comprehensive and comparative discussion, with the summary of the data from the various settlements constituting a partial analysis of the society in general (the "macro" level). The two chapters focus on the architectural finding, from various residential structures through public buildings up to the settlement plan. The small finds are discussed only in a few cases, mainly in order to demonstrate the problems raised in using them to deduce wealth, community organization, and economic structure. This problem, briefly discussed in the relevant chapters, receives a detailed discussion in the appendix to chap. 3.[2]

Chaper 5 examines the phenomenon of fortified structures in rural areas (usually identified as fortresses). The definition of these buildings justifies a separate discussion. If these were fortresses, they should be viewed as an urban element located in the rural sector,[3] but if they were estates or farms, they were agricultural sites. Despite the apparent similarity between estates and farms, the two options are very different: farms are part of the rural sector (and many of them are discussed in chap. 4), while estates, despite their geographic location and economic nature, constitute in many respects a branch of the city, since their "profits" and surplus reached the city. Also the social system of an estate is very different from that of a farm. The interpretation of these buildings thus has implications for the understanding of Israelite society as a whole.

---

2. Of course, pottery is the most important finding, as it teaches us about many topics (see, for example, in chap. 8). However, for the analysis to be significant, one must accurately reconstruct the place where the vessels were in use. In many cases one cannot know where the vessels were found during the excavation, either because the report is old and does not provide the required information or because there is no excavation report at all. In many excavations in which the data are available, the exposure is so limited that they are irrelevant to the study of most aspects of society (since this requires the excavation of complete structures, preferably more than one). This makes it difficult to use pottery (and small finds in general) for the purposes of this study.

3. The existence of a permanent army has implications for the social organization and structure, but the issue of the armies in the kingdoms of Israel and Judah, the source of the personnel in them, and other such issues have yet to receive a thorough study.

Chapter 6 examines several topics related directly to the "macro" level: monumental buildings, complex administrative and military organizations, and social and settlement hierarchies (assuming that the evidence reveals the degree of complexity of the societies under discussion). Checking the data concerning the kingdoms of Israel and Judah shows the similarities and differences and the developments that took place during the period. The data about the "macro" level are correlated with a more extensive analysis of the data from the "meso" level to provide a general picture of society.

Chapter 7 deals with cognitive analysis. The chapter examines the dominant residential house in Israelite society during the period of the Monarchy (the "four-room houses" of various types), the reasons for its exceptional popularity, and the social meanings it embodied.[4]

Chapter 8 deals with a difficult problem in archaeological research, the "pots and people" problem: can ethnic groups be identified in the archaeological findings? This chapter tries to evaluate the existence of various ethnic groups in the period under discussion, the complex relations between these groups, and the overall social structure. The starting point for this chapter is the rural sector, where it is easier to identify ethnic groups compared with urban settlements (where, in many cases, different ethnic groups resided together).

Chapter 9 briefly summarizes the process of change that Israelite society underwent from the end of the settlement period (the Iron Age I) onward, and describes how the social reality developed, the various aspects of which were described in the previous chapters.

It should be stressed that most of the discussions in this book are of a preliminary nature. Many questions are not discussed at all, while some of the analyses presented here are open to different interpretations. However, even if not all the conclusions are accepted in research, the strength of this book is in the extent of the discussion, the combination of the different analysis levels, and particularly the direction of the research.

---

4. The term *four-room house* is used in this book in its generic meaning and usually includes all the subtypes.

Chapter 1

Historical Inquiry on Israelite Society: Summary of Previous Research

Historians have comprehensively discussed the institutions of Israelite society in the period of the Monarchy and the social and economic changes that the society underwent between the period of Settlement (Iron Age I) and the period of the Monarchy (Iron Age II).[1] The various studies are, of course, based mainly on the biblical texts and to some extent on theoretical and comparative sociological analyses.[2] In this chapter, I will summarize the generally accepted positions of most past studies regarding the basic social structures—both what was regarded as the traditional social organization and the social organization that was modified during the period of the Monarchy—and regarding the main social changes that occurred over time, because many scholars assumed that the Iron Age traditional society experienced dramatic changes during Iron Age II.

The first part of the chapter will summarize studies that attempted to describe the traditional society, mainly on the basis of the biblical texts. The second part of the chapter will discuss the social reality during the Iron Age II, mainly toward the end of the period. The last part of the chapter will summarize the various studies addressing the processes that transformed Israelite society during the transition from the Settlement to Monarchy. Naturally, the majority of studies addressed in this chapter are based mainly, and in many cases solely, on the texts, usually on the Bible.

A Few Preliminary Notes

As noted above, this book discusses mainly the period of the Monarchy, especially the eighth and seventh centuries B.C.E. It is also necessary, for reasons that will become more apparent later in this book, to summarize the research regarding the "traditional" structure of the Israelite society—the structure that is attributed by most scholars to the Iron Age I. In this section, we will summarize the various views,

---

1. The results of many studies dealing with the social aspects of the settlement period (such as Gottwald 1979; Hopkins 1985; C. H. J. de Geus 1976; Lemche 1985) will not be summarized here but will be used for describing the "traditional" component of Israelite society during the period of the Monarchy (although such an exercise is not without problems; see chap. 9). It is worth noting that, while this chapter deals with the historical research, the subject matter sometimes requires references to archaeological studies as well (discussed in greater detail in chap. 2).

2. It should be remembered that most of the historical evidence (including the biblical texts) was written by members of the social elite, and naturally it focuses on this class (see, for instance, Coote and Whitelam 1987: 88–89). This bias influenced the range of topics covered and the references used in the studies based on these sources.

although many of these are based on written sources that most scholars today doubt are able to provide reliable information on this period. Nevertheless, they need to be treated, especially since, ironically, they may prove valuable to the study of Iron Age II (see more in chap. 9).

We should also note that such textually oriented studies took for granted, for example, the existence of the United Monarchy. While this issue is hotly debated today (e.g., Dever 1997a–b; 1998a–b; Lemche 1998; Finkelstein and Silberman 2001; 2006; Stager 2003; Bunimovitz and Lederman 2004; Faust 2004c; and many others), it is commonly agreed that the texts cannot be used for finely tuned reconstructions. It should therefore be stressed that the historicity of the United Monarchy is not our main concern here and is not directly related to the current discussion; even scholars who believe there was no United Monarchy in the tenth century agree that a kingdom was established later, and the social processes that they reconstruct will be at least partially similar to those suggested by scholars who dated these processes to the tenth century. In any case, it should be stressed that this chapter summarizes previous studies and reflects the state of biblical-historical research at the time it was initially written. Most of the studies discussed below were written before the influence of the minimalists on the discourse was felt, and some of the views are clearly dated and mirror the style of discussion that dominated biblical discourse until about a decade ago.[3] I have added a number of clarifications and updates, but I did not significantly change the nature of this chapter.

It is also worth stressing that the discussions in this chapter are usually intended to summarize different views in the field and do not necessarily reflect the conclusions of this work (for these, see chaps. 3–9).

And finally, the distinction between historical and archaeological studies is becoming more and more difficult, especially since more and more scholars have come to rely heavily on archaeological studies. Still, I address in this chapter mainly historical-biblical studies and wherever possible save the archaeological studies of Israelite society in Iron II for chap. 2.

Traditional Social Organization

Scholars are almost unanimous in defining the traditional framework of Israelite society as a kinship framework, meaning that society was organized on the basis of bloodlines (real or false). According to the accepted view, during the period of the Settlement and even at the beginning of the Monarchy, society was composed mainly of kinship units of various sizes: tribes, *mishpahot* (clans or lineages), *batei av* (extended families), and perhaps also nuclear families. The boundaries between the

---

3. The influence of the writing of the minimalists significantly changed biblical discourse, and while most scholars reject the outright minimalists' views on the historicity of the texts, the historical value of the texts for the period before the very end of the Iron Age is now questioned by most scholars and cannot be taken for granted. This is not the place to discuss the problematic nature of the minimalists' views themselves (see, e.g., Rainey 1994; Pasto 1998; Dever 1998b; 2000; 2001; Faust 2006b: 24–26 235–36, and references), but I should note that, despite dozens of books and hundreds of articles, they fail to present a viable picture of Iron Age society that is based on data of any kind; their writings are based on assertions and have therefore been addressed only partially in this chapter.

various levels of organization are not entirely clear (Halpern 1991: 49; Bendor 1996: 67; Pedersen 1926: 47, 53; Lemche 1985: 247–51; Cowling 1988: 191). Thus, for instance, there is a debate over the question whether the nuclear family actually constituted an independent level of social organization or whether it was an inseparable part of the extended family (C. H. J. de Geus 1976; Hopkins 1985: 25; Reviv 1993: 43–59; Halpern 1991: 49). It is even reasonable to assume that the theoretical division did not always match the actual situation: for example, *bet Av* X could be larger than *mishpahah* Y (Lieber 1968: 583). In any case, the members of such large kinship groups lived on their lands and jointly cultivated them. While certain scholars find hints of social and economic gaps already in Iron Age I (e.g., Bendor 1996: 223–24; Lemche 1985: 250), it appears that traditional Israelite society was generally a nonstratified society, without real classes, and can be defined as relatively egalitarian.[4] In the past, one popular opinion was that this equality resulted from an ancient nomadic ideal and that it is characteristic of nomadic societies (see, for instance, Lods 1932: 396), but today many scholars avoid seeking the origins of Israelite society in any nomadic background. At any event, it is accepted that the kinship framework typical of traditional Israelite society could have reflected the agricultural background of the Iron Age (see for example, Bendor 1996: 216–18).[5]

The Tribe

The picture of Israelite society arising from the Bible is based on a clear development scheme: the Israelite people started as a family (Jacob and his sons), continued as a federation of tribes, and reached its peak in the Monarchy. In this respect, the tribe was considered an intermediate stage and a central component of Israelite society, at least during the period of the Settlement. The currently accepted scholarly opinion is that, during the period of the Monarchy, the tribes did not constitute a real social organization level. The tribe, as part of the traditional structure,[6] was damaged by processes occurring at the beginning of the period of Monarchy, and its role became purely symbolic: identifying the population of the area that the tribe had historically settled. The tribal names in this period denoted merely territorial units (see, e.g., C. H. J. de Geus 1989: 21; Reviv 1993: 55–59; Harmon 1983: 143–44). There are also some more extreme opinions: on the one hand, there are those who claim that the tribe was never a real entity (see, for instance, C. H. J. de Geus 1989; Lemche 1996: 117) but merely an organization (or federation) of families (de Geus 1989: 156); and on the other hand, some believe that the tribe functioned as a social unit even in the period of the Monarchy (Bendor 1996: 87–93). This latter opinion seems exaggerated, and it appears that during the Monarchy the tribe had no social

---

4. Bendor 1996. Since there are no completely egalitarian societies (Price and Feinman 1995: 4–5; Lemche 1985: 223), perhaps it is preferable to use more cautious phrases, such as "societies with an egalitarian ideology" (Lemche 1985; see also chap. 7 below).

5. I do not wish to summarize the discussion on the origins of this population. For an extensive discussion, see Faust 2006b: 170–87, and many references).

6. I am not attempting to summarize here all the views on the social reality of Iron Age I, and it is quite clear that the tribes were not identical to the biblical description.

importance, except, perhaps, as a loose genealogical framework. This opinion will be discussed in more detail later.

The Mishpahah

The term *mishpahah* usually denotes a subtribal unit composed of several *batei av* (see for instance, Josh 7:14).[7] De Geus described the *mishpahah* as the most important form of organization and the most important way of life in ancient Israel (C. H. J. de Geus 1989: 137; Gottwald 1979: 115–316). The close connections between the *batei av* made the *mishpahah* into a real social unit. Hopkins believes that the solidarity between the different components within this unit were formed as a result of necessary cooperation between farmers. This ensured mutual help when needed and the optimal use of human resources (Hopkins 1985: 258). The *mishpahah* normally resided in one settlement or in neighboring settlements (as can be seen in the Samaria ostraca). Sometimes several *mishpahot* lived in one town (Harmon 1983: 127; de Vaux 1965: 21; C. H. J. de Geus 1989: 138; Hopkins 1985: 257). The land of the various households was owned by the *mishpahah*, which was also the body responsible for redeeming lands (see for example, Num 27:4, 11; Ruth 4:3–6; Hopkins 1985: 258).

Some scholars see certain texts (such as 2 Chr 4:21) as evidence that some craftsmen sometimes joined a "guild" and became a *mishpahah* with a fictive ancestor and genealogy (de Vaux 1965: 77; Demsky 1966; Reviv 1993: 52–53, and bibliography there; for a different opinion, see Vanderhooft 2008). Perhaps in this case there was indeed a *mishpahah* that made its living from a particular craft that was passed down through the generations (de Vaux 1965: 22). The more common opinion is that the *mishpahah* did not serve as an economic unit but concentrated the political power of the households (*batei av*) that it contained, since they were too small to have a role in the political game in themselves (Reviv 1993: 52–53). Some of the *mishpahah*'s roles may have had a ritual expression, at least in the earlier periods (see for example, 1 Sam 9:12; and especially 1 Sam 20:6, 19; see also Hopkins 1985: 257).

It appears that, unlike the tribe, the *mishpahah* retained its role in the period of the Monarchy. This statement applies particularly to the rural agricultural sector. Regarding the situation in the urban sector, it is reasonable to accept Reviv's opinion that "even if there was in the urban centers a sense of the individual's belonging to the *mishpahah*, this was, presumably, of historical rather than real value, just like belonging to the tribe, since in the urban sector, the individual's rise testifies to the decline or even disappearance of the *mishpahah*" (Reviv 1993: 33–34; on the *mishpahah*'s status, see also Lemche 1985: 248–70). Bendor has a different opinion: even in the urban sector the traditional *mishpahah* framework remained undamaged, and over time the city and the *mishpahah* simply merged. The city's collective responsibility grew out of the *mishpahah*, and the city elders were the *mishpahah* elders (Bendor 1996: 98–107). However, it seems that the changes inevitably occurred, and at least

---

7. Scholars define the *mishpahah* as a 'clan' (for example, Pedersen 1926: 46; C. J. H. Wright 1992: 761–62; Perdue 1997: 177), a 'lineage' (for example, Lemche 1985) or even a 'protective association of families' (e.g., Gottwald 1979: 257). These differences result from disagreement over the contents of the term (see the conclusions of chap. 4 below).

in the urban sector kinship ceased to serve as an exclusive cohesive principle (Lieber 1968: 586–87).

The Household (Bet Av) *and the Nuclear Family*

The accepted opinion is that the *bet av* (that is, the extended family) was the basic social unit in the period under discussion,[8] although some claim that the most basic unit was the nuclear family.[9] Nuclear families did indeed exist alongside the extended families, but scholars are divided regarding the degree of dependence of the nuclear family on the framework of the extended family. According to Lemche, most families were nuclear (Lemche 1985: 249–59; and following him, Rogerson 1989: 29–30; see also Martin 1989: 104–5).[10] For example, according to Lemche's interpretation, the story of the woman of Tekoah (2 Samuel 14) describes a nuclear family consisting only of a mother and her children (Lemche 1985: 244–59).[11] In his opinion, the expression *bet av* is used in the Bible both to denote an extended family and also to denote a nuclear family, and in some cases even to denote a larger lineage unit.

However, it seems that the *bet av*, in the sense of the extended family, was indeed the basic social unit in Israelite society (a production and residence unit, as C. H. J. de Geus refers to it, 1976: 135; see also Hopkins 1985: 253) and that the nuclear families existed within it. The expression *bet av*, literally, 'father's house' shows the patriarchal nature of the Israelite family as described in the biblical texts.[12] The genealogy is cited according to the father, and women are mentioned only rarely.[13] The father had total authority over his children, even the married ones, if they continued living with him. After the father's death, the family may have continued to live together, and in this case, one of the brothers, usually the oldest, became the head of the household (Stager 1985: 20). The usual composition of households was three or four generations, as transpires from the various bans (such as Lev 18:7–16), or the phrasing of the extensive responsibility for "the children unto the third and fourth generation" (Num 14:18; Deut 5:8; Weinfeld 1994: 77). The framework of several generations is also reflected in the stories of Gideon (see Hopkins 1985: 252).

---

8. For a definition of the extended family, see Yorburg 1975. On the *bet av* as an extended family, see Porter 1967; C. H. J. de Geus 1976: 133; Harmon 1983: 122–25; Hopkins 1985: 252; Chaney 1986: 62; C. J. H. Wright 1990: 53–55; Halpern 1991: 50; Reviv 1993: 47; de Vaux 1965: 20; Bendor 1996.

9. Bendor 1996: 121–23; Lang 1985: 85, 97; Holladay 1995: 386–87. Cowling (1988) even claimed that there was no evidence of the existence of the extended family. However, a study of the texts shows that the extended family, as the vast majority of scholars believe, was indeed the popular family type in this period.

10. This controversy too is related to the fluidity of terms; see above.

11. However, this interpretation can be disputed. Bendor (1996: 121–24) discusses other texts indicating social units smaller than the extended family.

12. Pedersen 1926: 46–81; Harmon 1983: 131; Stager 1985: 20; de Vaux 1965: 20; Reviv 1993: 44; Perdue 1997: 212–13 n. 9; Niditch 1997: 86–87, and many others. Some argue that Israelite society in Iron Age I had gender equality (Meyers 1997: 34), but it appears that this opinion does not accord with the evidence (see, for instance, Perdue 1997: 212–13 n. 9; compare Flannery and Marcus 1994). In any case, even Meyers agrees that in Iron Age II the society was not egalitarian (Meyers 1988: 189–96; see also Blenkinsopp 1997: 74–78). For the process during which gender inequality deepened with the establishment of the Monarchy, see also Faust 2002b.

13. Perdue 1997: 166. Since genealogy is determined by the male line, the biblical family is defined as "patrilineal," and since the wife moved in with her husband, the family is also "patrilocal." See for, example, Seymour-Smith 1994: 218–19.

Noah's family included the son's wives (Gen 7:1, 7), and Jacob's family comprised three generations (Gen 46:8–26). The *bet av* often included additions, some of them family members with various degrees of kinship, and others strangers (adopted children, hired staff, foreigners, slaves), such as Jephthah, who belonged to "his father's house" (or at least aspired to belong to it), despite being illegitimate.[14] An extended family could have included several dozen individuals.[15]

The Elders

The leadership of traditional Israelite society was held by the elders (for extensive details on this topic, see Reviv 1989). De Vaux defined them as: "the heads of families, who form a sort of council in every village" (de Vaux 1965: 69; see also Harmon 1983: 146; see, for example, 1 Sam 30:27–31). The elders constituted the local leadership level in ancient Israel (for example, 1 Kings 20) and in the ancient Near East in general. Their power stemmed from the patriarchal heritage, and they constituted a collective leadership at the level of the *mishpahah*. De Vaux noted the dialectical relation between this term and the term *sarim*: sometimes they are equivalent and sometimes opposed. Reviv believes that the elders were included in the various levels of judging both in Israel and in Judah. Their status declined during the period of the Monarchy compared with the previous periods, but they still constituted the local leadership. In his opinion, when the power of the central authority declined, the power of the local authority increased; thus, for instance, the elders and the *sarim* are represented in the local leadership in the story of Naboth's vineyard (1 Kings 21) and during the rebellion of Jehu (2 Kings 10).[16]

Land Ownership

In the Bible, land is perceived as the "patrimony," meaning family property that passes from generation to generation according to the inheritance law. The patrimony, plots of land of various sizes, was not supposed to be sold in traditional society (see, for instance, the story of Naboth the Jezreelite; Reviv 1993: 66–69).

Beginning in the nineteenth century, scholars accepted the view that in ancient Israel, as in other traditional Middle Eastern societies, there was a cyclical distribution of lands (Bendor 1996: 141–47; Hopkins 1985: 257–58; and also Dybdahl 1981). Following verses such as "the land shall not be sold for ever: for the land is mine" (Lev 25:23),[17] many scholars believed that the land was perceived as God's property,

---

14. De Vaux 1965: 20. For an extensive discussion of the texts, see Bendor 1996: 45–118. On the additions, see Reviv 1993: 47; Meyers 1997: 14. In this context, it is interesting to compare the *bet av* with the Mesopotamian *bitum*, which also included additions to real family members. See Gelb 1967: 6–7. For an extended discussion, see also Schloen 2001.

15. Between 10 and 30 people, according to Stager (1985: 20), and between 50 and 100 according to Gottwald (1979: 285), but see Lemche 1985: 248; Hopkins 1985: 253.

16. In Reviv's opinion (1989: 113), the elders were the heads of *am ha'aretz* (on this body, see below), although they are never mentioned together anywhere. According to him, the later historiography stressed "unity" and the "nation" and blurred the role of the elders (1989: 187–88).

17. This citation is attributed to the Priestly source of the Bible, the dating of which is disputed. In the common view, the Priestly source was written during the Persian period (see for instance, Clines 1993; Rofé 1994, and additional bibliography there), but many scholars now date it earlier, in the eighth–seventh

while those actually holding it were perceived as residents. This picture was also based on the texts in Joshua, describing the distribution of the plots during the Settlement period by lots (see, for example, Josh 15:1; 15:17–18; compare Num 26:53–56). Many scholars have viewed the laws concerning the Sabbatical year and the Jubilee as evidence of this sort of reality: the lands belong to the entire community (or actually belong to God), and the law ensures that the condition is reset periodically, by allotting the plots among members of the entire community. Bendor denied this evidence, because in his opinion the existence of a similar system in traditional Middle Eastern societies does not prove the existence of such a system in Israel, and the texts mentioned above can also be explained in other ways (Bendor 1996: 147). But he did accept, in principle, the argument that in ancient Israel a cyclical distribution of lands was practiced, and in this he relied on various texts, such as "My people's portion changed hands; how it slips away from me. Our fields are allotted to a rebel. We are utterly ravaged. Truly, none of you shall cast a lot cord in the assembly of the Lord" (Mic 2:4–5; for the text and for discussion, see Bendor 1996: 148); and "Hold up my goings in your paths, that my footsteps slip not. I have called upon you, for you will hear me, O God: incline your ear to me, and hear my speech" (Ps 17:5–6).[18]

However, it seems that in the reality of intensive agriculture, it would be unrealistic to have a system of land redistribution, because no one would cultivate a stranger's plot or invest in soil destined to become someone else's, so eventually the soil would become impoverished (Grossman 1994: 26). The (utopian?) laws of Leviticus are actually based on the assumption that there is private ownership of land (and it does not matter if this is individual, *bet av*, or *mishapah* ownership), and they are intended as a mechanism to preserve it (Meyers [1997: 19–20] also views the land as family property). Private ownership is also implied by verses such as: "Do not remove your neighbor's landmark" (Deut 19:14; compare Deut 27:17).

Israelite Society on the Eve of the Monarchy

It is widely assumed that society before the establishment of the Monarchy was organized in the traditional structure described above.[19] De Vaux saw the beginning of the Settlement period as a time when "all the Israelites enjoyed more or less the same standard of living. [. . .] Commerce, and the buying and selling of real estate for profit, were as yet unimportant factors in economic life" (de Vaux 1965: 72; however,

---

centuries B.C.E., and perhaps even earlier (see for example, Hurvitz 1974; Weinfeld 1982: 25–26; Friedman 1987; Halpern 1991; Kaufmann 1960). In any case, it is accepted that at least some of the texts were composed long before they were written down.

18. Bendor 1996: 154–55. Other texts he uses include: Isa 8:1; 57:6; Jer 37:12; Ps 69:28–29; 125:3. However, at least regarding Jer 37:12 ("Then Jeremiah left Jerusalem to go into the land of Benjamin to separate himself there in the midst of the people"), Eph'al (2000: 19) has shown that the text does not refer to the distribution of property at all, and so it is irrelevant to Bendor's argument.

19. Some scholars disagree over whether Israelite society in this period should be defined as a "segmentary society," meaning a tribal society composed of several equal groups lacking clear centers of power (R. R. Wilson 1977: 18–36; 1993; Rogerson 1986). But these studies were largely based on social-science research and anthropological comparisons and hardly referred to the reality in the land of Israel as reflected in the archaeological findings and the written sources. Some of the scholars even referred to the sources very freely according to their needs (R. R. Wilson 1993: 95).

de Vaux was aware of the existence of "exceptions"). In contrast, in Reviv's opinion, already in this period, "The subtribal unit moved over to the barter system to provide for survival needs and services, since the autarky system was not suited to the new conditions. Thus the economic gap grew and social polarity was revealed—a phenomenon accompanying any permanent society that is nonegalitarian in nature" (Reviv 1982: 93; compare Chaney 1986: 67; Fager 1993: 29).

It is clear that already in this period there were rich and poor Israelites, a fact expressed, according to many, in the descriptions of the "minor judges" (Judg 10:1–5; 12:8–15), whose property and status are described in detail (see also Bendor 1996: 223–24). Nabal the Carmelite was rich, and the title "great man" (for instance, 2 Sam 19:32) also refers to wealth. At the opposite pole of the social system, in this period one finds expressions such as "empty," "hasty," and "villains" reflecting the attitude of the population toward people who had been rejected by the existing social system (see Avraham 2000). But the majority of Israelites were situated somewhere between these two poles (Reviv 1982: 93–94), and thus "Israelite society in this period should not be defined as a class society. The relative balance and the absence of a clear class division stem from the processes of settlement—especially from the patriarchal lifestyle and the economic and social aim of the subtribal units, which maintained mutual responsibility and provision for the needs of their components" (Reviv 1982: 94).

While the social structure and reality of the traditional society seem more difficult to reconstruct, especially if viewed as reflecting Iron Age I, it appears that the reality in Iron Age II, especially near the end (while by no means simple) can be reconstructed on the basis of the texts with a higher degree of certainty. Let us move now to historical studies of the social structure at the end of the period of the Monarchy.

Social Organization at the End of the Monarchy

Most scholars believe that, according to the biblical evidence (particularly the criticism of the prophets), the kinship structure was destroyed by the end of the period of the Monarchy. The *batei av* and *mishpahot* disintegrated, and the nuclear family became dominant. Traditional leadership declined, and the elders lost their position to royal officials. The royal family accumulated vast property, and so did a small number of wealthy people and estate owners. Trade became a dominant factor in the economy. The vast majority of the population was composed of small, poor farmers who had been dispossessed of their lands and were in a constant state of impoverishment and became hired staff employed in the royal economy. In other words, in both kingdoms there was social polarization (Lods 1932: 397–98; Bertholet 1926: 233–36; Neufeld 1960; Bright 1972: 256–57; Elat 1982: 234 n. 2; Lang 1985; Chaney 1986; Bendor 1996: 210–15 and additional bibliography there).

According to this view, this polarization was also expressed in the stark contrast between town and country and between rich urban landowners and rural vassals:

> The rich demanded palaces modeled on those of the King, with winter and summer houses [. . . ,] feasts in which meat was a daily dish. [. . .] The women came to regard an enormous quantity of toilet articles and cosmetics as indispensable. [. . .] By right of

their rank they were judges, and used their position to oppress the litigants. Especially widows and orphans, who had no natural protectors were the prey of their rapacity. From small proprietors, who were compelled by misfortunes to borrow from them, they exacted ruinous interest, and in the end sold the insolvent debtor and his children as slaves and seized his land. [. . .] In this way small holdings gradually disappeared, and the country was covered with *latifundia*. [. . .] Thus there grew up a minority of nobles opposed to an ever increasing peasant proletariat. (Lods 1932: 397–98)

According to Chaney, the economic gaps were particularly severe: a small minority of two percent controlled and exploited the rest of the population (Chaney 1986: 56, 72–73).

According to de Vaux, in the reality of the eighth century B.C.E., rich landowners oppressed the weak and the poor (de Vaux 1965: 72–73), "(B)ut it would be a mistake to see in ancient Israelite society the contrasts found in other societies. [. . .] In Israel there never really existed social classes in the modern sense of groups conscious of their particular interests and opposed to one another" (1965: 68). Reviv accepts this position (Reviv 1982; 1989; 1993). In his opinion, the existence of gaps is undeniable, but the changes that the society underwent was not a disruption for everyone, stratification was more moderate, and in many cases the kinship structure continued as before (Reviv 1993: 52; compare Bendor's position [1996] that in this period Israelite society retained its kinship structure).

Houston (2004: 146) summarizes: "(W)e thus reach the conclusion that the eighth century in Israel and Judah offered the right conditions for the development of economic pressure on the peasantry sufficiently severe to be seen as unjust and denounced on that ground," and he concludes (2004: 147) that "there was a social crisis in the eighth century."

Thus, it appears that, regardless of the exact nature of the socioeconomic stratification, during the period of the Monarchy Israelite society became divided into what many scholars view to be three classes: upper, middle, and lower. There were also population groups existing outside this structure. Above the upper class was the royal family (Reviv 1993: 9; de Vaux 1965: 115–26), although its members had close ties with this class, first and foremost, marriage ties (such as the marriage of Jehoshabeath to the priest Jehoiada, 2 Chr 22:11; compare 2 Kgs 21:19, and others). Below the lower class were the slaves. Slavery was undoubtedly an inseparable part of society in the ancient Near East in general and in Israel in particular (as can be seen from the biblical laws; compare Jeremiah 34), but the economy of the kingdoms of Israel and Judah was probably not slave-based (Reviv 1993: 38–42; de Vaux 1965: 80–90; Mendelson and Aḥituv 1971: 1–13. For the situation in the ancient Near East, see Gelb 1967: 7). The following summary is based mainly on Reviv's analysis, with some expansion of the scope of the discussion (Reviv 1993: 5–40; compare de Vaux 1965: 68–79).

The Upper Class

The upper class was composed of the social, economic and political elites (Reviv 1993: 13). It included holders of positions such as senior administrative staff, senior

officers, the high priesthood, and the "king's servants" (1993: 24); the wealthy, such
as estate owners; and various "close friends," such as members of the court, and so
on. It seems that over time, these groups formed a sort of aristocracy (1993: 15–16).
In political terms, the members of the upper class usually supported the royal family
and its trends and engaged in a complex relationship with it (1993: 13; the complexity of this relationship is manifest in the story of Athaliah, 2 Kings 11).

The Bible mentions many members of the upper class, especially those who held
positions within the royal administration, such as the person known as "over the
household" (*majordomo*), the "scribe," the "recorder," and the "king's servant"—all
senior officials (see, for instance, 2 Kgs 18:18). There are also many references to this
group in epigraphic findings, such as stamp seals of the city governor (*sar ha'ir*) and
of various officials (Avishur and Heltzer 1996; Aḥituv 1993: 122–37). We also possess
a few references to the senior priests,[20] such as the seal "to Hanan, son of Helkiahu
the priest" (private collection, Paris), and perhaps also the seal "Mikniyahu, God's
servant," if this person had a role in the Temple (Aḥituv 1993: 131; the priestly bless-
ing from Ketef Hinnom may also be related to the priests; see Barkay 1989). The
biblical evidence for the existence of real noble families is quite indirect, although
the family of Shaphan, whose members served in senior positions for several generations, seems to be one of them (Aḥituv 1982: 252–53, and additional references
there).

Another question is whether large merchants were in this group. It is reasonable
to assume that they were (Reviv 1993: 21), but the Bible mentions very few merchants, and usually with a negative tone, so whether the merchants belonged to this
class is in doubt.[21] The negative attitude toward trade is apparent in the use of the
term *Canaanite* for trader (Hos 12:4 and other places; compare with the prophecies
about Tyre in Isaiah 23 and other places); it is reasonable to assume that, if trade had
been perceived positively, merchants would not have been treated as "Canaanites,"
a term that must have had a negative meaning (see also Faust 2006b: 57–58, and
references). In any case, according to Lenski and Lenski (197*: 243–45; compare Sjoberg 1960: 120–21), merchants in similar societies were not considered as members
of the elite.

The Middle Class

Reviv includes six groups in the middle class: (1) Holders of positions in the
royal administration, responsible for implementing the royal policy in administration, justice, military, the royal economy, and so forth. They sometimes developed
consciousness of a family lineage (*mishpahah*) and were appointed due to their connections, skills, and loyalty (Reviv 1993: 26–27). (2) The military officers (apart from
the senior officers, who belonged to the upper class). There is little reference to this
level of the military in the Bible, but much of the epigraphic evidence refers to this
group (such as the letters of Elyashiv, commander of the Arad fortress, or the "officer" mentioned in the Lachish letters; Aḥituv 1993, and extensive bibliography

---

20. Note the problematic nature of the unprovenanced artifacts discussed.
21. See the entry "trade" in *Encyclopedia Miqrait* (by the editors), col. 162–63.

there). (3) The population of the urban centers, and more precisely, the nonagricultural sector in these settlements: professionals, craftsmen, and service-providers, some independent and others dependent upon the royal economy. This group was presumably heterogeneous in terms of status and wealth. (4) The merchants dealing in mediation and marketing. These were mainly local merchants rather than the large merchants involved in international or large scale trade, whose status is not clear (see above). This group flourished as the standard of living in the kingdoms of Israel and Judah rose. (5) Urban population engaged in agriculture. (6) Nonurban groups that Reviv calls "wealthy farmers" (Reviv 1993: 30–31). In Reviv's opinion, the last two groups constituted the main part of the middle class and composed the body known as *gibbore ḥail* in the Kingdom of Israel and *am ha'aretz* in the Kingdom of Judah (though according to Reviv, farmers belonging to the lower class were also included in *am ha'aretz*).[22]

The Lower Class

This class includes, in Reviv's opinion, the weakest and most marginal groups in society, though they actually constituted the majority of the population, such as most of the rural-agricultural sector (including those with very little property) and the marginal elements of the free poor in the rural and urban settlements: "This refers to most of the population in these kingdoms, which can be called: 'the small peasants', and the 'marginal population' and should include nonagricultural workers whose residence and low economic status were similar to those of the peasants described above"[23] (Reviv 1993: 33). Even though these groups, as a whole, possessed a significant proportion of the land, their economic condition was poor. Those who kept their property were probably a main target for taxation and recruitment. Some parts of this sector had an unstable and variable economic basis, because they were gradually disadvantaged by the heavy burden. Presumably, this group experienced the age-old process of being expelled and becoming serfs, vassals, or hired laborers and tending to become attached to other people's farms as "foreigners" (*gerim*) or even slaves, although they undoubtedly constituted a significant factor in the economic system. The Bible and the epigraphic findings contain much evidence about the underclasses of Israelite society, such as day laborers (such as the reaper's letter from Mezad Hashavyahu; Naveh 1961; Aḥituv 1993: 96–100) and so on. In addition to these groups, the unemployed, beggars, and criminals should also be included in the lower classes (Lenski and Lenski 1974: 246–47).

Am Ha'aretz ('The People of the Land')

The meaning of the term *am ha'aretz* has been discussed extensively in the secondary literature (for a summary of various opinions, see Reviv 1993: 149 and

---

22. Reviv's division is schematic and should probably not be accepted as it is. In any case, Lenski and Lenski (1974: 246) state that in the urban settlements of agrarian societies there was indeed a sort of middle class that included groups such as artisans (between three and five percent of the towns' population) and so on.

23. Reviv 1993: 33–37, citation from p. 33. Later on, I will claim that Reviv was mistaken in his classification of many of the groups that composed the lower class.

bibliography there), and among the proposed explanations, the following two are
most prominent: the term denotes all free landowners in Judah; alternatively, it denotes a smaller body, the identity and essence of which are disputed. It appears that
the first opinion is more appropriate (compare de Vaux 1965: 70–71; Reviv 1993:
149–56), due to the wide coverage of the term *am* ('people') and the identification
of the groups not included in *am ha'aretz*: the royal family (e.g., 2 Kgs 16:15), the
"king's servants" meaning the royal administration (Jer 17:2), the priests and other
powerful persons (Jer 1:18), and the prophets (Ezek 22:25–29). According to Reviv,
"The unpropertied, hired laborers, workers, slaves, and other such social groups
who were never active in shaping the economy and the policy were also not included
in *am ha'aretz*" (Reviv 1993: 150), but even so this is a large and heterogeneous body,
including rich and poor (2 Kgs 24:14), urban and rural (Reviv 1993: 150; 2 Kgs 25:3),
and which should therefore be seen as a kingdom-wide group. Support for this view
can be found in the identification of *am ha'aretz* with *am Yehudah* ('the people of Judah'; 2 Kgs 14:11; 2 Chr 26:1). It appears that this body included most of the population of Judah, apart from the upper class and perhaps the lowest social groups.
De Vaux quoted the opinion that it refers to "the body of free men, enjoying civic
rights in a given territory" (de Vaux 1965: 70; presumably the elders, constituting the
traditional leadership, represented *am ha'aretz*; see above). It is possible that in the
Kingdom of Israel there was an equivalent body, also including landowners in the
countryside and in the city, known as *gibbore ḥail*.

Processes of Change in Israelite Society

The basic differences between the traditional social organization and the stratified structure typical of the period of the Monarchy suggest the need to examine the
possible causes of this change in the social reality. We have already seen that most
scholars view it as a gradual process correlating with the transition from the period
of the Settlement to the Monarchy. It is time to review some of the theories regarding
the changes that Israelite society experienced through time.

The Transition from a Nomadic Life to Permanent Settlement

Scholars who believed that the kinship structure preserved the ancient tradition
of the nomadic desert life-style considered the settling down and move to agriculture to be the main reason that the traditional structure was disrupted. Lods represents this opinion:

> According to the nomadic custom, pasture-lands and springs are the indivisible prop-
> erty of the entire *douar*. In the early period of their settlement in Canaan the Hebrews
> may have attempted to preserve this custom. But in historical times nothing remained
> of it but gradually disappearing traces. [. . .] [A] further consequence of the attach-
> ment of the Israelites to the soil was the growth of sharply marked social division.
> Among nomads the poorest is actually equal to the richest. [. . .] But this state of things
> underwent a complete change when the Israelites became sedentary agriculturalists.
> Thanks to the increasing security in tenure which prevailed in the land, skilful cultiva-
> tors were able to save their profits and use them to enlarge their property. [. . .] On the

other hand, there grew up, after the institution of the monarchy, a military aristocracy. [. . .] The exercise of power was a source of profit for the "elders" and for royal officials. (Lods 1932: 396–97)[24]

However, this opinion is no longer accepted, because many scholars reject the notion that the Israelites began as a real nomadic society (Bendor 1996: 217, 262–63; Dever 1993b; and many others. Some, however, still view Israel as emerging from semi-nomadic groups, though quite different from Lods's somewhat romantic view. For an updated summary of various views of Israel's origins, see Faust 2006b: 170–87, and references). Bendor stated very clearly that Israel had a sedentary background: "The kinship structure is rooted entirely in the sedentary agricultural Israelite society, and is not a remnant of a period or a system of nomadic shepherds. [. . .] This differentiation [. . .] is detached from historical reality and has its source in romanticism and idealization of the bedouin type" (Bendor 1996: 262–63). The currently accepted view is that agricultural society was the basis of the kinship structure, because most of the latter's features can be clarified against an agricultural background (regardless of Israel's origins). So, it appears that the biblical material reflects the reality of a permanent agricultural society (see, for example, Bendor 1996: 216–24), and therefore the settlement process was not responsible for the deep changes that traditional Israelite society underwent with the establishment of the Monarchy. Extensive study of the Settlement period resulted in attributing the changes to other causes: the establishment of the Monarchy itself and the processes accompanying this event, especially the formation of the royal administration and urbanization (see for example: Frick 1985; Hopkins 1985; Coote and Whitelam 1987; Finkelstein 1989).

The Establishment of the Monarchy and the Royal Administration

Following the written sources, many scholars believed that the royal administrative system was formed in the time of David and perhaps even before, during Saul's reign (see, for example, Aharoni 1962: 114–15; Elizur 1996).[25] The royal administration continued developing over time, acquiring more and more central power. Some noted that David's list of ministers (2 Sam 8:16–18; 20:23–26) still contained dualities, such as two military commanders (one for the popular army and the other for the mercenaries) and two priests. Solomon's minister list (1 Kgs 4:2–6), however, includes many more ministers but only one military commander (only for the mercenaries, not coincidentally) and one priest.[26] This shows Solomon's intent to strengthen the

---

24. In his opinion, another cause of the social gaps was Canaanite influence on the royal court.

25. Such text-oriented studies took the existence of the United Monarchy for granted, of course, and while this issue is hotly debated today, it is quite clear that the texts cannot be used for such fine-tuned reconstructions.

26. Chaney 1986: 67–68; he also adds that, prior to David's death, his heirs, Solomon and Adonijah, fought over the inheritance. Solomon was supported by Zadok, one of the two high priests from David's rule, and by the mercenary army, while Adonijah was supported by Abiathar, the other high priest, and Joab, commander of the popular army. Solomon's victory thus signified the victory of the administrative system and royal organization over the remnants of the popular tribal system. Solomon drastically changed traditional society by raising taxes, taking slaves, and more. David may have deliberately preserved this duality (hence the appointment of two priests and, especially, two military commanders), and Solomon's anti-traditional decision on this matter was one of the causes for the split in the kingdom.

royal administration. This intent is also reflected in the list of his officers (1 Kgs 4:7–19) and in the activities that involved the use of significant manpower. The administrative system formed during the Monarchy directly and indirectly caused a significant number of social changes.

Reviv lists three primary changes in Israelite society under the influence and initiative of the Monarchy (Reviv 1993: 98–102).[27] First, the tribal framework was broken. The list of Solomon's governors (1 Kgs 4:7–19) indicates that the Monarchy understood that its success depended on destroying the territorial-tribal framework. The movement toward centrality deliberately undermineed the population's traditional framework.

Second, many new classes emerged within the kingdom. With the establishment of the Monarchy, a class of people arose that was organizationally and economically dependent on the Monarchy (some identify them with the "king's servants" mentioned in 1 Sam 18:5; 2 Sam 2:13, and elsewhere). The various types of work performed by various artisans for the Monarchy (such as building projects) created and promoted new branches of the economy, thus increasing the importance of non-agricultural elements within the population. This class probably originated during the establishment of the royal administration and army and in line with the operation of the royal economy and its various branches. As the economic activity of the Monarchy increased, many additional positions were added to this class. The active involvement of the Monarchy in international trade brought merchants, sailors, and others into the royal system (1 Kgs 9:26–28; 10:15, and elsewhere). To this category one should probably add the Levites, who were involved in the administrative system in some manner (Reviv 1993: 19–20; B. Mazar 1974). The existence of the various groups close to the regime (and not involved in food production) placed a heavy burden on the state's economy, divided the population from the regime, and served as leverage for achieving the Monarchy's aims: "So it appears that the 'king's servants' helped break the tribal structure of Israel and promote the royal interests, as well as being a means for filling the regime's instructions" (Reviv 1993: 101).

Third, the Monarchy nurtured the urban population and its link to the crown. It appears that the Monarchy needed allies in its attempt to break the traditional frameworks, and it found them in the urban population, especially in its nonagricultural elements: merchants, military and administrative staff, artisans, and others. These sectors thrived in the royal economy and naturally supported its activities. It is also possible that the non-Israelite people who were conquered at the beginning of the Monarchy supported it, because they were dependent on its good will. The towns became the center, and the Monarchy directed most of its economic resources to them. The state had an ambivalent attitude toward the local authority systems of the towns, which were largely traditional. It appears that the state avoided harming the elders in order to prevent shock and also used them for its own purposes; thus

---

27. Notably, even if some scholars are correct that there was no United Monarchy during the tenth century and that the kingdom was established later, the processes that took place then must have been very similar to those described here (see below, chap. 9).

they were gradually integrated into the urban–royal authority layer (for a slightly different understanding, see chap. 9).

It seems that these processes had begun already during the period of the early Monarchy. At this stage the upper levels of urban society detached themselves from the traditional framework, and the process during which the wealthy acquired large agricultural estates began (Reviv 1993: 45, 64). This process developed throughout the period of the Monarchy, as the state continued to damage the traditional framework in various ways and taking parts of its roles for itself (compare Perdue 1997: 209–10).

Urbanization

Most scholars view the establishment of the Monarchy as a major factor in the acceleration of the urbanization process during Iron Age II. This process had begun during Iron Age I and probably reached its peak in the eighth and seventh centuries B.C.E. The biblical texts referring to the Settlement period do not mention urban activities not related to the tribe or other traditional frameworks, but presumably local interests detached from the kinship structure gradually began to form in the main settlements (Reviv 1989; 1993). The development of local interests was greatly influenced by economic specialization and by the increasing number of residents with defined professions. From the beginning of the period of the Monarchy, the city became a melting pot, creating new population compositions (Reviv 1993: 95, 97). The city began to be socially independent and was no longer perceived as part of the larger settlement and kinship fabric.[28]

The Changing Economic System

During the Settlement period, the economy was mainly autarkic, but already in this period conditions started to develop that contributed to the formation of production surpluses, which led to the formation of a barter economy based on supply and demand (Reviv 1993: 61). This development suited the period of the Monarchy and enabled the growth of the royal administration in a self-perpetuating process: the surplus enabled the development of a more complex system, and this in turn allowed the state to use the surplus to an even greater extent (see, for instance, Finkelstein 1989). The exchange system suited the purposes of the monarchy and the upper class, and allowed them to accumulate property and capital (Reviv 1993: 62).[29]

---

28. Stager (1985) explained the growth of the towns at the beginning of the Monarchy by an economic process he called the "closing of the highland frontier." According to his explanation, the settlements in the hilly regions reached the limit of possible cultivation. The lands were fully exploited and could not be further subdivided as part of the next generation's inheritance. The sons who did not inherit a family plot had three options: the army, officialdom, or the priesthood. This required relocation from the rural sector into the towns and created a demographic increase in the towns. However, this theory is difficult to accept. The settlement in the hills was much more intensive in the eighth century compared with the tenth century, even though there were no special technological developments over time. Thus it transpires that the land in the hill region was far from being fully exploited in the eleventh–tenth centuries, and probably even in the eighth century.

29. Reviv proposes that this economic system reflects Canaanite influence (compare Lods 1932: 397), but this is not necessary.

Even before the period of the Monarchy there were individuals with relatively great wealth, but from the time of the early Monarchy onward the transferral of land (of increasing size) to private ownership increased rapidly. The acquisition of capital and property by a minority led to the formation of private estates (according to Chaney [1986: 73], at least some of these estates specialized in the production of oil and wine). *Latifunda* sprang up increasingly in both Israel and Judah. Several factors fed this process of property and land acquisition by the minority: (a) royal grants expressing the king's gratitude to special people;[30] (b) deliberate colonization of new regions conquered during expansion; (c) the impoverishment of plot owners, leading them to sell their lands, or entitling their creditors to appropriate their lands, as was customary throughout the ancient Near East (Reviv 1993: 64).

The first two factors were probably more common during the early Monarchy, when many new territories were conquered (see Chaney 1986: 67–68, on the first factor). However, the third factor reveals the other side of the process in which the few amass property—that is, the impoverishment of the many. As the standard of living of the estate holders rose and their political power grew, so the independence of the impoverished farmers, who gave or sold their lands to the landowners, declined. They became serfs dependent on the people who had expropriated their land, and "in this respect, the rise of the latifunda was accompanied by the impoverishment of the population" (Reviv 1993: 65). The severe criticism of the prophets (such as in Isa 5:8–10; Mic 2:2, and elsewhere) shows that in the ninth to seventh centuries B.C.E. this process expanded and deepened.

Researchers have noted additional factors that helped concentrate land and capital ownership in the hands of a few members of the upper class. According to Chaney, beginning in the tenth century B.C.E. there were two parallel systems of land ownership. In the valleys and other recently conquered areas, royal estates were set up, while in the hill country the previous setting of independent farmers was initially preserved (Chaney 1986: 69). These two systems existed under unequal conditions. The regime imposed various taxes and, while the farmers had previously been able to keep profits from good years for use in bad years, now, following the raising of various taxes, there was no surplus left for this purpose. So the lands gradually moved into the hands of rich landowners.

Reviv noted that the surplus/profits produced were not distributed equally between the different classes: the lower the class, the smaller its share (if it received anything at all), while the well-off actually gained more, thanks to their control and supervision of the growing market economy. In parallel, the dependence of the lower classes on the wealthy increased, since the return they were forced to give for assistance kept increasing (Reviv 1993: 75). Thus the individual's or household's lands gradually moved into the possession of the few: "It transpires that the increasing dependence brought great benefit to the strong groups because it enabled the accumulation of additional capital and profitable economic involvement. In contrast, there

---

30. See 1 Sam 8:14, and note the complex relations between David, Ziba, and Mephibosheth (2 Sam 9:1–13; 15:1–4; 19:22, and elsewhere).

was a significant parallel impoverishment in the wide, weak margins of the population, especially in the large rural-agricultural sector" (1993: 76). The monarchic regime aggravated social polarization through the pressure of taxation, recruitment, and labor services (1993: 76; compare Coote and Whitelam 1987: 91; Blenkinsopp 1997: 86–88), while the rich acquired additional capital through providing loans, the repayment of which involved the payment of interest, giving pledges, and serfdom (Reviv 1993: 76–80).[31]

Chaney pointed out the correlation between the economic situation of the farmers and their worth as soldiers in times of need: as they were needed less, so their economic situation worsened (Chaney 1986: 70; compare Coote and Whitelam 1987: 115). This process of decreased demand occurred due to the rise of a permanent, standing army, begun during David's rule (the "Cherethite and Pelethite" battalions). But in David's time, there was still a commander of the popular army in parallel to the commander of the permanent army, while in Solomon's time the commander of the mercenaries was appointed as commander of the entire army (Chaney 1986).

Incidentally, it is worth noting that some scholars believe that in the final years of the Kingdom of Israel, the social gaps became less prominent due to the kingdom's military, political, and economic decline. This development hurt the elites in particular (Uffenheimer 1973; compare Weisman 1994: 20).

The Changing Family Structure

The social and economic changes also influenced the family structure, and we can see this as an indicator of the changes that took place in society as a whole (see also Faust 1995b; 1999b). According to Reviv, "some texts allow a view regarding the gradual disintegration of the *mishpahah* and the rise in the importance of the *bet av* and the individual. Other books preserve the call for the cancellation of collective responsibility, which could only be heard against the background of the loosening of this framework (2 Kgs 14:6; compare Deut 24:16; Ezek 14:12ff.)" (Reviv 1993: 103). Indeed, with the influx of the population into the towns and their employment in the new professions or the state administration, a new situation was created in which the relevance of the old kinship framework was lost. People who had just arrived in the city abandoned their extensive families and formed (or founded) only nuclear families. Officials or officers who were stationed in various remote places probably took only their nuclear families with them and left their *bet av*s behind, since an official cannot necessarily employ his sons and relatives in his same role. Even if the son of an official continued his father's career and turned to public administration, his position and place of work would be determined by the state's consideration rather than the family's wishes. The process was more severe among the lower classes. In contrast, presumably the effect of the change was milder (if it was even a problem) in the rural settlement sector, which maintained a more traditional character (compare de Vaux 1965: 22; Reviv 1993: 49–52; see also Faust 1995b; 1999b).

---

31. According to Chaney (1986: 68), this was the background for the development of the institution of the "redeemer," the role of which was to protect the family's lands.

Did Changes Occur in the Transition from
Settlement to Monarchy? An Alternative View

Bendor, in his book on the household, presented the opposite position of the accepted opinion presented above. In his opinion, Israelite society did not undergo any
destructive process in the period of the monarchy, and most of its citizens remained
farmers cultivating their own land. He believes that the Israelite city was unlike the
Greek *polis*, and its existence did not undermine the kinship structure. The *mishpahah*
continued to exist even in the city, in the framework of large kinship groups containing *batei av* (Bendor 1996: 216–24). In fact, apart from the capital cities, Jerusalem
and Samaria, the towns were agricultural and should not be contrasted to the rural
sector. The Israelite economy continued to be autarkic, and the rise in the importance
of trade and finance did not change this. The Monarchy did not abolish the kinship
structure at all, and the royal family constituted part of it. It did exploit the social
units (for purposes of recruitment, for instance) but did not destroy them: "The burden imposed by the monarchy did not break up the *bet 'ab*. It was only one among a
number of causes that affected the struggle for existence" (Bendor 1996: 115).

The kinship structure continued to prevail throughout the period of the Monarchy, and the biblical texts should be understood in this context, including those
that appear to indicate its collapse. Thus, for instance, according to Bendor, Isaiah's call, "Woe to them who add house to house and join field to field, till there is
room for none but you to dwell in the land!" (Isa 5:8), does not refer to the destruction of the traditional fabric of society, but to the internal tensions and struggles
within a household (Bender 1996: 130). Various processes detrimental to the weaker
population took place within the traditional households, since social and economic
differences existed even before the Monarchy, and so one should not accept the
argument that these were the results of the Monarchy and of urbanization (1996:
116–17). David Schloen has also suggested recently that the kinship framework was
preserved throughout the period of the Monarchy (Schloen 2001; and see also Stager
2003: 70–71).

Apparent support for this argument can be found in the words of Silver, who
examined the period's economy and determined that the archaeological record contains no evidence for the existence of particularly severe gaps in the eighth–seventh
centuries B.C.E.[32] In his opinion, this was a period of economic prosperity. A rise in
the general standard of living thanks to the economic prosperity can be identified,
but there is no evidence that the wealthy became rich at the expense of the poor
or contributed to social polarization (Silver 1983: 111–18, 248). He indicates that, in
times of prosperity, economic and political unrest tends to develop, and as a result
an altruistic ideology forms. Against this background, he sees the development of
classical prophecy, which dealt so extensively with social problems (1983: 234).

---

32. Fritz (1995) and Holladay (1995), who dealt with the subject from an archaeological perspective,
reached the conclusion that Israelite society was essentially "egalitarian" and that, apart from a thin layer
mainly connected to the Monarchy, no gaps in society can be identified.

Note, however, that Silver's arguments are not convincing. Thus, for instance, he claims that the economic situation during the Monarchy was reasonable but that the prophets—members of the elite (1983: 139–43)—succeeded in conducting the reform they preached and that this reform, contrary to any economic logic, destroyed the economy, weakened the kingdom, and eventually realized the prophecy of doom by bringing about the destruction of the kingdom (1983: 247–51). This argument is based on his deliberate (and conscious) attempt to oppose certain economic approaches (1983: 111–12, 134, 249), and it is not based on any real data. For instance, there is no reason to believe that all the prophets belonged to the upper class.

Between the Eighth and Seventh Centuries B.C.E.

Most scholars do not discuss the eighth and seventh centuries B.C.E. separately but treat them together (for example, Jamison-Drake 1991: 138, 141; Silver 1983: 117, 247; Dever 1995: 416). In contrast, Halpern stresses the differences between these two centuries (Halpern 1991). He thinks that theology developed from a concept of collective responsibility to a concept of personal responsibility. The idea of collective responsibility reflected a traditional society, where three or four generations lived in proximity, so it was natural for the extended family to bear responsibility for the individual members (for example, the punishment of sons for the sins of their fathers). The idea of personal responsibility, conversely, reflects a society in which the state has greater importance, because the state mechanism prefers personal responsibility and greatly reduces collective punishment (Halpern 1991: 17).

Halpern anchors this development chronologically, relying on the fact that Jeremiah and Ezekiel express the idea of personal responsibility and oppose collective responsibility in the seventh century B.C.E.: "In those days they shall say no more, 'Parents have eaten sour grapes, and the children's teeth are blunted.' But every one shall die for his own sins: whosoever eats the sour grapes, his teeth shall be blunted" (Jer 31:29–30); "What do you mean by quoting this proverb upon the soil of Israel, 'Parents eat sour grapes and their children's teeth are blunted'? [. . .] Consider, all lives are Mine. [. . .] The person who sins, only he shall die" (Ezek 18:2–4). The punishments are mostly personal, except for cases of betraying God (Halpern 1991: 11–13; but see Kaminsky 1995).

According to Halpern, Sennacherib's campaign of 701 B.C.E. was the turning point in the history of Judah that motivated this development. In the siege war imposed by Sennacherib, Judah needed consciously and deliberately to surrender the agricultural hinterland, and the strategic outcome was determined by reliance on the urban sector. The rural sector was abandoned, while the towns were fortified in the hope that they could survive until Sennacherib was forced to withdraw. The rural population was employed in fortification work and was partly relocated in the towns. At the same time, Hezekiah initiated cultic reforms, in which he destroyed only rural temples. Sennacherib reported that he destroyed the villages of Judah, and presumably exiling of people also seriously damaged this sector. After the campaign, the rural sector remained destroyed, and in fact only Jerusalem survived (Halpern 1991:

25–27). So, the rural sector was destroyed by both Hezekiah's actions and Sennacherib's campaign. In the new reality, the clans and rural landowners lost their power
to the court factions and the regular army. The rural priesthood also lost its power,
and the state now controlled the cult directly (1991: 59).

In the seventh century B.C.E., there was a gradual process of recovery in Judah.
There are signs of renewed settlement in the rural sector, but the nature of this
settlement is different from the nature of the earlier stage. Now it is a systematic
process, which indicates an interest in massive cultivation for defined economic
needs (Halpern 1991: 61). Judah moved from a traditional economy to an industrial
economy, and this change is also reflected in the greater number of epigraphic finds
from this period (1991: 63–64; compare Finkelstein 1994). The population of Jerusalem at this time was very dense, due to the *hamulahs*[33] that had arrived there from
other places during Sennacherib's campaign. The new settlements set up at this time
(such as in the Boqea Valley and at En Gedi) were too small to settle whole *hamulahs*,
and so presumably the price of renewed settlement was the dismantling of clans.
This process continued into the period of Manasseh.

Thus, in the seventh century B.C.E. the framework of the extended family was
broken, and the nuclear family became the dominant family type. Halpern supports
his reconstruction with archaeological findings: the cooking pots from this period
were smaller, probably because they needed to feed fewer people (but see Auld and
Steiner 1996: 72). The family tombs, at least apparently, contain fewer cells, probably
because the kinship groups were smaller, and for the first time there were individual
burials outside Jerusalem. At this stage, the state addressed its messages directly to
the nuclear family without the mediation of the clan. This is apparent in Deuteronomy, according to Halpern, where most of the state ideology is directed at individual
citizens rather than *hamulahs*. According to the new ideology, all citizens were equal
(for example, women could inherit property), and their fate no longer depended on
their fathers. In some respects, this was a period of alienation: the individual was
self-sufficient and was no longer perceived as an integral part of the extended family
(Halpern 1991: 71–89 and additional references there). The elements typical of traditional society were now perceived as inferior, foreign, and even pagan (1991: 90–91;
compare Silver 1983; for further discussion of the differences between the seventh
and eighth centuries, see chap. 2 below).

Between Israel and Judah

Although the issue was not thoroughly examined, in the past almost all scholars
discussed the kingdoms of Israel and Judah as one unit (e.g., Reviv 1993; Isserlin
1998: 7–8). Indeed, the kingdoms of Israel and Judah seem very similar from a social
point of view, and in many cases the situation in both kingdoms is simply discussed
together (Bendor 1996; Herzog 1992a; 1997a). This attitude is explicitly addressed by
Reviv (1982: 102; compare 1989: 102–3):

---

33. A "hamula" is a large kinship group. The term is Arabic but is used by many scholars today. I do
not want to translate with a modern anthropological term, since this would be a form of interpretation
(for this, see chap. 4).

Upon the division of the kingdom of Solomon, two political units were formed with shared historical, cultural, and social backgrounds. The division into "Israel" and "Judah," although it had some basis in the Settlement period and in the period of the United Monarchy, did not overshadow the elements unifying the Israelites. The limited information at our disposal, referring mainly to the Southern Kingdom, leaves no doubt that similar social development occurred in both the sister-kingdoms.

A much more cautious position was expressed by de Vaux. Having discussed the stability of dynasties in Israel and Judah, he stated:

> It is probable that if our information about the two kingdoms was fuller and more balanced, other institutional differences would come to light. One fact at any rate is very clear: Israel and Judah are sometimes allies, sometimes enemies, but they are always independent of each other, and other nations treat them as distinct entities. This political dualism, however, does not prevent the inhabitants feeling themselves to be one people; they are brethren (I K 12: 24; cf. 2 Ch 28: 11), they have national traditions in common, and the books of Kings, by their synchronized presentation of the history of Judah and Israel, claim to tell the story of one people. This people is united by religion. Like a man of God before him, who came from Judah (I K 13: 1f.) Amos the man of Judah preached in Bethel. (de Vaux 1965: 97)

Despite de Vaux's words, most scholars did not refer to differences in the social reality of the two kingdoms, although many studies noted that the kingdom of Israel was much larger and wealthier than the Kingdom of Judah (e.g., de Vaux 1965: 65–67; Oded 1984: 135).[34] Recently, some scholars (mainly archaeologists, or others on the basis of interpretations of archaeological data) suggested that the two kingdoms were two distinct entities, with little or no connection whatsoever (see, for example, Finkelstein 1999b).

Summary

Previous historical research has thoroughly encompassed the various social issues. Many scholars discussed them in light of the Bible and the Near Eastern sources on the one hand and using social-scientific theories on the other hand, and the survey provided here attempts to draw a continuous picture of the social history of Israel that represents the full range of opinions of the scholars who have discussed this period within its wider historical context. The various opinions presented will be examined extensively in succeeding chapters; before that, chap. 2 presents a summary of archaeological studies on Israelite society.

---

34. Chaney (1986: 70–72) did argue that Israel (at least in the beginning) had a different policy from the United Monarchy, due to opposition to the taxes of David and particularly of Solomon, but from the days of Omri onward there were processes that reduced equality in the Kingdom of Israel as well.

Chapter 2

History of Archaeological Study
on Israelite Society

We have seen that historical studies, despite their focus on political history, have extensively discussed issues related to society, its structure, and organization, mainly in light of the Bible. Archaeological publications, in contrast, have ignored this subject almost entirely (e.g., Hopkins 1985: 252; Dever 1995: 416). Most of the archaeological studies of Iron Age II have addressed issues of typology, chronology or political history, while the discussion of social issues remains in its infancy.[1] This attitude is noticeable in comparison with the opposite situation in the study of Iron Age I, where the great interest in the Israelite settlement has led to many social studies, dealing with various issues such as settlement distribution, the form and functions of domestic structures, and other subjects (e.g., Gottwald 1979; V. J. K. de Geus 1982; Hopkins 1985; Stager 1985; Lehman 2004; R. D. Miller 2005; and many others).

In recent years, however, many archaeological studies have been published about Israelite society in Iron Age II, especially on questions related to the formation of the Israelite monarchy (Hopkins 1985; Stager 1985; Finkelstein 1989; 1999b; 2005; Faust 2003a; 2007b, and additional bibliography there). However, the earlier of these studies, despite defining the transition of the central hill country to a statehood organization (compare Holladay 1995: 379), still constitute a supplement to the intensive study of the Settlement period, while the later studies became part of the debates over the United Monarchy and are not directly related to the issue discussed here. Certain aspects of society during Iron Age II have been discussed in a limited number of additional studies. This chapter will survey the various opinions and discuss topics of particular importance to the subject that will be dealt with in this book (some of the topics are also discussed in the later chapters of this book, where relevant).

General Studies

Most archaeological studies discussing Israelite society have referred to the subject in general and tried to identify characteristics of class stratification and levels of

---

1. Dever (1995: 416) expressed surprise about this state of affairs in view of the wealth of existing data. Chaney (1986) listed various reasons for scholars' avoiding the discussion of sociological issues, but he did not distinguish between historical and archaeological research (and as the previous chapter shows, one cannot argue that historical research has ignored the subject). Society during other periods in the archaeology of the land of Israel has not been studied properly either (T. E. Levy's 1995 edited volume is an exception that proves the rule), and where there is such research, it focuses on simple rather than complex societies (see Bunimovitz 1990: 1–7).

social organization (see also chap. 6 below). Jamison-Drake's book *Scribes and Schools in Monarchic Judah* (1991) discusses issues such as the administrative organization of the Kingdom of Judah, the existence of professional scribes, and so on. According to Jamison-Drake, the archaeological finds can testify, among other things, to social stratification in the Kingdom of Judah. First, a developed settlement hierarchy indicates a complex society, including decision-making centers and a concentration of surplus. In such a society, there would naturally be social stratification. Based on surveys and excavations conducted in the region, Jamison-Drake shows that in the eighth and seventh centuries B.C.E. there was indeed a very developed settlement hierarchy in the land of Israel and concluded that society was complex and stratified. Second, the existence of public buildings implies the existence of surpluses and of the managerial ability to organize them, meaning that there was a ruling class and an administration that built and used these buildings, signifying a complex, class society. Third, the finding of "luxury objects" indicates the use of surplus for trade. These factors indicate a society with a complex administrative system, requiring literacy, and relying on schools (the explicit subject of Jamison-Drake's book).

Despite its limited title, Jamison-Drake's study is a relatively wide-scale attempt to analyze the archaeological finds from Judah in social terms, and herein lies its importance. However, the methodological and practical faults of this study must be noted. Although the book was published in 1991, it was based on archaeological information that was out of date, such as the original excavation reports of many sites (Beth-Shemesh, Tell Beit Mirsim, and others), and the findings of the emergency survey from 1968. Not only is the information to be drawn from such sources very limited, the use of outdated material also led to serious flaws, such as not distinguishing between various levels (correctly identified many years before the book was written). Thus, for instance, Jamison-Drake attributes the hundreds of *lmlk* handles found on Tell Beit Mirsim to the seventh century B.C.E. (Jamison-Drake 1991: 216).

Jamison-Drake's book suffers from some other problems, in terms of both methodology and implementation. For example, although he discusses the Kingdom of Judah, his analysis refers to many sites that were not part of Judah, such as Ashdod (1991: 161), without noting the distortion of results that was likely to stem from this step. Furthermore, even when discussing the territory of the kingdom of Judah, Jamison-Drake used data of two types—results of surveys carried out in the hill country and results of excavations in the Shephelah—without attempting to base conclusions on their combination. Also problematic is his attempt to make inter-period comparisons throughout the entire range of time between the twelfth and the sixth centuries B.C.E., while ignoring the fact that there are some periods about which we have limited knowledge and also ignoring the difference in the preservation of finds in sites and levels that had undergone various processes of destruction and abandonment.[2] Another sort of problem is his habit of reaching conclusions without

---

2. This problem was recently noted by Na'aman (1996b). It is worth mentioning Lemche's extensive reference to Jamison-Drake's work (Lemche 1996: 107). After noting its importance, and even regretting that it had not received much recognition in research, he completely rejected the work itself, arguing that "it is not a major piece of work" and that "Jamison-Drake is dependent on material of low scholarly value,

presenting the data (apart from the graphs and tables at the end of the book). It is therefore difficult to know how Jamison-Drake analyzed the finds from each site and how he attributed particular finds to a certain period. The many mistakes that can be seen, despite the difficulty in presenting the material, warn us against using his conclusions. Thus, for instance, Jamison-Drake probably did not distinguish between finds from tombs and finds from settlements, as is apparent from the fact that the tables present findings from the sixth century B.C.E. at Beth-Shemesh, although in this century there was no settlement on this site, only a tomb.

It appears that Jamison-Drake was right in some of his conclusions about the eighth century, even if not necessarily for the right reasons. But his conclusion that Judah developed into a state much later in Iron II, probably in the eighth century B.C.E., does not necessarily follow from his already doubtful analyses (see further chap. 6 below).

Hopkins examined archaeological finds that manifest economic features, such as grand tombs, *lmlk* storage jars, and so on. In order to reconstruct social aspects of life in Judah, he included these finds in wide-scale historical reconstructions. In his opinion, Judah was actually composed of several societies—the urban elite, the regular urbanites, villagers, and nomads—and these groups differed from each other, as was the case during the Late Bronze Age. But it should be noted that Hopkins relied excessively on historical assumptions, some of which were not supported at all by the finds he referred to (for example, his argument about mismanagement [Hopkins 1985: 125] and other cases).

Dever recently delineated several guidelines for analyzing of Israelite society (Dever 1995). In discussing the renewal of urbanization in the land of Israel, he suggested distinguishing between three levels of settlement: large central settlements, medium-sized settlements, and small settlements (small villages and farms). Although most of the population lived in medium-sized and small settlements, the elite and decision-makers lived only in the central settlements. According to his premise, the processes of the centralization of power in the large settlements drove the urbanization process.[3]

Dever moves on to a more specialized discussion of the archaeological finds that testify to the existence of an upper class that possessed great wealth: tombs, public buildings, private homes of the "four-room-house" type, luxury items, and epigraphic sources. He assumes that the simple people were interred in simple inhumations that did not usually survive, while the monumental tombs that survived served members of the social elite. This means that these tombs reflect wealth and high status. The existence of monumental architecture is also evidence, in Dever's opinion, of central, sophisticated planning, because no private initiative could have performed these impressive construction projects (1995: 422–23). He briefly discusses the dominant house type, the four-room house, and suggests that the more spacious

dated archaeological reasoning, wrong or simply bad archaeology, misleading conclusions, and so on" (even though his method, in Lemche's opinion, was "faultless"). But after all this, Lemche warmly adopted the conclusions!

3. Later in his article (Dever 1995: 420–21), Dever also indicated the development of ethnic identity. This part of the article briefly, and even slightly speculatively, discusses general social processes.

homes of this type served as the villas of the upper classes. He also believes that the existence of luxury items indicates wealth. Dever also refers to literacy and argues that it was mainly the province of the elite, another indicator of social stratification. The epigraphic finds (the Samaria ostraca) also draw a picture of wealthy property owners, who, no doubt, accumulated their assets at the expense of the lower classes. Dever's article is almost the only attempt to discuss Israelite society as a whole in light of the archaeological evidence, which is the main reason for its importance. A different perspective on Israelite society was offered by Stager (e.g., 2003) and his students (e.g., Schloen 2001). According to this view, which is based on the concept of the patrimonial state, Israel and Judah remained kinship-based societies throughout their existence, and the backbone of the society was the traditional extended family (בית אב).

Economic Specialization

Various contradictory opinions have been expressed regarding the question of the economic specialization of city dwellers in Israel and Judah during Iron Age II. Fritz does not see any real sign of specialization and believes that all the cities' residents were farmers who provided for their own needs (although he seems to exclude the capital cities from this; Fritz 1995: 142). However, he seems to contradict himself by suggesting that the various towns contained soldiers' barracks (1995: 142–43). Presumably, a city in which soldiers were stationed also contained other professions (not just farmers). Moreover, the presence of an army (which is not a productive element and must be maintained by seizing the surplus) generates the concentration of various (specializing) service-providers around it.

Silver, who studied the economy in the period of the Monarchy in light of archaeological finds and written sources, reached the opposite conclusion, that in the kingdoms of Israel and Judah there was extensive specialization in the eighth–seventh centuries B.C.E. (Silver 1983: 247 and elsewhere). Other scholars support this conclusion. Eitan-Katz, for instance, identified in the archaeological record from Judah in these centuries various branches of economic specialization, especially in the field of agricultural production, as well as in other fields.[4]

Socioeconomic Stratification

Several types of archaeological finds have been perceived by scholars as indicating socioeconomic gaps: small finds, burial, and architecture.

Small finds: Many studies have referred, usually in passing, to pottery and small finds as indicators of economic status (poverty or wealth; for example, Yadin 1975; Elgavish 1994: 60). This attitude assumes, for example, that imported pottery or particularly fine ceramic vessels were owned by the wealthy. But this is a problematic assumption that has never, in the context of Iron Age Israel, been empirically

---

4. Eitan-Katz 1994 (see now also Katz 2008). It should be noted that she examined only finds from towns (and in Judah only). According to McClellan (1978: 280) there was economic specialization in various towns in the eighth century B.C.E. But he relied on the finding of dyeing installations in Tell Beit Mirsim, which most scholars currently consider to be an oil press rather than dyeing installations (see Eitam 1979). In his opinion, the farmers did not live in towns but in villages and farms around them.

tested and has never been based on systematic theoretical analysis.[5] In any case, the authors did not usually attempt to widen the scope from identifying the rich to learning about society as a whole, even on the level of individual settlements. The contribution of these studies, even if they are correct regarding individual cases, is thus of marginal value for understanding the total structure of a society.

A small number of studies are exceptions to this rule. Wood and Singer-Avitz tried to use the pottery and small finds to learn about the social reality. In his extensive study of Iron Age pottery, Wood argued that the number of vessels found in a house could indicate the wealth of the owners, but he did not try to apply his method in practice (Wood 1990): Singer-Avitz discussed this issue in a more concrete manner when she tried to learn about economic stratification in Beersheba based on small finds (Singer-Avitz 1996). Her study is singular both in its attempt to deal systematically with this issue and in its attempt to learn about the reality of a whole settlement without merely referring to one or two outstanding structures (for more detailed discussion, see the appendix to chap. 3).

Burial: Various scholars have considered the eighth–seventh century B.C.E. burial caves (known, for instance, from the Jerusalem region) to be evidence of social stratification based on the premise that these tombs were the burial places of the wealthy, while the poor were interred in simple inhumations that did not survive, and on the basis of differences among the excavated tombs (e.g., Dever 1995: 421; Hopkins 1996: 129; Barkay 1994; 1999). Other studies have proved this assumption to be true. For example, the various burials unearthed at Lachish, including many simple inhumations, enabled Barkay to establish this assumption regarding the social stratification in this town and in general (Barkay 1994: 148 n. 158). And a systematic analysis of the rock-hewn tombs also revealed sharp differences among them (e.g., Yezerski 1995; 1999; and see especially Barkay 1999). Thus, it appears that evidence from the various burials does indeed indicate social stratification.

Architecture: The first notable example of the use of architecture as a clear indicator of social stratification was probably supplied by de Vaux. In summarizing the results of his excavations at Tirzah (Tell el-Farʿah, north), he stated: "The houses of the tenth century B.C. are all of the same size and arrangement. Each represents the dwelling of a family which lived in the same way as its neighbours. The contrast is striking when we pass to the eighth century houses on the same site: the rich houses are bigger and better built and are in a different quarter from that where the poor houses are huddled together" (de Vaux 1965: 72–73; see also 1992: 1301). De Vaux did not just try to discover the degree of social stratification at the site on the basis of differences in the size and shape of the buildings; he also tried to understand the historical-social processes that took place during that period based on the differences among the tell's different levels (see Silver's criticism, 1983: 115–16).

Fritz presented an opposing argument. Having examined the plans of the various towns of the period and the buildings found in them, he reached the conclusion that there were no prominent gaps in Israelite society, and thus it should be seen

---

5. See the appendix to chap. 3, below. Even studies discussing terms such as "luxury items" (such as S. Geva 1989) did not define how to identify such an object (see also Hopkins 1996: 129–30).

as quite an egalitarian society (Fritz 1995: 188–89). In his opinion, the upper class that lived luxuriously was relatively small and included the royal family, property-owning families (from which high officials and senior officers were taken), courtiers, and perhaps small parts of the military. Most residents belonged to the lower class and were mainly farmers with houses and small plots of land. Fritz emphasizes the significant gap between the palaces and governors' residences in the capital cities (or administrative centers) and the private homes, and he states that the architectural uniformity in the residential towns of the period testifies merely to small differences between different population groups. In his opinion, the ordinary towns served the farmers (as a refuge), and "by no means constituted a contrast as in the case of 'town and country'" (1995: 189). The only real contrast was between villages and towns in the rural area and the capital and administrative cities. As a result, he concludes that poverty was shared by almost all the population, and very few escaped this fate.

This argument is supported by Holladay (1995). In his study of the economic organization of Israelite society, he claims that, "aside from palaces and clearly governmental residences, no residence from Iron II Palestine outstrips the average 'four-room house' by much more than a factor of two, or three at the outside" (1995: 392), which he believes is not a real gap and does not preclude the definition of Israelite society as egalitarian: it had wealth differences but no class differences (Holladay 1995: esp. pp. 391–92). While he accepts the existence of architectural differences (such as the "western tower" at Tell Beit Mirsim that overshadows the other structures at the site, or the large four-room houses found at Mizpah [Tell en-Nasbeh]), he identifies in the residential structures a continuity with the Iron I period, and in analyzing the function of the buildings he identifies wings that served as stables for animals. This, he believes, indicates that throughout the period the houses were occupied by families who operated independent economies. Holladay rejected the claim that the standard of living of the majority of the population declined in Iron Age II, because no extremely poor houses were found where the poor would presumably have lived, and he concludes:

> In short, on good present evidence, it is clear that Israel and Judah remained peasant economies (which characteristically display wealth distinction) throughout their independent existences, with independent household control of agricultural surpluses (after taxes, tithes, and possible rents or share-cropping costs) and—except for rulers' palaces and associated elite structures in the cities, and outsized houses with specialized storage facilities . . . [. . . there was] a remarkably limited range of household sizes. (Holladay 1995: 392)

McClellan, relying mainly on the finds from Tell Beit Mirsim, also noted that he hardly saw any evidence for poor quarters in the towns of the eighth century B.C.E. (McClellan 1978: 280). De Geus accepted de Vaux's analysis regarding Tirzah (Tell el-Far'ah, north) but noted that this was a unique case and that in general one could not identify economic differences between the various structures (for example, regarding Beersheba: V. J. K. de Geus 1982: 53–54; see also McNutt 1999: 158–62).

A return to the position of de Vaux is apparent in Campbell's study, which analyzes the finds from a residential house excavated in Shechem and reaches a generalized conclusion about the nature of the stratification of Israelite society (Campbell 1994). Campbell demonstrated the importance of the house under discussion by analyzing its size, the massive preparation undertaken for its construction, and the fact that the Assyrians went to the trouble of destroying it in particular. He concluded that it was inhabited by members of the elite. Campbell's conclusion is problematic, because it relies on the analysis of just one house, but he significantly clarified the discussion by considering factors other than the structure's size that had not been covered in previous studies: the degree of investment involved in constructing the building and the importance of the building as reflected in its location and surroundings.

Analysis of Residential Houses and Family Structure

Several works have discussed the structure of the family using a typological and functional analysis of residential houses. While these studies focused on the period of the Settlement (Iron Age I), they also referred to the period of the Monarchy (Iron Age II). The best-known among them is Stager's study "The Archaeology of the Family in Ancient Israel," which combines data from the Bible and from archaeological evidence and concludes that the basic family structure in this period was the extended family (Stager 1985). The extended family, according to Stager, did not live in one house but in a complex of structures, and the individual houses (usually of the four-room type) were inhabited by nuclear families (see also Schloen 2001; Brody 2009; see also chap. 3, below).[6]

This argument has been implicit in other studies that dealt with the subject of the family in passing, while analyzing the archaeological findings of the residential homes common in the Iron Age (mainly when attempting to calculate population),[7] and that suggested that these structures were inhabited by nuclear families (Shiloh 1970). In these scholars' opinion, this was usually a family of about five people (e.g., Broshi and Gophna 1984; according to Shiloh [1981: 279], there were eight people).

Holladay also studied the four-room house extensively and analyzed the functionality of this structure in detail (Holladay 1992; 1995). These and other studies tried to learn the function of each of the various spaces using ethnographic parallels and ethnoarchaeological research. Holladay concluded that this residential house suited the needs of a nuclear family of farmers, and due to the widespread distribution of this architectural type, he assumed that Israelite society was entirely a society of farmers. Because the structure continued to be the most common type during the period of the Monarchy as well, Holladay concluded that the character of Israelite society remained stable throughout the periods and did not undergo changes. This means that society remained agricultural, largely egalitarian, and without prominent socioeconomic gaps.

---

6. Compare Faust 1995b. Stager was preceded by Callaway 1983; and Harmon 1983. Harmon analyzed the finds from the hill region during the period of the Settlement (Kh. Raddana) and also believed that the individual houses were inhabited by nuclear families; the nuclear families were part of an extended family living in a cluster of houses (Harmon 1983: 122).

7. Many studies have dealt with the four-room house (such as Netzer 1992; Holladay 1992; 1995), but most of them dealt with functional analysis. As a result, and despite the social implications of an analysis of this sort, we consider it to be a typological and functional rather than sociological analysis.

Holladay's studies are important due to his use of the residential house as a sociological indicator, but this does not negate the problematic nature of his conclusions. His arguments that the four-room house was popular thanks to its functionality and that there were no changes in this functionality (or in the structure of society) during the periods under consideration are not convincing. This architectural type was common in both towns and villages and in fact was also the basis for the plan of public structures (such as the fortress at Hazor) and probably even for the Judahite Tomb. One can argue that this frequency is explainable not merely in functional terms (which differed between cities and villages) but also based on ideological reasons related to the special character of Israelite society (Netzer 1992: 199 n. 24; see also chap. 7 below; Bunimovitz and Faust 2002; 2003; Faust and Bunimovitz 2003; forthcoming). Thus, one should beware the conclusion that the continued use of an architectural form indicates an absence of social change.

Unlike the studies discussed thus far that analyzed mainly the architecture of the structures, a detailed discussion of the finds within some of those structures was carried out by Singer-Avitz (1996), including the finds in the houses of stratum II at Beersheba (more below). Additional studies were conducted by Hardin and Cassuto. Hardin (2001; 2010) analyzed in detail (more than any other study carried out so far) the finds in one dwelling unearthed at Tel Halif; Cassuto (2004) analyzed the finds in a number of structures from various sites in order to reconstruct the various activities that took place in them, and in an attempt to associate the various activities and spaces with gender-specific activities (this, in contrast to most studies of gender in ancient Israel, which were very general in nature and were based mainly on the texts).[8]

Also worth noting in this context is Eitan-Katz (1994), who examined economic production in towns in the Kingdom of Judah. She also reached the conclusion that the nuclear family constituted the basic economic unit.

Detailed Analyses of Specific Settlements

The only attempt to analyze the social nature of a specific settlement over a long period was Geva's study of Hazor in the eighth century B.C.E. (S. Geva 1989); it is very important because it was the first attempt of this kind in archaeology of the land of Israel. Geva analyzed the various strata of the city of Hazor and tried to understand social processes: how the local community dealt with the various dangers it faced; how it rebuilt its life after the various stages of destruction; how the state operated in the town of Hazor; and what relations were between the different elements in the city. Geva combined historical information with the archaeological finds, and tried to interpret the social processes that took place in the city in light of the various data. However, as in every preliminary study, various questions remain unexamined. Thus, for example, Geva did not deal with the question of stratification and socioeconomic classes or with issues of urban organization and planning (these issues will be at the focus of our discussion later).

---

8. Cassuto's study is part of a growing tendency to study gender in ancient Israel (see, for instance, the various works of Meyers [such as 1988; 2003]; see also Faust 2002b).

Another important study, though more limited in scope, was conducted by Singer-Avitz. She analyzed the pottery (and other finds) from a series of residential structures fully uncovered in level II of Tel Beersheba and reached interesting conclusions regarding the social nature of the various households. For instance, she tried to identify households that were wealthier than others. She also showed that certain structures were not consistent with a normal domestic life-style and proposed that they were inhabited by soldiers (Singer-Avitz 1996). In addition to arriving at conclusions regarding life in Tel Beersheba, with merely local applicability, this study is also an innovation in the archaeology of the region. For the first time, the small finds in residential houses were analyzed in detail in order to understand the functioning of the household. Thus her study bridged two levels of analysis: the analysis of a residential structure and its economic unit and the analysis of the entire settlement and its various quarters.

Between the Eighth and Seventh Centuries B.C.E.

Not all scholars discussing Israelite society saw the seventh century as a period worthy of discussion in its own right (e.g., Dever 1995: 416). However, archaeologists (or studies dealing with archaeological finds) even more than historians and biblical scholars tended to differentiate between these periods in terms of the general social context.

According to McClellan, in the eighth century B.C.E., Judah had a flourishing urban culture. Around the capital, Jerusalem, there was a network of fortified towns, all of which were planned in a similar and uniform manner, and thus rich houses could not be identified there. In contrast, in the seventh century B.C.E., the campaign of Sennacherib left extensive destruction in Judah, so that only Jerusalem remained standing, while in most of the other areas only fortresses and rural settlements survived (McClellan 1978). In this period, there was a decline in the standard of living of the population outside Jerusalem, and the rural residents were employed in cultivating the lands of large, wealthy landowners living in Jerusalem. Jerusalem itself grew significantly due to the arrival of many refugees who had lost their property. These processes formed new classes in society. In the eighth century, the economy was mainly royal, but in the seventh century, the rich exploited the economic decline to accumulate greater wealth and appropriated a sizable proportion of the economy (McClellan avoids using the term *latifunda*, because in his opinion there is no evidence of an accumulation of a surplus). In this period, the importance of the army within the economic system increased. McClellan summarizes the contrast between the periods by defining seventh-century Judah as a "city-state," in contrast to the eighth century, when it was a "nation state" (1978: 279).

Auld and Steiner painted a similar picture. In their opinion, the changes evident in area G (Shiloh's excavations) and trench A (Kenyon's excavations) in Jerusalem (the City of David) indicate that in the transition between the eighth and seventh centuries B.C.E. there was a parallel decline in power in the central royal regime and a rise in power of various elites, such as merchants (Auld and Steiner 1996). For instance, in the seventh century, the traders presumed to build private structures on the stepped stone structure that probably originally served as a podium for a royal building (note that this chronology is contested; see, e.g., Cahill 2003).

Eitan-Katz (1994) presented the opposite picture. She saw signs of a transition from a family-based economy in the eighth century to a centralized, royal economy in the seventh century. Beginning in the eighth century, various installations are found in the period's towns between and inside the buildings. Presumably these facilities were operated by the families who lived in the structures. In contrast, in the seventh century, settlements such as Gibeon and En Gedi had an economy based on the production of one product, indicating economic direction by a centralized regime (Eitan-Katz 1994; Katz 2008). The theory of the development of the economy in general and the royal economy in particular during the seventh century is also supported by a broader study of production and trade that showed that the economies of Judah and Philistia were highly integrated at the time, and both were incorporated within the wider Mediterranean economic system (Faust and Weiss 2005; 2011; Faust 2011a; see also Faust 2007c).

Other scholars stressed different elements. Finkelstein believes that, following Sennacherib's campaign, Judah in the seventh century had to deal with the reduction of its territory, because some of the most fertile areas it possessed in the past had been removed from its control. In his opinion, as a result of this, Judah intensively developed other areas, such as the Negev and the Judean Desert beginning in the time of Manasseh (Finkelstein 1994). Halpern also discusses the differences between the eighth and seventh centuries (Halpern 1991; however, archaeological evidence plays only a minor role in his discussion, which relies more on the historical study of the Bible): in the eighth century, there was a large rural sector and a largely traditional society, while in the seventh century, the rural sector was destroyed and traditional society ceased to exist. While most scholars believe that Judah in the seventh century was economically and demographically only a shadow of itself in the eighth century (e.g., Na^ɔaman 1993; 1994; H. Eshel 1991; Halpern 1991; McClellan 1978), this view is disputed (Finkelstein 1994; and detailed discussion in Faust 2008).

Summary

Most of the studies referring to Israelite society from an archaeological point of view discussed the issue rather generally. As a result, many potential directions for research have not been pursued, and essential questions remain unasked. Thus, for example, there has been no specific analysis of settlements from the viewpoint of their plan and organization (Geva's study of Hazor is an exception), and no one has tried to analyze any archaeological evidence from a social point of view in order to reconstruct Israelite society. In many of the partial studies published (that only implicitly deal with society), there are methodological flaws that cast a heavy shadow of doubt over the applicability of their conclusions. Thus, for instance, most scholars did not differentiate between Israel and Judah and dealt with both kingdoms together, implicitly assuming that these were similar societies (for example, Netzer

1992; Herzog 1992a; 1992b; Holladay 1995; Fritz 1996, and others).[9] This assumption needs to be acknowledged (e.g., Dever 1995: 416) and tested.

Worse, over the years, archeological works have tended to ignore the rural sector, which contained most of the population, and so far hardly any excavations have been initiated in rural sites for the period under discussion. Some scholars have been aware of this disadvantage (Holladay 1995: 391; Hopkins 1985: 252), and some of them have tried to bridge this gap by treating urban settlements as villages. Thus, for instance, Holladay treated Tell Beit Mirsim and Tell en-Nasbeh as large villages (Holladay 1995: 392). It appears that some of the problems in his analyses (and in the social analyses of other scholars) can be attributed to his lack of familiarity with the special features of this sector, which is the only explanation for the idea that urban sites such as Tell Beit Mirsim and Tell en-Nasbeh could represent the rural sector. A comprehensive study of the rural sector (usually from the accumulated data from salvage excavations) has only begun in recent years (e.g., Faust 1995b; 2000d; 2003a; 2003c; 2003d; this issue will be discussed in detail below, in chap. 4). So, let us summarize the state of archaeological research in Dever's words (1995: 416; see also above). After referring to a few good introductory books on the archaeology of the region, he summarizes thus:

> none makes any attempts to organize the data in terms of social structure, even though there are many suggestive possibilities. This is a serious deficiency in Syro-Palestinian and biblical archaeology, when one considers that the general field of archaeology has been moving toward social archaeology for 20 years or more. The orientation, however, reflects the typical bias toward 'political history.'

---

9. Several studies even expressed this assumption explicitly (e.g., Dever 1995: 416).

Chapter 3

Between Monarchy and Kinship:
Urban Society

This chapter discusses the archaeological evidence from the urban sector that relates to the structure of society. Most of the chapter is devoted to analyzing the various settlements at the site level (the meso level), and it concludes with a comparative discussion referring to the level of the entire society (macro level; see also chap. 6).

Definitions and Methodology

Definition of a City

Efrat stated that "the perception of a city changes from time to time and from place to place, and every civilization has its own definition of a city" (Efrat 1995: 57; for various definitions of cities today, see pp. 59–61; see also Osborne 2005: 5–8; R. G. Fox 1977: 29–38; M. E. Smith 2002). In his opinion, geographers in the past have not succeeded in finding a perfect definition for the phenomenon of the *city*. The question of the similarities and differences between *villages* and *towns* has also stood at the center of many studies (such as Herzog 1997a: 1–16; Enoch 1985; Grossman 1994; Osborne 2005: 5–8). In a fundamental article on the urban revolution, Childe listed several traits that in his opinion characterized the first cities, such as size and number of residents, presence of a nonproductive population, concentration of surplus, monumental construction, existence of a ruling class, and so on (Childe 1950; for additional urban characteristics, see also Reviv 1993: 85; for a similar discussion on another period, see, e.g., Safrai 1980: 10). This is not the place for an extensive discussion, but despite differences in the approaches of various studies, it is possible to generalize and state that the urban characteristics accepted by many scholars today are: the (relatively) large, dense, permanent concentration of a heterogeneous population; population mobility; complex division of labor; and socioeconomic stratification (Efrat 1995: 58; see also R. G. Fox 1977: 30; M. E. Smith 2002).

Notably, the early cities contained a significant agricultural population (e.g., Childe 1950: 9). According to many scholars, all the early cities were agricultural in nature, and the dichotomy between them and villages was a projection of a later reality (see, e.g., Sjoberg 1960; 1965; Frick 1970; Bendor 1996: 219). If these scholars are correct, there is no point in distinguishing between the urban sector (discussed in this chapter) and the rural sector (discussed in the next chapter). However, during the period of the Monarchy, as in many other societies, it does seem appropriate to distinguish

39

Map 1. Map of the urban sites discussed in chap. 3.

between town and country (e.g., Reviv 1993: 83–92; Herzog 1997a: 211–58, 275–78; and in general, Wirth 1965; Lenski and Lenski 1974: 259). The urban settlements were usually larger and denser than the rural settlements of the same society. Furthermore, in urban settlements one can find social stratification (as we shall see below) and economic specialization, which are conventionally considered urban features.[1] We can also find monumental construction in these settlements, even the smallest of them. A comparison of cities and villages shows that there were also significant differences in the social organization and family structure of these two settlement sectors. Although many of the city residents were farmers, it appears that the assumption that the premodern city was rural in nature is mistaken, at least for the period of the Monarchy. As Wirth put it:

It is particularly important to call attention to the danger of confusing urbanism with industrialism and modern capitalism. The rise of cities in the modern world is undoubtedly not independent of the emergence of modern power driven machine technology, mass production, and capitalistic enterprise. But different as the cities of earlier epochs may have been by virtue of their development in a preindustrial and precapitalistic order from the great cities of today, they were, nevertheless, cities. (Wirth 1965: 50)

---

1. Many scholars who discuss the various differences between cities and villages note that there was not a clear dichotomy that enables us to make a clear-cut, context-free distinction for each settlement type or assume that in each settlement we can expect the appearance of all the features of one particular type; there are general and culture-dependent characteristics that change from region to region and from period to period (Efrat 1995: 57; Safrai 1980: 110). The urban nature of a settlement or the extent to which it may be defined as clearly "urban" is therefore relative (Safrai 1980; see also R. G. Fox 1977: 30).

The distinction between city and village, even in ancient times and in agricultural societies, is thus accepted by many scholars. As we shall see below, there was another significant difference between a city and a village in the period of the Monarchy: the monarchy's intervention (see also Herzog 1997a: 276). In the cities of this period, there are signs of such involvement that distinguish them from the rural sector (see also below, chap. 9; for a historical-social analysis, see Reviv 1993: 85–86) along with other clear differences.[2] But one should not forget that the cities in agricultural societies, large and important as they were, contained only a small proportion of these societies' populations.[3]

Examining Social Stratification on the Basis of Residential Buildings

The discussion in this chapter and the next chapter is primarily about architectural finds, since architecture is the best tool we have for identifying economic and social differences (see, for instance, Blanton 1994; Crocker 1985: 52; Kemp 1977: 137; M. E. Smith 1987: 301, 327; M. E. Smith et al. 1989; and others; see also Holladay 1995: 377; this issue is extensively discussed in the appendix to this chapter). The discussion focuses particularly on the residential houses found in the period's sites. The public buildings discussed here are mainly mentioned in order to show the existence of a state-related organization and an upper class (and as a database for discussing political organization). In contrast to public buildings, which are prominent in preliminary reports and receive much scholarly attention, in many cases residential buildings have not received any detailed analysis, and this is the place to redress this imbalance. In cases where this is possible, we will use information from graves to learn about socioeconomic stratification.

Small finds are discussed only in cases where the site's excavators themselves discussed them or for purposes of demonstration (such as in Hazor). While there are different methods proposed for identifying degrees of wealth based on small finds, particularly pottery (Wood 1990; Singer-Avitz 1996; M. E. Smith 1987, and bibliography there), as can be seen in the appendix to this chapter, a test of suggested models in some of the sites discussed here does not corroborate them. Moreover, as we shall see below, a careful examination of the finds in one of the buildings in Hazor shows that simplistically basing degrees of wealth on small finds can be misleading. In any case, even scholars who stress the importance of small finds in identifying socioeconomic stratification agree that examining the architecture for this purpose is more efficient (M. E. Smith 1987; 1994). In analyzing residential buildings, I shall examine three major components.

1. The Area of the Residential Buildings. This component should indicate the standard of living and status of the residents (Crocker 1985: 52), as well as the number of residents or the type of family living in the building (following Naroll 1962,

---

2. These differences exist regardless of one's theoretical approach to the city (see Herzog 1997a: 2–7). For additional differences, see below.

3. According to Lenski and Lenski (1974: 241; see also Herzog 1997a: 1), the population of the cities comprised at most 10% of the population of advanced agrarian societies, and it was usually lower than this.

and others). In many cases, there is a correlation between these two factors (more below). For technical reasons, the buildings' walls have been included in the calculation of their area—meaning that the area we are referring to here is the gross area of the building.[4]

2. Construction Quality.   For purposes of this study, the quality of a building refers mainly to construction based on a plan and the extent of using square corners and walls, rather than to the quality of the materials (although this feature is also important and will be discussed in a few places). Plan-based construction indicates an economic level above a certain threshold and an ability to build while ignoring topographical features or the needs of other people in the area—an ability that implies a degree of power. The buildings will be rated according to their plan on a scale from 1 (lowest) to 5 (highest). Each building that was evidently built according to a plan, such as the four-room house plan,[5] will be rated according to its compliance with the plan. Buildings that were not built to any known plan but that manifest an orderly form (the corners are at 90 degrees, the walls are straight, etc.) will receive a high score. These scores are, of course, subjective and are determined in a way that cannot be measured accurately. But because the scores are given to buildings that can be compared, I believe that the possibility of differing opinions is very limited and that there will usually be agreement about which building is more nicely built.

3. The Sharing of Walls.   Shared walls are a means of saving. Using them saves both building expenses (because an existing wall is used, and there is no need to build a new wall) and space (because a double wall would take up twice the space of a shared wall). Using a shared wall, however, has legal implications and restrictions (see Sand 1994) and might therefore be avoided by the rich and wealthy. An examination of the plans of buildings in the land of Israel during the period of the Monarchy shows that very few were built without shared walls and that these buildings were usually larger and more nicely built. Thus, it appears that only the rich built houses without shared walls.

Wherever possible, these three components will be examined in light of the building's location on the site and its relation to other buildings (on the importance of this feature, see Gibbon 1984: 150; Blanton 1994: 14–15). A house's location close to a citadel or public complex may indicate that people connected to these public buildings lived in the house; houses built in separate neighborhoods may indicate clear social stratification and even segregation. Location is, therefore, another (fourth) architectural component to use in determining socioeconomic stratification. This will be clarified in the discussion below.

Graphic Presentation of Social Stratification

In order to help demonstrate the degree of stratification, I have quantified the data and presented them in graphic form using (freely) the Lorenz curve. The Lo-

---

4. The measurements were done by hand and were therefore approximate (but the potential for error is minor and will not be significant with regard to the analysis below).

5. As noted earlier, the term *four-room house* is a generic term, referring to a house type discussed in general, including subtypes such as three-room houses.

renz curve is a means used in economics for calculating inequality. The graphs present the degree of the centralization of property or income in the hands of part of the population. The data to be calculated are arranged in increasing order and presented on the graph cumulatively (for example, if one is presenting income data, one begins with the lowest income). The X axis presents the number of elements calculated, while the Y axis presents the data calculated cumulatively.[6] A graph with a straight diagonal line thus reflects equal distribution of the resource under discussion, because each segment of the population possesses the same percentage of the resource. A concave graph indicates inequality because, as the level increases, so does the cumulative percentage of the resource.[7] To provide additional visual information, at the bottom of each graph there is another curve showing the amount of the resource in the possession of each group in a noncumulative way.

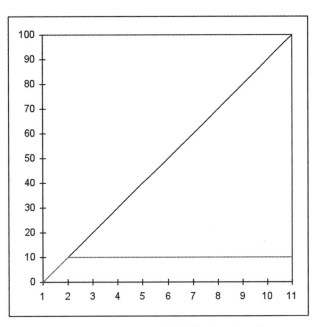

Graph 1. Graph showing an equal distribution of wealth.

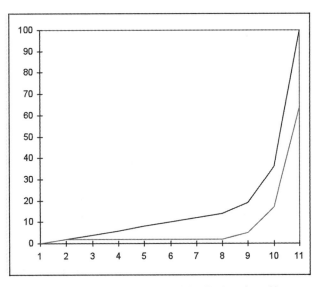

Graph 2. Graph showing an unequal distribution of wealth.

6. See for example Patinkin 1966: 16–17; Coulter 1989. For the implementation of this system for measuring plots of land, see for instance Fixler 1991: 75; 1992: 62–64. For an examination of differences based on architecture, somewhat similar to the method used here, see M. E. Smith 1994.

7. These graphs are usually calculated in percentages: the X axis represents the cumulative percentage of the owners of property or income, while the Y axis represents the amount of resource in a percentage. In order to avoid creating an impression of accuracy, I have not stated the percentages (more below).

To demonstrate, graph 1 presents 10 hypothetical groups (numbers 2–11) and a hypothetical resource with available units that add up to 100. As we can see, the first group possesses 10 units of this resource (at point 2, there are 10 units of the resource), and so does the second group (at point 3, there are 20 units of the resource, 10 of which are already possessed by the first group), and so on. Because each group possesses an identical amount of the resource, the society is egalitarian and the graph is straight.

Graph 2, which is not straight, shows that, of all the resources it represents, the first 7 groups (numbers 2–8) possess only 14 units, but the wealthy groups possess 65 units, representing 65% of the resource. So it is clear that this graph represents an extremely unequal society with regard to distribution of the hypothetical resource.

Due to the large difference in the data used by economists and the archaeological data at our disposal, it is important to stress that this is an **application** of an economic method to archaeology and that we are using it differently from economists.

The data (the "resource") presented in the calculations of the following graphs are residential buildings. For each settlement for which we have enough cumulative data, there are two graphs: the first graph calculates the area (size) of the buildings and examines only data that can be exactly and securely quantified. However, the use of solely the area of buildings presents a very partial reality, and the first graph, though it is the more objective of the two, is weak in indicating trends.[8] The second graph is a weighted graph that also takes into account the building's quality and the extent to which it shared walls. Since it also uses qualitative data, this graph is more subjective, but it presents a more complete picture of reality.[9]

To calculate the second graph, the building's size (the "objective" datum) is multiplied by its quality (the subjective datum) on a scale of 1 to 5. This measure is quite low, in order to prevent excessive distortion of the graph. In calculating the degree of use of shared walls, a value of 1 was given to shared walls and a value of 2 to separate or private walls (in this case, too, the data are "objective," although the figure is not). This measure is also quite low for the same reason. The inclusion of the qualitative data was not intended to produce a more accurate result (that is, a result that reflects the **degree of stratification**), but to achieve a better understanding of the **form and trends of the stratification**. Multiplying the various measures shows the

---

8. Palaces and fortresses were not included in the calculations, and perhaps this fact led to relatively moderate graphs. On the face of it, it would have been worth including them in the graphs, but I avoided this step to prevent concern that the method of calculation caused the concavity of the graphs. Because the purpose of the graphs is not to indicate the degree of stratification but its very existence and its nature, this self-imposed restriction does not detract from the study. Furthermore, in most sites, public buildings and grand structures have been excavated (and published) to a disproportionate degree compared with residential houses, so the calculation of these buildings would have skewed the upper part of the graph. It is also worth noting that for technical reasons the calculation of the buildings' area included their external walls. Since it was usually the larger buildings that had independent walls, in this case the method of calculation also helps reduce gaps, since for small buildings, the shared walls were calculated twice (for both buildings that used them). This datum also prevents, to some extent, the formation of concave graphs for subjective reasons.

9. Of course, the inclusion of these data still does not represent the full extent of social stratification, because it does not take into account the other elements that might reflect a stratified social reality.

different trends in different settlement sectors and different regions. These trends can always be distinguished by using simpler graphs and calculating with only one datum, but graphs of this sort are rather "shallow," while the weighted graphs are "deeper" and reflect the trends more clearly.

Cross-referencing data from different sites is very important. If in one site or one settlement sector the graph may be only slightly concave, it is arguable whether it actually indicates stratification. On the one hand, the statement that a concave graph shows stratification implies that a modest degree of concavity indicates relative equality; on the other hand, the graph reflects only part of the data, and the stratification in it may represent only some of the real stratification. Thus, the analysis of one settlement does not enable us to reach a clear conclusion or to decide between options. However, if another settlement produced a completely straight graph, one might conclude that complete equality could indeed be expressed in the findings, and thus even a slightly concave graph indicates at least some degree of inequality. In any case, the graphs are not intended to present accurate quantification of the data but merely quantitative estimates presented visually. In order to avoid creating the false impression of accuracy, I avoided noting the percentage of the "resource" or the degree of stratification (as required in a Lorenz curve) and found it sufficient to present the "raw data." What is important is the trend, not accurate results.

The Chapter's Structure

This analysis of the finds from various cities is divided into three parts: (1) The finds in the Kingdom of Israel, mainly from the eighth century B.C.E. Among the cities that are quite well known from an archaeological point of view are Hazor, Shechem, Shikmona, Tirzah (Tell el-Farʿah, north), Tel es-Saidiyeh and Megiddo, and to a lesser extent, Samaria, Dan, Gezer, En Gev, and Aphek. (2) The finds in the Kingdom of Judah from the eighth century B.C.E.: we have relatively extensive information about Mizpah (Tell en-Nasbeh), Jerusalem, Beth-Shemesh, Lachish, Tell Beit Mirsim, and Beersheba. (3) The finds in the Kingdom of Judah from the seventh century B.C.E.: we have information about Mizpah (Tell en-Nasbeh), Jerusalem, En Gedi, Gibeon, and Lachish.

Following a detailed analysis of each city, we examine the phenomenon (on the macro level) of public construction and urban planning in order to discover the degree of state involvement in the various sites and the nature of the local community organization. A detailed discussion will also be devoted to one type of public building (the public pillared building) that could have important implications for understanding the function of the urban system. Urban planning will also be examined from a new angle.

The final part of this chapter examines the family structure common in the city, the basic socioeconomic units, the nature of social organization in the city, and the mechanisms that influenced local society. The concluding discussion examines the differences between the cities of Israel and Judah and between the eighth and seventh centuries B.C.E., and proposes general conclusions regarding the structure of society in the urban sector.

The Cities of the Kingdom of Israel

Samaria

Samaria served as the capital of the Kingdom of Israel from the rule of Omri (878–871 B.C.E.) to the destruction of the kingdom. We know relatively little about the city during the period of the Monarchy. Its area probably reached several hundred dunams, but the area excavated includes primarily the royal complex in the heart of the city (for the excavation report, see Crowfoot, Kenyon, and Sukenik 1942).

Public Buildings. The royal complex is a sort of inner city (fig. 1), including the king's palace, storerooms, and administrative structures (Fritz 1995: 128–31). The fact that Samaria was the capital of a kingdom is clearly reflected in the archaeological finds: in the royal complex, there were monumental buildings constructed of ashlar stones, including fine capitals. Small finds that were discovered inside the buildings also indicate the site's importance: in one building ivory carvings were found,[10] and in another building the famous ostraca, known as the Samaria ostraca, were found. These ostraca indicate that a great amount of produce was concentrated in the site (but there is disagreement over its origins: Avigad 1982; Rainey 1988; see further discussion below). According to Chaney, the clear physical distinction between the royal complex and the rest of the city indicates that there was obvious social stratification in this site (Chaney 1986: 71).

Hazor

Hazor was an important city in the Hula Valley, close to one of the branches of the international highway (Yadin 1972; 1975; S. Geva 1989). It appears that during most of Iron Age II it served as a central administrative city, and various officials and position-holders (and perhaps also a military force) lived there (Herzog 1997a). The archaeological evidence also shows that in the eighth century B.C.E. the city occupied all of the upper tell.

Several levels from the eighth century B.C.E. have been excavated at Hazor. The following discussion concentrates particularly on the level in which the remains were most clearly uncovered, stratum VI, reflecting the middle of the eighth century B.C.E. (the days of Jeroboam II?), a period of economic prosperity (Yadin 1972: 179–85). Several public buildings and a large number of houses from this stratum were discovered in several excavation areas. In addition, a brief discussion of stratum V is also incorporated (but with caution) in order to increase the available information.

Public Buildings. The city in the eighth century B.C.E. was surrounded by a massive city wall, but the city gate from this period has not been discovered. At the highest point in the city (area B), a large citadel was discovered, with an open plaza in front of it. Perhaps this yard separated the royal section of Hazor from the other quarters of the city (S. Geva 1989: 93). Not far from the citadel was the city's large

---

10. The discovery of the ivories (small finds) in the grand palace does indeed indicate wealth, but the architectural context (the palace complex) speaks for itself, and the small finds such as the ivories only strengthen this interpretation. So, in this case there is a connection between the small finds and wealth; however, as in many cases, the architectural identification of wealth is more prominent (on this issue, see the appendix to this chapter).

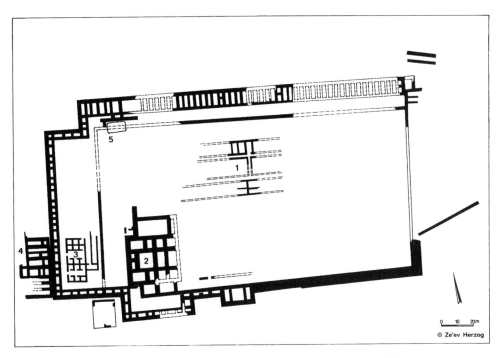

Fig. 1. Samaria: the royal compound (Herzog 1997a: 230). Reprinted courtesy of Ze'ev Herzog.

water-system (in area L). A large royal-economic complex was also unearthed in area G (Yadin et al. 1958–61; Yadin 1972; 1975; Ben-Tor 1996; S. Geva 1989). The importance of the city is also implied in the Bible, and it is listed among Solomon's construction projects (1 Kgs 9:15) and among the settlements conquered by Tiglath-pileser III (2 Kgs 15:29).

Residential Buildings. On the basis of an analysis of the excavated areas (revealing only a small proportion of the city's area), we know that there was a residential quarter in the center of the city. One house was also excavated near the water system, and another building was found near the complex in area G. The buildings are as follows:

1. Near the corner of the tell, in area G, a residential house of the four-room-house type (building 10037c) has been almost completely excavated (fig. 2). The building was well constructed and had two floors. Its ground-floor area is slightly over 70 square meters. At least on two sides, the building is not attached to other buildings, and it appears to be freestanding.

2. In the center of the tell, in area A (fig. 3), a four-room house was fully excavated (building 2a). The building is well constructed, and its ground floor area is about 160 square meters. According to Yadin, this was "the most beautifully planned and preserved building among the Israelite structures at Hazor. In fact, it represents the finest example of the Israelite 'corner-court pillared house' of that period ever found in Palestine" (Yadin 1972:

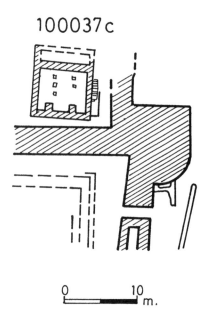

100037c

0   10
          m.

Fig. 2. Hazor: the structure at Area G (redrawn after Yadin et al. 1989: pl. 13; Geva 1989: fig. 16:3).

179). Geva also noted that "its orderly design, the right angles at the corners, the 'clean' outer lines, and its independence in relation to other buildings stand in dramatic contrast to some of the buildings later constructed around it" (S. Geva 1989: 46). Almost all of the building's walls are free, apart from its southwestern corner, where it seems that a similar building was attached to it (1989: 51). It is very likely that the building had a second floor (Yadin 1972: 180), like most of the four-room houses (Stager 1985: 15–17; C. H. J. de Geus 1986: 226–27; Netzer 1992: 196–98); thus, the difference between this building's area and that of many other buildings in Hazor is even greater.

3. Near the previous building excavated in area A (fig. 3), another structure was discovered (building 48), belonging to the three-room subtype. This house is quite small (its area is only 70 square meters), and its construction is poor. Although it belongs to the four-room type, its plan is irregular. Unlike its neighbor, most of its external walls are shared with other buildings.

4. Some other buildings have been discovered in area A that do not belong to the four-room type. Among them are the following three: (a) Building 14a, known as "the house of Makhbiram." Its plan is completely different: at the front there are rooms (probably shops), and behind them a paved yard, behind which are the house's two residential rooms, built one behind the other. The building is not large, and its total area does not exceed 70 square meters. If we deduct from this the area of the "shops," its size shrinks even further. In this building, there was no sign of planning either, and it also shares some of its walls with other structures. (b) Building 111, the area of which is about 70 square meters without the "shop" at the front (building 21a), or about 85 square meters including this shop. Some of its walls are independent, while others are shared. (c) Building 49, to the east of building 48. The area of the building itself is about 47 square meters, but Yadin and Geva include room 26 in it (Yadin et al. 1958–61; S. Geva 1989), and then its area increases to nearly 90 square meters. This building is small and unplanned as well, and its walls are shared with other buildings. It should be noted that in the first two buildings (14a and 111) the only free walls, built separately and not shared with other buildings, are the walls built alongside building 2a. The walls of this structure are self-standing, and the owners probably did not permit other people to use them. The third structure

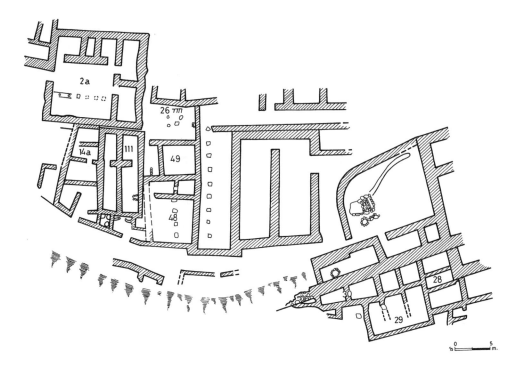

Fig. 3. Hazor: a residential neighborhood in area A (redrawn after Yadin 1972; Geva 1989).

(building 49) does not touch building 2a (apart from room 26), so it has no "wasted" walls, and all its walls are shared with other buildings. The fact that there is no "wasted" wall at the south of room 26, alongside building 2a, shows that this is not a room in the house but a sort of external yard, patio or lobby. Probably no additional wall was required because the external wall of building 2a was not used. Had this been a room in a building and there was a chance that the external wall of building 2a would be used, another wall would probably have been required here. This fact supports the suggestion that room 26 was not part of building 49.

5. In area A (fig. 3), close to where the city gate of stratum X ("Solomon's gate") had stood, some other buildings were found that were not of the four-room type (the numbering of these buildings is based on S. Geva 1989): (a) Building 28, the plan of which is similar to building 14a (1989: 55). Its area is about 55 square meters, including a casement that served as one of the walls. The building's walls are shared with neighboring structures. (b) Building 29, constructed from the remains of earlier buildings. According to Geva, its plan is similar to building 111. Its area is about 75 square meters, including a room and an especially thick wall that had previously served as a casement in the earlier city wall. The structure's walls are shared with neighboring buildings. In this area, the remains of other buildings were also found, but the scanty remains make it difficult to estimate their size, plan, and essence.

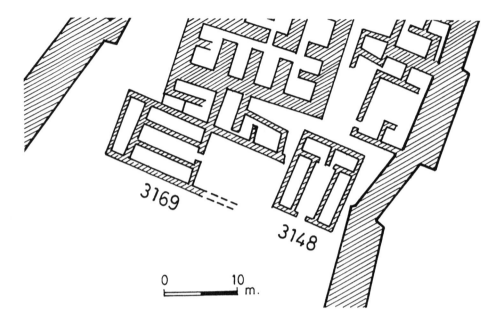

Fig. 4. Hazor: two four-room structures in area B (redrawn after Yadin 1972; Geva 1989).

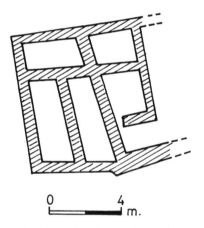

Fig. 5. Hazor: the structure in area L
(redrawn after Yadin 1972; Geva 1989).

6. At a slightly later stage, stratum V, two very similar four-room houses were built close to the citadel (fig. 4):[11] (a) Building 3169, a large building (its area is 120 square meters), built to a plan. (b) Building 3148, quite a large building (its area is about 100 square meters), with a clear and organized plan. Since both houses were built near the city citadel (in the plaza in front of the citadel), it is clear that they are not merely private homes. These buildings were probably built during the reorganization of the city's defenses (Yadin 1972: 187–89; S. Geva 1989: 41) and may have served for public purposes, although it is more likely that prominent leaders connected with the city's defenses on the eve of the Assyrian campaign lived there. The importance of these buildings and the status of their residents are implied by the use of ashlar stones (S. Geva 1989: 91).

7. Another four-room house was discovered in area L, at the head of the city's water system (fig. 5). Its area is slightly more than 50 square meters. The building was constructed before stratum VI, and during the period of this

---

11. These buildings existed in the eighth century B.C.E., but are later than the buildings discussed so far. However, these buildings help us understand the varied construction that existed in this period, and they expand our knowledge of upper-class homes.

Table 1. Buildings in Hazor in the eighth century B.C.E.[a]

Building	Area (approx.)	Plan (1–5)	Shared Walls	Location	Comments
Building 2a	160 sq m	5	No (except for a small section)	Probably the edge of a wealthy neighborhood	
Building 3169	120 sq m	5	No	Near the city citadel	Stratum V
Building 3148	100 sq m	5	No	Near the city citadel	Stratum V
Building 111	85–90 sq m (including shops)	3	Yes	Residential neighborhood	
Building 29	75 sq m	1	Yes	Residential neighborhood	
Building 10037c	73 sq m	5	Probably not	Near economic complex	
Building 48	70 sq m	3	Yes	Residential neighborhood	
Building 14a	70 sq m (including shops)	2	Yes	Residential neighborhood	Perhaps home of a cook (or servant), based on small finds
Building 28	55 sq m	1	Yes	Residential neighborhood	
Building 49	Less than 50 sq m	2	Yes	Residential neighborhood	
Building in area L	40–50 sq m	3	No	Near city water system	

a. At least some of the four-room houses had a second floor, but the table does not take this fact into account. If some of the other types of buildings did not have a second floor, the difference in area would be even greater. In addition, we should take into consideration the fact that the method of calculating the area of the walls increased (for technical reasons) the area of the small structures with shared walls (because in these cases the area of the walls was actually calculated twice).

level, its area was probably only about 40 square meters (1989: 90). Although this building belongs to the group of standard buildings, its construction is not particularly regular.

The above data are summarized in table 1.

Analyzing the Finds. The buildings may be categorized in three groups.

1. The first group includes grand structures such as building 2a, a large, fine four-room house where a wealthy family lived. The building has independent walls, unlike most of the buildings in Hazor in particular or Israelite cities in general, and

the excavators of Hazor stress the quality of its construction. Perhaps a few other buildings, not fully excavated, also belong to this group, such as the buildings to the west of Yadin's excavations, only the northwestern parts of which have been excavated (as can be seen in the plan of area A; compare S. Geva 1989: 51). The plan published following renewed excavations in this area indeed shows a large structure (over 150 square meters), of the four-room type, the plan of which indicates very organized construction and independent walls.[12] The two buildings excavated near the citadel probably also belong to this group. Their plan, the relatively short dura- tion of their existence, and the relative fineness of their construction indicate that prominent leaders lived in them (in this, they are distinct from building 2a, which was a private dwelling).[13] These buildings are also of the four-room type, and their external walls are not shared with neighboring buildings. So, people of position and wealth built large, grand houses based on a plan. They built their houses to be spa- cious and did not save resources in constructing the walls (there is almost no sharing of walls between houses), nor did they permit others to use the walls of their houses. These features indicate great power and influence, especially compared with the third group of buildings.

2. The second group comprises smaller four-room houses, which may have been inhabited by nuclear families. For example, building 10037c, which is well built and located near one of the city's economic centers, probably served as the residence of a senior official and his nuclear family. If a structure's size reflects the importance of an official, the size of this house probably indicates that this was a middle-level official. The building's regular shape shows that it was related to the nearby economic com- plex (Yadin 1975: 170). The other four-room house, in area L, very close to the water system, was probably the residence of the nuclear family of the official in charge of the site. Since the building is part of the water-system complex, its plan is rela- tively regular (a four-room house). Another building that may belong to this group is building 48, which was probably inhabited by a lower class or lower-middle-class family. In this case, it was constructed privately rather than by the state, which is why its plan is not regular or organized; in fact, it is based on using spaces between other buildings and using shared walls. Building 111, relatively regularly built, may also belong to this group.

3. In Hazor, more than in other cities, we can identify a third group of small, poorer houses. These buildings were discovered in area A. Their plans are irregu- lar, and in fact they lacked a plan. In any case, they were not built according to the four-room plan.[14] These houses are very densely constructed, with full utilization of

---

12. Ben-Tor 1996: 74. These excavations have yet to be published in an organized manner, and there is no accurate information about this building. However, the published plan shows that this house existed in the ninth–eighth centuries B.C.E., and we can assume that it also was located in level VI. Calculation of the area is very rough. This was confirmed recently, when two structures of this sort were reported (Ben-Tor 2008: 1773, 1775 [see especially the plans on p. 1733]).

13. This interpretation is further strengthened by the discussion on family structure in the urban sec- tor in the final section of this chapter.

14. In most other settlements in the kingdoms of Israel and Judah (such as Tell Beit Mirsim, Mizpah [Tell en-Nasbeh], Tirzah [Tell el-Farʿah, north], and perhaps also Tell es-Saidiyeh), the four-room (and par-

every available scrap of land, probably in order to save on building and land costs. So it seems that the poorest population lived there.[15]

Analyzing the architectural finds in level VI of Hazor enables us, therefore, to identify clearly two classes of the population—the wealthy and officials on the one hand, and the poor on the other hand—and perhaps a sort of middle class, consisting of minor officials and other residents.

The Location of the Buildings. An examination of the location of the buildings in the city helps us understand the social status of the inhabitants. Near the citadel, there were luxury buildings that probably served the most senior office-holders. Buildings reflecting the middle class were mainly in locations that probably served as residences of junior officials, near less-central state complexes such as the water system and the economic complex (on the eastern part of the city; see S. Geva 1989: 95). Additional buildings were exposed in area A, the main residential quarter excavated in Hazor: in the heart of the excavation area, there was a residential house that probably reflects the middle classes; at the edge of the area, there was a wealthy house (2a), apparently bordering a wealthier quarter (see also Ben-Tor 2008: 1773); but most of the houses belonged to the lower classes.

The conclusion that the types and locations of the buildings reflect a division into social classes is supported by the fact that what were identified as poor houses were not found near the royal complexes in Hazor. The poor structures were near the industrial area, sometimes built on the remains of public buildings that were no longer in use. This situation suited residences for the poor, who used any possible corner for housing (Faust 2003c; note that other parts of this abandoned public area were used to extend the wealthy neighborhood to the west; Ben-Tor 2008: 1775).

At the edge of area A, to the west of the "poor quarter," there are other buildings similar to building 2a (S. Geva 1989: 51; see also Ben-Tor 2008: 1773–75). According to the published plans, these buildings are constructed spaciously and at some distance from each other, which indicates that they did not share walls. Thus, it is possible that these are remains from a wealthy residential quarter; this sort of proximity between the poor quarter and the wealthy quarter was also observed in Tirzah (Tell el-Farʿah, north; see, e.g., de Vaux 1965: 72–73; 1992: 1301).

The Small Finds in Building 14a (the "House of Makhbiram"). This study focuses on architectural complexes due to the problems involved in the social analysis of small finds for the purpose of identifying wealth. These problems are demonstrated by an analysis of the small finds discovered in building 14a in Hazor, also known

---

ticularly the three-room) houses are the main construction type. In contrast, Hazor contains another type of house, which may have served people of the lowest classes or even servants. Perhaps due to Hazor's location near the distant northern border, there were more people of this class there (see also below, chap. 8).

15. The summaries and table above detailed the area of each structure. Because the buildings that belong to this group do not seem to have adapted a familiar plan to the needs of a particular type of family (such as a nuclear family), it is possible that more than one family lived in these structures. Perhaps one can even assume that each nuclear family lived in a single room, while the yards were used in common for purposes of cooking and so on. If this premise is true, their density was greater, and the poverty of their residents stands out even more clearly comparison with the city's wealthier families.

g to Makhbiram.'" [16] The many small finds in building 14a led Yadin to believe that the house's residents were affluent and that the entire residential quarter was a "bourgeois neighborhood" (Yadin 1975: 153–54; compare Holladay 1987: 290 n. 99). Many vessels were found in the building: cooking pots, a basin, a basalt bowl, six basalt millstones, an oven, bowls, basins, oil lamps, juglets, lamps, many storage vessels (one of which featured the inscription למכברם 'belonging to Makhbiram', to be discussed below), an ivory cosmetic spoon, a knife, a pestle, a casserole, and other items (Yadin 1975: 154; Naveh 1981: 302). Geva also identified the residents of this neighborhood as veteran, established families (both in building 14a and in the neighboring building 111), although she was aware of the stark contrast between them and building 2a (S. Geva 1989: 42, 44, 26). These conclusions, arising from the small finds, contradict the conclusions of the architectural analysis, presented above. The key to settling this contradiction lies in the reexamination of the inscription למכברם and the resulting reexamination of all the small finds (following Naveh 1981).

According to Yadin, מכברם is a personal name (unknown from other sources), containing two elements: the theophoric component רם, known from other West Semitic names (such as מלכרם or אדנירם), and the component מכבר, meaning 'master' or 'providing abundance' (Yadin et al. 1958–61: 68). But Naveh showed that, in Hebrew names that include the component רם, it is the other component that is theophoric, and thus Yadin's interpretation should not be accepted (Naveh 1981). According to Naveh, the fifth letter is ד rather than ר, and he reads למכבדם. Naveh believes that the inscription is similar to the inscriptions לשקיא ('to the drink servers') and לטב(ח)יא ('to the bakers') found in neighboring sites (En Gev and Tel Dan, respectively), meaning that the inscription refers to a title rather than a name. Naveh discusses the essence of the role MKBDM (מכבדים), and concludes that the intent was "the giving of a present, the bringing of an offering and sacrifice to God, and the serving of a meal to a guest." Because the מכבדים, like the bakers and wine-servers, were not members of the elite but service providers, Naveh turned to the small finds and showed that almost all the finds in this building, apart from the cosmetic spoon, are related to kitchens and food preparation and are thus more appropriate to servants than to the wealthy. This new interpretation matches the architectural analysis presented above, and the inscription למכבדם presumably refers to the servants who lived in the house and whose socioeconomic status was probably quite low.

Social Stratification in Hazor. Graphs 3–4 reflect clear gaps between the various strata of society in Hazor and indicate a significant degree of social stratification. However, the distribution does not reveal particular groups but represents a graded curve from the richest to the poorest. We should note that in Hazor quite a few buildings were discovered that belonged to the wealthy or to senior officials. This may be a result of the fact that the site was an administrative center, or it may just be the result of random findings, and in reality this group may have been smaller (see graphs 3 and 4).

---

16. For an extensive discussion of the small finds in Hazor, see the appendix to this chapter.

Stratum V. Stratum V was actually a rebuilding of the previous level, which had probably been destroyed in an earthquake (Yadin 1975: 149–50). This level represents the final years of the Kingdom of Israel, because Hazor was destroyed about a decade before the final destruction and disintegration of the kingdom. This was a period of instability and military and economic decline, compared with the previous period. Many of the residential buildings of level VI were rebuilt without significant changes (e.g., building 2a). In other houses, however, there were changes, and in "the house of Makhbiram," for example, the building's area was reduced. On this level, the two large four-room houses discussed above were built near the citadel in area B. A preliminary analysis of level V shows that social gaps remained and perhaps were even slightly exacerbated.

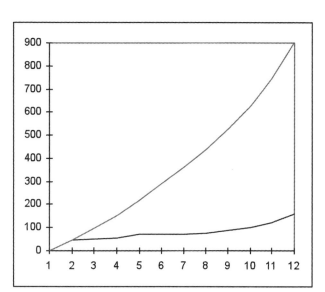

Graph 3. Hazor: size of buildings.

Kinrot (Tell el-Oreimeh)

The site of Kinrot lies on a hill overlooking the Sea of Galilee and was continu-

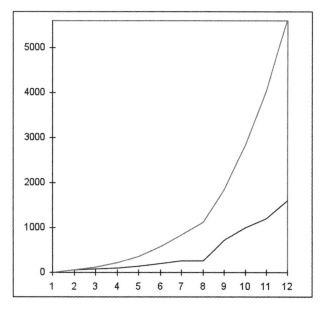

Graph 4. Hazor: weighted graph.

ously occupied from the tenth century B.C.E. onward. The eighth-century B.C.E. city (level II) was very different from its predecessors and was probably built after the destruction of the site (fig. 6). At this stage, the fortified settlement stood only on the hilltop, although several individual buildings seem to have stood outside the wall (Fritz 1990; 1993; 1995: 83–87).

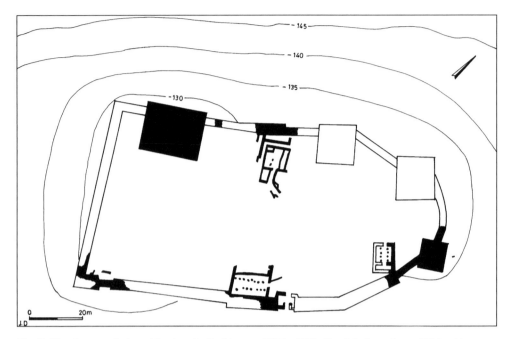

Fig. 6. Kinrot: general plan of the Iron II city (Herzog 1997a: 236). Reprinted courtesy of Ze'ev Herzog.

Public Buildings. A city wall with large towers was discovered on the site. Inside the wall, near the city gate, there was a large pillar building similar to buildings found in many urban settlements, such as Beersheba, Hazor, Megiddo and others. According to the excavators, the nature of the finds in the building rules out the possibility of it being used as a stable or storehouse, and it may have served as a barracks (Fritz 1993: 200; more below). The area may have served as the city's administrative center.

Residential Buildings. In the northwest of the city, there was "a private house built in Israelite tradition" (Fritz 1995: 85), and in the northeast of the site, a four-room house was discovered. Residential houses were built alongside the wall and parallel to it, and a road parallel to the wall surrounded the city. After level II was destroyed, perhaps during the campaign of Tilgath-pileser III (734 B.C.E.), a fortified settlement was rebuilt (level I), much poorer than its predecessor, and this settlement existed for a very short time and included various types of residential houses.

Only a few of the residential houses have been excavated. On level II, as we have seen, two buildings were discovered: one in area C, based on the four-room plan, with some changes (Fritz 1993: 200). The building's original area was 85–90 square meters, and after a room was added to it, its area reached over 100 square meters (fig. 7). The building's shape is irregular (it is rated 2). On two sides, the building faces the street, and it seems that on the other sides walls were shared with other buildings. A second building was partly excavated in area A, and the excavators considered it a four-room house (Fritz 1993: 92). The part excavated is just the north wing of the building, and it includes the entire length of the building (about 11.3

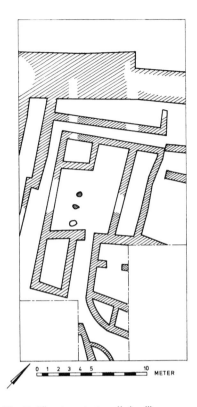

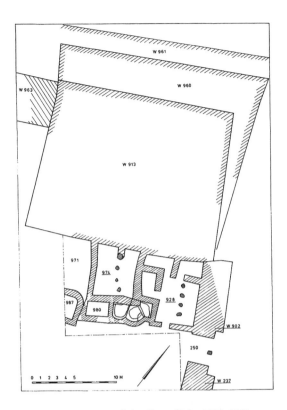

Fig. 7. Kinrot: a stratum II dwelling (Fritz 1993: 201). Reprinted courtesy of the Institute of Archaeology, Tel Aviv University.

Fig. 8. Kinrot: stratum I dwellings (Fritz 1993: 202). Reprinted courtesy of the Institute of Archaeology, Tel Aviv University.

meters; Fritz 1990: 380). Since the ratio between the length and width of a four-room house is usually between 6.25/10 and 8.5/10, we can assume that the width of this building was about 7.0–9.6 meters, and its area was between 80 and 110 square meters (probably closer to the higher figure). The part excavated shows that the house was quite nicely built. If it was indeed a four-room house, its plan was probably very regular (rated 4+). In the excavated parts, the house has no shared walls.

In level I, two poor three-room (?) houses were uncovered (building 974, area about 66 square meters; building 928, area about 65 square meters), constructed against one of the towers (fig. 8). The calculation of their area includes the walls, except for cases in which the buildings are built against exceptionally thick walls (such as the tower walls), and then the thickness of a normal wall instead of the thick wall was calculated.

The settlement that existed in level II included a massive wall with towers, a gate, and a pillar house, and it was obviously a city. The buildings excavated are of similar area but differ in their plans. One of the buildings is of a finer plan and probably had free standing walls. The other building underwent some changes, but its plan is less regular, and some of its walls are shared with other buildings that were only partially excavated. The settlement in level I was probably poorer. On this level, two neighboring houses were excavated. Their area was much smaller, their plans irregular, and their walls shared. This evidence is insufficient to reach decisive conclusions. It is difficult to compare the two levels, since the differences may stem from the differences in nature between a poor settlement and a city. Only on level II can one note certain differences between the buildings excavated.

Tell es-Saidiyeh

The Tell es-Saidiyeh site is located in the eastern Jordan Valley and is identified with biblical Zarethan. Several levels represent the eighth century B.C.E.; of them, level V is particularly important to the present analysis (Pritchard 1985; compare Tubb 1988).

Public Buildings. In the eighth century, the city was surrounded by a wall (Pritchard 1993: 1296), but it was only 1.5 meters thick. The wall had towers that protruded outward from the wall (Fritz 1995: 114–15).

Residential Buildings. In level V, a whole residential neighborhood was excavated, composed entirely of four-room houses (of the three-room subtype). The houses are almost uniform in plan (rated 4) and area (about 55 square meters), and together they create a sort of block surrounded by streets (Fritz 1995: 114–15). The uniformity in size of the buildings and their interior division show that the residents of this neighborhood belonged to the same social class. The excavator stated correctly that "this plan has no parallel in contemporary sites on both sides of the Jordan" (Pritchard 1993: 1296). Although the buildings themselves (in nature, plan, area, and the finds within them) were typical and very similar to buildings in other urban settlements in the land of Israel, especially in other provincial towns (Tell Beit Mirsim and Mizpah [Tell en-Nasbeh]), there is no real parallel to its overall planning. In the city of Nippur, which included several different quarters, excavations also revealed one planned, uniform neighborhood. Based on documents found in the buildings, this quarter was attributed to the temple staff (Stone 1987: 126). Is it possible that in Tell es-Saidiyeh all the residents of the planned quarter also belonged to one organization?

Tirzah (Tell el-Far'ah, North)

Tirzah was the capital of the Kingdom of Israel for a short period of time during the ninth century B.C.E. until the construction of Samaria in about 879 B.C.E. (Chambon 1984). The two levels relevant to us are level VIId from the eighth century B.C.E. and level VIIb, which was dated to the tenth century B.C.E.

Public Buildings. In the eighth century B.C.E., Tirzah was an important city. In the quarter excavated, some grand residential buildings were discovered that were probably not public buildings, as well as a building that may have had an administrative function near the city gate (de Vaux 1992: 1297; but it seems that, contrary to his opinion, the gate was not functional during this period; see Herzog 1997a: 217–18).

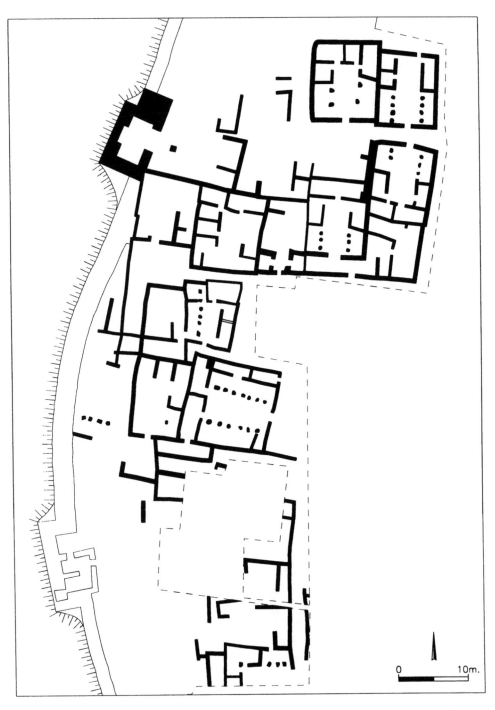

Fig. 9. Tirzah: the Iron Age IIA settlement (Herzog 1997: 219). Reprinted courtesy of Ze'ev Herzog.

Table 2. The Buildings at Tirzah (Tell el-Far'ah, North) in the eighth century B.C.E.

Building	Area (and Net Area)	Plan	Shared Walls	Location	Comments
328	113 (86)	5	Yes	Wealthy quarter?	
327	150 (103)	5	Partially	Wealthy quarter?	
362	65 (53)	3	Yes	Poor quarter?	
336	90 (78)	4	Yes	Poor quarter?	
366	76 (62)	4	Yes	Poor quarter?	
148	150 or more	5	No	Wealthy quarter?	The area stated does not include attached rooms and yards, which would greatly add to the total area.

Residential Buildings. In the tenth-century B.C.E. level (level VIIb), one can identify some relatively large four-room-type buildings, some of them with a yard in
front of them (fig. 9). In the final report of the excavations of Tirzah, Chambon included a table listing the data from 13 of the many structures found in this level
(Chambon 1984: 32). Their net area is between 53 and 121 square meters (the gross
area of most is 65–110 square meters and reaches even 150 square meters or more).
Despite the differences in the buildings' size, they are similar in plan: they share
walls, and it is hard to distinguish them without a thorough examination. Even an
analysis of the buildings' locations shows that their distribution throughout the area
seems random.

In the eighth-century level (level VIId) as well, a relatively large area was exposed, and many residential houses were found there (fig. 10). Their plans are varied,
and some of them are quite large compared with other structures on the same level
and with buildings known from the previous level. Chambon's table includes only 5
buildings, and their net area is between 53 and 103 square meters (1984: 44).[17] These
buildings do not include the large, grand buildings constructed in the northern area
(the area of which is 150 square meters and more). As is apparent from the plan, the
differences in the quality and planning of the buildings match their size and location, so we can identify separate neighborhoods on the basis of these criteria (Fritz
1995: 96–98). According to de Vaux, these gaps do not appear in the tenth-century
levels, and the differences in appearance are the result of social processes (de Vaux
1965: 72–73; 1992: 1301). This is how de Vaux describes the eighth-century level:

> [...] nicely-built private structures were also excavated, built to the plan [of the previ-
> ous level] . . . but they are slightly larger and their construction method is improved.
> Their walls are more regular and they are made with two properly chiseled faces, and

---

17. The various buildings in the two strata at Tirzah, including the small ones, are almost always
larger than usual for houses in other cities of this period.

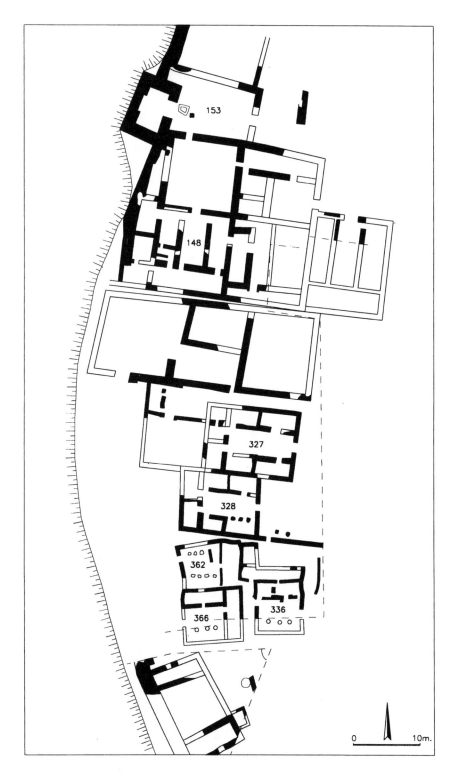

Fig. 10. Tirzah: the Iron Age IIB settlement (Herzog 1997: 231). Reprinted courtesy of Ze'ev Herzog.

the corners are well interlocked. These are the houses of the rich, separated from the poor quarter by a long, straight wall. In the poor quarter, small, poorly constructed houses are heaped together. The great difference between the houses of the rich and poor, compared with the uniformity of the residential houses from the tenth century B.C.E. fits what we know about the social development in Israel during that period. (de Vaux 1992: 1301)

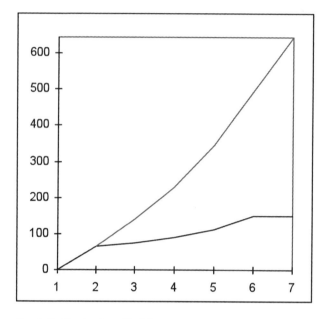

Graph 5. Tirzah: size of buildings.

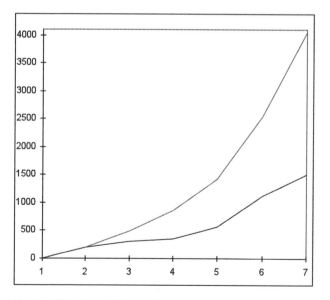

Graph 6. Tirzah: weighted graph.

We can deduce that during the eighth century B.C.E. there were several defined quarters in Tirzah. In the south of the excavated area, there were several relatively small, poorly constructed buildings. North of them, perhaps behind a separating wall, were two larger buildings, constructed to a regular plan. In the north of the excavated area, two more buildings with large yards were unearthed. We can assume that the southern part of the site was occupied by members of the lower class and that these buildings (362, 336, and 366) belonged to a poor quarter. It is worth noting the difference between this quarter and its equivalent in Hazor: in Tirzah, even the poor structures are four-room houses. The reason for this may be the veteran population of Tirzah, who maintained its construction tradition (on the different situation in Hazor, see below, chap. 8). The larger and better-built buildings, located north of the poor quarter beyond the wall, probably belonged to a more affluent residential neighborhood, and the wall may have been intended to divide these quarters from each other, as de Vaux believed. The even grander buildings in the north of the excavated area may be a continuation of the affluent quarter, but they may also be the residential neighborhood of the senior administration officials and similar persons. It is reasonable to infer that the variety of finds represents three different groups: the ruling class, wealthy families, and poor families (see graphs 5 and 6; see also Herzog 1997a: 232).

The graphs reflect the social stratification in the site. This stratification is spread throughout the social spectrum, and it is hard to point to a clear cutoff point between the different strata. However, it should be stressed that the sample in Tirzah is smaller than in the other sites. We should also remember that the poor houses in this sites were of medium size compared with other urban settlements.

Shechem

Shechem is located at an important crossroads and probably served as an administrative city in the eighth century B.C.E. (G. E. Wright 1965; Campbell 1994: 34).

Public Buildings. According to Campbell, a large silo found on the site indicates the city's importance (Campbell 1994: 34), and some believe that this implies that the city was a tax-collection center (G. E. Wright 1992: 1526). During the period of the Monarchy, the city was probably surrounded by a wall, even though it was probably less important than it had been during the tenth century B.C.E., when the Bible informs us that it served as the kingdom's capital.

Residential Buildings. Building 1727 excavated on the site is a large, nicely-built four-room house (rated 5) with added wings. The area of the central unit is about 85 square meters; together with the partially excavated wing 12, the built area increases to 110 square meters, and along with the other (reconstructed) units, it approaches 150 square meters. On the three sides excavated, the building has no shared walls. According to Campbell, the building's size and plan and the preparation and leveling of the ground conducted before its construction indicate great wealth. In his opinion, the inhabitants of this house (or similar houses), who were wealthier than others, were the target of the prophet Amos's criticism (Campbell 1994). However, building 1727 is the only complete residential building from Iron Age II that has been published, so we cannot deduce the existence of social stratification in eighth-century B.C.E. Shechem solely from it. Compared with other urban sites, this building is indeed impressive, and it was probably inhabited by a wealthy family, but this site has no extant proof of social stratification.[18]

Shikmona

In the settlement of Shikmona, located on the Carmel coast, several settlement levels from Iron Age II have been excavated (Elgavish 1994: 49–72). The discussion below refers mainly to the city plan of Iron IIA, due to a lack of sufficient information regarding later levels.

---

18. Campbell argues that the building's importance is also indicated by the selective destruction of the area by the Assyrians, especially since other buildings were probably not damaged. For the excavation results, see now Campbell 2002.

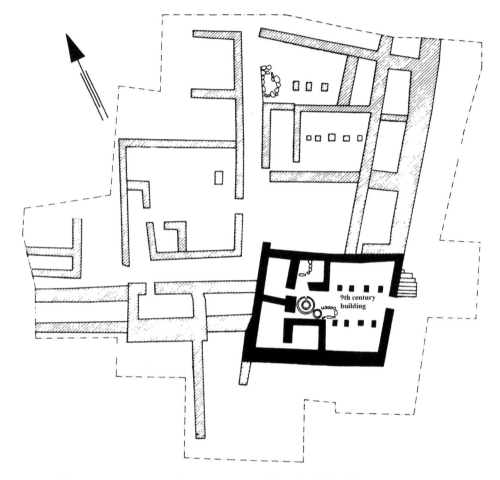

Fig. 11. Shikmona: general plan of the excavated area (Elgavish 1994: 49).

Urban Plan. On level 12, the southeastern section of the town was fully excavated, including the surrounding casement wall, two streets, and several residential
homes (fig. 11).

Residential Buildings. The southeastern side of the casement wall was lined by
typical four(three)-room houses, and along the front was a street parallel to the wall.
In the southwestern part of the city, there was a road alongside the casement wall
itself. Three residential houses were fully excavated: two of them are three- or four-
room houses, built perpendicular to the eastern wall, and a mirror image of each
other (the broad room of one is at the front rather than the back). The area of each of
them is about 55 square meters. At the corner of the wall is a third, larger four-room
house (over 150 square meters; Elgavish 1994: 49–51). In the plan, one can see another fairly large building nearby. However, its plan is uncertain, and the excavator
did not make clear whether it had been fully excavated, so it will not be analyzed.

Table 3. Buildings in Shikmona in the Tenth Century B.C.E.

Building	Area	Plan	Shared Walls	Location	Comments
North	55	2	Yes	Circumference street	
Central	55	2	Yes	Circumference street	
Corner	150+	5	Yes, but only with fortifications	Corner, combined with fortifications	The building existed during several levels. Many imported vessels found.

Already at the beginning of Iron Age II (tenth century B.C.E., according to the excavator), socioeconomic gaps are apparent in Shikmona. Perhaps, being a coastal town, Shikmona was settled by administrative officials from the beginning of the period of the Monarchy (Elgavish 1994: 56–57), and this is one of the reasons for the existence of economic stratification from the very beginning (see below, chap. 9). Unfortunately, we do not have detailed plans from later periods of the city's history, but the plan of the large building did not change. Since this is a large residential building by any standard, it is reasonable to conclude that the economic gaps persisted in the following periods. In this impressive building, which continued to be used in the ninth and eighth centuries B.C.E., remarkable finds were discovered, such as a wide variety of fine and even imported pottery, which in the excavator's opinion indicated the wealth of its inhabitants (Elgavish 1994: 61–63; but see the appendix to this chapter).

Megiddo

Megiddo is located in a very fertile agricultural area and is near the international highway that connected Egypt with Syria/Mesopotamia. During the period of the Monarchy, it served as an important administrative city (Kempinski 1989; 1993). According to accepted opinion, Iron Age II is represented mainly by levels IVB–VA and IV. These levels include mainly grand public buildings and only a few residential houses. The discussion will focus on the finds in level IV (for various views on the chronology see, for example, Shiloh 1993b; Kempinski 1989; Finkelstein and Ussishkin 2000).

Public Buildings. Impressive fortifications were discovered at the site: an inset-offset wall (wall 325) and impressive four- and six-chamber gates. Many luxury buildings were also found (building 1482, building 1616, and palace 338). Two large stable/storehouse complexes were excavated, one in the northeast of the city, the other in the south. Many buildings were constructed using a technique that combined ashlar pillars with unhewn stone fills. The city of level IV was a planned city with four central quarters (fig. 12): a residential quarter to the west of the gate, stables to the east of the gate, an administrative quarter around building 338, and another quarter that included the water system and building complex 997.

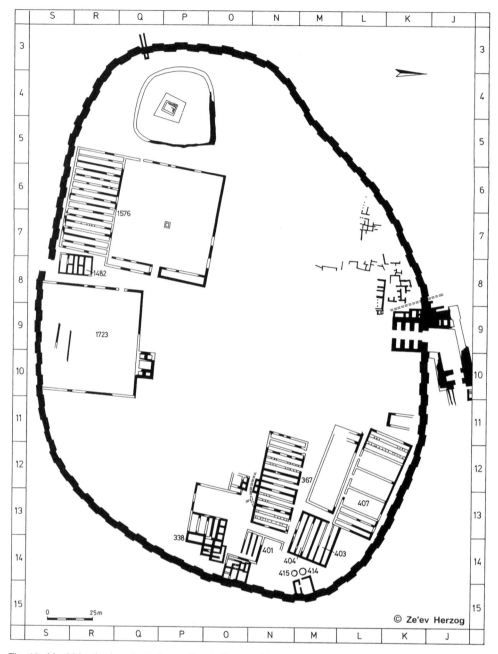

Fig. 12. Megiddo: the Iron II city (according to Herzog; Herzog 1997a: 227). Reproduced courtesy of Ze'ev Herzog.

Residential Buildings. From Iron II, some four-room-type residential houses (or subtypes of this group) are known at Megiddo, but there are also some other buildings that are similar to typical Bronze Age courtyard houses. According to Kempinski, this is because "in Megiddo where the local Canaanite segment of population was probably stronger, the traditional house form of the bronze age absorbed the

new form" (Kempinski 1989: 127). Most of the Iron Age II private structures excavated and published (of both types) are very large, and their area is around 100–160
square meters. However, due to the paucity of published material about the residential houses, and because in most cases the published information refers to the
beginning of this period (level VB) or to its end (level III), it is not possible to analyze
the buildings of this period, and Kempinski's conclusion that the population had a
high standard of living (1989: 133–35)—a conclusion that accords with the area of the
buildings compared with the area of buildings in other urban sites—must suffice.

Other Sites

In the Kingdom of Israel, several other sites have been excavated that contain
levels from the period discussed here, but we do not have extensive information
about their residential buildings. The findings only indicate the city's status and the
existence of public buildings. Among the prominent sites, we can list Dan, Jokneam,
Gezer, En Gev, and Aphek (Antipatris).

Dan. Dan was an important city in the northern Jordan Valley. In this large
city, which was surrounded by a massive wall, a central place of worship was found
(Biran 1992). The city's gates (interior and exterior) were also discovered. Outside
the city, a large square was found, and beside it were several buildings. According
to the excavators, these were the *husot* (markets) mentioned in the Bible (Biran 1996;
for another possible understanding of the finds, see Faust 1996). Unfortunately, no
residential buildings were published, so it is difficult to study the structure of society
in the city.

Jokneam. On this site, part of an Iron Age II city was discovered. The main components excavated are massive fortifications, which underwent many changes during the Iron Age II (Ben-Tor et al. 1987: 7–8). Nearby, what may have been the city's
water system was discovered. We have little information about the residential buildings (1987: 8). Some residential homes were built during this period, and at least one
of them probably followed the four-room plan (1987: 8).

Gezer. The city, located near the border of Israel and Judah, probably belonged
to the Kingdom of Israel (A. Mazar 1990: 415–16; Dever 1998c). This was an important city, and it contained fortifications, a massive gate, a water system, and so on.
But despite the intensive excavations conducted on the site by Macalister and, later,
the Hebrew Union College expedition (led by G. E. Wright, W. G. Dever, and J. D.
Seger), the information about the city plan and its residential houses is very limited
(Dever 1993c; 1998c; Herzog 1997a: 234), though a few four-room houses were reported (Ortiz, Wolff, and Arbino 2011).

En Gev. During Iron Age II, there was a fortified settlement and fortress at En
Gev. The new excavations have discovered public buildings of the pillared building
type (B. Mazar 1992b; Kochavi 1993b).

Aphek (Antipatris). At the site, very few remains from Iron Age II were discovered. Several four-room residential buildings (area 70–80 square meters), which
probably survived from a dense residential quarter, were discovered. They were
dated to the tenth century B.C.E. (Kochavi 1989a: 86–91). It is possible that later in the
period of the Monarchy this site was partially or completely abandoned.

Summary

Many cities have been found from the Kingdom of Israel, especially from the eighth century on the eve of the kingdom's destruction. The distribution of the excavated sites is uneven, and many of them are concentrated in the northern valleys. This spread may reflect the state of research and the difficulties in excavating sites in Samaria, but presumably the population was also concentrated in the valleys because the valleys were geopolitically and economically strategic (Broshi and Finkelstein 1991: 7, 17).

The period's cities were fortified and surrounded by massive walls of various types. Gates were found in the city walls and were usually quite impressive. In some of the cities, additional public buildings were found: storehouses or stables (on this type of building, see further below), citadels, water systems, and so on. It is clear that these public buildings were constructed by the state (or kingdom). The cities served as state control and tax-collection centers. In such a city, there was probably a governor, and in some cases there was also a garrison. Due to their administrative importance and because a relatively large population was gathered there, defense was important, and this is why there was such a great investment in fortifications. The city also served as the state's cultural agency, and for this reason great effort was invested in public works that served to glorify the regime, to enhance its legitimacy, and even to convey certain messages (Whitelam 1986).[19] As we shall see below, this state involvement—one of the cities' features—created social processes that increased the difference between cities and villages, in which similar processes did not occur.

The most common residential house in the cities was usually quite small, but there were also larger structures. It appears that most of the buildings discovered were inhabited by nuclear families (Faust 1995b; 1998; 1999b; Stager 1985, and additional bibliography there. See also Holladay 1992; 1997).

In cases for which we have sufficient data, we can state that in the Kingdom of Israel there was a relative socioeconomic continuum. This means that there were clear differences between the different strata but not a polarized reality of a few rich and many poor; between these two groups there appears to have been a middle class.

Cities of the Kingdom of Judah in the Eighth Century B.C.E.

Jerusalem

In the tenth century B.C.E., Jerusalem, the capital of the Kingdom of Judah, was concentrated around the City of David and the Temple Mount (Steiner 2001; Cahill 2003; see also Faust 2004c; A. Mazar 2006b; Finkelstein 2001; 2003). Over time, and particularly during the eighth century B.C.E., the city underwent a demographic and geographical expansion. Jerusalem spread to the west, and the western hill (the present-day Jewish and Armenian Quarters and Mount Zion) was settled and surrounded by a wall (fig. 13). During this period, Jerusalem could have been defined as

---

19. However, the absence of inscriptions (Faust 2006b: 94–95, and references; see also Rendsburg 2007) indicates that this sort of self-glorification may have been less common.

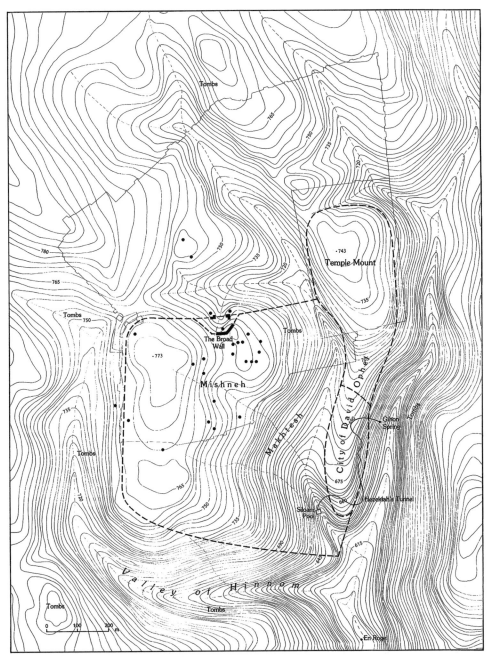

Fig. 13. Jerusalem: the eighth-century city (Shiloh: 1993a: 707).

a "primate city" (see also Barkay 1988). This process was probably not only the result of natural population growth but, during the final third of the century, some refugees came to Jerusalem (a few from the territory of the destroyed Kingdom of Israel and others from the devastated Shephelah), and they contributed to the population increase in the city (Barkay 1988). After Sennacherib's campaign, the growth rate increased during the seventh century B.C.E. (Faust 2005b; 2008), but this period will be discussed separately.

Public Buildings. From the description of the palace that Solomon built near the Temple (1 Kings 7), it appears that Jerusalem, like Samaria, had a royal compound— a sort of acropolis (Fritz 1995: 130). There were many public buildings in this area, including first and foremost the Temple (its importance during this period gradually increased), and the king's palace. Information about these structures is derived from the Bible alone, and no archaeological remains of them have survived. Eilat Mazar recently excavated a large building in the upper part of the City of David (E. Mazar 2007a; 2007b) and, while she attributes it to King David, it is far more likely that it is an Iron I building that was still in use in Iron II (see also A. Mazar 2006b; Faust 2010b; contra Finkelstein et al. 2007; Finkelstein 2011). If it was indeed used in this period, then this large building presents us with one of the largest public buildings of Iron Age IIA.

The only other large public building in the area with surviving remains is the building excavated at the eastern edge of the excavations to the south of the Temple Mount. At this site, identified as part of the Ophel, remains were discovered of a storehouse and perhaps of the Ophel gate (Mazar and Mazar 1989; E. Mazar 1991; 2011). However, the remains of some other impressive public works have been excavated that demonstrate the city's grandeur, including the water systems. These public works included the Warren's Shaft system (which at this time incorporated the shaft itself; Faust 2003e; 2007a; contra Shimron 2004) and, toward the end of the eighth century, also included Hezekiah's tunnel (for further details, see de Groot 1991b; Reich and Shukrun 1999; Faust 2000a; Abells and Arbit 1995; and additional bibliography there). Another important find is a section of approximately 200 meters of the city wall, discovered on the western slope of the City of David (Shiloh 1984; de Groot 1991a: 46), as well as a few dozens meters of city wall on the western hill (the "broad wall"; Avigad 1983). The thickness of the wall is impressive: 5 meters in the eastern wall and over 7 meters at the western hill. Another wall has recently been discovered near the Kidron Valley that probably surrounded the neighborhoods previously believed to be located outside the walls (Shukrun and Reich 1999; Reich and Shukrun 2008).

Residential Buildings. Most of the few buildings known to us today from the City of David are those destroyed by the Babylonians in 586 B.C.E., such as the buildings in area G (Shiloh 1984: 14). However, many of the buildings were erected in the eighth century B.C.E. and probably even earlier. For instance, the "house of Ahiel," a relatively fine residential house (some 100 square meters), built originally in the tenth century (Cahill 2002; 2003); or "the house on the lower terrace" in area E1 (Shiloh 1984: 13). This structure is near the city wall and measures about 8 × 8 meters. Each of the building's three spaces is built on a different terrace.

During the period under discussion, there were also some residential quarters on the lower, eastern slopes of the City of David. In the past, these quarters were considered to have been located outside the walls. However, following the recent discoveries by Reich and Shukrun (e.g., Reich and Shukrun 2008), we may assume that these neighborhoods were surrounded by a wall.

In the large trench dug by Kathleen Kenyon in the 1960s, the remains of many buildings were found (Auld and Steiner 1996: 38–39), and it appears that, from the tenth or ninth century onward, buildings were constructed on the eastern slope of the City of David: "[T]his seems to have been a quarter where the common people lived, the small traders and artisans, who. . . . sold their produce to the farmers. These were certainly not rich or important people; the buildings were simple and small, and nothing valuable was found in them" (Auld and Steiner 1996: 38; for the excavation reports, see Franken and Steiner 1985; Eshel and Prag 1995; Steiner 2001). Behind these buildings, several caves full of complete vessels were found. Because the pottery repertoire discovered included cooking pots, jugs and drinking cups (but very few storage vessels), this location may have been the kitchen of an inn. Auld and Steiner suggest that these structures served as part of a guesthouse that served traders and holiday pilgrims who were visiting Jerusalem (Auld and Steiner 1996: 39; however, one would expect an inn to contain storage vessels). In their opinion, from this stage onward Jerusalem became primarily a residential city.

Another building excavated was probably a blacksmith's workshop. Under the building's floor, three ostraca were found, dated to the end of the eighth century B.C.E. (Auld and Steiner 1996: 68). Recently, a few other buildings have been excavated on the eastern slopes of the City of David's, but no details are available (Shukrun and Reich 1999: 15). Other residential houses were found on Mount Zion and the western hill (below the "broad wall") and have been partially excavated (Avigad 1983; Broshi 1973). According to Shiloh (1984: 28):

> A phenomenon peculiar to stratum 12 is the construction of poor, simple dwellings on the rock-terrace of the city-wall. . . . Those buildings, similar in their construction and in their sparse 8th century B.C.E. pottery. . . . There is no doubt that this special phenomenon, of construction outside the city-wall, was a side-effect of the overall process of the expansion of Jerusalem during the 8th century B.C.E.

The different types of buildings discovered in the different areas demonstrate the socioeconomic stratification in Jerusalem from the tenth century B.C.E. onward (Cahill 2002; 2003). These gaps were still present (and may even have widened) during the later part of the Iron Age (see below regarding the seventh century B.C.E.).

Tombs. Burial caves have been discovered in many areas around the settled part of Jerusalem (e.g., Barkay 1991a: 117; 2000; Reich 1994: 106). The caves, dated mainly to the eighth–seventh centuries B.C.E., represent the most common type of burial in Judah—that is, family burial in simple graves. The graves are cut into the rock and contain benches (on which the bodies were laid) and a repository, where the bones were later gathered (Barkay 1994; 2000). These tombs probably served one family over several generations. One can identify several levels of ornamentation and quality in these tombs. In addition, simpler graves were also discovered: shaft graves cut in the stone (Reich 1994: 103). Most of the deceased were probably interred in simple graves, which did not usually survive (Barkay 1991a: 103; 1999: 99).

However, not only normal family tombs and poor graves were discovered. In Jerusalem, there was also a magnificent burial method that was employed by the most senior officials. In the village of Siloam, east of the City of David, we find grand tombs of this sort, some of them individual or couple graves, in contrast to the usual family burials. This method was probably used by individuals with positions so senior that they received a private burial, contrary to the norms of the period. One example of this method is a tomb containing the inscription [. . .]יהו אשר על הבית ('. . . yahu over the house'), which probably belongs to this period (Ussishkin 1993b: 325–28). The Bible also states that fine burials were typical of senior officials, such as Shebna, who was "over the house" (Isa 22:15–16; this is probably not the individual buried in the grave just mentioned, however). The use of grand tombs probably began in the ninth century B.C.E. (Ussishkin 1993b: 286–87). Barkay distinguishes between three types of tomb in this cemetery, but all are of very high quality (Barkay 1991a: 105–11).

On the basis of the prominent differences in the plan of the tombs, their usage, and the quality of the cutting, one can identify signs of clear social stratification that existed in Jerusalem during this period, similar to what we were able to learn from the residential houses. Thus, we can identify the tombs of the most senior officials, grand family tombs (of noble families), ordinary family tombs, poor family tombs, and even simple graves. The poorest people were probably interred in simple trench graves. This evidence of the highest classes is unique to Jerusalem and is not found at other sites.

Mizpah (Tell en-Nasbeh)

Tell en-Nasbeh is located north of Jerusalem and was continuously settled throughout the period of the Monarchy (McCown 1947). It was a provincial town that grew and became more central due to its military importance (see the events described in 1 Kgs 15:17–22; Broshi 1992: 1080–81; Herzog 1992b: 263; 1997a: 239; Zorn 1999). The site has recently been studied extensively.[20] Stratum III existed throughout Iron Age II and contains no sign of destruction or rebuilding. This stratum is divided into three phases, differing from each other in certain details, but most of the buildings survived throughout the period. Stratum IIIA dates from the middle of the eighth century B.C.E. up to 586 B.C.E. (Zorn 1993: 114). The main area of the town in this period included residential houses of various sizes that were very similar in their construction method.

Public Buildings.   From the ninth century onward, the city was surrounded by a massive inset-offest wall, probably containing one gate (fig. 14). This wall was built only after the stratum III city was founded, and so it was placed outside the existing buildings. The gap between the city's houses and the wall was therefore the main area for growth in subsequent periods. In this area, several buildings were constructed, including large, fine four-room houses that may have served for

---

20. For example, Zorn 1993, and other publications. Zorn's stratigraphy is different from that of previous studies; some of the changes are not relevant, others will be discussed below.

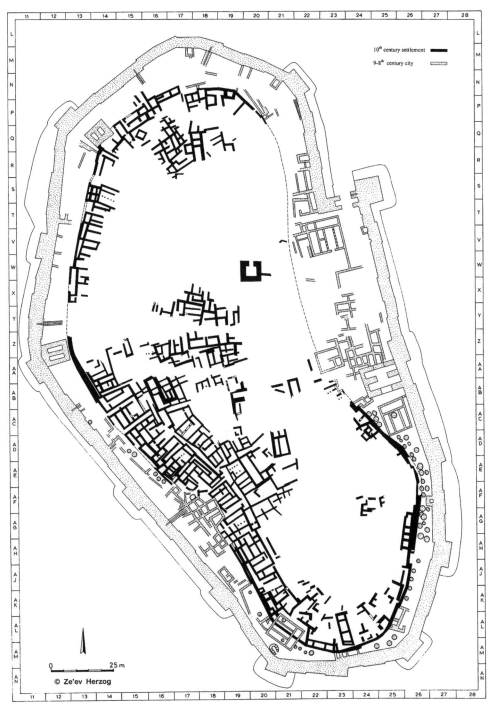

Fig. 14. Mizpah: general plan of the Iron II city (Herzog 1997a: 238). Courtesy of Ze'ev Herzog.

administrative purposes or as residences of senior officials.[21] Apart from these, almost no public buildings were unearthed on the site. Perhaps the reason for this is that the center of the tell did not survive. The city plan shows lines of massive, long, straight walls in the center that may have belonged to public buildings.

Residential Buildings.   As noted above, most of the town's area contained residential houses of various sizes. Zorn analyzed the architecture of the remains of 73 different buildings: 71 buildings, constituting 29% of the limited settlement area of the Iron Age, and 2 more buildings located outside the wall (Zorn 1993: 116–20). On the basis of 23 buildings, the plans of which can be accurately measured, we can conclude that the average area of a residential house (including the walls) is about 65 square meters (in a later publication, Zorn uses the figure 58.3 square meters; see Zorn 1994: 39). Zorn classified three types of buildings based on size (53–54 square meters, 70–79 square meters, and over 100 square meters) and suggested that they represent a social system with three classes (Zorn 1993: 153–54).

Table 4 is based on Zorn's data (Zorn 1994: 39), with the addition of the details relevant to the current discussion (plan quality, shared walls, location). The table includes the 23 buildings whose plans can be identified and also the 3 large four-room houses (120–30 square meters) that may have served as residences of senior officials (as noted, Zorn dated these buildings to the Neo-Babylonian period).

---

21. Branigan 1966; see also Herzog 1997a: 237–39. The dating of these buildings to Iron II (from the ninth century onward) was accepted by practically all scholars, but recently Zorn (1993; 1999) has claimed that these buildings were only added at the end of the Iron Age and that they belonged to the city of the sixth century B.C.E.—that is, after the destruction of Judah. Zorn's analysis of old material is exemplary, but his stratigraphic analysis raises problems, and his evidence is largely circumstantial. Thus, for example, some of the circumstantial evidence that Zorn believes makes it doubtful that the buildings existed during the Iron Age, such as the location of several buildings in the entrance of the internal gate (Zorn 1999: 60), is also evidence against the gate's existence during the period that Zorn refers to; according to his theory, whoever came in through the wide city gate would have been forced into a narrow alley immediately after passing through the gate. Furthermore, while one of the buildings (110.01) contained pottery found in situ indicating that the building ceased to be used in the fifth century B.C.E. (i.e., the Persian period, which suits Zorn's analysis, 1999: 61), the picture was different in the other buildings. In a neighboring building (125.01), pottery was found that was identical to pottery from the destruction levels of Jerusalem and Lachish (in 586 B.C.E.). Zorn tried to argue that the use of large storage vessels lasted a very long time and that the structure was built immediately after 586 B.C.E. However, if this was pottery that was used for a very long time, why not assume that such vessels were made a long time before the destruction of Jerusalem and Lachish and used up to their destruction? Thus, this pottery does not indicate the construction time of the building where it was found, as Zorn argues, but rather its destruction time, as is the case in the equivalent sites that Zorn refers to (for a new analysis not accepting Zorn's late dating of the buildings, see also Herzog 1997a: 237–39). Furthermore, if Zorn was correct and the Iron Age storage vessels were used in the Persian period, why was not any Persian period pottery found in association with it? The finding of this Iron Age pottery, therefore, simply shows that the house it was found in was destroyed in the late Iron Age (as was claimed in the past). The exception is of course the house in which Persian period pottery was found, and this late pottery most likely arrived at the house when it was reused during the Persian period (reuse of buildings was very common in the Persian period; see, e.g., the reuse of Iron Age houses during the Persian period at Tel 'Eton and Kh. el-Qom; Faust 2011c: 204, 214; Dever 1997c: 392, respectively). We should note that almost all of the four-room houses known in research were built in Iron Age II and not thereafter; but due to the proximity of the destruction of Judah and the building of the later city, as suggested by Zorn (probably immediately after the destruction of Jerusalem), this does not in itself disprove Zorn's suggestion.

Table 4. Buildings at Tell en-Nasbeh (Iron Age II)

Building	Area	Plan	Shared Walls	Location	Comments
125.02	60	1	Yes	City center; residential quarter	
141.01	90+	2	Yes	Near casement wall; residential	
141.02	57	2	Yes	Near casement wall; residential	
141.03	70	3	Yes	Near casement wall; residential	
141.04	60	2	Yes	Near casement wall; residential	
141.05	44	2	Yes	Near casement wall; residential	
141.06	30	2	Yes	Inner city	
142.01	120	2	Yes	Near the wall	
142.02	50	2	Yes	Inner city	
142.03	52	3	Yes	Inner city	
142.04	47	2	Yes	Inner city	
142.05	55	2	Yes	Inner city	
142.06	57+	1	Yes	Inner city	
142.07	43	1	Yes	Inner city	
142.08	47	2	Yes	Inner city	
142.09	54	1	Yes	Inner city	
142.10	49	2	Yes	Inner city	
142.11	63	2	Yes	Inner city	
159.01	56	3	Yes	Near wall	
159.02	65	2	Yes	Near wall	
159.03	90	2	Yes	Near wall	
159.04	42	3	Yes	Inner city	
159.05	41	3	Yes	Inner city	
379[a]	180	5	No	Near city gate	Probably a later addition to the previous buildings
226	125	5	No	East of the city	Probably a later addition to the previous buildings
23	115	5	No	South of the city	Probably a later addition to the previous buildings

a. The calculation of the area of the 3 four-room houses is based on the plans in Braemer 1982: 74, 80.

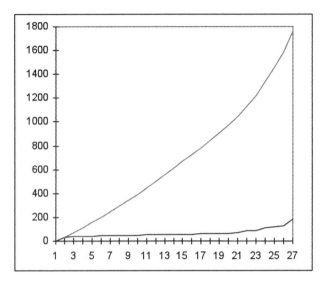

Graph 7. Mizpah: size of buildings.

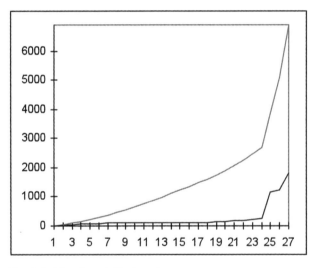

Graph 8. Mizpah: weighted graph.

The large four-room houses and the other large, simpler structures are concentrated on the edges of the tell, and Zorn suggested that this area was a preferred residential quarter (Zorn 1993: 153–54). This is a different picture from other sites (such as Beer-sheba, below), and perhaps this difference should be attributed to local circumstances. Thus, for example, perhaps in contrast to other sites whose area was defined by the topography and existing city walls, at this site there was the possibility of expansion and growth, and so the affluent preferred to leave the center of the tell and to build their houses in the new area on the edges of the settlement (on similar processes in a number of Iron Age II sites, see Faust 2003c). In other places, the wealthy had no reason to leave the center, so they remained there. Alternatively, the arbitrary nature of the findings may influence this impression: there may have been an important quarter at the cen-

ter of the tell, containing public buildings, but due to the bad preservation of the tell's center we do not know this part of the city. Indeed, it is possible that in the center of the site the remnants of a very large, impressive building can be identified.

Graphs 7–8 show a small group of buildings with an area much larger than the other buildings. This fact is apparent in the first graph but especially in the weighted graph. It is reasonable to conjecture that the differences in the residential structures that Zorn treated as class differences were actually differences in the wealth of members of the same class. Real class differences can be detected only between the

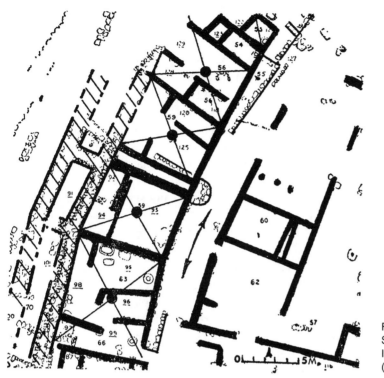

Fig. 15. Beth-Shemesh: a group of Iron Age dwellings (Shiloh 1978: 40).

large buildings added at the edge of the settlement and the rest of the town's buildings (compare A. Mazar 1990: 437).

Beth-Shemesh

Beth-Shemesh was a central city in the Shephelah and is located in the Soreq Valley. Three expeditions have excavated the site: Mackenzie's expedition (on the margins and south of the site), Grant's team (most of the tell's area), and Bunimovitz and Lederman's team (mainly on the northeast and south of the tell). Several phases were dated to Iron Age II.

Public Buildings. In the past, scholars considered Beth-Shemesh to be a provincial town (e.g., Herzog 1992b: 264), but in the northeastern corner of the city evidence has recently been excavated showing that at least this part served for public purposes: the city wall, a gate, the water system and even a large public building from Iron Age II were discovered (Bunimovitz and Lederman 1997; 2008; 2009). Perhaps, therefore, a better definition of the settlement would be an administrative town. Many residential quarters were discovered in the remaining areas of the city. Most of the buildings are subtypes of the four-room house, but in these quarters too, some public buildings were found, including a grand structure, a storehouse, and a very large silo (Grant and Wright 1939: 68–70; G. E. Wright 1970; Bunimovitz and Lederman 2009: 136; for a reflection of the city's importance in seal stamps, see Garfinkel 1984).

Residential Buildings. Several problems make it difficult to analyze the findings, despite the intensive excavations and the many plans published (Shiloh 1978: 40; Bunimovitz and Lederman 2009). First, the site presents serious stratigraphic problems. Second, the plans published are very fragmentary, and it is difficult to be certain about the location of the edges of each building. The publication of the small finds also refers to each space separately without referring to other parts of the building or even trying to clarify its nature (i.e., whether it was a residential room, a yard, a street, and so on; e.g., Grant 1934). So it appears that an analysis of most of the residential houses is impossible.

Shiloh analyzed (architecturally) four residential houses from Beth-Shemesh (fig. 15), which were dated to the tenth century B.C.E. (Shiloh 1978: 40). At least two of them are four-room types. Their sizes (north to south) are:[22] 45 square meters (rated 2; with shared walls); 52 square meters (rated 3; shared walls apart from one side); 52 square meters (rated 3; shared walls apart from one side); 80 square meters (rated 2; with shared walls). It should be noted that Shiloh's interpretation of the last building is doubtful, and it is more likely that one of the spaces (space 66) does not belong to this building (see below). Thus, the area of this structure would be only 67 square meters, and only some of its walls were shared. In any case, these buildings are in stark contrast to the large building mentioned above (G. E. Wright 1970; Bunimovitz and Lederman 2009).

Lachish

During the period of the Monarchy, Lachish was a very important city and probably served as a central administrative city in the Kingdom of Judah, perhaps even a second capital (see, e.g., Tufnell 1953; Aharoni 1975; Ussishkin 1978; 1993a; 2004; for its place in the settlement hierarchy see, e.g., Herzog 1997a: 217).

Public Buildings. The stratum III city, dated to the eighth century B.C.E., was surrounded by a double wall (fig. 16). In the center of the city, there was a large, magnificent palace, and beside it there were storehouses and stables (Ussishkin 1993a; 2004).

Residential Buildings. The fact that only a few residential buildings have been excavated makes it difficult to understand the social situation in Lachish. Parts of many residential buildings have been uncovered along the street leading from the city gate toward the palace (Tufnell [1953: 103] interpreted some of these remains as shops; for another interpretation, see Eitan-Katz 1994: 39–40). Parts of many other buildings have been found in various parts of the tell, but we cannot know their complete plans, except for just one building on level III, which contains rooms 1013–17, 1039 (Tufnell 1953: pl. 115). If this is indeed one building, its measurements are approximately 11 × 11 meters, but the quality of its construction is not particularly

---

22. The calculation of the buildings' area includes the houses' external walls. Because in this case the buildings lean against the casement wall (but are not part of it), the casement wall is not included in the calculation.

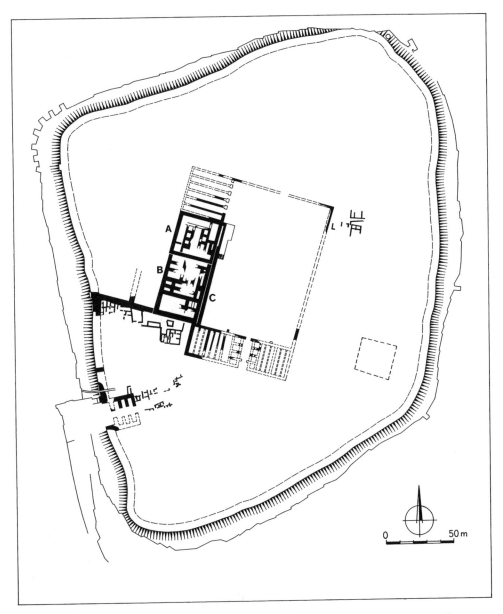

Fig. 16. Lachish: general plan of the Iron Age II city (Herzog 1997a: 240). Courtesy of Ze'ev Herzog.

high. According to Olga Tufnell (1953: 103), the poor quality of construction is common to all the residential houses, but she noted that this latter building (like its neighbors) was built on a relatively prominent area topographically.

A few other buildings were uncovered near the meeting point of the external wall with the wall of the palace complex. The many rooms discovered in this area probably belonged to three or four buildings (Ussishkin 1978: 49, 51–53):

1. The lower building: its area is about 45–50 square meters, and it is composed of several rooms around a paved yard. It contained vessels typical of a private residence complex (for an analysis, see Eitan-Katz 1994: 39). The building does not follow any known plan (rated 2), and all its walls were probably shared.

2. The middle building: includes unit 1009 (excavated earlier by the British expedition) and locus 3525 (excavated by Ussishkin's expedition). Its plan and the boundary between it and the upper building are difficult to define and identify (rated 2). Its southern part has yet to be excavated. This building also contained a range of everyday finds (pottery vessels, weights, etc.). Due to the problem in identifying the building's boundary, it is difficult to reconstruct its size and shape, but it is certainly the smallest of the three buildings.

3. The upper building: includes units 1001–2, 1005–8. This is quite a large house, with no clear boundary between it and the middle building. It is not built to any known plan (rated 2). It is questionable whether room 1002 (area: 85, rated 3) actually belonged to the building containing the other rooms or whether it was a separate unit. If so, rooms 1001, 1005–8 belonged to a fourth building, constituting the largest unit in the building complex (area: at least 105 square meters).

The various residential houses exposed in Lachish were not built to any known plan and are not similar to each other in plan or area. This seems to support Tufnell's opinion that the various building parts excavated housed "the poorest members of the community" (Tufnell 1953: 103). Although there are significant size differences between the buildings, there are no clear gaps based on the other criteria, and it seems that in this case too what we can see are differences within the lower class rather than different classes. So far, no affluent houses have been excavated (apart from the palace, of course), but presumably, if the excavation area is extended and the residential quarters are excavated, such buildings will be found. At any event, the presence of the palace, surrounded by poor buildings but isolated from them by a massive wall, reveals extreme socioeconomic gaps.

Tombs. Many tombs have been exposed near the tell (Barkay 1994: 148). The magnificent burial caves of the type unearthed around Jerusalem (monumental individual graves and multiroom family tombs) are completely absent from the site. Most of the caves discovered (40.5% of the graves on the site) are regular and contain more than one room. The single-room caves constitute another 13.5%. Irregular caves and reused caves account for only 2.8%. Most of the graves (52.6%) are simple inhumations cut into the rock or dug in the ground. According to Barkay, this division is "a faithful socio-economic mirror of the socioeconomic stratification of Lachish's population" (Barkay 1994: 148 n. 158). One should also take into account the possibility that many of the simple graves have been destroyed and have disappeared over time (and in the past, their proportion would have been higher than the percentage mentioned above).

The picture arising from the analysis of the graves complements the analysis of the residential houses. The graves show that Lachish was inhabited by both rich

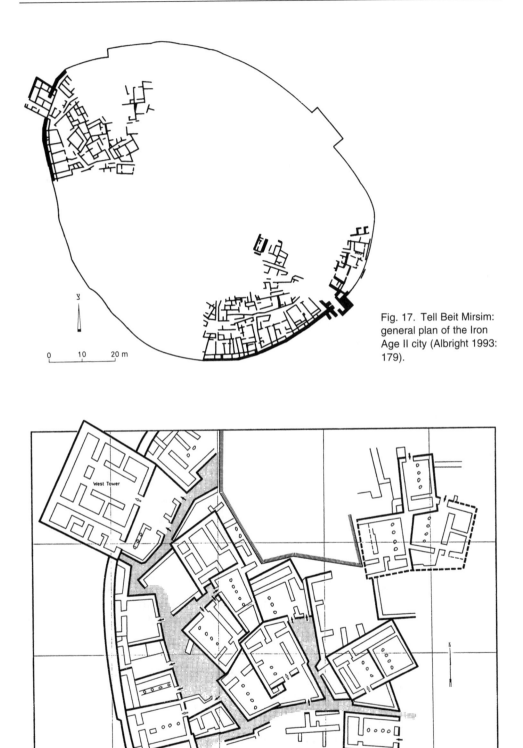

Fig. 17. Tell Beit Mirsim: general plan of the Iron Age II city (Albright 1993: 179).

Fig. 18. Tell Beit Mirsim: the northwestern quarter (Shiloh 1970: 187).

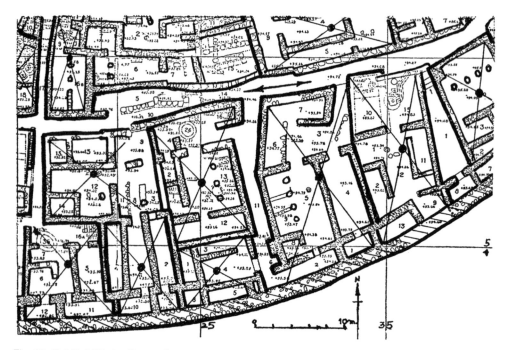

Fig. 19. Tell Beit Mirsim: the southeastern quarter (Shiloh 1978: 38).

and poor and that they were buried in different graves. If all the residential houses excavated in the tell indeed belonged to the poor, their percentage was even greater than the graves reveal (although, even there, they had an absolute majority). The excavation revealed that Lachish was also inhabited by the most senior elements of the population: the monarchy and its attendants. They lived in the palace but were probably buried in Jerusalem in the multiroom family tombs.

Tell Beit Mirsim

This site of Beit Mirsim (fig. 17) is located in the southern Shephelah (Albright 1943), and in the eighth century B.C.E. it was a provincial town (Herzog 1992b: 261).

Public Buildings. The excavations revealed the city walls, the gate, and perhaps also a tower in the western wall (Albright 1943). There are also hints that a store-house was present on the site (Barkay 1993), but this is far from certain. In the city center, the remains of a massive structure were noted; the excavator saw it as a public building or fortress, but its excavation was never completed, so we cannot know its full plan (Albright 1943: 48–49).

Residential Buildings. The buildings are small and lack fine planning. The vast majority of them belong to the four-room type, and most of them are actually three-room houses. An examination of the buildings' size and quality shows that most of the residents probably belonged to the lower class. It appears that the "western tower" (photograph 1) was actually a large four-room building, perhaps belonging to one of the city's wealthy residents or to the governor (Holladay 1992: 316–17; Shiloh 1970:

186). Residential houses have been excavated in two neighborhoods, which were exposed on the north-west and southeast areas of the tell. In the northeastern excavation area, 16 build-ings with plans that can be completely or almost com-pletely understood have been excavated (apart from the "tower"; Albright 1943: pls. 6, 7), and so have parts of other buildings (fig. 18). Most of the buildings are of the three-room subtype. Shiloh divided the quarter into buildings (Shiloh 1970), and his division is generally convincing.[23]

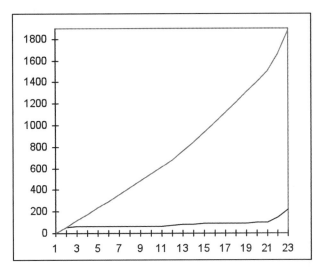

Graph 9. Tell Beit Mirsim: size of buildings.

Additional buildings were excavated in the southeastern excavation area (fig. 19). Many build-ings were excavated in this area, and about 15 of them have a plan that can be analyzed satisfactorily (Al-bright 1943: pls. 3, 5). We only note here the buildings with a relatively clear plan.

Settlement Plan.[24] The main characteristics of Tell Beit Mirsim's plan are the belt of houses that was built along the city wall and the

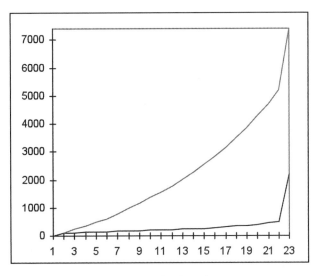

Graph 10. Tell Beit Mirsim: weighted graph.

23. However, his proposal that several units of residential houses should be viewed as one build-ing should not be accepted. The main factor in his proposal was the absence of openings in some of the buildings (based on the published plan), and so he suggested that they were entered from neighboring residential units. But in some cases there is no sign in the plan for an opening connecting the rooms as he suggested. In the absence of signs of an entrance to a residential unit, it is preferable to reconstruct an opening facing the street rather than an opening through a neighboring building. As a result, all the resi-dential units should be separated, and Shiloh's proposal of seeing several units as one complex should not be accepted.

24. See Shiloh 1970; Holladay 1992: 317.

Table 5. Buildings in Tell Beit Mirsim in the eighth century B.C.E. [a]

Building	Area	Plan	Shared Walls?	Location	Comments
31: 10, 11	80	4	Yes	Residential neighborhood in northwestern quarter	The building has a front yard.
31: 7, 8, 9	60	2	Yes	Residential neighborhood in northwestern quarter	
32: 5, 6, 7	65	2	Yes	Residential neighborhood in northwestern quarter	Subtype of the three-room type
32: 9, 12	65	2	Yes	Residential neighborhood in northwestern quarter	
22: 10	100	2	Yes (except walls facing the street)	Residential neighborhood in northwestern quarter	
22: 9, 11	60+	2	Yes	Residential neighborhood in northwestern quarter	The plan is slightly distorted since the building was probably built in the space between previous buildings, but it tries to follow the accepted plan.
32: 1, 3, 4, 15	95	3	Yes	Residential neighborhood in northwestern quarter	Quite similar to a four-room house
21: 11, 12	85	3	Yes	Residential neighborhood in northwestern quarter	Front yard (shared)
22: 9, 10	90–	3	Yes	Residential neighborhood in northwestern quarter	Front yard (shared) (not fully preserved)
22: 4, 5, 13, 14	95	2	Yes	Residential neighborhood in northwestern quarter	Irregular four-room house, probably a combination of rooms
11: 4, 5	60	4	No	Residential neighborhood in northwestern quarter	
11: 2, 3, 8, 9	65	3	Yes	Residential neighborhood in northwestern quarter	Front yard (shared)

Table 5. Buildings in Tell Beit Mirsim in the eighth century B.C.E. [a]

Building	Area	Plan	Shared Walls?	Location	Comments
11: 1	60+	3	Yes	Residential neighborhood in northwestern quarter	Front yard (shared)
12: 2, 3, 8, 9	90+	4	Yes	Residential neighborhood in northwestern quarter	Its western part is reconstructed, quite regular construction
13: 1	150	3	Yes (probably)	Residential neighborhood in northwestern quarter	Only partially excavated
13: 8, 9	63	4	Yes	Residential neighborhood in northwestern quarter	
Western tower	220+	5	No (only with fortifications)	Grand structure on the city wall	Today considered a four-room house used as a residence of the city governor or a wealthy family. Area over 220 sq. m (without the attached unit; taken together, the area is nearly 300 sq m).
51: 5, 6	60	3	Yes	Residential neighborhood in southwestern quarter (near the gate)	
4: 1, 2, 4	55+	2	Yes	Residential neighborhood in southwestern quarter (near the gate)	Front yard (?). Probably built using existing spaces.
24: 3, 4, 5	70	3	Yes	Residential neighborhood in southwestern quarter (near the gate)	
23: 12, 13	90	4	Yes	Residential neighborhood in southwestern quarter (near the gate)	Four-room house with fine front yard
33: 9, 11, 12, 13	100	4	Yes	Residential neighborhood in southwestern quarter (near the gate)	Four-room house with fine front yard

a. As noted, the calculation of the buildings' area includes the houses' external walls. For the buildings located in the tell's circumference belt, the calculation includes the external walls and also the casement rooms, but the external city wall that these rooms lean against is not included in the calculation.

Photograph 1. The Western Tower at Tell Beit Mirsim.

ring road that meandered parallel to it (compare Shiloh 1970; see also Holladay 1992: 317; more below). The areas excavated in Tell Beit Mirsim were mainly residential neighborhoods. The only exceptional building is the western tower. This is a very grand, regular, symmetrical building. It appears that the builders of this structure had not only financial means but also political power, because the building was constructed over the city wall. It is possible that, at some stage, as the system of local authority in provincial towns developed, it was decided to establish a "governor's house," and due to the dense occupancy of the tell, this location was chosen. Alternatively, perhaps a wealthy individual used his power and influence to build a sort of palace in the only available space on the tell (for further discussion, see Faust 2003c).

The other buildings represent standard residential quarters. There are some differences in the area and size of the houses, but apart from the western tower, there are no houses clearly belonging to a different sector of society. It is worth considering whether this resulted from the site's being a provincial town or from the random nature of the findings (which means that on other parts of the tell a different picture might be discovered). A clue in the latter direction can be found in Barkay's suggestion that there was also a large storehouse on the tell, which was robbed in later years, and another clue is the large public building, a small part of which was excavated by Albright (Albright 1943: 48–49). Thus it is certainly possible that there is an area on the tell that has yet to be excavated where the public buildings and perhaps the fine residences of the administrative officials were located.

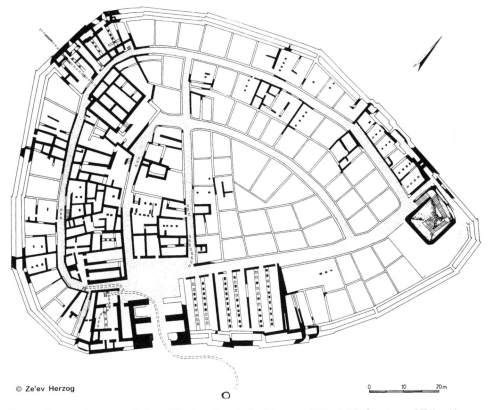

© Ze'ev Herzog

0 _____ 10 _____ 20m

Fig. 20. Beersheba: general plan of the Iron Age II city (Herzog 1997a: 247). Courtesy of Ze'ev Herzog.

Graphs 9–10 show that only one building (representative of a small elite group) is exceptionally different from the other buildings. This fact is reflected in the weighted graph, but the trend can also be identified in the graph representing only building size. The buildings' data show a lack of uniformity, and there are gaps in terms of size and quality between the other buildings as well. However, since these buildings reflect the same socioeconomic stratum, the differences cancel out and thus are not deeply expressed in the curves presented here. The sublayers within the large group (belonging to the lower class) can be identified in the lower graph at the bottom of graph 10: there are three subgroups identifiable there.

Beersheba

Stratum II at Tel Beersheba (probably biblical Sheva; Na'aman 1980; 1987: 4) was a small and well-planned administrative town in the eighth century B.C.E. (Aharoni 1973; Herzog 1997a: 244–47).

Public Buildings. The city was surrounded by a wall with a gate (fig. 20). A series of public buildings of the pillared-building type were found near the gate (photograph 2) and were interpreted as storehouses. Opposite the gate, there was a large residential house, which the excavators identified as a governor's residence. Several

Photograph 2. Pillared buildings, Beersheba.

other buildings were discovered in this area. Another large building, the "basement house," was found in the city center. Residential houses were located in most of the city. At the northern end of the city, not far from the storehouses, was a large water system that was filled from the outside by flood water. The city as a whole is well planned, which implies public-royal construction.

Residential Buildings.[25]   In the western quarter, three buildings (75, 76, 26) were excavated alongside the casement wall, and their entrances were on the circumference street, or the ring road (Beit-Arieh 1973):

---

25. For a partial analysis of these buildings, see Singer-Avitz 1996. In many cases, I disagree with her division of the buildings, and I believe that most of the buildings that she interprets as four-room houses should be considered three-room houses, with the fourth room probably being an alley leading to the city wall (see detailed discussion in Faust 2002a; 2004e; see more below). In a recent publication, Singer-Avitz (2011: 282) attempted to reject my interpretation, mainly in light of pottery and installations that were unearthed in those alleys or corridors, and suggested that they should be regarded as part of the adjacent houses. This is a very problematic suggestion. Mobile artifacts (as well as ovens and even some small walls) can be instructive about the usage of a space in the final stage prior to the destruction but not during its original phase. It is very likely that when refugees flooded the city on the eve of Beersheba's final destruction, many of the corridors (about their significance, see later in this chapter, in the discussion of urban planning in Beersheba and in the section on urban planning) were partially used by people, and the finds that Singer-Avitz refers to represent this phase. The fact that there is no physical connection between those corridors and the adjacent buildings (see also the plans in Singer-Avitz 2011: 283) disproves any attempt

1. Building 75: According to Singer-Avitz, this is a four-room house. She adds to the two long rooms (75 and 77) another long room (28) (Singer-Avitz 1996; following Beit-Arieh 1973: 33–34). The building's area, including the three long rooms, the two casements, and the front yards is about 85 square meters; without the front yard, it is 65–70 square meters. The house was planned together with the wall and the street, but its plan is not very regular (rated 3). Its walls are shared with the neighboring buildings and the city wall. It is more likely, however, that room 28 was not part of the residential building (see further below), and in this case the plan is more attractive and regular; the house's area is reduced to 70 square meters including the yard (60 square meters without it), and the back walls continue the front walls (rated 4).[26]

2. Building 76: The house has two (or according to Singer-Avitz, three) long rooms, a front yard, and a broad space composed of two casements. The building's area is about 67 square meters; without the front yard, the area is less than 60 square meters. The house was constructed together with the street and the city wall (and has shared walls), but despite this, its plan is not consistent or symmetrical (rated 3).

3. Building 25: The building included a front yard (reconstructed), a broad room (casement), and two long rooms. Its area is about 75 square meters; without the front yard, its area is only 60 square meters. The building is not symmetrical, and it probably connected rooms and casements (rated 3). The attempt to add room 28 as one of this building's rooms raises problems (see below).

In the southwestern quarter, two buildings with similar plans (607, 630) have been excavated and can be identified and analyzed:

4. Building 607: According to Singer-Avitz, this is a four room house, but an examination of the plan makes it more likely that it was a three-room house. The plan does not demonstrate how the broad room (the "casement") ends in the south, and since the northern casement wall seems to continue the house's northern wall, the area is calculated on the assumption that the same is true for the southern wall. The building's area is just over 70 square meters; without the front yard, it is only 50 square meters. The building's plan is fine and symmetrical (rated 4).

5. Building 630: A structure with three rooms and a front yard. Its area is slightly over 70 square meters; without the yard, its area is about 50 square meters. The building is very similar to its neighbor, and it too is nicely built (rated 4).

---

to connect them, because nobody would intentionally build rooms that cannot be approached from the house itself or that would require the inhabitants to go to the main street in order to reach them (more below). Furthermore, the fact that such a phenomenon exists in the outer belt of houses (the houses that were built adjacent to the wall) of many cities in Judah shows that this was a general characteristic of Judahite city planning.

26. The area calculated in the tables does not include room 28, the area of the yard in front of it, or the casement behind it. The area includes the building's walls apart from the external city wall.

Two other buildings (855, 812) were found in the city's interior (in discussing the following buildings, I had to rely only on the small-scale plan that was published, so there may be relatively large deviations in the calculation results).

6. Building 855: Its area (including the walls) is about 110 square meters, and there is a large yard in front of it in which stairs and an oven were discovered. The building is very nicely built and is divided into four symmetrical spaces (rated 5). The building's walls are probably shared only on one side. The nature of the finds inside the house is unusual: these were many serving vessels and a large range of vessels and small finds. According to Singer-Avitz, this was a particularly wealthy household (Singer-Avitz 1996: 172; more below).

7. Building 812: This building was less well preserved than the previous one, and so it is difficult to estimate its plan and area. According to the reconstructed plan, its area is about 105 square meters, but another space may need to be added to the reconstruction, which would increase the building's area.

In the north quarter, five other three-room buildings were examined (529, 522, 526, 673, 770), with the city wall's casement rooms serving as their back rooms:

8. Building 529: Its area is about 60 square meters, and its plan is quite regular (rated 3). Most of its walls are shared.

9. Building 522: Its area is about 65 square meters, assuming that only half of the casement area should be calculated, because in the city plan this casement seems to be shared with building 526. Its plan is slightly less regular (but still rated 3). All its walls are shared.

10. Building 526: Its area is less than 50 square meters, including half of the back casement (see above). Its plan is not regular (rated 3).

11. Building 673: According to Singer-Avitz, this building too is a three-room house, but the plan appears to show it as a slightly distorted four-room house (rated 2), and its area is over 70 square meters. If the fourth space does not belong to the building, its shape is more symmetrical (still rated 2), and its area is reduced to about 50 square meters. Its walls are shared.

12. Building 770: The building is probably of similar size (65–70 square meters). It is not clear how the back space was used, because the casement's interior wall divides it (the area stated is obtained by continuing the imaginary lines of the existing walls and including the area formed as a broad room). The plan is irregular (rated 2).

13. Another building typical of Beersheba is building 430, a three-room house with a front yard, built close to the city gate area (Herzog, Rainey, and Moshkovitz 1977). Although it has only three rooms, this house is very large, and its area is about 140 square meters. Apart from the two long rooms, the front yard, and the casement rooms, this building has a real broad room located at the back of the house before the casement rooms. In this building as well there was no precise match between the casement rooms and the

building's width, probably due to the use of the casement room next to the gate (which was accessed only through this building in any case). The house's location close to the gate indicates its importance and that of its residents. The building is quite nicely constructed (rated 4).[27]

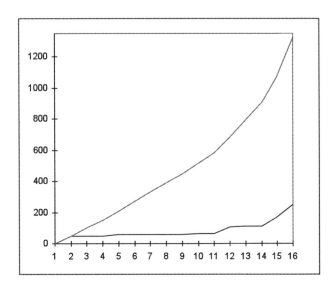

Graph 11. Beersheba: size of buildings.

Two more buildings have also been excavated that were used for public purposes, according to the excavators (Herzog 1993: 172):

1. The "basements house": This building received its name from the basements uncovered beneath its floor. The excavators assumed that in the levels prior to stratum II, the city temple stood on this site, and the basements were constructed as a result of its complete dismantling. They assumed that, at the time of stratum II,

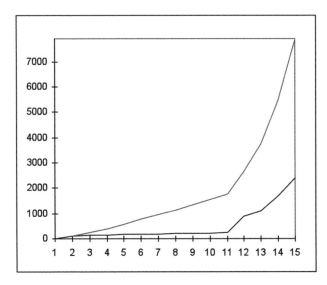

Graph 12. Beersheba: weighted graph.

wine was stored in the basements, and the house may have belonged to an official responsible for the storehouses (Herzog 1993: 140). In any case, the building is a large four-room house that was probably used as a residence, either of a private individual (wealthy, in this case) or of an official (as

---

27. Yadin (1978) suggested that this building contained Beersheba's "gate altar." His suggestion is interesting but does not seem likely, because it would necessitate changing the accepted date of Beersheba's level II by more than a century, which is not convincing. See, e.g., Herzog, Rainey, and Moshkovitz 1977.

Table 6. Buildings in Beersheba in the eighth century B.C.E.

Building	Area	Plan	Shared Walls	Location	Comments
75	70 incl. front yard; 60 excl. it	4	Yes	Western quarter	
76	65–70 incl. front yard; 60 excl. it	3	Yes	Western quarter	Considered a three-room house
25	75 incl. yard; 60 excl. it	3	Yes	Western quarter	Considered a three-room house
607	70 incl. yard; 50 excl. it	4	Yes	Southwestern quarter	Considered a three-room house
630	70 incl. yard; 50 excl. it	4	Yes	Southwestern quarter	Considered a three-room house
855	110 excl. front yard	5	Only partially (considered no)	City center, near basements house	Large house with large front yard
812	105	?	At least partially (considered yes)	City center	The plan is not fully clear.
529	60	3	Yes	Northern quarter	
522	65	3	Yes	Northern quarter	
526	50–	3	Yes	Northern quarter	
673	50–70	2	Yes	Northern quarter	Area calculation depends on plan analysis.
770	65 (?)	2	Yes	Northern quarter	Situation in the broad room is unclear.
430	140 incl. front yard; 110 excl. it	4	No	Near city gate	Area excl. the part of the casement beyond the wall line.
Basements house	140 excl. south wing; 170 incl. it	5	No (?)	City center	Probably also had a front yard
Governor's house	250	5	Partially	Near city gate	Uses ashlar stones

the excavators suggested). The building's area is nearly 140 square meters without the southern wing and over 170 square meters with this wing and is very attractively constructed (rated 5).

2. The "governor's house": A large and very nicely constructed building discovered near the city gate area. Its plan is not familiar from other places (rated 5), and its area is about 250 square meters.[28] It is partially built of ashlar stones and overlooks the city gate (Reich 1992: 211).

Social Stratification. According to Singer-Avitz (1996), in the north quarter of Beersheba there were relatively small houses. On the basis of an analysis of the pottery found in the buildings and due to the absence of cooking facilities and weights, Singer-Avitz concluded that this quarter served as the residence for a male population that did not prepare its food (in contrast to the other quarters), perhaps soldiers who received their food from a central cooking facility. The other buildings constructed alongside the city wall do not imply great wealth, and in her opinion they were inhabited by the lower classes. In one case (building 76), she suggested that a house was the house of a potter and that potters in ancient societies were in a lower class of the population. The buildings inside the city (located away from the city wall) served a more affluent population, in her opinion, and this is how she interprets the small finds from building 855.

An analysis of the city plan of Beersheba shows that the lower classes (soldiers or civilians) indeed lived around the circumference in three-room houses. Members of higher classes (senior officials and the wealthy) lived in the city center. Most of the public buildings were near the city gate.

Graphs 11–12 reflect a distinction between a group of large, high-quality buildings and the rest of the houses. This first group is larger in Beersheba than in Tell Beit Mirsim and Mizpah (Tell en-Nasbeh), probably because Beersheba was an administrative town.

Urban Planning. According to Singer-Avitz, three-room houses were located only in the northern quarter, while the rest of the buildings on the site were four-room houses. But as we have seen, all the buildings in the city's circumference, which are the majority of the houses discussed here, were three-room houses (see also Zorn 1993: 138 n. 245). The different analysis of the individual residential houses influences the understanding of the entire city plan. It is well known that the whole of Beersheba was built almost according to a master plan, and it is the best example of a planned Iron Age settlement. So it appears that the houses around the edge were intended to be three-room houses, and their rear space was one of the casements in the city wall. Behind each pair of houses, there was a sort of narrow corridor serving as access to another casement. The corridor and the casement did not belong to any building. They probably served public (or administrative) needs and may have

---

28. According to Aharoni (1973), the building's area is about 15 × 18 meters, while according to Reich (1992: 210), it is 10 × 18 meters; a study of the plan shows that the measurements are closer to Aharoni's, and the building's area is over 250 square meters. Notably, it is possible that the plan is reminiscent of a four-room house, if an entrance were reconstructed in its northeastern part.

been used for storage and for access to the city wall.[29] This, for instance, is the role of spaces 28 and 87 in the southwestern quarter, of the "fourth space" that Singer-Avitz probably attached to building 630, and so on. It should be noted that in the northern quarter such corridors were not found, and this supports Singer-Avitz's suggestion (based on the small finds) that soldiers lived in this quarter, since the buildings were used for public purposes, and there was no need to leave spaces for these purposes (access to the city wall and storage; see below).

It is worth mentioning that in Nippur several residential quarters of a different character were discovered. A planned, uniform quarter was found that the excavator believed served as the residences of families working in the temple, and there was also a private quarter where the buildings differed in size and quality (Stone 1987: 126–27). The partial similarity to Beersheba enables us to suggest that, despite the overall planning apparent in Beersheba, and although some of the buildings were used for public and state purposes, some of the residential houses were built privately, within the constraints imposed by the overall urban planning (streets, passages, and so on). This is why there are some houses in the city in which construction is irregular and unattractive, despite the careful overall planning (Faust 2002a).

Other Sites

There are additional sites that were excavated, and the finds might contribute to the present discussion. These include Aroer (in which parts of many buildings were unearthed along with the city wall and where the finds indicate the existence of various social and ethnic groups; Thareani 2011), Tel ʿEton (where parts of a number of upper- and middle-class dwellings, including the governor's residency, were excavated, as were parts of the city's fortifications; Faust 2011c), and many others, but the data are not detailed enough for the purposes of the present study and will not be addressed in detail here.

Summary

The period's cities,[30] including the provincial towns (A. Mazar 1990: 435; there, he includes Beersheba among the provincial towns), were well defended by city walls (of various types) and gates. In some of the settlements, there were also water systems, citadels, storehouses, and so on. As in the Kingdom of Israel (compare Herzog 1997a), the state was responsible for the construction of all of these. Most of the cities' residents lived in rather small houses, in most cases three-room houses.

---

29. Compare Holladay (1992; 1995: 388), who treats the houses as three room houses with an alley beside them. For a detailed analysis and a clarification of the importance of leaving access to the city wall, see Faust 2002a; 2004e.

30. Tel Batash is not discussed here, because it is not clear whether it belonged to the Kingdom of Judah (A. Mazar 1993: 155; Mazar and Panitz-Cohen 2001: 279–81; see also Kletter 1995: 44–50). While there may have been Judean involvement in the construction of the fortifications of stratum III (A. Mazar 1985a: 306–9), this is not certain, and in any case this does not make the site Judean. Furthermore, there is very little information about the eighth-century B.C.E. residential houses from this site (Kelm and Mazar 1995: 135; see also A. Mazar 1997b: 256–63, where all strata II–III architectural elements are discussed together, but the only dwellings discussed are from stratum II [1997b: 260–62]).

The family structure was probably the nuclear family (Stager 1985; Holladay 1992; Faust 1999b and additional bibliography there; more below).

The findings show that in the cities of the Kingdom of Judah there were clear socioeconomic differences. A narrow stratum of society was the wealthy elite,[31] while the rest of the population was in a much worse economic condition. At the same time, within both of these classes one can see substrata. Thus, for example, Zorn identified three lower classes at Tell en-Nasbeh (apart from the elite). The wealthy minority was not uniform either, and one can distinguish, for example, between the royal family and its entourage and other wealthy families, as is apparent in the differences at Beersheba between the large houses and the "governor's house."

Cities of the Kingdom of Judah in the
Seventh Century B.C.E.

Jerusalem

In the seventh century B.C.E., Jerusalem reached its peak and the city's area encompassed 60–100 hectares (see fig. 13, above, p. 69). The reason for this is that Jerusalem was one major settlement that was not damaged during Sennacherib's campaign (though not the only settlement; see Faust 2008), and it served as a haven for many refugees from other places in Judah that were completely devastated, mainly in the Shephelah. These refugees came to Jerusalem, not only because their homes had been destroyed, but also because they saw Jerusalem as a safe location that could never be destroyed (see, for example, McClellan 1978; H. Eshel 1991; following texts such as Jeremiah 26).

Public Buildings. The city was surrounded by a massive wall (long sections of which have been exposed in the Jewish Quarter and the City of David) and also contained an impressive water system. The Temple flourished at the end of this period, and the Ophel building (discussed above) was still in use. The palace and Temple have not been excavated,[32] but other public buildings have been discovered. The growth of Jerusalem was also reflected in the city's agricultural hinterland (Faust 1997; 2003d).

Residential Buildings. Private houses have been discovered in several excavation areas in the City of David. In area G, an entire residential quarter has been excavated. This quarter may have come into being during an earlier period (probably the tenth century B.C.E.), but most of our information about it is from the remains of the end of the period. In this area, a four-room house of approximately 100 square meters ("the house of Ahiel") has been excavated, one of the few fully excavated residential houses in Iron Age Jerusalem (Shiloh 1984: 18). The finds in the building, such as a toilet, indicate a high standard of living. The remains of 37 storage vessels were found in the building's back room (Auld and Steiner 1996: 69).

---

31. In some places, such as Tell Beit Mirsim and Mizpah (Tell en-Nasbeh), the socioeconomic situation was quite egalitarian until larger and more prominent buildings were constructed. But it is not clear when they were built, and they seem to have existed for a long time.

32. See above regarding "David's palace." Note that late Iron Age II remains there were not found in situ (E. Mazar 2007b: 67–69).

Parts of some other buildings were found on top of the stepped-stone structure in the same area. Only a small part of the building known as the "Bullae House" has been excavated. Fifty-one bullae were found in this house that were burned when the house burned down during the city's destruction in 586 B.C.E. According to many scholars, this building served as the royal archive, because the names on the bullae are not repeated. Others believe that this was the home of a trader, mainly due to the household pottery found in situ (Shiloh 1984: 15–16; Auld and Steiner 1996: 42, 67). Remains of burned decorated furniture were found in the "Burnt Room" (Shiloh 1984: 19; Auld and Steiner 1996: 69).

Kenyon's excavations also revealed late construction stages in the same area (Auld and Steiner 1996: 42). In one building, 37 stone weights with inscriptions were found, along with work tools such as hammers and anvils. These finds are typical of a blacksmith's workshop, where small products such as jewels were made and sold (1996: 42). This building also contained ostraca from the end of the eighth century B.C.E. Another building contained ceramic "foot baths," probably intended for washing feet. Eighty-eight fish bones were found, brought from the Mediterranean, the coastal rivers, and perhaps also the Jordan River; presumably, importing fish to Jerusalem was expensive (1996: 69–70). These data indicate that this was the house of a wealthy family. Another building contained 120 loom weights, probably implying commercial weaving (1996: 70).

The quarter in this area (Shiloh's area G and Kenyon's trench A) was probably planned and contained a main street from which alleys split off (1996: 70). This fact along with the evidence of trade and the various pieces of hygienic evidence (toilets and baths) indicate that this was a prestigious quarter, according to Auld and Steiner. They believe that the construction of the residences of traders and artisans on top of the stepped building, which originally served as a royal compound, reflects the rise in the power of this population group compared with its status during the eighth century B.C.E. (1996: 65–66; note, however, that at least some of these buildings were already built in the early stages of Iron II).

Some buildings from the seventh century have also been discovered in area E. The "ashlar House" is impressive in the quality of its construction, the thickness of its walls, and the ashlar stones set in its corners. Its size (13 × 12 meters) is much greater than the other buildings discovered nearby (Shiloh 1984: 11; Auld and Steiner 1996: 42). It may have been a public building or perhaps a wealthy home (Margreet Steiner expressed this opinion in a lecture at Bar-Ilan University on November 26, 1997). Another building that remained during the seventh century B.C.E. was the house on the lower terrace (Shiloh 1984: 619; see above).

Alon de Groot tried to explain the difference between the House of Ahiel (in area G), which was located on the slope, requiring great effort to construct it all on one level, and the house discovered in area E, where the surroundings required that it be constructed on several terraces. In his opinion, this difference shows the socioeconomic gap between the residents of the two buildings: the first building, located in the north of the City of David, was probably inhabited by members of the upper class, while the second building belonged to people of lesser status (de Groot

1991a: 48–49; Shiloh [1984: 18] also remarks that the quality of the "house of Ahiel" is notable in comparison with the buildings found in area E). In this context, we should remember that Auld and Steiner also stressed the difference between the "ashlar House" and the rest of the buildings in area E (Auld and Steiner 1996: 42; most of the buildings in the lower quarters, once considered outside the city walls, were probably abandoned during this period; see Shiloh 1993a: 704–5).

According to Auld and Steiner (1996: 34–64), many imported products were discovered in the excavations in and around the city: wood and wooden furniture imported from northern Syria, ivory from Mesopotamia, decorated shells from the Red Sea, wine jugs from Greece or Cyprus, pottery from Assyria, scarabs from Egypt, fish from the Mediterranean, and so on. They believe that in this period Jerusalem was a wealthy city, and its wealth originated in trade.[33] In their opinion, most of the commerce was controlled by the monarchy, but during this period private traders became involved and benefited from it.[34] They believe that many of the city's residents were wealthy traders and artisans, living with their families and servants, while the royal court, senior officials, and priests lived in the Temple Mount and Ophel area. They think that the poor lived outside the city walls (on the traders and artisans, see Auld and Steiner 1996: 70–72; see also Shiloh 1984: 19), but it is more likely that they also lived in other quarters of the large city.

Tombs. In this period, the cemetery at the village of Siloam was still in use, mainly for the burial of senior officials. Very grand (multi-) family tombs were found in Ketef Hinnom and in the St. Ettienne area (e.g., Barkay 1994, and discussion and bibliography there), and they testify to the elite families, their financial power, and the extended family structure they maintained. In contrast to the typical burial systems (with one room) used for members of an extended family (*bet av*) over several generations, the grand burial caves (with many rooms) reflect a family structure that maintained the *mishpahah* framework (clans; on this term, see chap. 1 and chap. 4). The *mishpahot*'s economic strength allowed the families to maintain this framework, and this in turn helped them to protect their power. In one of the cave complexes in Ketef Hinnom, one cave was found with a series of parallel tombs in a room used for multiple burials (Barkay 1994: 117). This room may have been used for the burial of "additional" members (residents, servants, etc.) who were allowed burial in the family tomb (see chap. 4). The simplest family tombs imply another economic standing (Hopkins 1996: 129–30), and, when compared with the Siloam tombs and the impressive tombs at Ketef Hinnom (and similar tombs), seem to have belonged to the middle classes, perhaps free citizens belonging to *am ha'aretz*. In Mamilla, such family tombs were found, as were even simpler, shaft tombs, which served the lower

---

33. Some of the evidence is weak. An analysis of the evidence and the significance of trade is beyond the scope of this chapter, but see chap. 8 (see also Faust 2006b: 49–64).

34. The evidence presented by Auld and Steiner for the traders is scanty. The fact that certain imported items reached Jerusalem does not show how they arrived and does not indicate private trade. For an extensive discussion, see Auld and Steiner 1996: 63–71. On the southern Arabian inscription that they attribute to a trader, see Shiloh 1987a.

classes. It is likely that a large proportion of the population was interred in simple inhumations that were not preserved.

Analysis of the tombs shows significant stratification, perhaps more severe than in previous periods, and the picture that arises from them complements the findings from excavations in the city itself. In seventh-century B.C.E. Jerusalem, the entire range of classes was represented, from the wealthy and senior office holders through the families of priests and other wealthy families, artisans, independent and free families that maintained their status throughout the period, and up to the simplest people, probably day laborers. This varied reality is reflected in the finds, despite their fragmentary and partial nature; in fact, only one (the House of Ahiel) or two (if we consider the Ashlar House) residential houses have been fully excavated (and published in a manner that allow us to discuss them). This unprecedented stratification may have happened because of the fact that some of the residents of Jerusalem in this period were refugees who arrived in the city (following Sennacherib's campaign) empty-handed (McClellan 1978: 282; see below, chap. 9).

Lachish

Lachish declined in the seventh century in comparison with the eighth century B.C.E. Although it gradually recovered from its destruction and returned to serve as an important town in the Kingdom of Judah, it did not regain the grandeur it had previously known. A few relatively scattered remains of dwellings were found on the site (Ussishkin 1993a: 909; 2004: 91), but we have insufficient information to discuss the social composition of the city.

Mizpah (Tell en-Nasbeh)

According to Zorn, the transition from the eighth to the seventh century B.C.E. created no changes at the site, and thus the analysis of the situation during the eighth century presented above also applies to this period (Zorn 1993). This means that the socioeconomic gaps in the city were still present.[35]

En Gedi

In the excavations of En Gedi, only a limited part of the small tell was unearthed. According to the excavators, stratum V represents the end of the seventh century B.C.E., and the settlement was completely destroyed during the Babylonian conquest. The excavations revealed structures of a uniform plan: a yard with two small adjacent rooms on one side. The settlement's economy was probably based on one special component. Due to its small size and unique nature, it should probably not be termed a *city* in the accepted modern sense of the word. In the yards near the buildings that were burned and buried under collapsed bricks, special sunken barrels were found in the ground, and around them were many pottery vessels. The excavators explained the unusual finds by proposing that the settlement's economy

---

35. Notably, the highlands were only partially devastated in Sennacherib's campaign, especially when compared with the Shephelah (Faust 2008).

was based on cultivating perfume plants, particularly persimmon (B. Mazar 1992a; see now the final report, Stern 2007).

Other Sites

In the seventh century B.C.E., the Shephelah was devastated, and large tracts of land were transferred to Philistine control as a result of Sennacherib's campaign. Other areas did not suffer as much however; many new settlements were also established, mainly in the marginal areas of the Kingdom of Judah (for possible reasons, see Finkelstein 1994; see also Faust and Weiss 2005; Faust 2008). Our knowledge of these settlements is very sparse (usually not even one residential house has been excavated or fully published) and is not sufficient to generate an analysis of the social conditions there.[36]

Summary

Judah in the seventh century B.C.E. was different from Judah in the eighth century. The Shephelah was devastated, while other regions flourished. Unfortunately, most of our archaeological information comes from the Shephelah, and our data on the seventh century is therefore limited (Faust 2008, and references). The findings clearly show that during the seventh century B.C.E. the importance of Jerusalem increased, and this was apparent also in the sharp increase in surrounding settlements (Faust 1997; 2005b; compare Feig 2000). The many settlements established on the margins of the kingdom also testify to the great changes that had occurred. But the available archaeological finds do not provide clear evidence of a change in the social structure compared with the eighth century B.C.E. In the excavated cities of this period, one can identify clear social gaps. In Jerusalem, these gaps are wider, and one notes the presence of several classes, from the poorest to the wealthiest.

Discussion:
Public Buildings

Evidence for public and monumental construction was discovered in all the cities discussed here. All the urban settlements in the period of the Monarchy, including provincial towns, were surrounded by walls of various types. These walls, despite the variety of shapes and thickness, were all quite massive and were undoubtedly constructed and financed by the monarchy (A. Mazar 1990: 435; compare Dever 1995: 423; on Hazor, see S. Geva 1989: 107). The walls contained gates that were usually quite impressive. Buildings related to the administrative system (such as governors' houses), citadels, and so on were also discovered. The sites have only been partially excavated, of course, and presumably there were other public buildings that have yet to be excavated.[37] However, it is clear that the administrative

---

36. The situation at Aroer, for example, is an exception (see, e.g., Thareani 2011), but the discussion is less relevant for most issues addressed in this book.

37. It is worth considering Tell Beit Mirsim, which may have contained a storehouse that was not excavated (see Barkay 1993) and a public building, only the edges of which were excavated (above), and which is rarely mentioned in the research literature. Beth-Shemesh, too, should serve as a warning against the

towns (and, of course, the capital cities) contained many public buildings, while the provincial towns had few public buildings apart from a wall and gate (compare Herzog 1992b: 248; A. Mazar 1990: 436). The presence of various public buildings implies a stratified society (see below, chap. 6) and royal involvement of the sort that was typical of urban settlements (compare Herzog 1997a: 276). This involvement was one of the factors contributing to the social processes that took place in the cities and caused social stratification.

The City Gate as an Urban Community Element

City gates and their various roles have been studied thoroughly, and many works have been devoted to their military roles, architectural development, chronology, and so on (e.g., Coogan 1982; Herzog 1976, and additional bibliography there). Many scholars have discussed some of its social aspects. The following discussion reexamines the social role of the city gate and the physical implications of this term.

Social Roles

The city gate is mentioned in biblical and other texts in many contexts. Many gates from the Iron Age have been excavated and subjected to detailed analyses. From the various texts and the archaeological evidence, we know that the gate and the square in front of it were a "focal point for public life in the city" (Coogan 1982: 232). The gate was the most appropriate place for public activities that involved a large number of people (see, e.g., Herzog 1976; Coogan 1982: 231–36):

> Place of justice: This role of the gate originated in the Canaanite period. The city elders probably operated there. In the ancient Near East, the city gate was the site for gatherings, and there is a wealth of evidence, both biblical and other, that legal proceedings were conducted at the gate (see Coogan 1982: 234–35).
> Punishment: Following from the previous role, the gate also served as a site for punishing criminals by stoning, as stated in the biblical laws regarding rebellious sons, rapists of engaged girls, and so on (Coogan 1982).
> Commerce: Extensive evidence indicates that commercial activity took place in the city gate, the natural arena for such activity. It is possible that the Hebrew word שער ('gate') received its additional meaning, 'rate', during this period (Coogan 1982: 235).
> Worship: Various types of evidence show that the city gate was the focus of ritual activity (Coogan 1982: 236; Emerton 1994; and especially Blomquist 1999), and this is stated explicitly in the report of Josiah's reform: "He also demolished the shrines of the gates" (2 Kgs 23:8; but see Fritz 1995: 140).

These activities have been extensively discussed in the past, and since they are familiar and do not change what we know about the structure of society during the period of the Monarchy, we do not need to expand upon them here, except for the obvious question: where exactly did they take place? Herzog, for instance, suggested that the signing of witnessed agreements and other civilian activities were conducted within the gate's chambers, which in many places were equipped with

---

conclusion that there were only a few public buildings. Even after most of the site had been excavated, the accepted opinion among scholars was that this was a provincial town, with residential buildings covering most of its area; only new excavations in the northeastern corner of the site revealed the public quarter located there (Bunimovitz and Lederman 1997; 2008).

benches of some sort (Herzog 1992b: 271). Other activities, such as commerce, could have taken place in the square facing the gate, which was probably considered part of it. However, these suggestions raise problems. Although some of the activities could take place in the gate's plaza, others require a different location. Thus, for example, regarding judiciary activity, even the chambers of the largest city gates are too small and were not suitable for public trials, especially if one takes into account that any such proceeding would have blocked access to the gate itself. This and other similar activities must have necessitated additional space.

In this context, it is worth mentioning that Eph'al and Naveh have recently identified another function of the gate (Eph'al and Naveh 1993). Following the discovery of several inscriptions that mentioned the "jar of the gate," they suggested that in each city there was a system of weights and measures "of the gate," a sort of *agoranomos* familiar to us from later periods. This phenomenon reflects commercial activity but also hints that the city gate was more important than the gate structure itself and even more important than the financial transactions taking place there. The gate was a social institution that the city's residents respected because it represented order, a concept of great importance in human society in general and in the Israelite society of Iron Age II in particular (see below, chap. 7). This institution should not be restricted to the physical gate structure.

In light of the above, and based on additional arguments to be presented below, I suggest that the biblical term "the city gate" did not refer only to the gate structure but to a whole area or quarter that included the gate building, the adjacent square or plaza, and the public buildings nearby—all of which served as an arena for the activities discussed above and more to be mentioned below.

Public Buildings Near the City Gate

Archaeological research has shown that various public buildings were located near the city gate. These buildings are often of the long "pillared-building" type. Aharoni, who excavated a long pillared building near the city gate in Beersheba (see photograph 2, above, p. 88), noted parallels of this phenomenon in Tell el-Far'ah, north (Tirzah), Beth-Shemesh, Tell en-Nasbeh (Mizpah), Hazor, and Arad (Aharoni 1973: 17). Not all the examples he mentioned are accepted by all scholars, but in the meantime, the city gate and adjacent public buildings have been excavated in Beth-Shemesh (Bunimovitz and Lederman 1997), and buildings of this sort have been found at Tel Kinrot (Fritz 1993: 200), Jerusalem (Mazar and Mazar 1989: E. Mazar 1991), and at Tel 'Ira (Beit-Arieh 1985, 1999b), and it appears that a public building also stood near the city gate in Gezer (Shiloh 1978: 49). Some of the buildings are of the type discovered in Beersheba: buildings divided into three long spaces by rows of pillars. The location of these buildings is no coincidence (apart from Aharoni, mentioned earlier, see also Borowski 1987: 80; Currid 1992: 53; Herr 1997: 138), and presumably they constituted part of the gate complex.

The long pillared-building type, typical of many of the public buildings found near the city gates, has been found in the land of Israel in Iron Age levels, from the end of Iron Age I and throughout Iron Age II. In fact, this type is one of the prominent public architectural elements in the period of the Monarchy. The first building of this type was discovered at Tell el-Hesi, and ever since then there has been debate regarding the nature of the pillared building.[38] The long pillared buildings and their role have been discussed extensively by scholars, and several main explanations have been proposed: stables (e.g., Yadin 1975; Holladay 1986); storehouses (e.g., Currid 1992; Herzog 1992a, and extensive bibliography there); barracks or soldiers' residences (Fritz 1995: 142–43); and trade centers, markets, or custom houses (Kochavi 1992; 1998; Blakely 2002; respectively).

Most scholars accept one of the first two possibilities, and there is also an intermediate proposal that the pillared buildings were constructed deliberately, to provide a place for both purposes (Kempinski 1993: 103; A. Mazar 1990: 477–78). But neither of the first two explanations suits the small finds discovered in these buildings, which were mainly everyday vessels. In most cases, there was no evidence of the presence of horses or of storage. A representative example can be seen in loci 221 and 222 in the pillared buildings at Beersheba, which were well preserved (Herzog 1973: 25). The finds included 136 complete vessels, including 35 bowls, 5 deep bowls, 1 krater, 21 cooking pots, 36 storage jars and hole-mouth jars, 2 flasks, 1 stand, 4 lamps, 30 juglets, jugs, and decanters, and 1 strainer.

The find at Kinrot is similar: in one of the side rooms, excavators discovered 26 bowls, 10 kraters, 40 cooking pots, 17 storage jars, 12 jugs, 5 juglets, and 2 lamps. Another room, which was only partially excavated, contained 17 bowls, 2 kraters, 5 cooking pots, 6 storage jars, 2 small jugs, 1 amphora, and 1 lamp (Fritz 1993: 200).[39]

The finds at Tel Hadar do not match what would be expected in a storehouse or stable either (Kochavi 1992). Fritz summed up the finds: "(T)he numerous vessels, which were mainly found in the side rooms, make it most likely that the latter was used for habitation; thus the possibility that they were used as stables or as storerooms is excluded" (Fritz 1995: 142). This is probably why the other explanations were suggested.

Some scholars have proposed that the buildings were indeed stables or warehouses but later served for other purposes (Yadin 1982: 242 n. 78; Ahlström 1982b: 138). This explanation is not convincing, because the everyday finds were discovered in most cases, not just in exceptional cases requiring a special explanation. Notably, the public buildings near the city gate that contained many storage vessels (as in Tel ʿIra and Jerusalem) were not pillared buildings of the type discussed here. It transpires that the long pillared buildings were not used (only) for storage. The third explanation (barracks) is possible, and so is the last explanation (trade centers or markets). It appears likely that these buildings discovered near the city gates constituted part of the gate quarter, and some of the activities taking place at the city gate took place in them.[40]

---

38. The debate refers to both the building at Tell el-Hesi and the many similar buildings discovered since then; for a summary of previous opinions, see Currid 1992.

39. Similar findings were discovered at Megiddo; see Pritchard 1970: 273.

40. The buildings were probably multifunctional (see Herr 1997: 138; A. Mazar 1990: 477–78; Kempinski 1993: 103; and even Yadin 1975: 62). Some of them, such as the building at Tel Hadar, were built prior to the period under discussion here, and thus they are clearly not "Israelite" in essence. Our discussion of this famous archaeological type is only partial and focuses only on Iron Age II buildings existing in "Israelite"

Another Role of the City Gate

The Bible notes another role of the city gate that has yet to be treated in scholarly literature: the place where the wretched and oppressed gathered. Many writings mention the presence of the poor and mistreated at the city gates, and in many cases this is related to the gate's being a place of justice.[41] Thus, for instance: "they turn aside the poor in the gate" (Amos 5:12), "they are crushed in the gate; neither is there any to deliver them" (Job 5:4), and "rob not the poor because he is poor; neither oppress the afflicted in the gate" (Prov 22:22). Other texts contain no reference to the judicial role of the gate, but perhaps the gate represents the whole city or a place of settlement in general, such as: "If there is a needy person among you, one of your kinsmen in any of your gates in the land" (Deut 15:7).[42] Other texts explicitly state that the lowest elements of society, such as the strangers, were present at the city gates: "the stranger who is at your gate" (Deut 14:21), and perhaps also "the stranger who is within your gate" (Exod 20:10); "Gather the people together—men, women, children, and the strangers in your gates" (Deut 31:12).[43] Deut 14:28–29 states, "At the end of three years, bring out the full tithe of your yield that same year, but leave it in your gates. Then the Levite, who has no hereditary portion as you have, and the stranger, the fatherless, and the widow in your gates shall come and eat their fill," implying that this was the regular location of all who needed food.

There are verses where it is difficult to interpret the gate as a symbol of the city, and they should be understood literally: "You shall not turn over to his master a slave who seeks refuge with you from his master. He shall live with you in any place he may choose in one of your gates" (Deut 23:15–16). The servant escapes to a particular city, so "one of your gates" cannot mean "one of your cities." "You shall not abuse a needy and destitute laborer, whether a fellow countryman or a stranger in one of the gates of your land" (Deut 24:14). "When you have set aside in full the tenth part of your yield—[. . .] the year of the tithe—and have given it to the Levite, the stranger, the fatherless, and the widow, that they may eat their fill in your gates" (Deut 26:12)—interpreting this as "they may eat in your cities" would void the verse of meaning.

---

areas. The function of other buildings not discussed here may have been similar, but their analysis is beyond the scope of the discussion. The wealth of information about the long pillared buildings has created extensive research, but the discussion below refers only to the pillars buildings that were public buildings located near city gates.

41. It is immaterial for our purposes whether people ever obeyed these prescriptions, or even knew of them. As King and Stager (2001: 7) wrote, "[F]or our purposes, then, it matters little whether the biblical accounts are 'true' in the positivistic sense of some historians and biblical scholars. It is enough to know that the ancient Israelites believed them to be so. The stories must have passed some test of verisimilitude, that is, having the appearance of being true or real. In this sense the biblical account and many other ancient accounts, however self-serving and tendentious, become grist for the cultural historian's mill" (see also Burckhardt 1998: 5). The existence of the discussed structures, however, might indicate that in this specific case the texts reflect at least some reality (see below).

42. Compare Deut 5:16; 17:2; 28:52; and see also Shupak 1996: 40. However, if the use of "gate" to mean "city" was common in the Bible, one would expect a wider range of contexts in which it is used, but the contexts where the gate is mentioned are mainly about judicial affairs or the marginal elements of society.

43. Though perhaps the words "thy gates" refer to all the people mentioned earlier, and not only to "thy stranger," and then the gate should be interpreted as symbolizing the whole city.

In this way, one can reinterpret Jer 17:27: "But if you do not obey my command to hallow the sabbath day and to carry in no burdens through the gates of Jerusalem on the sabbath day, then I will set fire to its gates; it shall consume the fortresses of Jerusalem and it shall not be extinguished"—if the gates of the city served as a residence for the underclass, the prophet is contrasting them with the palaces of the wealthy and the nobles. On the face of it, one can interpret the verses as meaning that the poor lived outside the gate,[44] perhaps within the plaza. But this interpretation has no support. The words "needy," "stranger," and "poor" are not mentioned in connection with the *migrash* (compare Faust 1996). Hence, the poor should be sought in the actual city gate.

What is the "gate" where the city's poor and strangers resided? The attempt to identify the gate's chambers as the area of activity, as Herzog argued when referring to the legal function, is not convincing. Not only should the space be larger, it is also not logical that the poor lived in the city gate structures, which were important for defense. As long as one understands the term "city gate" to refer only to the gate structure, one cannot understand the texts literally, because none of the activities mentioned above could have taken place in the limited space of the gate building. However, if the "city gate" was a whole quarter or area of the city that also included, besides the gate structure and adjacent plaza (as many believed, such as Herzog 1976), the neighboring public buildings, then there is no difficulty in assuming that many people and goods were housed in this area. Legal proceedings could take place in the area's buildings and not in the gate structure itself, just as these buildings could house the poor, strangers, widows and orphans. Other public buildings located near the gate, even buildings that were not of the pillared-building type, could serve for the same purposes, and it is possible that some of the public market–related activities, the "jar of the gate" and so on, were organized there.

The problem of the poor in the city, arising so starkly from biblical descriptions and many prophecies of reproach,[45] is familiar in scholarly literature dealing with agricultural societies. According to Lenski and Lenski, "the unemployed, the beggars, and the criminals" constituted between one-tenth and one-third of the population of urban centers in advanced agrarian societies (Lenski and Lenski 1974: 247). This proportion does not include unskilled laborers and day workers, who constituted a large group in these settlements and presumably often needed aid themselves. Lenski and Lenski note the severity of this social problem and note that: "[N]o agrarian society found a solution for this problem. But then, the leading classes were not especially interested in finding one" (1974: 247). In many cases in these societies, positions were purchased to produce financial benefits. Justice was also bought, and whoever paid more won (1974: 228). At the same time, as we shall see, it is possible that Israelite society treated the problem slightly differently.

44. Perhaps this appears to be the case in the reference to the lepers in Samaria, "outside the gate" (2 Kgs 7:3), but lepers probably did not belong to this class and had to stay outside the settlement.

45. See for instance, Reviv (1993: 120–24) and references to the Bible and other sources there. For an extensive discussion on the poor as one of the marginal groups in biblical Israel, see Avraham's comprehensive study (Avraham 2000).

Justice and Righteousness in Biblical Israel

The picture presented here seems surprising. Is it possible that the state pro-vided a residence for the oppressed elements of society? Moshe Weinfeld has shown that the concept of "justice and righteousness" is often related to the concept of "mercy and lovingkindness" and is aimed at ameliorating the condition of the un-derprivileged.[46] He notes that "the execution of justice and righteousness in the royal domain refers primarily to acts on behalf of the poor and less fortunate classes of the people. These were carried out by means of social legislation, initiated by the king and ruling classes" (Weinfeld 2000: 8–9). Doing justice and righteousness is the task of leaders and monarchs (2 Sam 8:15; 1 Kgs 10:9; Psalm 72; Jer 22:3, 15; 33:15; Ezek 45:9; compare also Weinfeld 2000: 35; Whitelam 1979: 29–37; Whybray 1990: 117). Weinfeld discusses mainly texts dealing with the liberation of slaves, both in the Bible and in the ancient Near East, but this commitment must also have had a practical aspect. It is not farfetched to assume that the care for lower social classes was also expressed in allocating an area where they could stay; the commandment to bring them food may be explained by the commitment to justice and righteousness of the individual.[47]

Many scholars have discussed this commitment of the monarch or the state to providing for the welfare of the poor and helpless. According to Perdue, "(T)he royal distribution of charity was designed to transfer the loyalty of the underclass and perpetual poor to kings. . . . The monarch as supreme judge and national benefactor established courts to administer the king's justice in the royal state . . . thus rivaling the system of justice carried out by the households, clans and tribes" (Perdue 1997: 210; for further discussion, see also Malchow 1996). Even if this system did not ac-tually benefit the poor in practice, its very existence and pretension are important.

Blenkinsopp also noted "the public charity and 'the social security system' of the triennual tithe (Deut 14:29; 25:12–13)" (Blenkinsopp 1997: 91). In this context, it is worth noting that in Weinfeld's opinion the tithe deposited at the gate for the Levites, strangers, orphans, and widows was not a tax but "a support for the penni-less." Giving the tithe was probably perceived in Israel as a philanthropic act, while in the rest of the ancient world it was usually considered a tax (Weinfeld 1973: 129, 130).

According to Mary Douglas, in biblical terms the reality of poverty threatened and detracted from the "world order" (identical to biblical "righteousness"; Doug-las 1993, and bibliography there). This perception demonstrates the importance of

---

46. Weinfeld 2000. The concept of *justice* has often been discussed in relation with the gate (in light of verses such as Deut 17:18; Amos 5:15; and Zech 8:16). Weinfeld believes that justice and righteousness are synonymous. While this derives from many biblical verses, one can sometimes separate between "justice" in its literal sense and "righteousness" that expressed itself in concern for the poor and weak (both were realized at the gate).

47. Although there is no clear legal expression for the duty to care for the poor and provide them with dwellings and food, it is likely that the law does not express the desirable but merely the required minimum for which those who do not follow are punished, while desirable behavior was required by biblical ethics. For an extensive discussion of the gap between the law and expected behavior in the Bible, see Wenham 1997.

justice and righteousness in Israelite society during the period of the Monarchy and may explain the efforts made in Israel and Judah to deal with the problem of poverty.[48] Several biblical verses explicitly link the gate to justice and righteousness. Thus, for instance, Jer 22:2–3,

> Hear the word of the Lord, O king of Judah, you [. . .] and your courtiers and your subjects who enter these gates. Thus said the Lord: Do what is just and right; rescue from the defrauder him who is robbed; do not wrong the stranger, the fatherless, and the widow; commit no lawless act, and do not shed the blood of the innocent in this place.

Verse 3 interprets the meaning of justice and righteousness (translated here 'just' and 'right') as caring for the weaker sectors of society, with reference to the king's duty. This verse also mentions the gate as the site where justice and righteousness take place. In this case, it is difficult to interpret the word "gates" as a symbolic term for Jerusalem, especially in light of the connection we have noted between the oppressed, orphans, and widows and the gate. It is reasonable to assume that the verse refers to the gates of the king's palace, serving a similar role to the city gates and demonstrating even more intensely the king's commitment to justice and righteousness. This connection may also be reflected in Ps 118:19, "Open the gates of righteousness for me" (here the term "gate" is also used in the literal sense, because it says "open . . . for me," and this may be deliberate word-play), and Ps 118:20, "the righteous shall enter through it" (the gate).

In Biblical Hebrew, the terms 'justice' (משפט) and 'righteousness' (צדקה) are nearly identical. Since it is generally accepted that 'justice' (in both the modern sense and the biblical sense) took place at the gate, it is reasonable to assume that the second term, 'righteousness', was also realized at the same place. The result of this is that all the evidence that appears to be dealing only with justice is probably related to both justice and righteousness (for an extensive philological discussion, see Weinfeld 2000; Gossai 1993). Furthermore, most of the texts referring to justice at the gate deal with the poor and lower classes. Presumably, only a small number of legal proceedings in the city were related to the poor, and thus one would expect most of the texts mentioning the term "justice" to refer to various proceedings, not simply to justice for the poor. The fact that the poor are mentioned in connection with justice in a very large number of cases indicates that at least in some cases the term "justice" was indeed synonymous with "justice and righteousness."

This new understanding of the term "(city) gate" may help explain its difficult appearance in Prov 23:6–7, "Do not eat the bread of the stingy; do not desire their delicacies; for as he thinks in his heart, so is he. 'Eat and drink!' he says to you; but he does not really mean it" (in Hebrew, "thinks in his heart" is "like a gate in his soul"; for various interpretations of the word 'gate' here, see Shupak 1996: 154–55). Perhaps the meaning is: do not eat a miser's food, because his hospitality is like a city gate—he gives food and tells you to eat and drink, but in his heart he does not mean it. In any case, the mention of the gate in connection with food and drink is

---

48. On the importance of this in terms of the cosmic order, see also Whitelam 1979: 29–30; on the importance of order in Israelite society, see chap. 7 below; Faust 2001.

interesting. Understanding the nature of a city gate also allows us to propose an improvement on the explanation of the inscription אחך ('your brother') engraved on a bowl found in grave 8 in Beth-Shemesh. According to Barkay, who analyzed this find, the inscription is referring to "your poor brother." In his opinion, the bowl was used to serve food given to the poor and was originally located in the Temple (Barkay 1991b). His explanation accords with the care for the poor during Iron Age II (in opposition, for example, to Hopkins 1996: 132), but perhaps the bowl was originally located in the city gate rather than in the Temple (and given the wide exposure of Beth-Shemesh, it is likely that no Iron Age II temple existed there; see Bunimovitz and Lederman 2009; see also Faust 2010a).[49]

The City Gate as a Liminal Space

If the state did indeed devote a special place to the poor and downtrodden, why was the city gate, the most public place, chosen for this purpose? The city gate constitutes a "liminal space" or a "transitional space" (not the gate structure only but the whole gate quarter was a transitional space, because people passed there on their way home when entering the city, and vice versa). Many anthropological studies have noted the problems that this type of space raises and have shown that it requires special attention or defense (see also Blanton 1994; Parker-Pearson and Richards 1994: 25–29 and references there; for a discussion of biblical evidence and ethnographic examples of the importance of such spaces, see Frazer 1918: 1–18). The city gate was a dangerous, vulnerable place and thus required special security arrangements. The location of justice and righteousness at city gates may have been perceived as helpful, because good deeds could make a dangerous place safer (on the importance of transitional spaces as expressed in the architecture of various societies and the range of ways to protect them, see Parker-Pearson and Richards 1994: 24–29).

About 75% of Iron Age city gates face east (Faust 1999a; 2001). In Israelite society, east was considered God's place, and so it was considered a welcoming and perhaps also a safe direction. It is worth noting that many societies in the ancient Near East attributed responsibility for moral justice, law, and order to the sun (for example, Ps 37:6; compare Sarna [ed.] 1996: 186–87). It is therefore likely that both the eastern orientation of the gates and the "exhibition" of "justice and righteousness" at the gate were both meant to protect this vulnerable location. Moreover, Nachum Avraham has shown that the poor and other marginal persons in Israelite society are in a liminal state, which is a sort of transitional condition (Avraham 2000, particularly the introduction; for a comparison of liminality, see 2000: 9). The gate space, being a transitional space, is thus appropriate for the poor. Neither the gate quarter nor the population residing there was an integral part of the community or the city to which they apparently belonged. In addition, a more prosaic reason can be suggested that

---

49. This background may also explain the parallel between poverty and the gate in Ps 9:13, "Have mercy on me, O Lord; see my affliction at the hands of my foes, You who lift me from the gates of death" (but this may not necessarily be the intention of the text).

the poor were at the gate: there was a greater chance that people would see them there and aid them.

The Gate Quarter as a Public Space

Roberts defined three types of spaces: private, communal, and public (Roberts 1996: 65–69). His definition can apply, *mutatis mutandis*, to Iron Age settlements, where one can observe the private space that was limited to members of the community, residents of the city; the public space where anyone could move freely; and the communal space where members of the community could move freely, and outsiders could enter if invited. The residential areas of the town were certainly private spaces, while the area beyond the city wall was perceived as a public space; there were probably privately owned lands, but the landscape in general was public, and anyone could travel between settlements. The city gate was a liminal space: guests, visitors, traders, and so on could visit it, but the fortified city gate structure prevented free entry, and presumably people could only enter if permitted to do so. This liminal space also included the open area outside the city gate, where many of the trade and commercial activities probably took place (there was a similar perception of the space in residential homes; see chap. 7 below). In merely functional terms, a communal space (the city gate quarter) was the most suitable part of the city for providing assistance to the poor.

Summary

The biblical term "city gate" refers to a public quarter located near the gate structure itself. This quarter included the gate structure, the open space in front of it (the plaza), and the nearby public buildings. Some of these buildings, for example, at Tel ʿIra and Jerusalem, provided for storage, and similar buildings must have existed in all settlements. But most of the buildings excavated served other purposes, at least in their final stages: conducting public trials (and the punishments were probably conducted in the gate square) or providing hospitality for the poor, strangers, visitors, and so on. The buildings may also have served as markets, at least sometimes during the winter. The buildings were probably often used for more than one purpose; thus, for example, an Iron Age I building at Tel Hadar (not discussed here) had one wing used for storage, while another wing contained evidence of food preparation (Kochavi et al. 1992: 37–38). Other buildings may have been residences for officials related to the city's operation, such as the city's governor or a sort of *agoranomos*.

Stratum II at Beersheba provides an appropriate example. This was a planned city, containing all the elements expected in a "standard" Israelite city: the city gate was found in the southeastern part of the city and had an adjacent plaza. North of the gate, complexes of long pillared buildings were found, usually interpreted as storehouses (see photograph 2). Diagonally opposite the gate was a building that probably served as a senior official's residence, generally considered the governor's house. The area alongside the northern edge of the pillared building has not been excavated, but north of that the city's impressive water systems have been excavated, and presumably there were other public buildings in between them. All these buildings constituted the city gate quarter, and it appears that the activities discussed above (law, punishment, commerce, justice and righteousness, and perhaps also worship) were conducted in this quarter.

The Israelite concept of "justice and righteousness" entailed (among other things) caring for the weak and oppressed. This duty applied both to individual people and to the leader (the monarch). From the Bible it appears that a place was allocated to society's underprivileged and that their place was the city gate. Since this clearly does not mean the chambers of the gate structure itself, I have attempted to show that some of the activities took place in the public buildings near the gate, perhaps the enigmatic pillared buildings found near the gates of many settlements of this period.[50] The presence of many poor people was a problem in the urban settlements of all agrarian societies without attempts being made to solve it (Lenski and Lenski 1974: 247), but it appears that Israel and Judah did try to deal with it.[51] Although we have no direct evidence linking these buildings to the city's poor, the finds discovered in them are of an everyday nature. The other suggested interpretations of these finds—such as the buildings being trade centers, markets or barracks—have no support from the written sources, and in any case are not preferable to the suggestion presented above (on the maintenance of these structures, see below).

Urban Planning

Urban planning has been extensively studied elsewhere, and there is no need to discuss it in detail here (see, for example, Shiloh 1978; Herzog 1992b; 1997a; on various aspects of urban planning, see Faust 2002a; 2004e; for city development, see Faust 2003c). For our purposes, it is sufficient to note that, even in cities that were apparently not planned, there are some elements that reflect planning (besides the very existence of public buildings, a city wall, a ring road, and so on, as discussed in the studies mentioned above). An analysis of the plans of a few cities shows that, despite their great congestion, and although the buildings were sometimes built without any real planning, using any available space, one can identify the existence of a guiding hand in the use of space and in preserving spaces for public needs between the private buildings.

Thus, for example, at least in some quarters of Tel Beersheba, some of the private residences were separated from each other by corridors leading to the casement rooms. I suggest that these corridors were public spaces, intended for storage and/or easy access to the city's fortifications. This explanation is appropriate to a planned city such as Beersheba, which undoubtedly served a role in the kingdom's administration. It could also apply to other towns. One can identify similar corridors

---

50. This is not to argue that all the buildings of this type discovered in the land of Israel served this function. In some sites (such as Tel Hadar), the buildings were used for different functions, but at least in some cases they served the suggested purpose.

51. Elements of Israel's religion, cosmology, and world view were shared by many groups in the ancient Near East. But each group had its own unique ideas, and the distinctive features of the various groups should not be underestimated. Concern for the poor was the king's responsibility in some other societies, and they may also have tried to deal with this social problem, but we have no evidence of this.

between the buildings in a partial analysis of the plan that Shiloh published of one of the quarters in the period of the Monarchy at Beth-Shemesh (Shiloh 1978: 40; see plan 15 above). In contrast to Beersheba, the casemates in Beth-Shemesh did not serve as rear spaces of the buildings but were closed, and so presumably the corridors provided access to all the casemates in the city wall. A similar phenomenon appears at Tell Beit Mirsim (see the plan analyzed by Shiloh 1978: 38; see fig. 19 above) and at Mizpah (Tell en-Nasbeh; see McClellan 1984; see fig. 14 above). These sites were also found to have corridors leading to the casemate rooms. Because the casemates were open (as in Beersheba), they presumably served for storage, and the corridor was not used only for defensive purposes (see extensive discussion in Faust 2002a).[52] In other cities, mainly in the Kingdom of Israel, the city wall was accessible from the circumference street (sometimes called the ring road) along its entire length (Faust 2002a; and see there for an extensive discussion of urban planning in this period). Keeping the passages clear may have been achieved by community organization, but it is more reasonable to interpret it as part of the city/royal organization (more below).

Conclusions

Building Size and Family Structure

The factors that influence the size of buildings and the relationship of building size, number of inhabitants, and wealth has received a great deal of scholarly attention (e.g., Healan 1977; Kramer 1979; Netting 1982; Blanton 1994; M. E. Smith 1994; M. E. Smith et al. 1989; Cameron 1999; and see also various papers in Coupland and Banning 1996). Wason proposed three explanations for large buildings: first, a large building may demonstrate wealth and luxury; second, its size may result from the number of inhabitants; and third, large buildings may have served for special purposes requiring a large space (Wason 1994: 140). An analysis of the size of buildings should take into account these three possible explanations, but we should remember that almost all the buildings discussed in this chapter and the next served as residences and did not have special or exceptional functions.

Many scholars believe there is a high correlation between the size of a residential house and the number of inhabitants, and since Naroll's study it has been considered acceptable to assume a factor of ten roofed square meters per person (Naroll 1962; compare Kramer 1979; Stager 1985; for other estimates, see also Ember and Ember 1995; B. M. Brown 1987; for further discussion, see below). Although one should not presume a fixed ratio in all societies, there is a degree of truth to this assumption, which has been verified in many studies in this region. In any case, it is likely that, within one society, the factor (whatever it is) was constant. In many cases, there is also a correlation between a family's wealth and a family's size, meaning that affluent families would have been larger (see Netting 1982; Kramer 1979). One possible explanation for this correlation is that the wealthy could afford to have a large, ex-

---

52. Perhaps in Beth-Shemesh the casemates were also used for storage, but the products stored were brought in from a slightly higher level, as is sometimes the norm in storage spaces. In any case, the casemates in Beth-Shemesh did not constitute part of the houses.

tended family, while the poor could not (compare Sjoberg 1965). Wealthy households also acquired additional members not belonging to the biological family, such as servants (Netting 1982). According to Yorburg (1975), who analyzed the situation in agrarian societies, the wealthy in a city lived in extended families. In Iron Age II cities, there was indeed a correlation between wealth and family structure. The city's affluent usually lived in larger and grander buildings and had larger households.

The residential buildings found in the various cities were mostly of the four-room-house type, or more precisely, the three-room-house subtype. The vast major-ity of these houses were quite small: the area was between 40 and 70 square meters (gross; these data apply to both Israel and Judah, to all layers of the urban scale, and probably to both the eighth and the seventh centuries B.C.E.).[53] Based on the usual methods for calculating area, this was sufficient for four to seven people, and most scholars have concluded that these houses were inhabited by a nuclear family (e.g., Stager 1985; Broshi and Gophna 1984; 1986). The small number of residents in urban buildings is particularly noteworthy compared with rural buildings (see be-low, chap. 4). The question why the period's cities were inhabited mainly by nuclear families will be discussed below, but even at this stage we can see that one of the

---

53. The idea that during Iron Age II several small buildings typically constituted a compound that was inhabited by an extended or joint family (e.g., Schloen 2001: 51; see earlier, Stager 1985; Callaway 1983; Harmon 1983: 122) does not withstand scrutiny, and in reality, hardly any compounds of this sort can be reconstructed. This can be seen very clearly by the various settlement plans discussed above (as well as in other sites; see also the discussion of rural sites in chap. 4, below). Notably, even the examples these scholars present for Iron II compounds do not stand up to examination. Although this is not the place for extensive discussion, one has only to look at the example that was chosen by Brody (2009; 2011) to demonstrate the existence of compounds, a cluster of structures at Tell en-Nasbeh. Even a brief glance at the plan shows that this is not really a compound. Brody simply chose a row of five structures built one after the other along one side of one of the city's streets. In order to move from one house to another, the inhabitants needed to go to the main street, join other pedestrians, and then enter the other house (Brody 2009: 47). This is not a compound but an arbitrary selection of houses, and there is nothing in the architecture that even hints that the houses were part of a single unit. Brody's attempts to prove the con-nection between the various separate houses on the basis of the artifacts found in them also does not stand up to scrutiny. First of all, he relies on the distribution of sherds (and not vessels), and this is problematic, because different sherds might come from different phases in the use of the house (as he himself realizes, e.g., on p. 53). This is especially true in the case of "old" excavations such as this. Moreover, not only is the analysis dubious, but even the results presented by Brody seem to disprove his case. The finds indicate that each separate unit was independent, and vessels used for storage, cooking, serving, and so on, were found in every one of the units! The differences between the various units, as observed by Brody, are to be expected, and similar differences were found between adjacent domestic buildings in every settlement and in every period (see the differences between the structures discussed in the appendix to this chapter, as well as those discussed by Singer-Avitz 1996; Mazar and Panitz-Cohen 2001; and see now a detailed discussion of many houses in Aizner 2011). In the few, relatively rare cases in which a number of buildings can be grouped together (e.g., buildings 21:11, 12, and 22:9, 10 at Tell Beit Mirsim), it appears to have been architectural limitations that forced the builders to use a shared courtyard, rather than social reasons. Fur-thermore, as can be seen in this monograph, the current discussion (above, in the discussion of the urban settlement sector, and below, in the discussion of the rural sector) can account for the existence of all types of families in Israelite society without positing such compounds. It is possible that compounds of this sort were prevalent in Iron Age I (the main period discussed by Stager, Callaway, and Harmon), but this is beyond the scope of the present monograph (if these compounds were prevalent in Iron I, then the change that occurred during the transition to the Iron Age II could have been a result of the changes in settlement patterns that took place at the time; see chap. 9, below). In addition, Schloen, Brody, and others ignore the evidence regarding the inner division of the structures, the economy of the various kinship units, and other lines of argument discussed in this book.

reasons was state intervention in the city, which led to an increase in the importance of hired laborers (compare Greenfield 1961), and probably also the development of commerce and the economic changes that had already occurred in simple agrarian societies (Lenski and Lenski 1974: 216).[54]

A few very large buildings were also discovered in various cities. These were probably inhabited by wealthy families, some of which maintained an extended family structure (on the existence of extended families among the urban elite in agricultural societies, see Yorburg 1975; compare Blenkinsopp 1997: 52; Frick 1970: 106–8). This size implies (based on the above ratio) that they housed some 12 to 16 people, and because many houses also had an upper floor, the number should be even larger. Some of the large, fine buildings in urban settlements are divided into many subunits, more than the basic four (or three) rooms.[55] This fact implies a great diversity in the nature of the activities in these buildings and the need for subdividing them according to the needs of the various nuclear units living in the building as part of an extended family. The life cycle of the extended family probably had an impact on the amount of subdividing because the size and composition of a family may change, but the size of the structure does not (see below, chap. 4). Some of the other grandest buildings were subdivided hardly at all beyond the most basic division. It is possible, of course, that the reason for this was that the extended families living in these houses were at an earlier stage of their development cycle (on the life cycle of the extended family, see Wilk and Rathje 1982). However, buildings with schematic, uniform subdividing (such as the buildings near the citadel and economic complex at Hazor and the large buildings at Mizpah/Tell en-Nasbeh) were usually assumed (based on their location or history) to have had official functions rather than just being (wealthy) family residences.

The Basic Economic Unit

The economic systems of the kingdoms of Israel and Judah have not been a subject for many comprehensive studies. John Holladay, for instance, analyzed the residential buildings, the storage options, and so on, and concluded that the basic economic unit in these kingdoms was the nuclear family (Holladay 1995). Hayah Eitan-Katz examined economic specialization in the Kingdom of Judah and collected data regarding various production facilities (Eitan-Katz 1994). Small installations scattered between or within buildings were found at Beth-Shemesh, Tell Beit Mirsim, Mizpah (Tell en-Nasbeh), and other places. Based on the size and distribution of these facilities, Eitan-Katz reached the same conclusion, that the basic economic unit in these settlements was the nuclear family. Private facilities were also found in the cities of the Kingdom of Israel—for example, in the large four-room house in Shechem (G. E. Wright 1992: 1529; Campbell 1994: 41–43), in a similar house in Shikmona (Elgavish

---

54. Their distinction between a simple agrarian society and an advanced agrarian society is real and important, but the dates and developments that Lenski and Lenski propose should not necessarily be accepted (more below).

55. Notably, the term "four room" is misleading, because the basic plan of the house relates to the number of spaces, whereas the number of actual rooms can vary even within the same subtype, because many of the spaces can be further subdivided. See more in chap. 7.

1994: 59–67), and probably also in Hazor (e.g., Ben-Tor 1999: 33; compare Ben-Tor 1992: 254–56). So it appears that Eitan-Katz's conclusion also applies to the cities of the Kingdom of Israel, and that there was also a private economy there based on nuclear families. The private family system probably operated in the cities parallel to the state system, which dominated the economic scene, as manifested in the many storage structures as well as some larger installations and facilities. Thus, Shulamit Geva interpreted the economic facilities found in Hazor as part of a state-owned system (Geva 1989: 96–97; however, there were probably also some private facilities). So it appears that this parallel, private and state economic system was typical of the kingdoms of Israel and Judah (see also Faust 2007c; 2011b).[56]

In sites where many agricultural-industrial facilities were discovered (mainly olive presses), they were not found in all the buildings. This fact shows that not all the city's population made its living from production using similar facilities, and perhaps some of the population worked with other installations (such as wine presses) that were usually located outside the city (Faust 1995b: 53, 65, 88). Some of the people whose houses did not contain installations may have been employed as senior officials or as day laborers. The distribution of the facilities and the variety of their nature indicate occupational diversity (on specialization in Judah, see also McClellan 1978: 280; Katz 2008).

Community Organization

In all the cities discussed here, evidence has been found of state activity, but no signs have been discovered of a local community organization. The economic system was state-run or private (at the nuclear family level), and there is no indication of any intermediate level. The maintenance of public spaces was probably also the responsibility of the state-urban system.[57] Most of the evidence indicates an administrative organization rather than a community organization, and only a little of the evidence can be interpreted in either way. This situation is in contrast to the rural sector where, as we shall see, there is archaeological evidence of community organization.[58]

---

56. We have insufficient evidence to consider the situation during the seventh century B.C.E., but at least some of the finds from Jerusalem show that the reality was the same in this period. At Mizpah (Tell en-Nasbeh), there was also no change in the economic reality in the transition from the eighth to the seventh century B.C.E.

57. Even if the two systems coexisted, it is safe to assume that the urban-state system, which was stronger, took over many of the functions of the community system. Several historical sources refer to city watchmen (Song 3:3; 5:7; perhaps also Ps 127:1), but their dating is uncertain, and there is no certainty that this refers to the reality of the period of the Monarchy. On the range of opinions regarding the dating of the texts, see Sarna 1982a: 447; Sarna [ed.] 1996: 21–22; Pope 1977: 22; Goulder 1986: 72–74; Zakovitch 1992: 19; M. Fox 1996: 24; Avishur 1996: 22–23; Hurvitz 1996: 23–24; Weinfeld 1982: 52–53. It is also unclear who was responsible for organizing the watchmen—the local community or the state administration (which is more likely). Furthermore, the term *'ir* (usually translated 'city') mentioned in the sources may also refer to a village (Faust 2009b, and additional references there).

58. In an important study about wealth and poverty in Proverbs, Whybray (1990: 114) distinguished between texts composed by rich urbanites (esp. chaps. 1–9 and 22:17–24) and texts composed by rural dwellers (mainly 10:1–22:16; chaps. 25–26). In his opinion, the texts belonging to the first group reflect an ambition to succeed but no concern for the poor, "though the urban poor were no doubt in as much need as

In light of these conclusions, we may assume that the city-gate system (which, among other things, aimed at caring for the poor and oppressed) does not reveal community organization either, and was probably the responsibility of the kingdom. This explanation suits the strength of some of the buildings, particularly their inclusion in the city's fortification system, which was certainly not the responsibility of the local community. This system realized some of the monarch's duties of justice and righteousness.

The finds do not help solve a separate question: who maintained these buildings? I am not referring to physical maintenance (such as repairing walls and ceilings, dividing the space for markets, and so on), which was probably the city administration's responsibility, but I'm referring to the question of providing for the everyday needs of the people who used these buildings. This question has clear implications with regard to the extent and level of community organization, if it existed at all. There are three possible answers: the state, the local community, or individual local residents. The first two possibilities are improbable. While the state allocated the space and built the buildings, it is unlikely that it would have granted resources for ongoing needs. The responsibility for this may have been transferred to the community, but, as noted, we have no evidence for the existence of this level of organization. The most likely possibility is the third. The state provided for the "public housing" of the poor and the buildings that served other public functions, but the poor and the strangers living there were largely dependent on the good will of the city's residents, as part of an individual's commitment to "justice and righteousness" (this explanation matches Barkay's interpretation of the bowl with "your brother" inscribed on it, mentioned above).

Social Stratification

In the various cities discussed, both in Israel and in Judah, the calculated area and quality of residential houses reveals clear social stratification. However, despite their great importance, the residential buildings are only one component in calculating social stratification (for example, palaces were ignored in the above discussion), and it appears that the socioeconomic gaps were actually larger. In some cases, the gaps can be explained as mere wealth differences (such as the three classes identified by Zorn at Tell en-Nasbeh), but in other cases there were undoubtedly more significant differences. This applies both to the buildings added at a later stage in Tell en-Nasbeh and particularly to other sites, such as Hazor, where there were prominent differences between the various buildings and perhaps even different residential neighborhoods (and also at Tirzah). Another component that should be taken into account in analyzing socioeconomic gaps is the value of the land. The existence of separate neighborhoods reinforces the stratification.

---

the rural poor. There is no sense of a caring community here." The poor are not mentioned at all in chaps. 1–9, at least partially composed during the Iron Age; on their dating, see Shupak 1996: 11–12, 27; Whybray 1995: 150–57; see also Friedman 1987: 213; compare Goulder 1986: 73. Whybray's study accords with my conclusion that there is no evidence for the existence of a real urban community.

Some scholars believe that there were only two social classes in the city (the richest and the poorest; London 1989); in their opinion, the cities in the ancient Near East were not real cities, and between these two classes there was no middle class (Coote and Whitelam 1987: 89–90). An examination of the data does not support this argument. In some of the cities (such as Hazor and Jerusalem), the entire socioeconomic spectrum was present. But in some towns (such as Mizpah [Tell en-Nasbeh] and Tell Beit Mirsim), there were probably only two main classes. In any case, due to state involvement in these settlements (leading, among other things, to an increase in hired labor; compare Greenfield 1961; see more below), the period's cities should not be treated as large villages (contra Holladay 1992: 317; 1995: 392) but should be seen as towns or cities in every respect (Wirth 1965; compare Lenski and Lenski 1974: 259).

Another tool for examining social stratification is the analysis of tombs, particularly in Judah. Examination of the type and nature of tombs in Jerusalem and Lachish pointed to large socioeconomic gaps within the population and pointed up the distinctions among grand individual tombs of members of the ruling circle, grand family tombs, simple family tombs, individual trench graves, and simple inhumations (as we have seen, there are also many biblical references to social stratification).

According to Lenski and Lenski (1974: 241–48), in advanced agrarian societies, the urban settlements were inhabited by (in declining social order) the upper classes (and their servants), traders, craftsmen, a large group of unskilled laborers, and beneath them a large group (between one-tenth and one-third of the population) composed of the unemployed, beggars, and criminals. This last group included, among others, many of the members of the previous group who were forced to cease working as day laborers due to their health and so on. We cannot examine precisely the proportion of the population in each group in the cities discussed here, but this sort of division seems reasonable for central sites such as Jerusalem, Hazor, and others (see more below).

The issue of social stratification will be discussed further in chap. 6, below.

Provincial Towns versus Capital and Administrative Cities

It appears that, as one ascends the urban scale, the percentage of wealthy and officials in the population increases. In provincial towns, only a few structures were found indicating this population segment, while in the more central cities and administrative towns, a relatively large percentage of such buildings was found. We do not possess accurate figures, and in light of the partial excavations we cannot make precise calculations, but the data we have are sufficient to indicate clear (and predictable) differences between the types of cities.

Israel versus Judah

As most researchers have recognized, the situation in both kingdoms is similar, but the current findings, despite their partial nature, enable us to identify certain differences between Israel and Judah. An analysis of the settlements shows that at the end of the eighth century B.C.E. there were usually only two classes in Judahite cities (except for in Jerusalem, particularly in the seventh century B.C.E.): a lower class including the vast majority of the population (composed of various groups of course), and a very limited upper class of the very rich.[59] In contrast, in Israelite cities there was more of a spectrum between the richest and the poorest. The socioeconomic gap in Israel was no smaller, but there were also middle classes.

In terms of size, the cities in Israel were one order larger than those in Judah. This datum may indicate a more developed socioeconomic scale and indicate the differences in the character of the kingdoms of Israel and Judah (see below, chap. 6).[60]

Another matter worthy of study is the fact that most of our knowledge about urban settlements in both kingdoms comes from settlements in the valleys or the Shephelah, although central cities such as both kingdoms' capitals were located in the hill country. Two explanations can be offered for this phenomenon, and they do not exclude each other. One possibility is that this results from an uneven concentration of archaeological excavations in Israel. Intensive archaeological research has been conducted in the lower regions of the country, because the higher areas (most of the area of the kingdoms of Israel and Judah) were barred to Israeli scholars for a long time, and because it was dangerous to excavate there even during the British Mandate period. Even after these regions were opened up to Israeli research (which constitutes most of the archaeological work in the region) following the Six-Day War, many surveys were conducted in these regions, but unfortunately only a few excavations were carried out (Shiloh and to a limited extent Hebron are exceptions in this respect).

The second possibility is that there were indeed many cities concentrated in the lower regions of the land of Israel, which are more agriculturally fertile than the mountains. These regions are closer to major roads, which increased their trade potential, and they were also the settlement centers of the country during the Bronze Age. Although during the Iron Age the political power centers moved to the mountains, we still should not expect a drastic reduction in the importance of these key regions. The Bible also mentions more cities in these regions (except for Jerusalem, of course), even though the books were probably written and edited in the mountain area. This awareness is important in understanding the processes that took place in the area with the beginning of reurbanization in the Iron Age (chap. 9).

The Kingdom of Judah in the Seventh Century B.C.E.

Obvious changes occurred in the Kingdom of Judah in the transition from the eighth century to the seventh century B.C.E. These changes, extensively discussed in previous studies, were manifest by a drop in settlement intensity in some important areas (the Shephelah) and by an increase in the importance of the marginal regions.

---

59. The upper class in Judah was probably composed of several different groups, such as the monarchy and its entourage on the one hand, and the wealthy on the other hand. However, due to the limited extent of the elite in Judah, it is difficult to distinguish between these two groups, and in any case this was a very small elite group in relation to the entire society.

60. It is not likely that the differences between Israel and Judah are due to the arbitrary nature of the finds or due to the Israelite settlements' being more central in terms of settlement scale than the Judean settlements examined in the Kingdom of Judah. The sample of settlements was quite large and included all the settlements that had been sufficiently excavated. Furthermore, the differences in socioeconomic stratification match gaps in other areas (see below, chap. 6).

In this part of the discussion, the paucity of excavation in the cities of this period and the resulting lack of information about them is notable,[61] but the main differences between the eighth and seventh centuries B.C.E. are clear. Following Sennacherib's campaign, a total change occurred in settlement distribution (see Halpern 1991, though his suggestion that there was a deliberate policy of the Kingdom of Judah to destroy the traditional framework is unlikely; compare Finkelstein 1994). However, despite the many changes in settlement following the destruction of 701 B.C.E., we have no evidence at present that there were changes in the basic structure of society in the urban sector, and important features persisted in the seventh century B.C.E. Presumably, the structure of urban society remained similar and was based on nuclear families and on clear social stratification. The evidence is fragmentary and partial, so it is best to wait until further information becomes available before drawing final conclusions. The conclusions presented here are tentative, and further study should be devoted to this issue.

Appendix:
Small Finds and Social Stratification

As mentioned at the beginning of this chapter, wealth and social stratification are reflected mainly in architecture rather than in small finds. Many studies have remarked on the difficulties raised by the use of small finds to identify wealth and social status (see, for instance, Blanton 1994; Crocker 1985: 52; Kemp 1977: 137; compare M. E. Smith 1987: 302). Even scholars who believe that wealth can be identified on the basis of small finds (and, despite the problems, it definitely can be) usually agree that architecture is more reliable in this respect (e.g., M. E. Smith 1987: 301, 327; 1994: 151; note that some of the studies mentioned below are based on Smith's work). In this chapter itself, architecture was used as a tool to identify social stratification, while here in the appendix we shall try to examine the connection between small finds and social stratification and wealth. On the face of it, there is no doubt that the contents of a house indicate the affluence of its residents (M. E. Smith 1987). However, several problems overshadow this assumption—even beyond the problems that Smith noted—related for one thing to the fragmentary nature of archaeological finds.[62]

Pottery as a Luxury Item

Pottery is the most common small find. Vickers and Gill argued that pottery did not serve as a symbol of status or wealth in the ancient world, because it was always cheap (e.g., Vickers and Gill 1994). In their opinion, scholars who attribute importance to pottery are projecting present-day reality onto the past, because only in recent centuries has pottery (particularly imported) become valuable.

---

61. There are sites in the highlands of course, but the information is very limited. There were many more large-scale modern excavations in the Shephelah, but at this time specifically, the region had only limited settlement.

62. The following is by no means intended to be an exhaustive discussion but aims at presenting a few cautionary notes.

Even if we reject this opinion, partially or completely, there is no doubt that in the ancient world pottery was not the most expensive possession in the house.[63] The most valuable items that could be a better indication of wealth (such as various metal items) were not usually preserved at all, because they could be reused (by remelting and so on); their high price made preservation worthwhile (if they were damaged, it was worth repairing them), and some of them were made of perishable materials. We should remember that there were only small numbers of valuable items in the house in the first place and, due to the above, "real" luxury items are rare in the archaeological record. Pottery is not a suitable substitute.

The Nature of the Finds in Relation to the Processes of Destruction and Abandonment

Any attempt to learn about differences in wealth based on the small finds is based, to some extent, on quantitative data. Any comparison between assemblages must take into account the fact that there are clear differences between finds in a house that was suddenly destroyed and those in a house that was abandoned. Any attempt to compare assemblages from buildings that have been destroyed or abandoned is doomed to failure, because this factor is difficult to measure or quantify. One can only compare assemblages that have undergone similar processes, and this is a datum that is difficult to prove (on this issue, see Nevett 1999: 58–59). It is even possible that different buildings abandoned at the same time underwent different processes. Thus, for example, Wason discusses a case in which the Natchez abandoned camp hastily but took with them the household possessions of the chief (Wason 1994: 111). People mistakenly believed that the chief's house, although large (further evidence for the importance of architecture), was poorly furnished. Wason concluded from this case that evaluating only the discovered objects may lead to a fatal mistake in assessing the social differences in the society examined.

The Portability of the Small Finds

On the face of it, if we know how to identify luxury goods (such as expensive metals), we can make conclusions from their discovery about the wealth of the residents of the houses without depending on the number or quantity of the goods. However, luxury items raise other problems. Such finds are transportable and could have reached the location where they were discovered in various ways. This problem can be demonstrated using Hall's study (M. Hall 1992; cited by Orser and Fagan 1995: 193–94). The study dealt with the historical period in South Africa when pottery was already considered a luxury item. In the Dutch East Indian Company, there was a sort of pottery hierarchy. At the lowest levels, cheap red vessels decorated with green and yellow glazing were common. Above them were crude porcelain vessels imported from Indonesia. The most prestigious vessels were made of fine

---

63. This opinion is accepted by the majority. See, for instance, Orton et al. 1993: 30; Morley 2007: 31. This is not the place to discuss all the conclusions of Vickers and Gill (published in many articles, apart from the book mentioned above) or the argument that arose following their publications; see, e.g., Stissi 1999: 90–91, and additional bibliography there.

porcelain imported from Indo-China. These items were not just useful and elegant. They were used at complex social ceremonies of tea drinking and formal dinners and in many cases constituted a status symbol. It is not surprising that fragments of these vessels were discovered in structures populated by the elite of the Dutch East India Company.

However, fragments of the fine vessels were also found in slave dwellings along with the crude red vessels, while crude porcelain, used for example by Dutch soldiers, was absent from the assemblage found in the slave quarters. One would expect the slaves not to use the type of pottery used by the soldiers, but how do we explain the presence of fine porcelain in the slaves' dwellings? Discussing Hall's suggestion that the slaves stole these vessels is not relevant here (though I tend to accept it).[64] The point is that the vessels that should have been a clear indication of wealth were found in the slaves' quarters. If Hall is right, this demonstrates even more forcefully how unreliable the attempt is to use transportale pottery to learn about the wealth of its users. It is much safer to rely on architectural features, because the slaves' dwellings are very different from the homes of the rich.

The Problem of Context

According to Orser and Fagan, who discussed Hall's study, fine porcelain had a very different meaning to slaves and to masters (Orser and Fagan 1995: 194). Slaves saw stealing fine pottery as a means of struggling against oppression (resistance) rather than as an indication of wealth (although of course the two issues were related). Without clear information about the social context, one cannot know the significance of any particular object.

The issue of the overall context raises another problem, which makes the use of small finds for the evaluation of wealth more difficult. The discovery of a luxury item or status symbol in archaeological finds does not *necessarily* indicate the status of its owner, because an item can indicate prestige without itself being very expensive. Even if we reject the suggestion of Vickers and Gill regarding the low price of pottery, we should still remember that small finds in general, and pottery in particular, were much cheaper than structures (even in terms of the investment of work days). Thus, it was easier for people to obtain transportable luxury items and status symbols than to purchase (or build) an expensive house. Once again we are forced to conclude that residential houses reflect the social status of their owners more reliably. To use an example proposed by Blanton, a person may be able to buy an expensive suit to create an impression of wealth (for purposes of business or deception), but presumably he or she could not afford to buy a house in a wealthy area, because

---

64. It is possible to imagine other scenarios in which small finds that indicate wealth might be found in the residences of the lower classes. Thus, for instance, in English manor houses, the butler was responsible for cleaning and maintaining the silver and gold items; when they were not in use by the manor owners or their guests, they were kept in the servants' quarters, near the butler's room (see Girouard 1980: 280). These items were intended to demonstrate the wealth and status of the owners during formal dinners and other events. However, if the manor house was destroyed and archaeologists were to excavate its contents, the silverware would probably be found in the servants' quarters (compare Deetz 1996: 199).

of its high price (Blanton 1994: 14). Only a person who could afford such a house can be assumed to be wealthy.

The Problem of Identification

In many cases, status symbols were clear to contemporary observers, but archaeologists cannot always identify them. Presumably, in the past, as today, there were sorts of "brands," meaning luxury items worth more than their material value; in fact, this is the assumption of anyone believing that certain pottery vessels were more valuable than others. But to date there is no simple method of identifying luxury brands if the raw material is cheap.[65] Blanton demonstrated this point using the example of modern-day men's suits (Blanton 1994: 14). In the eyes of most observers, two men wearing similar pinstripe suits are of a similar class. However, one of them may be wearing an expensive designer suit while the other is wearing a simple suit bought at discount. Only observers who are aware of the subtleties of the fashion world could spot the difference, and it is unlikely that future archaeologists would be able to perceive these differences. Furthermore, it is problematic to label luxury items as a sign of wealth even if the raw material is relatively expensive. Thus, for instance, in a study of Aztec sites in Mexico, Smith discovered items made of jade—which one would expect to have been expensive—in all the houses in the sites he examined. Thus, they are not a simple indicator of wealth (M. E. Smith 1994: 153).

Methods of Identifying Wealth Using Small Finds

Despite these reservations, many emphasize the importance of small finds for identifying social stratification. In the context of the archaeology of the land of Israel, two research methods have been suggested: one viewing the quantity of vessels found in each building as a means of measuring wealth (Wood 1990: 90), and the other viewing the variety of vessels found in the house and the number of serving vessels as parameters for measuring the inhabitants' wealth (Singer-Avitz 1996: 166–67, and additional bibliography there).

The discussion above shows that these two methods are problematic, first and foremost in principle. Thus, for instance, the first method, relying on the number of vessels found in the house, cannot deal with find differences that resulted from destruction or abandonment of the site. A house that was abandoned may have been deliberately emptied of its contents by the owners, while a house that was destroyed suddenly would be found with all its contents. And even if various houses in the same site were abandoned, it is possible that the houses of the rich and the leaders would be emptied more thoroughly. The second method, which relies on the variety of vessels and the number of serving vessels would not identify the wealthy quarter in an English manor house, for example, because the household's valuable serv-

---

65. The argument that imported pottery served as luxury items needs to be proved in each case, and, despite M. E. Smith's general claim (1987: 320), proof has yet to be provided in the cases discussed here and perhaps also in other cases (this issue is related to the question whether any type of pottery was actually valuable). It is worth noting that Singer-Avitz (1999) showed that the few imported pottery vessels found in stratum II at Beersheba were discovered scattered among different buildings and probably did not belong to wealthy households in particular.

ing items (and other valuables) were usually kept in the servants' quarter (compare M. E. Smith 1987: 310, 312).

However, it is worth examining the validity of these methods regarding Israelite society in Iron Age II. We cannot examine the finds in all the building on all the various sites because of the scope of this task and also because in many cases the reports do not enable us to "return" the items to the houses (cf. Daviau 1993: 26). Instead of a general examination, we will have to make do with a few examples from sites that provide us with sufficient information: eighth-century B.C.E. Hazor and Beersheba, and seventh-century B.C.E. Tel Batash.[66]

Eighth-Century B.C.E. Hazor

In her comprehensive study, Shulamit Geva discusses the small finds discovered in the various levels and buildings of Hazor (Geva 1989: 117–32). She divides the small finds into several groups: cooking utensils, vessels for preparing food, storage vessels, utensils for various other purposes (in fact: serving vessels),[67] luxury vessels, various small finds, and unclassified items (the group Geva defines as "various small finds" is not sufficiently clear to use in the current analysis). Below is an analysis of the finds from Hazor in light of Geva's data, with an emphasis on the group that includes serving vessels and luxury items.

An analysis of the finds from stratum VI (destroyed in an earthquake, according to Geva) shows a very partial correlation between the size of the building and the number of vessels found there. The only building that probably belonged to a wealthy family did indeed contain more vessels compared with the other buildings, but we should remember that this building was two or three times larger. The number of luxury vessels or kitchen/serving vessels does not present a clear picture, either. While house 2a contained more vessels (of all groups), building 10037 contained very few vessels (20, only 4 of which were serving vessels); the location and plan of the building obviate the conclusion that this was one of the poorest buildings in Hazor. Indeed, above I suggested on the basis of architectural considerations that a state official may have lived there perhaps an official responsible for the nearby economic complex.

There is an even more extreme contrast in stratum V. Above, we discussed buildings 3169 and 3148, built near the citadel. These were relatively large buildings, with an accurate plan, constructed with ashlar stones, which testify to their quality. However, in building 3169 only 10 vessels were found, of which 2 were luxury items

---

66. Any attempt to use the small finds to learn about wealth differences (or for any other purpose) can only take place when the finds are from the same site and the same stratum. Any other comparison could distort the picture due to the nature of preservation that varies from site to site and from level to level with regard to the nature of activity in the area and the processes of destruction or abandonment that the site had undergone.

67. S. Geva 1989: 147–49. In fact, there are certain differences between this group and what Singer-Avitz defines as "serving vessels." Geva includes flasks in this group, but Singer-Avitz states (1996: 171): "even flasks were sometimes used for serving, but they were also used for additional purposes such as storage, and so were not taken into account." In a comparison between different buildings on the same site, this does not make any difference, because the criteria for examining the buildings are the same.

Table 7. Finds from Stratum VI at Hazor.

Bldg.	Area	Nature (based on architectural analysis)	No. of Vessels	Luxury Vessels	Kitchen/Serving Vessels (percentage of total finds)
2a	160	Wealthy house	99	2	32 (32)
14a	70 incl. shops	Lower class (servants' house?)	50	0	16 (32)
111	85–90 incl. shops	Lower class	36	2	9 (25)
48	70	Middle-lower class	23	1	8 (35)
49	Under 50	Lower class	30	4	10 (33)
29	75	Lower class	15	0	1 (6.666)
10037	75	Middle official	21	0	4 (19)

and 2 others were serving vessels. In building 3148, 53 vessels were found, only 2 of which were luxury items, and 10 were serving vessels (a very low percentage). The investment in the construction of these two buildings was great, and they were probably inhabited by important people, but these qualities were not apparent from the small finds (according to the criteria examined here). One cannot argue that these buildings were evacuated and abandoned before the destruction, because they were built shortly before the destruction as part of the preparation for the coming war, and so it is unlikely that they were evacuated before the war. Furthermore, this argument would support the argument that small finds cannot indicate wealth, given the portability of the vessels; thus, it undermines the very attempt to learn about wealth from the small finds. A similar (or even larger) lack of correlation was found in the other buildings in stratum V.

Eighth-Century B.C.E. Beersheba

Singer-Avitz examined the degree of wealth of the households in Beersheba (stratum II; Singer-Avitz 1996: 171–72). This is the first study of its kind in the archaeology of the land of Israel and the only study that examines the method of identifying wealth in archaeological finds in the region on the basis of the number of vessel types, the number of find types, and the percentage of serving vessels from the ceramic assemblage.

The buildings that Singer-Avitz analyzed are summarized in table 8.[68] As she says, "an examination of the vessel types (not their numbers, but the types of finds, without reference to their quantity) showed that 14–22 types of pottery vessels were found in each building" (Singer-Avitz 1996: 171), and she apparently agrees that the number of pottery-vessel types is not a successful indicator of wealth. Later she

---

68. The chapter analyzed a few other buildings, but so far their findings have yet to be published, and so they are not included in the table.

Table 8: Finds from Eighth-Century B.C.E. *Beersheba.*

Bldg.	Area	Nature (based on architectural analysis)	Vessel Types	Find Types	Percentage of Serving Vessels within Finds
75	60 (excl. yard)	Normal building	22	10	16
76	60 (excl. yard)	Normal building	14	11	15
25	60 (excl. yard)	Normal building	20	13	27
630	50 (excl. yard)	Normal building	18	7	16
855	110 (excl. yard)	Wealthy building	20	23	38
812	105	Wealthy building?	14	8	16

states that "the small finds that were not pottery vessels show a different picture: in building 855 there were 23 types of finds, while in the other buildings there were 7–13 types of finds" (1996: 171). Building 855 is thus exceptional both in the percentage of serving vessels and in terms of the variety of small finds, and in her opinion this reflects a wealthy household.

In this case, there is a correlation between Singer-Avitz's conclusion based on the small finds and my conclusion based on the architectural analysis, because the size of the building is much larger than the size of all the other buildings (the building's area is only slightly larger than building 812, but the latter has no front yard; moreover, building 855 is of much higher quality). But her use of the two criteria (the number of types of small finds [apart from pottery] and the percentage of serving vessels) raises some questions. Because she does not note the number of vessels found, the percentage of serving vessels may be misleading. According to her method, a house in which 20 vessels were found, 8 of them serving vessels (that is, 40% of the finds), would be defined as a "rich house," while a house of the same plan and size, where 150 vessels were found, of which 20 were serving vessels (only 13.3% of the finds), would be defined as a "poor house"! But in absolute numbers, the second house contained many more vessels in general, and serving vessels in particular, and so it seems that this one should be defined as a "rich house." According to Smith (on whom she is relying) as well, the quantity of serving vessels is more important than their percentage within the entire assemblage (M. E. Smith 1987: 313; compare Singer-Avitz 1996: 166).

Above, the problem of the small finds was demonstrated using building 14a in Hazor (the house of Makhbiram). In stratum VI, 50 vessels were found in the building, and 32% of them were serving vessels. In stratum V, representing a later stage of the building's history, only 18 vessels were found, but the percentage of serving vessels rose to 44.4%. Could one argue that at this stage the building's owners were wealthier than in the past? The number of vessels dropped to 36% of their previous number, and the number of serving vessels dropped to half (from 16 to 8). Thus, the presentation of the serving vessels as a percentage alone creates a seriously skewed

picture, as in the case of presenting the number of types of small finds without re-
porting the number of vessels found. So it appears that also in Beersheba, despite
the coincidental partial similarity between the results of the small-finds analysis and
the architectural-spatial analysis, the small finds cannot serve as a simple indicator
of wealth.

The problematic nature of small finds for identifying wealth is further demonstrated by the new data published on Beersheba by Singer-Avitz (2011).[69] In this
extended English version of her original Hebrew article (1996), Singer-Avitz defends
her attempts to determine wealth differences using small finds and downplays the
significance of architecture (2011: 294-98). While her work on the finds in Beersheba
is very important, and her original work (1996) can be seen as pioneering in many
ways, her discussion of wealth is very brief and ignores most the problems inherent
in the use of small finds for this sort of exercise (see, for example, the various points
discussed in this appendix). The data themselves, furthermore, reveal the problems
inherent in the use of small finds for such purposes. Thus, for example, Singer-Avitz
claims that one of the wealthiest houses in Beersheba was a tiny structure of 33
square meters (building 1441, not discussed in this chapter because no data were
available at the time), simply because 80 pottery vessels were unearthed there. Suggesting that a tiny house of this sort is one of the wealthiest in Beersheba on such a
basis does not make much sense to begin with but, even if one is willing to consider
this idea, the comparison she makes with other buildings completely refutes it. Notably, Singer-Avitz compares the finds in this small building to the finds unearthed
at the (very) large governor's palace, in which only 71 vessels were found (2011:
295-96). She maintains that the latter structure was the governor's palace, which is
in itself sufficient evidence to disprove her theory that the number of vessels can
serve as in index of wealth (since the large residency contained fewer vessels than
the tiny [1441] building).[70] The new data presented by Singer-Avitz are, therefore,
just another indication of the danger that lies in any simplistic attempt to use small
finds in order to determine wealth.

Seventh-Century B.C.E. Tel Batash

The ethnic identity of the residents of Tel Batash in this period is uncertain, but
this is irrelevant to the clarification of the issue at hand. We have quite complete data
regarding a few of the buildings found in stratum II (based on A. Mazar and Panitz-
Cohen 2001: 163–72).[71] Building 743 is a fine building (77 square meters)[72] adjacent

---

69. The data were published only after this book was in page proofs; thus, they could not be incorporated into the discussion of the finds in Beersheba above.

70. This also shows that there is not always a direct correlation between a structure's size and the
number of finds (although this correlation may hold true in most cases), further demonstrating the problem of generalizing on the basis of small finds.

71. The discussed figures are slightly updated from those published in Kelm and Mazar 1995: 146–50,
to which I referred in previous publications.

72. This figure includes the walls (the eastern wall belonged to another, larger building, and we calculated only a typical wall). The net area, as published by Mazar and Panitz-Cohen (2001: 163) is 51 square
meters.

to a public building and constructed following the three-room plan. Ninety-eight pottery vessels were excavated in this building, including 35 bowls, 1 chalice, 10 kraters, 12 cooking pots, 14 storage jars, 9 jugs, 7 juglets, 6 bottles, 1 lamp, and 3 stands. The pottery was accompanied by a large number of additional finds (5 votive vessels, 6 stone objects, 3 weights, 6 iron objects, 1 bronze object, 1 bone/ivory object, 1 scarab, 3 whorls, 1 pendant, 2 beads, and 47 loomweights).

Building F608 was not excavated in its entirety, but since most of it was exposed, we can discuss it here. The building seems to follow the three-room plan, though it is less nicely constructed than building 743 (its estimated size is 65 square meters).[73] Sixty-seven vessels were unearthed in the building, including 25 bowls, 4 chalices, 5 kraters, 2 amphorae, 4 cooking pots, 16 storage jars, 3 jugs, 4 juglets, 3 bottles, and 1 lamp. Other finds include 1 stone object, 4 iron objects, 1 bronze object, and 8 bone/ivory objects, along with 66 loomweights. An adjacent building, F607, was smaller in size (49 square meters)[74] and also followed the three-room plan. Sixty-two vessels were found in the building, which include 23 bowls, 5 kraters, 1 amphora, 6 cooking pots, 5 storage jars, 10 jugs, 8 juglets, 1 bottle, and 3 lamps. Additional finds include 3 votive vessles, 2 stone objects, 2 weights, 1 bronze object, and 52 loomweights. Additional buildings the finds of which were reported, include building 950, but since it was only partially exposed, it cannot be discussed in detail here, and the information will be referred to only in commenting on general patterns.

When examining the number and percentage of possible serving vessels (bowls, bottles, jug, juglets, and chalices), the following picture emerges: building 743 had 58 vessels (59%), building F608 had 40 vessels (almost 60%), whereas building F607 had 42 vessels (almost 68%). The number of serving vessels in building 743 is larger than any other building, just as the size of the building itself is larger. When we examine the percentage, however, the smaller building is prominent (although the differences are not striking). If we apply the term *serving vessels* only to bowls, it transpires that in building 743 they constituted 36% of the finds, while in building F608 they were 38%, and in building F607, 37%. The smaller buildings had a slightly larger percentage of bowls (however, the difference is insignificant). What is clear, however, is that the expected differences did not appear. The number of finds (and, generally speaking, also the type of finds) increases with the size of the building (not surprisingly of course), and this is true also for building 950, not discussed here (Mazar and Panitz-Cohen 2001: 163). It is also worth considering the extent to which the calculation method influenced the results. If the term *serving vessels* includes juglets, bottles, and so on, the result changes significantly. And again, the architecture is the element with which we can (and should) compare the conclusions based on the small finds (in an attempt to verify them).

Sites outside the Land of Israel

Crocker examined both architecture and small finds at Tell el-Amarna, and he also concluded that wealth was reflected reliably only by the first type of evidence

---

73. Its net area is 46.2 square meters (Mazar and Panitz-Cohen 2001: 163).
74. The net area is 32.4 square meters (Mazar and Panitz-Cohen 2001: 163).

(Crocker 1985). In contrast, in analyzing finds from Nippur, Elizabeth Stone identified a connection between the small finds and the size of the buildings (Stone 1987: 73). In the earlier levels of the site, the houses were similar in size and also in the finds discovered within them. As time went by, a gap developed between buildings of different sizes, plans, and construction quality and also in the finds unearthed in them. The wealth differences were also reflected in the written finds discovered in the various buildings. Another site where a correlation was found between the analysis of the small finds and the architecture in examining indicators of wealth was Tell Jawa in Jordan. At this site, the excavators analyzed the assemblages from building 800, a large building with a relatively impressive quantity of small finds (Daviau 1996: 93). But despite the exemplary analysis of the finds, discussion of only one building is insufficient, and we must include other buildings in the analysis before final conclusions can be reached about socioeconomic differences.

Another study relevant to this issue was conducted at several Aztec sites in Mexico (M. E. Smith 1994). It turned out that no item or vessel was used *only* by the rich, and no find was discovered that could be seen as a status symbol used only by them—not even jade vessels (1994: 153). However, a statistical sampling shows that certain finds were more common in wealthy households. These vessels had no qualities that could link them to the wealthy; they were everyday vessels. However, these are only statistical data, and there were opposite cases, and these vessels were found in large numbers in houses that were not wealthy (1994: illustration 71). In any event, in these sites as well, the main indicator of wealthy houses was the architecture (1994: 151–52).

Conclusion

Sometimes there is a correlation between wealthy houses and the number of pottery vessels found in them, and sometimes there is also a correlation between wealthy houses and the percentage of serving vessels. However, these correlations are not sufficient for determining wealth. Additional correlations also appear unhelpful. In order to determine whether a building belonged to the wealthy or not, one needs complete data, meaning all the information about the house's contents; partial and processed data are not sufficient. These data should be processed carefully, and each case should be examined on its own merits. In any case, this sort of analysis can only complement an architectural analysis; it cannot replace it. Likewise, it is impossible to reach valid intercultural generalizations (with the exception of items made of expensive materials such as gold);[75] any conclusion applies only to one place and time, and one cannot assume a priori that it applies to other situations.[76] At the same time, the many reservations against using small finds to determine wealth

---

75. It is the added-value that is difficult to evaluate.

76. The interpretation of the existence of many more vessels in larger buildings raises a methodological problem. Even though this fact is predictable, it may have risen from several causes. It is possible that wealthier people lived in the buildings, who kept more vessels (as we have assumed above). It is possible that more people lived in them (based on the assumption of a fixed density of people in a covered space), and thus they used more vessels. In fact, these possibilities are not mutually exclusive. There is a certain correlation between the wealth of a household and the number of members (see above, and also chap. 4;

(especially considering the difficulty in comparing different strata and sites) should not preclude the fact that there is no substitute for this type of find when it comes to analyzing the use of space and other similar matters (see recently: Singer-Avitz 1996, in the section not dealing with social stratification; compare Daviau 1993, and additional bibliography there).

Finally, I should stress that some small finds were used mainly by the rich, and the items, when identified, can serve as an indication of wealth. However, they are not universally used only by the wealthy (unless the material is expensive, of course), and their usage is culture-specific. We may (and should) look for these sorts of items, but we may not assume that what appear to us to be nice-looking pottery vessels were used exclusively (or even mainly) by the wealthy in other societies. Searching for these items should be part of a wide-scale attempt to learn about an ancient society—an attempt to learn not only about wealth but also about the economy, organization, gender issues, and ethnicity of the society, and more.[77] Only in this way can we hope to unearth the meaning of the various items used by the members of the society examined. As far as wealth is concerned, it is likely that a comprehensive study of this sort will examine the various items in relation to architecture which is the best indicator of wealth.

---

compare Netting 1982; Kramer 1979; M. E. Smith 1987: 323); the quantity of vessels may thus indicate both the number of residents and their wealth. But one should remember the above reservations.

77. And in relation to various types of finds (for a sophisticated study of wealth, see the above-mentioned study by M. E. Smith 1994).

Chapter 4

Community and Family: Rural Society

Most of the world's population has always lived in rural settlements (see, e.g., Lenski and Lenski 1974: 241; Perdue 1997: 165). Despite this fact, the rural sector of the land of Israel has not been the object of many studies, probably due to the tendency of archaeology in Israel to excavate tells, which are more "promising" sites in terms of archaeological findings and are considered more important historically—especially the tells identified with settlements from the biblical period (e.g., Reviv and Kuchman 1986; C. H. J. de Geus 1986: 227; London 1989: 41; Ahlström [1982a: 25] even considered Syro-Palestinian archaeology to be "tell minded"). Due to the relative scarcity of excavations in the rural sector compared with their number in the urban sector, the following discussion is not based on regional divisions (such as Israel and Judah in chap. 3) but on settlement types: farms, villages, and large villages (see also Faust 1995b). This part of the discussion is mainly on the "meso" level, meaning the level of the individual settlement. Later on, the data from the various settlements will be compared and analyzed on the basis of geographical and regional characteristics.

Definitions and Methodology

The Definition of a Village

Compared with the definition of a city, which seems relatively clear, the definition of a *village* is disputed among geographers (Grossman 1994: 1; see also chap. 3 above). The controversy is over the question whether to use a functional definition, enabling an integrated perception of the village as a closed system of residence and land use or, alternatively, to refer to the nature of the land and space. In the first definition, a village is a functional unit, economically and socially. The settlement is not merely a group of buildings, but is a community of people with a central occupation. Humans, not just buildings, are part of the definition. The second definition refers to the nature of the landscape and surroundings without attributing any importance to the essence of the human activity in this space. This second definition is more popular in modern geographical research. It sees the village as a place of residence, and the main criterion for defining it is the ratio between buildings and open space. Because this definition does not depend on the use of the land surrounding the residential houses, the village is not necessarily perceived as an agricultural area (Grossman 1994: 1–2). This approach does not observe the essential difference between town and village.

Sociologists, too, are concerned with the question of defining the village, and according to some of them, we should return to this definition: a settlement characterized by a landscape of primary production (Gilbert 1982; Grossman 1994: 3). Sociologists' interest in this question focuses on the gradual disappearance of the social and economic features of the village and the penetration of urbanization, as a particular life-style, into the way of life of village residents (Grossman 1994: 3). However, it appears that the functional definition, perceiving the use of land as an active production element, is more appropriate to ancient villages (1994: 4), while a definition that focuses on a ratio between buildings and open space is relevant only to the modern era, when the life-style of many rural residents has become urbanized. During the ancient era, all villages probably served mainly as agricultural production centers, even if the partial findings we possess cannot confirm this assumption for every settlement.

Some scholars solve the question of the definition by elimination: the village is a settlement that is not a town (Grossman 1994: 2). In the previous chapter, we listed some of the accepted criteria for identifying an urban settlement, and if we eliminate them, we obtain the following characteristics of a village: limited area, low population density, homogeneity of life-style, proper internal relations, and the absence of a distinct class division (see, for example, Reviv 1993: 90). One may also assume that the character of the village, being a relatively isolated and closed place, was more conservative. These features are indeed the opposite of characteristics of the city, which were listed in the previous chapter. However, this is a case for stressing certain criteria that exist in both forms of settlement. Perhaps it is better to avoid a comprehensive definition and to make do with examining each case individually (see also Safrai 1980: 110; Grossman 1994: 17).

Several scholars believe that the distinction between towns and villages is modern and has no basis in the periods before the Industrial Revolution, when cities were largely rural, and the life-style of their residents was similar to that of villagers (Sjoberg 1960; 1965; Frick 1970; Bendor 1996: 219; see also pp. 98–100). However, we have already seen (and this will be further supported later in this chapter) that during the period of the Monarchy there were clear differences between town and village, partly resulting from the various processes that took place in these two settlement sectors (compare Wirth 1965; Lenski and Lenski 1974: 259). In the urban settlements, state involvement accelerated the processes of change in traditional society and increased the proportion of nonproductive residents in the population (soldiers, officials, day laborers of various types, service providers, and so on). Many residents of the cities were engaged in agriculture, but the social processes there worked to their detriment, and their proportion and importance decreased. As a result, the way of life in cities and villages was very different. The differences between the two forms of settlement are also indicated by their different levels in the settlement hierarchy of the period: most of the rural settlements discussed below were very small villages and farms, and only a few were large villages. So, besides the above definitions and distinctions, it appears that there is no denying that the sites discussed in this chapter belong to the rural sector.

The Chapter's Structure

The research method used here is similar to the method used in the previous chapter. The following analysis divides the rural settlements into four types based on size and nature:[1] (1) small villages or hamlets; this group includes some extensively excavated sites (for instance, Beit Aryeh, Kh. Jemein, and Hurvat Rosh Zayit), some reasonably well-known sites (such as Kh. Kla, Kh. Jarish, and Tel Zeror), and sites known only partially from surveys (for example, Kh. Maiyaseh and Kh. Umm Kahal); most of the villages of this type are from the territory of the Kingdom of Israel; (2) villages located at the foot of fortresses (Hurvat Uza, Tel Arad, Kh. el ʿId, and Kh. Abu et-Twein), which have some special features (see also below, chap. 5); (3) large villages or townships, such as Deir el-Mir and Kh. Banat Barr;[2] (4) farms excavated or surveyed mainly in the southern foothills of Samaria and around Jerusalem; some additional farms have been discovered in Benjamin and in the Hebron hills; most of the farms are from the territory of the Kingdom of Judah, and they are dated to the latter part of the Iron Age (some of them only from the seventh century B.C.E.).

Following a detailed analysis of the sites, several levels of community organization are examined: family structure (relying on an analysis of the residential houses), economic organization (based on an analysis of the production facilities discovered), community organization (as manifested in systems of terraces, collection and storage facilities, communal construction. and the organization of security), and socioeconomic stratification. The last part of this chapter draws conclusions regarding social structure in the rural sector, and the archaeological evidence is compared with the biblical descriptions and the known situation in the ancient Near East.

Villages

From the descriptions below,[3] one can detect several elements that were shared by all villages: (1) the villages were nucleated and were usually located on a hilltop or on a hillside; (2) the space comprised approximately one hectare; (3) all the villages were surrounded by a boundary wall; (4) in almost all cases where building plans can be determined, they were four-room houses; (5) the residential houses were large, usually 120–30 square meters; only in exceptional cases were the buildings larger (or smaller) than this (note that the area of buildings within the sites themselves is usually identical, and no real gaps between them can be identified); (6) villages specialized in a number of agricultural domains (usually oil and wine production) and probably participated in the market economy (compare Faust 1995b:

---

1. We should distinguish between these settlements and the villages discovered in various sites in the northern valleys (Tel Qiri, Tel Hadar, and Nir David), which belonged to a different social and cultural world than the rest of the villages (see below, chap. 8).

2. Originally, on the basis of Dagan's (1993) survey, I considered Kh. Qeiyafa to be such a settlement, but the recent excavations by Garfinkel and Ganor (2008) seem to indicate that it was a town or a large fortress, with clear evidence of royal involvement (see also Garfinkel and Ganor 2010; Garfinkel et al. 2010).

3. This chapter does not include a full list of all the Iron Age rural sites excavated to date but instead describes only sites on which the information is sufficient for a social analysis.

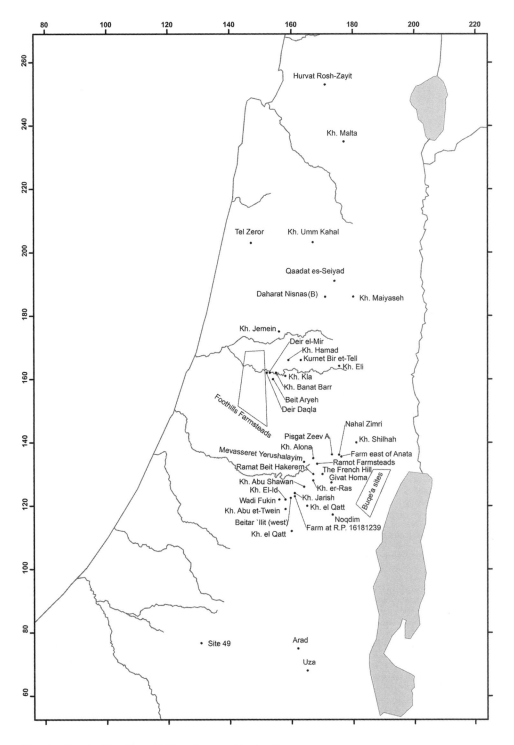

Map 2. Map showing the rural sites discussed in chapter 4.

51–54), as is evident from the fact that the production facilities were found in large concentrations or were particularly large in size and clearly produced surpluses; (7) usually, no public buildings were identified in the villages, though in some of them there were small storehouses (see map 2).

Rosh Zayit

Hurvat Rosh Zayit is located in the Lower Galilee, about 10 kilometers south-east of Tel Akko. A tenth–ninth-century B.C.E. fortress was discovered there. After the fortress was destroyed, a village was founded at this site, and it survived until approximately the beginning of the last third of the eighth century B.C.E. (for the final report, see Gal and Alexandre 2000). The village contained pillared houses of the four- and three-room-house type. According to the excavator, the fortress was Phoenician, but the settlement built later was an Israelite village, and it was destroyed during the campaign of Tilgath-pileser in 732 B.C.E. (Gal 1992b: 12–13; 2001). The village's economy was based on olive-oil production. The oil-press building was also of the four-room-house type. The oil-press installations discovered included a pressing area and collection pit carved in the yard and a crushing basin carved in a rock (Gal 1993a; Gal and Frankel 1992; Gal and Alexandre 2000: 161–67). The area of the four-room house exceeds 150 square meters (excluding the yards in front of it) and is nicely built in shape. Around the peak, there was a terrace surrounding the remains of the settlement. According to the excavator, this terrace may have been the remains of the perimeter wall (Gal 1993b: 1289). There was no natural water source at the site, and the settlement used water from cisterns discovered at the site. Another building excavated contained two rooms, and its total area was about 45 square meters. However, this was probably part of a larger structure, and there was at least one more room on its western side (Gal and Alexandre 2000: 153–55). Portions of other buildings were uncovered in area C, but their roles and usually also their plans are unclear (Gal and Alexandre 2000: 179–82).

Hurvat Malta

The site of H. Malta is located in the Lower Galilee Mountains, near Nazareth (Covello-Paran 1998; see now also Covello-Paran 2008). Its area is about one hectare, and the remains of several buildings have been excavated there. On the upper terrace, a typical four-room house has been discovered, with an area of about 120 square meters and its long spaces separated by two lines of pillars (fig. 21). Various installations have been discovered on the site, and in area A (on the west of the site) there was probably an industrial area. The remains of a fortification system were discovered in the north, east, and west. The fortification included a rampart (4 meters wide), built in sections with unhewn stones, but with planed stones at the end of each section.

Khirbet Umm Kahal

The site of Kh. Umm Kahal is on a hill in Samaria, south of the Dothan Valley, and its area is 0.6 hectares. The place was discovered in a survey and has not been excavated (Zertal 1984: site 43). Iron Age II pottery constituted about 80% of the total

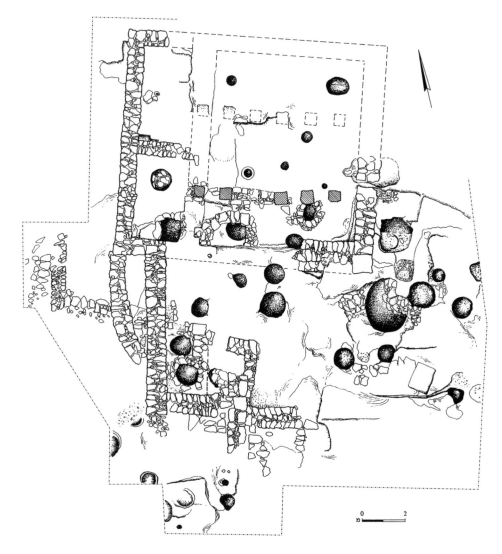

Fig. 21. H. Malta: a four-room house (Covello-Paran 1998).

finds. There was a wall surrounding the site, built of partially chiseled stones. The surveyor noted that "this wall may have served as a fortification" (1984: site 43). The remains of four houses were also discovered, probably of the four-room type, the average dimensions of which are about 8 × 10 meters (although, according to the surveyor, in personal communication, these measurements are very general and should not be used for calculations; I thank Prof. Zertal for this information), and contained monoliths that probably served as pillars. There were five cisterns on the hill.

Tel Zeror

The site, located in the Sharon region, was an Iron II village located on an ancient mound (Ohata and Kochavi 1966–70; Kochavi 1993d). The area of the fortified site is about 0.5 hectares, and it contained a tenth-century B.C.E. storehouse. In the ninth–eighth centuries B.C.E., the settlement spread to the southern peak (area B), but this area remained outside the fortifications. Four-room houses from this period were discovered on the northern peak (area A), surrounded by a boundary wall about one meter thick. The wall was supported on the inside by posts about half a meter thick. In area E, a well was discovered that probably belongs to this period.

Daharat Nisnas B

Daharat Nisnas (B) is located in the Manasseh hills and was discovered in a survey. The site's area is approximately 0.2 hectares. Thirty percent of the pottery finds from the survey were from Iron Age II, and the rest were from the Iron Age III (Zertal 1992: 435–36). In the south and east, a wall about one meter thick was discovered. The wall surrounded the site and included a tower and perhaps also a gate. Ten cisterns were discovered in the area.

Qaadat es-Seiyad

Qaadat es-Seiyad is in the Manasseh hills, located on an artificial plain. It was found in a survey (number 258). Its area is about 0.6 hectares. Seventy-five percent of the pottery is from Iron Age II and the rest is from Iron Age I (Zertal 1992: 465–66). The artificial plain is supported by a high wall of large unhewn stones. This wall served both to support a terrace and as a fortification. It was discovered to the west and north of the site, and its highest preserved height was two meters. The surveyor suggested that the settlement was probably entered from the southwest. A collapsed tower was found on the western side of the site and, north of the terrace wall, another particularly large tower was identified. The remains of buildings have been found both inside and outside the wall.

Khirbet Maiyaseh

Khirbet Maiyaseh is located in Samaria, and its area is one hectare (Zertal 1992: 479–80). Sixty percent of the pottery finds were from Iron Age II, 30 percent from the Persian period, and the rest from Iron Age I. The site is surrounded by a terrace about one meter high that may have served as a base for a wall. On the hilltop, there are remains of a large building, the area of which was about 30 × 15 meters. Other buildings can also be seen, some of which spread down the southern slope.

Khirbet Jemein

Khirbet Jemein is a late Iron Age village in western Samaria. The settlement was almost fully preserved on a rocky hill near the entrance to Maaleh Shomron (fig. 22). The ruins are spread over an area of about one hectare (Dar 1986a; 1986b: 36–37, 77–80). The settlement included about 20 buildings of the four-room type (photograph 3), most of them in an excellent state of preservation, and it was surrounded by a boundary wall that is preserved on the east and south. In the southern part of the site, the buildings' walls served as a boundary wall. In the northern region of the site, a lime kiln, a blocked cave, an oil press, and a wine cellar were discovered.

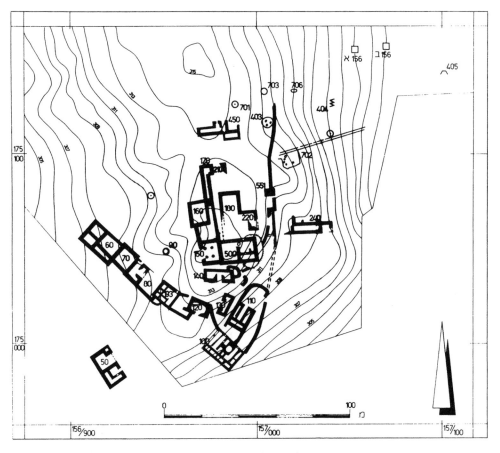

Fig. 22. Kh. Jemein: general plan of the Iron Age II village (Dar 1986a: 14).

About a dozen plastered cisterns were found around the site and on its slopes. Many terraces built in this period were found surrounding the site (Dar 1986a: 36). In addition to the residential houses (table 1), the following buildings were excavated:

Building 450: This was the northernmost building excavated. An empty area separates it from the rest of the buildings. The complex's length is about 21 meters, and its width is uneven. According to the excavator, the building served as a storehouse for the produce of the nearby oil press. The building was composed of halls that may have held standing storage jars.

Locus 551: This was the settlement's boundary wall, of which a length of about 15 meters was unearthed. A small structure was built into the wall, which may have served as a guardroom. The excavator believes that this was not a real "city wall" but only a small defensive or boundary wall. It would have been sufficient against uninvited guests but could not have withstood an army.

Wine cellars: On a rock surface in the northeast of the settlement, three hewed openings were found, close to each other and equidistant (fig. 23). It would have been possible to cover them with a stone or wood lid and to seal them hermetically. It was identified as a wine cellar based on its similarity to the wine cellars unearthed in Gibeon, and its dissimilarity to the water cisterns found at Jemein.

Table 1. Buildings in Khirbet Jemein

Building	Area	Plan	Shared Walls?	Location
100 south	125	5	No (only within the complex and with the boundary wall)	In the corner of the site
100 north	117	5	No (only within the complex and with the boundary wall)	In the corner of the site
50 south	117	5	No (only within the complex)	South of main settlement
50 north	122	5	No (only within the complex)	South of main settlement
500 east[a]	121	4+	Only within the complex	On the hilltop
500 west	134	4+	On some sides	On the hilltop
193	121	4+	On two sides; incorporated into the perimeter wall	Incorporated into the perimeter wall

a. According to the excavator, the whole of complex 500 is one building, different from the rest of the buildings in the site. It is larger and is not built as a four-room house. In his opinion, this was not an ordinary residential home, and perhaps this was the house of the village leader or chief (Dar 1986a: 15–17). However, a study of the plan (see also fig. 22) shows that building 500 was probably just another double four-room house, like most of the buildings excavated on the site, and its area is very similar to most of the others. Not only are the dimensions and overall plan similar to the other double units, even the inner division of the eastern unit is that of a four-room house (the western building was not preserved like the others due to its position at the top of the hill, so its inner division cannot be determined; the outer plan, however, is almost identical to other four-room houses at the site).

Photograph 3. A four-room house, Kh. Jemein.

Oil press: About 20 meters south of the wine cellar, an agricultural installation was found (locus 720), which probably served as a public or communal oil press. A smaller, private oil press was also found.

The buildings found at Kh. Jemein were large and well built. They are very similar to each other, and no real differences can be found in size, structural plan, use of shared walls, or other qualities. Graphs 13–14 reflect almost total equality. This is particularly notable in the second (weighted) graph, which in the urban sector usually reflected very severe gaps. This comparison indicates that the concavity of the graph in the urban sector is not merely the result of artificial distortions in the calculation method, because in the rural sector the graph is not concave; where there is equality, it is indeed manifest even in the weighted graphs.

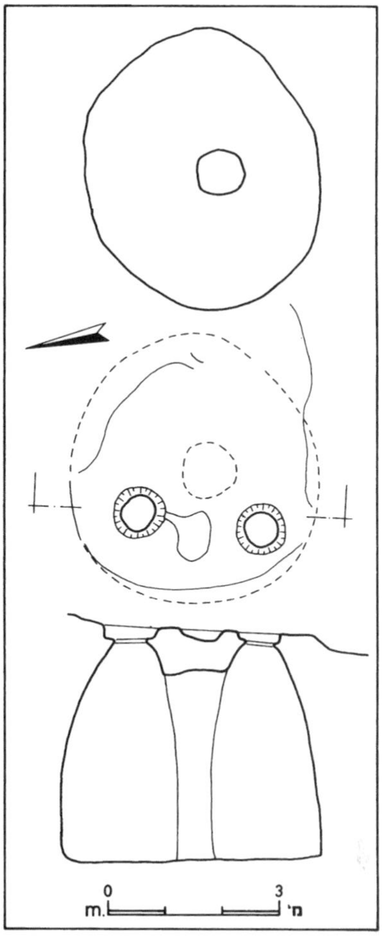

Khirbet Deir Daqla

Khirbet Deir Daqla is located in western Samaria and was discovered in a survey. About 60% of the pottery finds were from Iron Age II. A boundary wall was found at the northern edge of the site, probably from Iron Age II. A wine cellar with five openings was also found (Eitam 1980: 49). The site was recently excavated in salvage excavations (Har-Even 2011; private communication) that exposed segments of the settlement's boundary wall, parts of Iron Age dwellings, and an industrial area.

Fig. 23. Kh. Jemein: the wine-cellar (Dar: 1986a: 30).

Beit Aryeh (Khirbet Hadash)

Khirbet Hadash is located on the southern bank of Nahal Shiloh, inside modern Beit Aryeh (fig. 24). This is a rectangular settlement, with an area of about 0.5 hectare. David Eitam surveyed the site, and Shimon Riklin excavated it (Eitam 1992a; 1992b; Riklin 1993; 1997). The site was surrounded by some sort of casement wall, and the gate was located in the northeastern corner. The site contained about 10 residential structures of the four-room house type. The buildings were adjacent, and their rear spaces usually formed the casements of the wall (Riklin 1997). Thirty-three agricultural installations (mostly for the production of olive oil) were found in and around the site, and 27 of them are typical of this period (photograph 4). Water cisterns and a quarry were also discovered. Calculation of the installations' production indicates

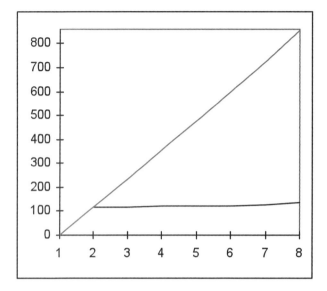

Graph 13. Kh. Jemein: size of buildings.

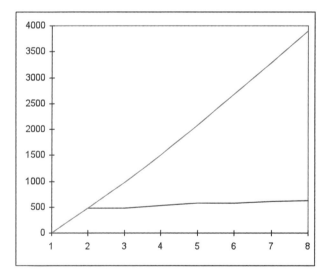

Graph 14. Kh. Jemein: weighted graph.

a large surplus (Eitam 1992b; for calculation of the surplus, see p. 178).

According to David Eitam, the first to survey the site, the wall and industrial zone indicate that this was a fortified royal village (Eitam 1992a; 1992b). However, based on a comparison of the finds with finds in other villages, it was an ordinary Iron II village. A large number of residential structures were found.[4] Apart from these residential houses, there were several other buildings on the site. In the center of the site, two relatively small, adjacent buildings (570, 590) were partially excavated. Their plan is different from the other dwellings at the site, hence indicating a different function. The excavator, who initially considered the site to be of a royal nature, thought at the time (oral communication) that they were not private houses, but "scribes' chambers" (see Herzog 1992a). Given the nature of the site, a more modest interpretation of

4. Riklin 1997. The publication of the site contains several errors. The measurements described in the article do not match those in the plan published or those in the previous publication (of building 340; Riklin 1993). This issue was clarified with the excavator, Shimon Riklin, who told me to rely on the plan, and that there were errors in the measurements published in the article. He even kindly gave me the original plan of the site (scale 1:100) as well as additional, unpublished information. The measurements quoted here follow the original plan. I am grateful to Shimon Riklin for his assistance and the extensive and useful information that he gave me.

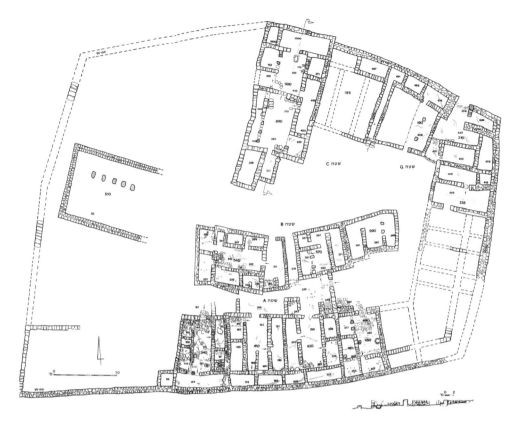

Fig. 24. Beit Aryeh: general plan of the Iron Age II village (Riklin 1997: 8).

Photograph 4. An installation for the production of olive-oil, Beit Areyh.

Table 10. Buildings at Beit Aryeh

Bldg.	Area (excl. front yard)	Plan	Shared Walls?	Location	Comments
340	105	4+	Yes	Settlement periphery	Front yard; area published 115 sq m[a]
410	120	5	Yes	Settlement periphery	Front yard
420	110	4+	Yes	Settlement periphery	Front yard, perhaps also one or two rooms.
450	85	5	Yes	Settlement periphery	Three-room house;[b] front yard
540	105	4	No	Settlement center	In front of the building there is a large, closed courtyard[c]
190	110	4	Yes	Settlement periphery	Near gate, two long rooms found, but apparently, were originally three
900	120	4	Yes	Settlement periphery	
890	105	3 (4–)	Yes	Near bldg. 900	Leaning on bldg. 900[d]
195 (497)	130	5–	Yes	Settlement periphery	Only partially excavated

a. See also Riklin 1993.

b. This is the only three-room house found on the site. This house type is rare in the rural sector.

c. Building 540 is the only structure that does not share walls with other buildings, and it seems that this is a result of its location in the center of the open space inside the settlement.

d. Buildings 890 and 900 are interconnected. The area of building 900 is about 120 square meters, and the area of building 890 is about 105 square meters (without the front rooms, which are clearly a later addition; compare Riklin 1997: 7). It seems that, originally, building 900, a large four-room house, stood there. It was entered from the edge of the central space through an opening in Wall 11, but this entrance was later blocked (the original entrance can be identified both in the published plan and in the field, because the blocking is somewhat thinner than the original wall). Wall 11 should be reconstructed as continuing eastward and cutting across the middle of the unit that was excavated as locus 450 (indeed, in the field one can still identify a large rock protrusion that continues the wall in this direction, partially cutting through locus 450). In this scenario, it is a typical four-room house in size and plan (note that the western wall of the building was originally fully built, and despite the opening of an entrance there at a later stage, as discussed below, in the field one can still see the foundation courses that run all along the western side of the building). Later on, building 890 was constructed beside it, blocking the original entrance and leading to the opening of the entrance in the southern edge of the building's western wall, as can be seen in the plan. This resulted in a somewhat atypical plan for building 900. The new building 890 was composed of only three long rooms and, although there may also have been a broad room at the end of the structure, it did not survive, and there is no clear evidence of it. The entrance to building 890 was from the south, through the central space (afterward, two rooms—loci 331 and 338—were built near the opening of this building, from the outside). If this was indeed a structure with only three long rooms, then its plan is unusual, unless we reconstruct an additional broad room, which would improve the plan.

the structures as serving some communal purpose (perhaps some sort of storage, different from that in the western building, below) is more likely (given the fact that the entrance to one of the structures was not found and given that the structures were only partially excavated, it is possible, though not plausible in my view, that we are discussing a single structure rather than two different units). An examination of the finds inside the buildings could have helped solve the problem, but they were not excavated down to their floors. However, even if these are small residential houses of a different plan, this changes the general homogeneous picture only to a very small degree. The reality on the site is still very egalitarian compared with the city, though the gaps here may be slightly larger than expected.

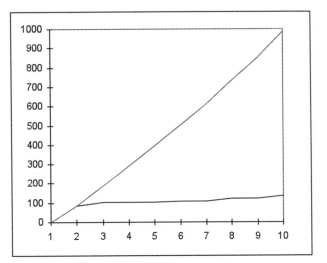

Graph 15. Beit Aryeh: size of buildings.

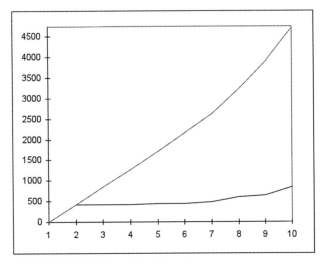

Graph 16. Beit Aryeh: weighted graph.

At the western edge of the site, the remains of a large structure were identified but not excavated. It had massive walls and was probably similar to the buildings familiar in many Iron II sites that served as storehouses, stables, and so on.[5]

At the entrance to the settlement there was a sort of gate and alongside it a guardroom (as at Kh. Jemein). The wall beside the gate is the most massive wall on the site. Between the buildings numbered 6 and 9 in the publications, there is a sort of corridor with a casemate room at its end, which according to the excavator served

---

5. Riklin 1997: 12. On some buildings of this type in the period's cities, see above, chap. 3. The proposal I raised there for the interpretation of some of these buildings is not relevant to the discussion of rural society, however.

as a guardroom overlooking the gate. This reconstruction is not convincing, but it is worth noting the similarity between the corridor leading to the casemate and the reconstruction that we proposed for the city plan at Tel Beersheba, for example.

Graphs 15–16 reflect a high degree of equality in Beit Aryeh. The main distortion in the second graph is a result of the fact that building 540 did not have shared walls. The reason for this was probably purely technical, and so even the slight concavity of the graph is to some extent artificial.[6]

Khirbet Kla

Khirbet Kla is located on a hilltop in western Samaria (Eitam 1980: 69–70; 1987: 24–25). This was a fortified settlement of about 0.65 hectares, surrounded by an agricultural area of about 5 hectares. Near the site, there was an industrial area that included agricultural installations, cisterns, a cave, and a quarry. Around the site, there were terraced fields, and the fields were crossed by a road. The settlement was protected by a wall and a gatehouse with towers. The surveyor suggested that the site itself is divided into two parts. Its western part, occupying about one-third of the area, may have been used for public purposes. This area contained a secondary industrial area, two cisterns, and two large yards. In the eastern part of the settlement, the buildings were denser. Alongside the gate, there were long buildings that may have served as storehouses. In the site's center, there was a large, two-level building with eight rooms that was used for storage and residence. According to the excavator, this building was constructed as a public initiative.

Hurvat Hamad

Hurvat Hamad is located in western Samaria and was discovered in a survey (Dar 1986b: 38–42; 1993: 1314). It probably existed continuously from the Iron Age until the Hellenistic period, but most of the remains are from the later period. A few Iron Age agricultural installations were identified in the site and perhaps also a storehouse from this period (Dar 1986b: 40–41).

Kurnet Bir et Tell

The site of Kurnet Bir et Tell is located in Samaria, and its area is about 0.3 hectares. Remains of solid walls and collapsed buildings were discovered. A wall surrounded almost the entire perimeter of the site. Iron Age olive-crushing installations were found to the south of the site (Finkelstein 1988b: 166; Finkelstein, Lederman, and Bunimovitz 1997: 447).

Mevasseret Yerushalayim

The site is located inside present-day Mevasseret Yerushalayim. It was founded in the second half of Iron Age II. A 30-meter-long section of the settlement's 3-meter-thick perimeter wall was discovered. Agricultural installations and terraces from

---

6. B. Routledge (2009) had recently questioned my interpretation of the finds at Beit Aryeh. I address the issue in this chapter, below, where I discuss the family structure as reflected in residential houses.

this period were also discovered (Mevasseret Yerushalayim 1979; Edelstein and Kislev 1981: 53–54).

Khirbet Jarish

Khirbet Jarish is located in the northeastern Hebron hills, and its area is approximately 0.3 hectares (fig. 25).[7] It was a small village from the end of the Iron Age. The site includes building complexes, the external walls of which are part of the perimeter stone wall. This wall is build of planed unhewn rocks made of hard limestone. The building complex in the north of the site includes a multiroom structure (building A), and it is connected to the building at the center of the site (D). A few buildings were also discovered in the

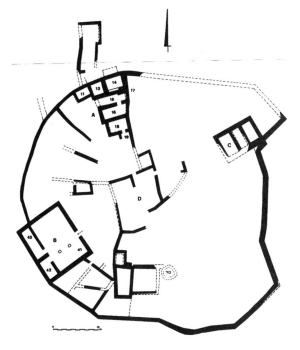

Fig. 25. Kh. Jarish: general plan of the Iron Age II village (with later remains; Amit 1989–1990b).

western part and one small defensive (?) building (C) was uncovered in the eastern part. North of the wall, there are remains of walls that end at the foundation of another building (perhaps an external tower).

Building B, a unit typical of this period, was probably divided into three rooms. Its area is 12 × 13.5 meters, and its proportions are different from the usual plan. It is difficult to evaluate the plan, however, because the only plan published was of the entire site, but it seems to be tidily constructed. The building is integrated with the western part of the perimeter wall. Another series of rooms has been excavated in the northern section of the site, but it is difficult to determine their plan from the publication. According to the excavator, there were many open yards in the site, but according to Ofer, the site was more densely constructed (Ofer 1993: 89, appendix 2).

Fortress Villages

Several additional rural sites from the end of the Iron Age were located at the foot of fortresses or fortified structures (on their nature, see chap. 5; see also Haiman

---

7. Amit 1989–90b. The site was first discovered in the emergency survey of 1968, and was dated to the Persian period (Kochavi [ed.] 1972: 38). Later examinations showed that the pottery belonged mostly to the eighth–seventh centuries B.C.E. (Ofer 1993: appendix 2, pp. 88–89; Amit 1989–90b). A final analysis of the finds (Amit and Cohen-Amin in press), however, shows that the site also contains some Persian material. It is possible that the differences between this rural site and other sites result from the (limited) activity that took place there during the Persian period, which changed its form to some extent.

1988; Faust 1995b: esp. 85–87). Although they are rural in nature, they deserve to be classified as a separate group due to the following factors: (1) the sites are scattered and not nucleated (apart from the settlement at H. Uza), they are unfortified, and they are located on the slopes below the main structures; (2) they did not have large concentrations of production installations; (3) no storehouses were identified in them. It is worth noting that we have little information regarding their residential buildings, but it seems that at least some of them were four-room houses.

Khirbet Abu et-Twein

Khirbet Abu et-Twein is located on a saddle southeast of the Iron Age fortress excavated by Amihai Mazar. The remains of the small, unwalled settlement were discovered in a survey (A. Mazar 1982: 89). The settlement consisted of several residential houses that were built on the natural rock. Their walls were built solidly of stone and in some cases survived to the height of one meter or more, and the remnants of monolithic stone pillars can be seen. The survey showed that the settlement included a few buildings—no more than ten—that were scattered over a large area, and between them there were open spaces. One building is on the rise between the saddle and the fortress, and another building (in which three pillars can be seen) is a few hundred meters from the settlement. Only Iron Age II pottery was discovered on the site, and Mazar assumed that the place was inhabited by soldiers or farmers connected to the fortress. Beyond the southwestern corner of the fortress, there was a cistern that probably served the residents of the village.

Khirbet el-ʿId

Khirbet el-ʿId is located west of Beitar Ilit. During Iron Age II, there was a rectangular casemate fortress there. Below it, the remains of a small settlement were discovered. The pottery finds show that the fortress and the settlement below it were settled from the eighth century B.C.E. up to the destruction of the Kingdom of Judah (Baruch 1996: 4; 1997).

Tel Arad

Examination probes conducted in the early 1990s alongside the road leading to the peak of the mound at Arad found the remains of Iron Age II residential houses (Gitert and Amiran 1996: 112–15). According to the excavators, "[T]he appearance of residential houses on the hill slope, outside the fortress, is interesting and very significant. Perhaps one could hypothesize that this phenomenon shows that the residences of the soldiers' families were on the hill slope, outside the fortress limits" (1996: 115).

Hurvat Uza

Hurvat Uza is located ten kilometers southeast of Arad. At the end of the Iron Age, there was a Judahite fortress there, and below it was a settlement spreading over about 0.7 hectares (Beit-Arieh 1986: 36; 1991: 126; 2007). The settlement is located on the slope north of the fortress and almost touches the gate's supporting wall (for the fort, see chap. 5, fig. 34 below). One can observe blocks of buildings built on artificial terraces, and some of the buildings are particularly large. Between the blocks of buildings, there are passageways that probably served as roads. During the excavations, a block was uncovered that contained two buildings with a shared wall; some of the walls also served as terraces. The southern building was fully excavated and proved to be a large building (6 × 14 meters) that included a western wing with three rooms. Between the paved yard and the long room there is a row of pillars. According to the excavator, the choice of the slope, which was difficult to build on, may have been due to security considerations. At the peak of the settlement, a cistern was found. Beside the fortress, there were additional cisterns, and there may be other cisterns buried in the rubble, all of which served the site's residents.

Khirbet el-Qatt

Khirbet el-Qatt is located in the Hebron hills. A square fortress (about 30 × 30 meters) was discovered with a yard in the center, and nearby were the remains of a village. Only a few pieces of Iron Age pottery were discovered on site (Kochavi [ed.] 1972: 50), but according to Mazar, it is likely that the fortress itself was built already during the Iron Age II. The neighboring village contained pottery from this period (Mazar 1982: 106–7 and n. 17), but we have no further information about the settlement.

Note that these villages differ in structure and essence from the rest of the villages discussed in this chapter, and they will be discussed further in chap. 5.

Large Villages or Townships

Before discussing this group, we should note that large villages and townships are underrepresented in archaeological literature. On the one hand, due to their rural nature, no planned excavations are carried out on sites of this sort. On the other hand, they are too large to be excavated in salvage excavations and are usually avoided when construction or building activities are undertaken (Faust and Safrai 2005; forthcoming). It is not surprising, therefore, that this group includes only two sites. Despite this, a few special features can be cautiously learned from these two sites: (1) the sites are spread over quite large areas, sometimes even larger than some of the period's cities; however, their houses are not densely constructed but spread out; (2) the sites were defended or encompassed in some way; at Kh. Banat Barr, which was naturally protected, possible security structures appear at important points; (3) the residential houses that have been identified were built to the four-room house plan; (4) most of the buildings are quite large, though some smaller buildings can also be identified, and there were clearly some differences among the various buildings; (5) the sites contain concentrations of agricultural production installations along with individual installations that are scattered in or between the buildings.

Deir el-Mir

Deir el-Mir is located in western Samaria, and its area is about 5 hectares. The survey located about 75 buildings in the site. The general plan of two buildings was

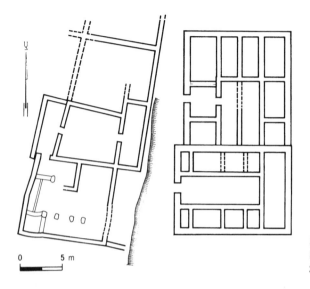

Fig. 26. Two dwellings surveyed at
Deir el-Mir (Gophna and Porat 1972:
207).

published (Gophna and Porat 1972: 207), which showed that both were four-room
houses (fig. 26). One was relatively quite poor, and its area was about 100 square
meters. The area of the other, a well-built house, was about 140 square meters. An
examination of the site plan (yet to be published) enables us to identify many buildings, some of them four-room houses, the average area of which is about 130 square
meters (I would like to thank Prof. M. Kochavi and Prof. I. Beit-Arieh for their per-
mission to use the unpublished site plan). The site was probably surrounded by a
wall (Sharon Survey 1973). In a saddle south of the peak, there is a rock surface
of about 0.1 hectare, where there are the remains of five agricultural installations.
Farther north, there are additional installations, one of which was inside a building
(according to Eitam [1987: 24] the site was large and planned, but an examination of
the plan does not support this suggestion).

Khirbet Banat Barr

Banat Barr is located on the northern bank of Nahal Shiloh in the western hills of
Ephraim (fig. 27). Some identify it with Zeredah, the city of Jeroboam, son of Nebat
(Kochavi 1989b). The buildings are spread over a strip of about half a kilometer along
the cliff and on a pointed slope (Eitam 1980: 64–67).

Six quarters and areas have been distinguished in the settlement:

1. The main section of the ruins (2.9 hectares) is located at the top of the slope.
   The buildings are mostly buried under heaps of stones. Northwest of the
   complex, there is a concentration of six hewn-rock agricultural installations
   and two cisterns.
2. On the peak of the cliff above, the remains of rock-hewn agricultural
   installations, and two pools were found. In this area, the remains of terraces
   were discovered, and it appears that the buildings were mainly on the lower
   terrace and were supported by a retaining wall.

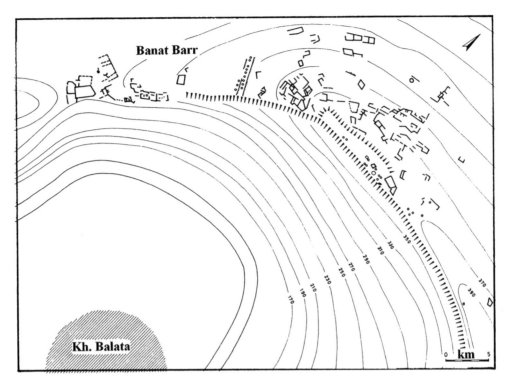

Fig. 27. Kh. Banat Barr: general plan of the Iron Age II village (Kochavi 1989b: 199).

3. Along the back of the narrow branch are the remains of a few buildings. Along the top terrace, two houses of the four-room type were identified (their measurements: 14.8 × 11.6 meters, 11.1 × 7.7 meters). Some of their walls were integrated into the stone terrace, while others were built of rows of unhewn stones that survived to a height of 0.7–1.5 meters.

4. On the saddle at the bottom of the slope, a complex was discovered that probably served to protect the southern entrance to the settlement. South of the path was a building with three large spaces. South of this building, two more spaces have been preserved. On a nearby rock surface, an olive press was found. Parts of additional buildings were discovered nearby. The plan is not completely clear, but the structure may have protected the southern approach to the settlement.

5. On the upper terrace at the foot of the cliff and south of it, the remains of some poor buildings were identified. Natural caves and niches in the cliff, and a concentration of agricultural installations were also discovered.

6. On a rock surface to the east, beyond the pointed cliff, another concentration of agricultural installations was found. The wall surrounding the site at the west incorporates a cave, the walls of which had been planed. Nearby, an olive press was found. There may have been other industrial buildings in this area.

In addition to these six areas, about 370 meters from the eastern edge of the cliff, there was a single structure that overlooked the nearby wadi. The building was surrounded by thick walls and was fortified with two towers. This building belonged to the site and may have been responsible for guarding the eastern entrance.

The large village at Kh. Banat Barr was, therefore, a settlement of "several dozen houses that relied on the natural fortification that nature provided for protection" (Kochavi 1989a: 201). The settlement was built along the cliff, and the distance between its outermost buildings is about 500 meters. On the cliff rock at the center of the site and on the rock shelves at its feet, about 30 agricultural production installations were found, organized into groups. The site is unique in its topographic features, in the spread of its construction, and in the fact that there may have been a distinction between the ruling center at the top of the cliff and the rest of the settlement (1989: 200–201).

Farms

This group includes mainly the farms discovered in the hill country. They seem to have consisted of a complex located in the center of fields: buildings or building complexes constructed on an agricultural estate that belonged to an owner. This was probably the settlement type that the Bible calls *haserim* (חֲצֵרִים; Lev 25:31; see below). The farms contained quite a large residential house (usually 130 square meters or even more),[8] usually of the four-room-house type, and additional buildings that probably served as animal pens, as storage for tools and produce, and so on. The buildings usually form a complete complex with a yard at its center. The ancient farms around Jerusalem include all these components but not the built complex with the yard,[9] but this does not alter their other features that are in common with other farms.

Note that this group does not include dozens of farms from the late Iron Age that are located on the western slopes of Samaria, from Um Reihan to the Ayalon Valley in the south (Finkelstein 1978; 1981; Dar, Safrai, and Tepper 1986; Faust 1995a; 2006a). These farms, the "foothills farms," have been discussed previously,[10] and only the main issues are repeated here. The farms are of various types (figs. 28–29). The farms of northwestern Samaria are sometimes surrounded by casemates and sometimes include other buildings (Dar, Safrai, and Tepper 1986). The rest of the farms are nucleated, isolated complexes that stand alone in the agricultural area. Their plans are not uniform, and the size of the structures and complexes is not identical, but they had some common features. On most farms, there was a wall surrounding a square (or irregularly shaped) yard; within or beside the yard, there was a square room

---

8. If the three-room house in H. Alona was built in the Iron Age, the area of the smallest house is about 95 square meters. However, as we shall see below, the dating of this building is uncertain.

9. Elsewhere (Faust 1997; 2003d: 100), I have tried to show that this was for economic and security reasons.

10. For a summary of the material and additional bibliography, see Faust 1995a; 1995b: 35–37, 64–69; 2003d; 2006a; see also Finkelstein 1978; 1981; Riklin 1994; Scheftelowitz and Oren 1996: 3–5; Yeivin and Edelstein 1970.

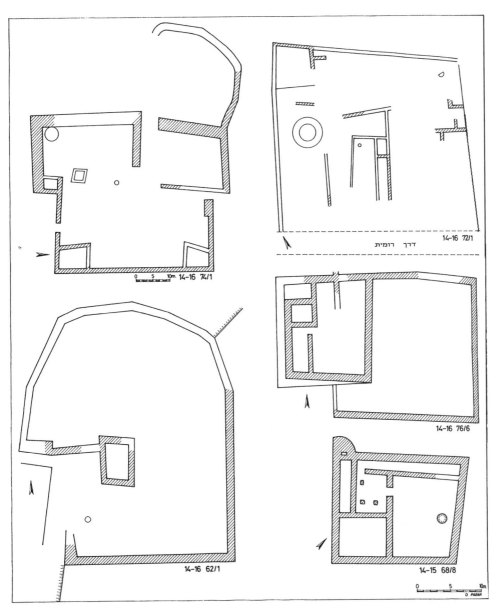

Fig. 28. The foothills farmsteads: selected plans (Finkelstein 1981: 333).

or several rooms, ranging from 2.5 × 2.5 meters to 5.5 × 7.5 meters. The yards were unroofed; it is possible that the surrounding wall was not very high and served only as a boundary. Construction used medium and large unhewn stones. Inside (and sometimes outside) the yard, there was one or more cistern. The yards usually had only one entrance, and sometimes there was a pen adjacent to them. Near the farms, hewn wine presses and parts of olive presses were found (Finkelstein 1978; 1981).

According to Finkelstein, who was the first to survey the farms in western Samaria, the residents of the farms were refugees from Samaria who settled in this

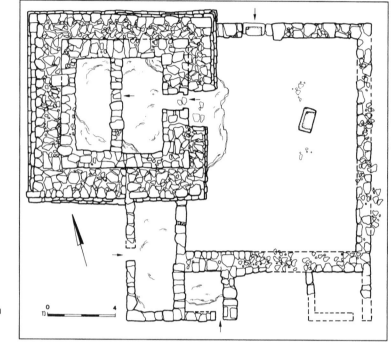

Fig. 29. The Ofarim farmstead: plan (Riklin 1994).

region, which is ecologically inferior, because the better lands in the Trough valley were in use (Finkelstein 1978: 71). According to Dar, the farms should be seen as an ancient settlement phenomenon related to the Israelite settlement (Dar 1982: 59). According to Eitam, the farms constitute part of the flourishing of the settlement in the central hills in the eighth century B.C.E. (Eitam 1992b: 177). Elsewhere I have tried to show by using the dating of the farms, their settlement history, and their form that this was a settlement phenomenon that was not related to the hills but to the coastal plain, and that the founders of the farms should be sought there (Faust 1995b; 2006a). In my opinion, the farms were established by residents from the coastal plains after the destruction of the Kingdom of Israel in order to expand the agricultural hinterland of their settlements while exploiting the damage to the settlement in the hill area. In addition, it is likely that some of the settlers were exiles from Mesopotamia who were settled there by the Assyrians (Faust 2003b; 2006a; Na'aman and Zadok 2000). These farms thus were not connected to the Kingdom of Israel (and certainly not to Judah), were probably not established until after its destruction, and I therefore will not include them in this context. The farms relevant to our discussion are the hill farms, discussed below.

Hurvat Eli

Hurvat Eli is located northwest of Shiloh (Hizmi 1998). At the end of the eighth century B.C.E., there were probably two buildings on the site (fig. 30), a large four-room house (174 square meters) and a house that may have been of the three-room

subtype (140 square meters).
The buildings were prob-
ably connected to a subter-
ranean water system. In the
seventh–sixth centuries B.C.E.,
the buildings were rebuilt to
the same plan and were integrated into a complex. The
smaller building was part of
the complex, while the larger
four-room house was outside
it and was connected to it by a
system of walls and a corridor
that also incorporated several
caves. Finds from the eighth
century B.C.E. were also discovered in the complex, which
means that the complex may
be only slightly later than the
buildings and that for most of
the time they coexisted. The

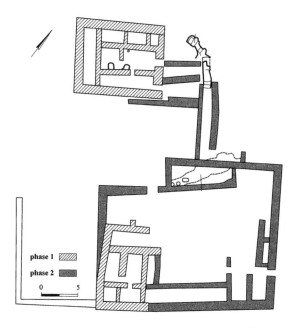

Fig. 30. Kh. Eli: plan of the farm buildings (Hizmi 1998).

site's nature is unclear, but its interpretation as an agricultural farm is likely.

Hurvat Shilhah

The site is located in the eastern part of the Benjamin region (Mazar, Amit, and
Ilan 1996). Near the hilltop, a single, square, Iron Age II (seventh-century B.C.E.)
building was discovered. The building was probably composed of a central yard
surrounded by rooms (fig. 31).

Three components can be identified in the complex: (1) A central yard, which
occupies most of the area. (2) In the southwestern part of the complex, there is another architectural unit that was integrated into the complex. Two of the walls of
this unit are the external walls of the whole structure. The external measurements
of this unit are 13.2 × 9.9 meters. This is in fact a typical four-room house that was
built symmetrically (rated 4+), but its walls are quite thin. The front space is divided
into three spaces by two rows of pillars. The space south of the pillars is paved with
stones. In the southeastern corner of the floor, there is a silo made of a row of small
stones. Some other installations were found near the row of pillars. The broad space
was also divided. In one of the rooms, a cistern was found; this is the lowest part of
the site, which was probably why it was located there. This appears to have been the
main residential unit of the entire complex. (3) Around the edges of the yard (but not
along its entire perimeter), there were rooms, parts of two of which were excavated.
Some of the rooms may have served as animal pens.

Several suggestions have been made regarding the nature of the complex: (1) It
was a royal fortress on a main road, where a garrison was stationed to patrol the

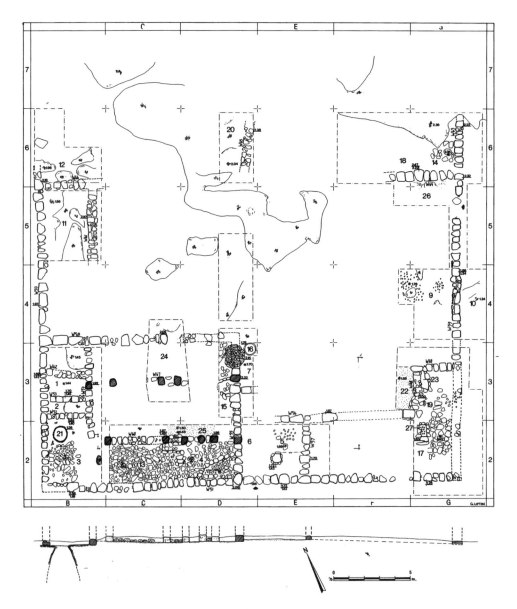

Fig. 31. Kh. Shilhah: plan (Mazar et al. 1984: 239).

road. (2) It was an inn for caravans that passed along the road: the large yard served for stabling animals, and the rooms around it served for storage and resting, while the inn's operators or owners lived in the main building. (3) It was the center of an agricultural estate, royal or private. The structure can be seen as a residential house at the center of an agricultural estate that subsisted mainly on herding and perhaps on some cultivation along the river banks. The excavators were not decisive about the various suggestions but noted that some combination of them may be closer to the truth.

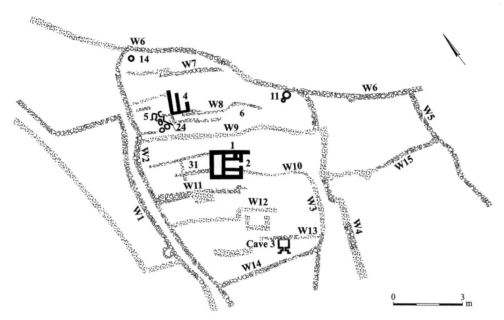

Fig. 32. Kh. er-Ras 1: plan of the farmstead and its surroundings (Edelstein 2000: 40).

Nahal Zimri

Nahal Zimri is located near Jerusalem and is dated to the end of Iron Age II (mainly the seventh century B.C.E.; Maitlis 1989; 1991). A large four-room farmhouse (12.2 × 9.8 meters) was excavated there; it was nicely built and symmetrical (rated 5). A cave incorporated into the farm was also discovered, and so were a cistern with a square pool, a wine press, and terraces from this period.

French Hill

The site is located near the French Hill neighborhood of Jerusalem. A large farm with an agricultural area of about 1.2 hectares was surveyed and excavated on the site (Mazor 2006). Within the area enclosed by stone fences, there were agricultural terraces, an ancient road, cisterns, and agricultural installations. According to the excavators, the farmhouse (11.5 × 10 meters) was basically of the four-room type, although it differs from a typical house in having some installations (a wine press or storage facilities) inside its northeastern part (2006: 2*–3*; according to the plan [2006: 2*], the house is indeed based on the four-room plan but with some deviations). The system included a wine press, a cistern, a treading surface, storage pits, and pressing facilities. Northeast of the treading surface, another cistern was found. It seems that the farm was established during the eighth century B.C.E. and existed to the end of the Iron Age.

Khirbet er-Ras

Khirbet er-Ras is located on the southern slope of Manahat Hill (Kh. er-Ras 1982: 28–29). Excavations and a survey at the site showed that this was a farm unit that

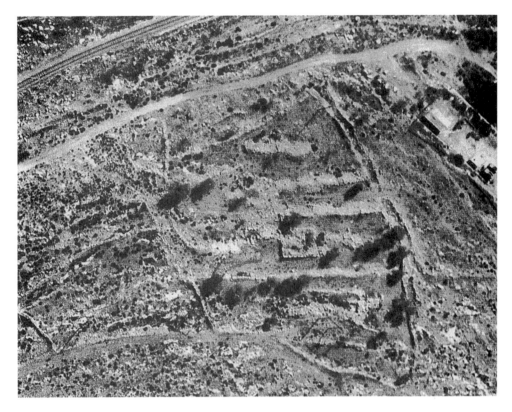

Photograph 5. An aerial photograph of the farm at Kh. er-Ras (1): the farmstead is located in the middle and is surrounded by its fields (Edelstein 2000: 40).

included three or four buildings, caves, pens, and an agricultural area composed of terraces that were surrounded by a fence and various agricultural installations, dated to the end of the Iron Age (fig. 32; photograph 5). A central four-room house was excavated (13 × 10 meters). The building had a stone-paved yard, and its plan was regular (rated 4+). About 20 meters north of the building, another building was excavated, of which only one room was preserved. In the southern part of the site, a cave was discovered in which there were finds, most of which were from the end of the Iron Age (including some *lmlk* handles).

New excavations conducted on the site later uncovered several more buildings (Feig 1995; 1996). About 40 meters from the previous buildings, another well-pre-served four-room house was excavated (Kh. er-Ras 2). Its area was nearly 165 square meters, and it too was built symmetrically (rated 4). About 300 hole-mouth jars were found *in situ*, and it appears that the broad space was used as a storeroom. Near this building, to the south, an industrial installation that contained two spaces was hewn into the rock: one space with a stone floor surrounded by walls that served as a storehouse, and another space with four recesses and a collection pit that probably serviced an olive press. This complex also was first built during the eighth century B.C.E. and continued in existence until the end of the Iron Age.

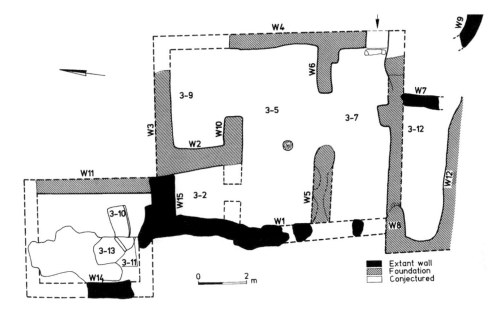

Fig. 33. Pisgat Zeev A: plan of the farmstead (without the reconstructed broad room; Seligman 1995: 65).

The findings of the new excavation and the discovery of the remnants of additional buildings up the hill led the excavator to believe that this was "not just a single farmhouse as was initially thought, but an agricultural settlement, an established village, on the southern margins of Jerusalem at the end of the First Temple period" (Feig 1995: 6). The data derived from the two excavations seems to negate Feig's suggestion and, given the distance between the two structures (40 m; Feig 1995: 5; 1996: 3, 4, fig. 1), it is likely that the two were separate farmsteads, part of a dense concentration of farms surrounding the capital city of Jerusalem (see Faust 1997; 2003d; more below). The site is being reexcavated now, however, and the first season was carried out in the summer of 2011 by Yuval Gadot. According to Gadot (2011: 46), the distance between the two above-mentioned structures is only some 10 m, and he actually unearthed parts of additional walls in the area adjacent to the buildings and between them (see especially his figs. 1–2 on pp. 45–46). Although it is not clear what the actual distance was between Kh. er-Ras 1 and Kh. er-Ras 2, if Gadot is correct this seems to support Feig's suggestion that the site was a village, but we need more data in order to classify it.

Pisgat Zeev A

The site is located in the Pisgat Zeev A neighborhood of Jerusalem. A residential house, a wine press, and a cave that probably was used for storage were discovered there (fig. 33). The farm was probably established during the eighth century B.C.E. and ceased to be occupied at the end of the seventh or beginning of the sixth century (Seligman 1994).

The excavator noted that the residential house (10 × 8 meters) had a different plan from the other farms in the Jerusalem area (1994: 73). The building was badly preserved, and only a few sections of its walls survived. A study of the plan shows that, despite the subrooms, the structure had three spaces and functioned as a broad building. This construction form is rare in this period, but it is possible that the broad room, originally located in the western part of the house (an area completely eroded), simply did not survive. If this suggestion is correct, we have a relatively fine long building with four spaces, like the other buildings found in this area. Its reconstructed area is 120–30 square meters (based on the ratio between the house's fully preserved width and its reconstructed length), and in this way as well it is similar to other buildings on other sites in the region.

Hurvat Alona

The site is northwest of Jerusalem. During Iron Age II, there were several farmhouses scattered around the site (Weksler-Bdolah 1999). One of them was excavated, and it turned out to be a three-room house (12.5 × 7.5 meters) with a large rectangular yard in front (1999). The building is quite well constructed. A closer examination of the pottery, however, showed that it was from the Persian period. It is unclear whether the building is also from the Persian period or whether the pottery finds only reflect a later phase of the use of the building.[11] It is best, therefore, to treat the site's data with caution.

Givat Homa

The site is located on a hill south of Kibbutz Ramat Rahel in Jerusalem. A pillared house was discovered (15 × 10 meters), in which there was a small wine press from the end of the Iron Age (Mai 1999). The building, which is probably of the three-room type, is very well built.

The Ramot Farmsteads

The Ramot farmsteads (sites 32, 36, 48, 50, 51) are five isolated structures located in the agricultural area that were discovered and excavated by a Hebrew University team (Davidovitz et al. 2006). Sites 32, 36, 48, 50, and 51 were interpreted as late Iron Age dwellings (2006: 68–69, 70–72, 72–75, and 77–79, respectively). The excavators stressed that the buildings are significantly smaller than their contemporaries (2006: 91–92), and have made several suggestions for the function of the structures:

1. The structures were used only seasonally, not throughout the year (2006: 92).
2. The structures were used by extended families, but the occupant density was much higher than in other structures. They find this explanation to be unreasonable (2006: 92).

---

11. Personal communication with Shelomit Weksler-Bdolah and Alon de Groot. Most of the farmhouses discovered in the Jerusalem area are quite uniform in size, and this building is much smaller than usual. This fact may perhaps be explained by its later date (at least in its present form).

3. Each house was used by a nuclear family. The excavators attempted to reconcile this suggestion with previous studies that suggested that the extended family was predominant in the rural sector. They therefore suggested that all the structures uncovered in the Ramot forest were used by one extended family, but the family did not live in one large structure; instead, they used many smaller structures (2006: 92).

While tempting, the last suggestion seems to me to be problematic. Not only does it leave problems in other sites (as they are aware; Davidovitz et al. 2006), but the data from the Ramot structures rule it out. Notably, structure 32 is more than half a kilometer away from the nearest house (structure 36; see map 2; 2006: 39), and this precludes its being part of the same unit. As far as the other structures are concerned, they are much closer to each other, so the interpretation is possible. However, it is important to stress that one of the buildings, which is approximately in the center of this group of structures, is fairly large and covers some 120 square meters. Davidovitz and others (2006: 92; see also p. 75) consider part of it to be an open courtyard and therefore believe its size is only 49 square meters, but there is nothing to support this suggestion. It is more likely, if indeed all the structures were part of the same unit, that we are discussing a regular farmhouse (structure 48) with additional structures that were used for storage, and so on around it (structures 36, 50, and 51). Structure 32 could have been part of a different farm.

It is also possible, however, that each of the structures was a separate farmstead and that some of them were used by nuclear families, which is at variance with the general rule in the rural sector. If this is the case, perhaps this can serve as evidence for the social processes of change that were already in operation around the Jerusalem metropolis (see below). The fact that the structures were not of the four-room type can also support this suggestion.

Khirbet Abu Shawan

Khirbet Abu Shawan is a farmstead that was excavated near Beit Jala. The farm was composed of several buildings, two of which were excavated. The eastern building is about 85 square meters large, and the western one, only the western part of which was excavated, seems to have measured some 95–100 square meters at least. The second building seems to have been the central one, but later construction destroyed parts of it, and it is difficult to assess its plan (although a four-room plan is possible based on the walls that were unearthed). A cave and a wine press were also found nearby. The complex is dated to the late Iron Age (Baruch 2001; see now also Baruch 2007).

Ramat Beit Hakerem

In the Ramat Beit Hakerem farmstead, poor remains from the late Iron Age (seventh century), Persian period, and early Hellenistic period were discovered. Although the structure was poorly preserved, its dimensions are clear (16 × 11 m), and it encompassed approximately 175 square meters (Davidovitz et al. 2006: 80–82, 86–87, 93–94). Since the eastern room was not further subdivided, the excavators

suggested that it was an open courtyard (2006: 82), but in the absence of any supporting evidence I think it is better to treat this as part of the house. Although this
is a long structure, its plan did not follow the four-room type, but this might be due
to the later occupation and use of the building.

The Buqeah Sites

Several sites have been discovered in Buqeah Valley in the Judean Desert. They
may be military fortresses (Cross and Milik 1956), or semi-military sites, meaning
they were agricultural farms located in areas of importance in terms of security
(Stager 1976). The sites show signs of advanced agriculture, including dams, cisterns, and more. Scholars agree that the sites were constructed at the same time,
probably by the central regime, during the seventh century B.C.E., and were in existence only for a short time (for example, Cross and Milik 1956; Stager 1976).

Khirbet el-Qatt

Khirbet el-Qatt is located on Mount Hebron (Amit 1989–90a). The complex is
spread over an area of about 350 square meters. The building includes three adjacent
rectangular spaces and a square tower. West of the tower, there is a stone surface
at the edge of which a wine press is carved that comprises a treading surface and
channels leading to a collection pit. Additional wine presses from this period have
also been found. The pottery fragments discovered indicate that the site was in use
from the Iron Age up to the Persian period (the seventh to fifth centuries B.C.E.). Not
far from it are four or five other Iron Age buildings.

Farm Southeast of the Village of Wadi Fukin

This farm site is in the northern Hebron hills. The complex (860 square meters) is
composed of several units (Amit 1992; Amit and Cohen-Amin in press): the central
unit (20 × 15 meters) is probably a four-room house. To its west was a large yard
(22 × 16 meters), and at its edges the remains of walls were discovered, perhaps
walls of rooms. In the northwestern corner, on a raised level, a square tower was
constructed (9 × 9 meters) that overlooked the nearby agricultural lands. Another
tower may have protected the northeast wing. The finds show that the site was in
use during the eighth–seventh centuries B.C.E.

Farm at Reference Point 16181239

This farm is located in the northern Hebron hills (Amit 1991; Amit and Cohen-
Amin in press). A square complex (28 × 25 meters) built of unhewn stone was uncovered. In the southwestern corner, there was a yard, and in the northern space, a
water reservoir was hewn into the rock. The pottery unearthed is dated mainly to
Iron Age II.

Additional Farms

Since the final manuscript of this book was submitted to the publisher, a few
more farmsteads have been brought to my attention, the more well-preserved of
which will be briefly described. At Site 49 (Ramot neighborhood, Beersheba), part

of an Iron Age IIb farm complex was excavated, including a large, eastward-facing, four-room house (17 × 10 m) and, beside it, another structure that was apparently used for storage (Feder and Negev 2008). At Noqdim (Peleg 2004), another Iron Age IIb farm complex was unearthed and partially excavated. The complex incoporated a number of structures including a small three-room house that served as a stable (unit 300) and two additional, larger structures that may have served as dwellings. It seems to me that the main farmhouse was unit 400, the area of which was 11.5 × 14 m but, because it was only partially exposed, no other details are available (the additional unit—unit 200—was larger, but most of this area was probably an open yard, and it is likely in my view that its purpose was storage). The last site to be discussed is the late Iron Age farm complex that was uncovered east of Anata (Reuben and Peleg 2009). The main farm building identified in the excavations was a large three-room house (8.8 × 11 m), accompanied by agricultural installations and a cave. It must be stressed that many additional farmsteads were partially excavated and published in recent years (e.g., the farm unit near Beitar Ilit [west] that was partially excavated by Har-Even [2009]), but since the data from most of them are too sparse for a social analysis, they will not be discussed here (see discussion of many such sites in Faust forthcoming).

Discussion:
Social and Community Organization in the Israelite Village

Family Structure as Reflected in Residential Houses

Most archaeologists who dealt with the Israelite family structure or with the residential houses typical of the period (four-room houses) believed that the common family structure was the nuclear family (for instance, Shiloh 1981; Broshi and Gophna 1986; Stager 1985).[12] These scholars discussed the archaeological finds familiar from many of the cities in the eighth–seventh centuries B.C.E. (Tel Beersheba, Tell Beit Mirsim, Mizpah [Tell en-Nasbeh], Tirzah [Tell el-Farʿah, north], Tell es-Saidiyeh, and other sites such as Hazor) and concentrated on the size of the common residential houses (30–70 square meters), a size sufficient for a nuclear family that comprised a father, mother, and two or three unmarried children.[13] A few, however, presented an opposing view, in which the four-room houses were inhabited by extended families (Dar 1986a; Maitlis 1989). Relying mainly on sites that they had excavated themselves, they argued that the four-room house was inhabited by a family of several dozen souls.

---

12. See also Faust 2000c; 2000d. Elsewhere (Faust 1998; 1999b), I have analyzed the size of houses in villages compared with the size of houses in the cities during Iron Age II and have shown that the family in the rural sector was an extended family. This section repeats the main conclusions and expands on other matters.

13. For the accepted density coefficients, see, for example, Naroll 1962; Ember and Ember 1995; B. M. Brown 1987; and the discussion in chap. 3 above. It is important to stress that scholars at both ends of the gamut of opinions discussed here used the same density coefficient. See further below.

The arguments raised by both sides have some justification; however, without noticing, both sides referred only to one part of the settlement continuum. Most scholars examined urban settlements, while the sites analyzed by Dar (Kh. Jemein) and Maitlis (Nahal Zimri and Kh. er-Ras) are rural sites. The average area of the houses on these sites is about 120 square meters, which is more than twice the area of the average residential house in the city. A comprehensive examination of some 35 four-room houses discovered in the rural sites that we reviewed above shows that their average size is near 130 square meters (see table 11).[14]

Based on the size of the buildings in villages and on farms, it is indeed reasonable to assume that they were inhabited by extended families (for exceptions, see below),[15] including parents, married sons and their children, unmarried daughters, unmarried aunts, and other relatives who remained living there for various reasons, slaves (?), agricultural workers, and others. Thus, it seems that each of the above-mentioned scholars concentrated on only one aspect of the settlement system. Some houses were inhabited by nuclear families (in the city), while others were home to extended families (mainly, though not solely, in the rural sector).

Another indicator of the differences between the family structures in the city and in the country is the number of rooms in the buildings. Most of the urban buildings have three spaces, while most of the rural buildings have four spaces. This difference was not necessarily essential, and may have been the result of construction requirements related to roofing such large buildings (but see chap. 7 below). However, while the three-room houses were indeed usually divided into only three rooms (often with an additional yard at the front), the rural buildings were typically divided into many subdivisions.[16] The number of rooms in a (ground floor of the) four-room house (not including the front yard) was between four (in very few cases) and eight (in many cases). The large number of rooms indicates the complex activities that took place in the buildings and the need for separate quarters that probably did not exist in most of the urban buildings, such as separating the various nuclear units

---

14. Note that the building at Ramat Beit Hakerem does not follow the four-room plan (although this may be the result of later activity at the site). Not included in the calculation are the Ramot farmsteads (see more below).

15. It is very possible that the ratio between roofed area and the number of inhabitants is not a universal constant but is culture-dependent (see Hayden et al. 1996; for additional references, see also chap. 3 above). However, even if this ratio varies from culture to culture, this does not detract from the scenario presented here, which is referring to the differences between two settlement sectors of the same culture and society. Presumably, the ratio in both sectors was close, even if other factors were involved. As we have seen, Wason (1994: 140) suggests several reasons for the existence of large buildings: (1) they reflect status or wealth; (2) they had a large number of residents; (3) additional functions took place there. In the case discussed here, the first option is clearly irrelevant, since we are discussing the rural sector whose members were not wealthy and all of the houses are relatively similar, and the third option, as we shall see below, is also irrelevant. The second option is the one proposed here to explain the differences. However, we have already seen that in certain cases the different explanations do not contradict each other, and several may be used in combination (thus, for example, some of the large urban buildings were probably inhabited by a family that was both wealthy and large).

16. It should be noted that we are discussing only the ground floor of buildings that probably contained more than one floor. As noted in chap. 3, above, the term "four rooms" refers to the basic configuration and is somewhat misleading, because many houses contained more rooms.

Table 11. Data on the size of buildings in the rural sector.

Site	No. of Buildings (approx.)	Average Area (Square Meters)
H. Malta	1	120
Kh. Jemein	7	110–20
Beit Aryeh	9	110
Kh. Jarish	1	160
Deir el-Mir	2 published (more can be identified in the site plan)	100–140
H. Shilhah	1	120
Kh. er-Ras	2	130, 165
Nahal Zimri	1	130
French Hill	1	115
Givat Homa	1	150
H. Eli	2	140, 174
Pisgat Zeev	1	80 as excavated, 125 reconstructed
Kh. Abu Shawan	1	100
Ramat Beit Hakerem	1	175
Farm near Wadi Fukin village	1	300
Site 49 (Ramot, Beersheba)	1 farmhouse	170
Noqdim	1 farmhouse	161
Farmstead east of Anata	1 farmhouse	97

residing in the same home (Kramer [1979: 155], for example, studied a culture in which one room was sufficient for a nuclear family, which would not be the same for an extended family).

Not only the large number of rooms in the four-room houses, but also the lack of uniformity in the subdivisions (compared with the relative uniformity of the subdivisions in the three-room houses in the cities) support the interpretation that these were houses inhabited by extended families. The needs of a nuclear family are relatively regular and stable, while the needs of extended families undergo drastic changes throughout their life cycles, because the total number of family members and the nuclear units, in particular, change over time (Wilk and Rathje 1982: 626; Seymour-Smith 1994: 76). The differences in the subdivisions of the various buildings probably resulted from these changes. Each of the families living in the different houses was probably at a particular stage (different from that of other families) in its life cycle at the time of destruction and abandonment, when the architectural picture "froze," from an archaeological point of view.

I should also mention that most of the large four-room houses in the cities, which are usually interpreted as residential homes of elite families (and most accept that they were inhabited by extended families), are also further subdivided. The main rooms (spaces) in the large urban buildings, which we suggested served as the residences of officials (such as the buildings near the fortress and the economic complex in Hazor, or the three large four-room houses at Mizpah/Tell en-Nasbeh), are not subdivided or are only slightly subdivided.

On the face of it, the significant differences in the area of the buildings in the cities and the villages can be explained as resulting from the differences in land usage in the different sectors. According to one possible explanation, population density in the city necessitated a reduction in the size of the buildings, while in the country people could build without area restrictions. In other words, land in the rural sector was more available.

It appears that in planned cities such as Beersheba, the planners could take the settlement's limited space into account and built relatively small buildings so they could include more houses in the city's limits. This argument is relevant to planned cities (though it is doubtful that the officials of the population were forced to live in such density), but it does not explain the small area of the buildings in unplanned cities such as Mizpah (Tell en-Nasbeh) and Tell Beit Mirsim. While it can be argued that at these two sites the untidy construction forced the density on the builders, this argument ignores the fact that at least some of the buildings were constructed before there was high density, when it was still possible to build these houses to the size that the owners wished. The fact that in both planned and unplanned cities there were usually small houses of similar sizes shows that these arguments do not really explain the phenomenon. Furthermore, most of the rural buildings were not houses of the wealthy and contained no signs of conspicuous consumption. So one cannot assume that they were larger than the functional needs of their residents required, and presumably their large size reflected the inhabitants' needs.

Another possible explanation is that sites of an agricultural nature require additional space and larger buildings to accommodate livestock and agricultural produce. But this argument also fails the reality test: in the villages, there were often yards in front of the houses and alongside them, and some special storehouses have also been discovered. Furthermore, most of the farms contained not only yards but also additional structures or buildings that probably filled this function (Maitlis 1989: 64). In the cities, such buildings have not been found, even though some of their residents worked in agriculture. It appears that, when city residents owned agricultural produce or livestock, they were stored in the buildings themselves or in *migrashim* outside the city (Portugali 1984: 283; Faust 1996). The conclusion is that the significant differences in the area of residential houses in the cities and in the villages cannot be explained by the cost of land, or by planning (or lack of planning), or even by the agricultural needs of the rural sector.

The differences are probably caused by social factors. The differences between the city and country with regard to family structure (nuclear versus extended family) have already been discussed by Bible scholars such as de Vaux and Reviv, although they were not familiar with archaeological finds from the rural sector (de Vaux 1965; Reviv 1993; compare Hatt and Reiss 1965; Yorburg 1975). In this conservative sector, the traditional family framework was preserved, while in the urban sector there were alterations to the family structure (see also chap. 9).[17]

Presumably, life expectancy also influenced family structure and size. Our knowledge of this issue is limited, but from a preliminary study in Central America, it transpires that the residents of rural areas or village cultures lived longer than residents of large urban centers (Rathje and McGuire 1982: 710–11). If this conclusion is also correct regarding the place and time we are discussing here, we cannot deny the impact of this factor on family size, and this is another reason for the larger size of rural families (Lenski and Lenski 1974: 249–50; also note the health problems in the city, which were detrimental to life expectancy there; compare Basset et al. 1992).

Interestingly, the structures unearthed in Ramot are mostly smaller than the rural houses discussed above, and while the small houses could have been secondary structures of a large farm, it is also possible that they were used by nuclear families. While it is difficult to decide which explanation is more likely, we should bear this datum in mind, and it is possible that this is evidence for processes of social change around the Jerusalem metropolis (see more below).[18]

---

17. As noted in chap. 3, above, the idea that extended or joint families lived in compounds during Iron Age II (e.g., Schloen 2001; Brody 2009; 2011) does not withstand scrutiny. Not only are such compounds absent in the Iron II archaeological record, but a broad examination of the period's society reveals that such compounds are superfluous, because the existing spectrum of houses can account for all types of families in Israelite society. Although this is not the place for an extended discussion of the compound theory, we can now, in light of the data presented in this chapter (see also chap. 3), point to some of the issues that seem to have been ignored by Schloen and Brody but are accounted for by the explanation forwarded here: (1) the existence of large four-room houses in the cities (e.g., the various large structures discussed in chap. 3): these houses were not needed if extended families lived in compounds; (2) the differences in the division of space inside the houses in the urban and rural sectors: these could only result from differences between the kinship units that inhabited the houses in these two settlement sectors; (3) the differences in the distribution and size of agricultural installations, which (again) indicate differences in family structure between cities and villages, revealing that extended families did not live in compounds but in large houses (and see more below); (4) even the differences in the sizes of the structures in cities and villages were not seriously addressed. A broader treatment of Israelite society would have showed them that there were clear differences between the urban and rural sectors, and extended families lived in large, complex four-room houses and not in compounds.

18. Recently, B. Routledge (2009) discussed the question of variability in houses' size during the Iron Age. Thus, for example, in addressing some works (by others as well as by me) he correctly questioned the use of an "average" size for houses without discussing the full range of the existing structures, noting that the term "average" can disguise large differences in the size of buildings and may be misleading. Part of Routledge's article dealt with my work, and on the basis of some of my previous publications he challenged some of the basic conclusions of these works. Most of Routledge's criticism concern Beit Aryeh (Kh. Hadash). He attempted to use the published plan of the site to show that large differences in the size of structures did indeed exist within small rural sites, and he subsequently used this insight to study social structure at large. This is not the place for a detailed discussion of the arguments raised by Routledge in this important article, but a few brief comments are in order. First of all, there are clear differences between houses in cities and houses in villages, and this is apparent not only on the basis of average size (which I discussed in some of my previous publications) but also on the basis of the spectrum of structure sizes that existed in these settlement sectors (as can be seen in chaps. 3–4 of this monograph). Thus the smallest rural houses are larger than the larger "typical" urban houses (with the exception of rare, exceptionally large urban houses that represent the urban elite and also differ from smaller urban houses in quality). This means that differences in "average" sizes are significant and meaningful, and the gaps between the two settlement sectors as far as structural size is concerned are real. Furthermore, there are differences in

The Basic Economic Unit and the Distribution of Production Installations

Several studies have recently discussed the structure of the basic economic units in the land of Israel during Iron Age II based on the distribution of the production installations. Hayah Eitan-Katz (1994) discussed the size and distribution of the production installations in the various cities of the Kingdom of Judah during the eighth century B.C.E. The fact that the relatively small installations in the cities were distributed inside the various houses and between them without any order or organization led her to conclude that each of them provided for the needs of only one nuclear family and thus that the basic economic unit was the nuclear family (Eitan-Katz 1994). Holladay, who discussed the ancient economy of the kingdoms of Israel and Judah, reached similar conclusions. From an analysis of the residential houses and the storage capacity of the various installations, Holladay concluded that the basic economic unit in Israelite society was the nuclear family (Holladay 1995). However, Holladay focused only on the urban sector and was not familiar with the

---

the use and division of household space between the two sectors, and this is accompanied by differences in household economy and community organization. All those lines of evidence further support the distinction between the urban and rural sectors that was initially based on the size of houses. Routledge ignored all these facets of information (even though some of it was already published in my early articles on this matter), which clearly support my initial conclusions.

More specifically, Routledge questioned my calculation of house size at Beit Aryeh, noting that in light of the differences between his measurements and mine it is "unclear how exactly [my] divergent figures were calculated" (B. Routledge 2009: 47 n. 18). His criticism is surprising. It is based on using a scan of the small-scale published plan (apparently without even using the information contained in the text of the published [Hebrew] article itself). Not only is the published plan small and very difficult to use (when attempting to calculate the size of individual units within the village), but it was spread over one and a half pages of the journal; photocopying or scanning it would result in distortion of some portions of the plan. My own calculation of the size of the houses at Beit Aryeh was based on the original 1:100 plan provided to me by the excavator (more below), and hence errors (which inevitably occurred because the measurements were done by hand) were relatively minor. Routledge, furthermore, mixed different types of buildings (he does not refer to the observations of the excavator, and it seems that he did not read the brief publication itself, whether it is correct or not). Thus, for example, he includes in his discussion of houses what appears to have been a large communal storage building (see above). This, of course, leads to artificial differences (furthermore, it must be stressed that the structure was not excavated, and its size is merely an estimate). He also treats what appear to be two separate units (units 890 and 900) as one, hence creating a new, large unit. Although this is a possible interpretation (because there appears to be an opening connecting the two units), he should have wondered why the excavator gave the structures separate numbers and should have given more thought to my suggestion that they were indeed two separate units (see also the discussion earlier in this chapter). On the other side of the spectrum, he included small units in his discussion of dwellings, which probably were not used for habitation (units 570 and 590), hence increasing the gap between the various structures even further. And all this is without the distortion that was undoubtedly created by using a small-scale scanned plan. I must stress that, although my analysis could of course be wrong, it is based not only on the published report but also on a number of discussions with the excavator (Shimon—not Shmuel—Riklin), who also gave me the original 1:100 plan of the site along with a number of unpublished manuscripts and even a more-detailed plan of some of the houses, as well as on a number of visits to the site. All this does not guarantee that my conclusions are correct, but it is essential for anyone who wishes to study the community living at Beit Aryeh, let alone use the data from this village to draw conclusions on society at large.

And this brings me to my final comment on this issue. It is dangerous to base far-fetched conclusions about social structure on an analysis of one element (house size) of one site, even if this analysis is flawless. What is required is a large-scale study based on various types of finds, from many sites. I hope that the more detailed study of which this footnote is one part will answer Routeldge's queries.

findings from the rural sector.[19] The conclusions of Eitan-Katz and Holladay are therefore valid for the urban sector but do not suit the rural sector, where the situation is completely different.

In the villages, the production installations were concentrated in "industrial areas" and were, at times, very large and perhaps even communal in nature:

- *Kh. Jemein*: Near the edge of the settlement, an area was discovered that revealed several agricultural installations. Prominent among them was a particularly large oil press, which the excavator interpreted as a public oil press. Next to the oil press there, were pits for storing oil, with a capacity of thousands of liters. A large wine cellar was also found there (Dar 1986a; 1986b).
- *Beit Aryeh*: Near the edge of the settlement, an industrial area was discovered in which were found over 20 oil production installations (Eitam 1992b).
- *Kh. Kla*: Two industrial areas were discovered on the site, each evidencing a concentration of agricultural-industrial installations. The main area was on the east side of the site, and the other was on the west (Eitam 1980: 69–70).
- *Deir el-Mir*: The site probably had several industrial areas with concentrations of installations (Eitam 1980: 69–70).
- *Kh. Banat Barr*: Four industrial areas were discovered on the site that had concentrations of installations (Eitam 1980; Kochavi 1989a).
- *Kurnet Bir et Tell*: Near the edge of the settlement, an industrial area was discovered with some 10 rock-cut installations for the production of olive oil (Finkelstein 1988b: 166; Finkelstein, Lederman, and Bunimovitz 1997: 447).
- *H. Malta*: The excavator reported "various rock-cut installations, attesting to the presence of an industrial zone here" (Covello-Paran 1997: 40).

In addition to the sites discussed above in more detail, concentrations of production installations were also found at Deir Daqla (Har-Even: private communication), Sheikh Isa (Finkelstein, Lederman, and Bunimovitz 1997: 389; the olive presses were observed on a visit to the site on August 3, 2008), Kh. Tibnah (Finkelstein, Lederman, and Bunimovitz 1997: 367; many installations were observed on a visit to the site on August 3, 2008), and other places (see also Faust 2011a).

It transpires that, in the rural sector, there was organization in the production of agricultural produce from the agricultural-industrial facilities. In some cases, the installations are quite large (perhaps communal), which indicates organization beyond the extended family. In most cases, however, the installations are concentrated in industrial areas, in contrast to the lack of organization and random distribution of the installations in the cities. This fact also reveals organization in the production. It appears that the villages preserved large kinship and social frameworks. Responsibility for production was in the hands of a social unit even larger than the extended family—a unit that the Bible calls *mishpahah* ('lineage/clan'; this issue will be discussed extensively below). In many villages inhabited by just one *mishpahah*, there was only one industrial area, because the village's entire produce was processed together, and

---

19. In Holladay's opinion, Tell Beit Mirsim and Tell en-Nasbeh were fortified villages, but he admits that the rural sector is not known in research. However, these two settlements are not villages but provincial towns (Faust 1995b; Herzog 1992b; see also Faust 2002a; 2003c, and chap. 3, above).

in any case the village elders (who were also the elders of the kinship group) made the decisions regarding the produce. In some of the villages (mainly the large ones), there were two to four industrial areas. These settlements were inhabited by two or more *hamulah*s or *mishpahot*. Each unit had its own industrial area, and each of the units was economically communal.[20] This does not mean that all the crops and produce were communal as in a modern kibbutz but that at least some of the crops were processed communally or in an organized manner. Each household used its produce independently, but there were also communal mechanisms in place.[21]

Community Organization as Reflected in the Terrace Systems

Terraces contribute greatly to agricultural production: they enable the cultivation of land on steep slopes, prevent land loss, maintain soil humidity, and aid root penetration (Moody and Grove 1990: 183). Terrace systems have been discovered around many villages, and in several cases they have been dated to Iron Age II. This is the case at Kh. Jemein (Dar 1986a: 36; 1986b: 36–37, 77–80), Mevasseret Yerushalayim (Edelstein and Kislev 1981), and probably at Kh. Kla (Eitam 1980: 69–70). The construction of terraces has been extensively discussed in scholarly literature in connection with social structure (Stager 1985: 5–9; Hopkins 1985; Coote and Whitelam 1987; Broshi 2001; and others; almost all the studies dealt with this issue in the context of Iron Age I). Most scholars dealing with this topic believed that the construction of a terrace system was an operation requiring the cooperation of a large number of people. Thus, for example, Edelstein and Kislev thought that the construction of terraces around Mevasseret Yerushalayim was a state operation organized by the central regime (Edelstein and Kislev 1981: 55–56). In contrast, Broshi believes that the construction of the terraces was a very long process that was conducted by families, perhaps even nuclear families (Broshi 1996: 96; 2001: 65). Most scholars hold an intermediate opinion. They do not attribute terrace construction to the central regime but to large supra-household social groupings that cooperated (Hopkins 1985: 269), as Renfrew and Bahn put it: "activities like terracing involve cooperative effort on the part of a whole community" (Renfrew and Bahn 2004: 207). Thus, the very existence of the terrace systems is another important indication of organization at the *mishpahah* level.

20. It is possible that there were intermediate situations in the large villages or townships: the lineages were responsible for the production and the economy in general, but there were also small, private installations for use by people who were not necessarily part of the kinship units. For a different interpretation, see Eitam 1987: 24.

21. According to Eitam (1992a; 1992b), the sites at Beit Aryeh and Kh. Kla were royal (industrial) villages for olive oil production. This interpretation is based on the concentration of installations found there and on what seem to be relatively impressive fortifications for a rural site. Eitam was probably not familiar with other rural sites and thus was unaware of the similarity between these two sites and "ordinary" villages. Even if we accept the common opinion regarding the "estates" that developed in the Kingdoms of Israel and Judah in this period that specialized in oil and wine production (since a "royal village" is a sort of "estate"), the sites discussed here are very different from the typical "estates" (see below, chap. 5). According to Chaney (1986: 73), the sale of cash crops was detrimental to the living conditions of the rural population engaged in agriculture. An analysis of the villages in terms of the buildings and organization clearly shows that they were not poor settlements or estates that plundered the lands of the rural population, as in the view of proponents of the accepted historical approach.

Community Organization Reflected in Storage Facilities

In many of the villages, storehouses and various storage facilities were identified: At Kh. Jemein (storehouse, large wine cellar, and cisterns, the location of which outside the built complexes could indicate their communal nature), at Kh. Kla (long building interpreted as a storehouse; Eitam 1980: 69–70), at Beit Aryeh (large pillared building that may have been a storehouse), at Deir Daqla (wine cellar with at least five openings), at H. Hamad (storehouse; Dar 1986b: 40–41; 1993: 1314), at Sheikh Isa (a wine cellar; see, e.g., Frumkin 2005), and more. These are small, simple buildings and installations compared with the storehouses and facilities discovered in the cities, but we should remember that the urban storehouses were state-built and served state needs. The construction form and quality show that the poorer storage structures in the villages were built by the local residents. These facilities indicate the existence of a local system that took care of storing and preserving the produce. It appears that this system was also operatiang at the level of the *hamula-mishpahah*, just like the system that was responsible for the agricultural production itself (this sort of reality may also have existed in a provincial town such as Gibeon [see Demsky 1987], but it is more likely that the storage there was part of a royal system). The *mishpahah* elders (in small villages, these were also the village elders) must have been responsible for redistributing the produce. It is possible that the storehouses held the communal produce of the village or the produce of different households, and this produce may have remained in the ownership of these households. It is also likely that not all the village's produce was stored in the communal installations and that part of it was stored elsewhere, such as in residential houses (some of it was clearly stored there).

Settlement Organization

The existence of an organizing system can also be deduced from the form of a village. In contrast to the common opinion (such as Frick 1970: 90), very few of the villages of the period were unwalled; in fact, most of them were surrounded by a perimeter wall. Perimeter walls were discovered in many cases, such as the following rural sites: Kh. Jemein, H. Malta, Tel Zeror, Beit Aryeh (Kh. Hadash), Kh. Kla, Kurnet Bir et Tell, Deir Daqla, Deir el-Mir, Kh. Jarish, Kh. Umm Kahal, and Kh. Maiyaseh. These walls are, of course, much more modest than those of the period's cities, since they were built as a local enterprise, rather than being initiated and constructed by the state. The perimeter wall was usually formed by joining the buildings on the edge of the village, but sometimes a freestanding wall was built, the sole purpose of which was to serve as a boundary wall. In at least one case, both methods were used together (for example, Kh. Jemein). In a few sites, a small gatehouse was also found (Kh. Jemein and perhaps also Beit Aryeh and Daharat Nisnas B).

The construction of a defensive wall of any type is impossible without a body that can decide the matter and oversee its realization; thus, the mere existence of village walls is another indication of the presence of some sort of governing body. Some of the villages with boundary walls were quite large villages and contained more than one industrial area. If indeed these settlements were inhabited by two or

more *mishpahot*, presumably the body responsible for security was larger than the
group responsible for the economy.

Despite great variety in the forms of boundary walls, their presence can be
treated as a clear characteristic of a village. Presumably, relatively thin walls were
not intended to defend against an army but against raiders or other irregular threats.
However, there may have been additional explanations. Rowlands listed several possible reasons for building a boundary wall (Rowlands 1975: 299), such as guarding
livestock, gathering water, defining private space, and more. Walls and gates also
had symbolic-magical significance, such as preventing the entry of ghosts and demons (compare Rapoport 1969: 31; Hingley 1990; Parker-Pearson and Richards 1994:
24; Faust 1995b: 82–83; 2000c; 2000d). According to Hingley, "Enclosures can be defined as boundaries of social exclusion" (Hingley 1990: 96); boundary walls can also
serve as symbolic representations of the social boundaries separating the local social
units from "other" groups and society as a whole (Bevan 1997: 184–86). According
to Warren, who excavated a Bronze Age village in Crete, "The defensive arrangements of the exterior wall . . . are the most specific indication of independent status,"
meaning that a boundary wall symbolizes independence from the external world
(not necessarily formal independence; Warren 1983: 255).

According to Thomas, who analyzed the situation in Britain during the first millennium B.C.E., walled settlements sometimes symbolize a distinction between different components of society; they serve as a clear marker of "us" and "them" and
are typical of societies where there is a clear separation between groups (Thomas
1997). A division of this sort is usually characteristic of agrarian societies with intensive agriculture and where there is a strong sense of land as property. The clear
boundaries reflect, in his opinion, the process of the intensification of agriculture and
the rise in the importance of the land as a resource and also reflect changes in the
family structure, particularly the transition to requiring marriage to be within the
group, aimed at keeping the land in "our" hands. Prior to the intensification process,
when land was still not such an important resource, marriage outside the group was
more common, because there was no anxiety about the land changing hands. According to Thomas, the intensification of agriculture led to changes in the form of
settlement through the mechanism of changes to the family structure, and walled
settlements reflect this change.

Most of the components listed by Thomas were present in the land of Israel during the period of the Monarchy. Here, too, there was a process of agricultural intensification, and here also the settlements were walled.[22] From the sources, we know
that Israelite society preferred endogamous marriages, meaning marriages within
the kinship group (see, for example, the story of Zelophehad's daughters, Numbers
36; see also de Vaux 1965: 30–31; McAfee 1993: 690). Thus, the existence of a boundary wall also indicates "togetherness" and the communal nature of a site.

_____

22. Rural settlements surrounded by defensive walls were present in the region already during Iron
Age I (see Faust 1995b, and additional bibliography there), and the process of agricultural intensification
also began in this period (see, e.g., Stager 1985). There is great similarity between the settlement forms in
Iron Age I and II, despite the lack of settlement continuity. On this issue, see further below, chap. 9; see also
Faust 2003a; 2007b; contra Finkelstein 2005.

Socioeconomic Differences

In most of the rural sites examined, we cannot identify social and economic stratification, even though in two villages (Kh. Jemein and Beit Aryeh) there are extensive architectural finds that could easily have shown socioeconomic differences, were there any. The relative uniformity of the site of the residential houses can be seen not only in an intra-site analysis (the main tool for examining these gaps) but also in an inter-site comparison in which no clear gaps can be identified. A clear example of this statement can be found in an analysis of the farms around Jerusalem: Nahal Zimri (farmhouse area about 120 square meters), Kh. er-Ras (two structures were found with areas of 130 square meters and 165 square meters), Pisgat Zeev A (residential house area reconstructed to 120–30 square meters), French Hill (building area about 115 square meters), Givat Homa (150 square meters), Ramat Beit Hakerem (175 square meters), Kh. Abu Shawan (100 square meters), and Alona (about 95 square meters, if indeed it should be dated to the Iron Age). Although we are not discussing solely one site (so discrepancies are expected), the overall differences are relatively small when compared with differences within cities (possible exceptions to this rule will be discussed below).

The typical rural house of this period was a large four-room house (almost always of the main type, with four clear spaces), the area of which was usually 120–30 square meters (and rarely was outside the 100–160 square meters range), and the quality and shape of which were quite similar in all the sites.[23] The great similarity between the buildings indicates a high degree of equality in this society, especially given that the sites are distant from each other. But we should not assume absolute equality, which is impossible (see, for instance, Wason 1994: 1). In equivalent analyses of the period's cities, the archaeological finds showed clear socioeconomic stratification. Thus, the gaps that probably did exist in the rural sector (but were not identified in the archaeological finds), were small. Presumably, these gaps were apparent to the local residents, but outside observers and later anthropologists would find them hard to identify (see, e.g., Tod 1974). Perhaps there is no evidence of social stratification due to the presence of social mechanisms that prevented the display of wealth. In many traditional societies, it is unacceptable to display wealth (Lees 1979: 271; Wilk 1983: 112; see also Blanton 1994: 188), and high social status was not reflected in residential houses or in clothing but in other ways, such as contributions to public events (such as the church). In any case, these gaps, even if they existed, were smaller to begin with (for an egalitarian ethos in Israelite society, see also Faust 2006b, especially 92–107, and references).

Finally, we should mention the possible exceptions to the above "rule." At sites such as Deir el-Mir and Kh. Banat Barr, despite the limited data available, there

---

23. As we have seen, Dar identified building 500 in Kh. Jemein as the village head's residence, but it is clear that this was just a double four-room house similar to other buildings on the site. In Beit Aryeh as well, a building was found that was larger than the rest, but there it was probably two houses. In any event, even if we treated this house as one house that was the residence of the village leader, differences would still be minimal (and we would simply have one house that was larger than the others, which are quite homogeneous). We must note that this is irrelevent for Kh. Jemein, where building 500 was clearly a typical double house unit.

seem to have been some differences in both quality and size between the various structures. These differences, which were larger than at other settlements (even if we consider the "exceptions" in those villages [such as building 890 and 900 at Beit Aryeh] as indicating social stratification), may indicate that in the large villages processes of social change were operating, probably as a result of their large size and exposure to the political and economical forces of the state.

Additional possible "exceptions" can be seen in some of the farmsteads around Jerusalem. The possibly unique characteristics of the Ramot structures were discussed above, and although it is possible that the main building there was just another typical farmstead (and the other buildings were simply secondary structures of this farm), this is not certain. Therefore, the possibility that the small size of most of the buildings indicates that a nuclear family lived there cannot be ruled out. One should also consider the fact that most of these structures do not follow the four-room plan, and this may also be indicative of their low status.[24] If these structures should indeed be treated as exceptions to the common reality in the rural sector, the reason behind it was probably their location in the hinterland of Jerusalem; it is likely that the large metropolis influenced the social structure of its surroundings as some of the residents of the city acquired more and more land. The inhabitants of the small structures at Ramot and similar houses may have worked the land of others.

Although very speculative, the evidence from the few houses in the Jerusalem region along with evidence from the large villages seems to indicate that the processes of social change were in operation also in the rural sector. Socioeconomic stratification in Israel and Judah will be discussed further in chap. 6, below.

Conclusions

The Village as a Community

In a recent article, Kolb and Snead turned their attention to an archaeological analysis of the community (Kolb and Snead 1997: 611). They identified three important components of all communities: (1) Social reproduction: "the role of the local community as a particular node of social interaction . . . forming a principal arena in which sociopolitical relationships are negotiated or played out." The community has a minimal number of components, demographically, some of which conduct regular interactions, and "the repeated interactions socially reproduce the group." (2) Subsistence economy, which is "a central element in community life. Local communities serve as a focus of subsistence labor and are principal arbiters of access to productive resources." The communities are important economic factors, although they are not necessarily units of economic organization. Communities create conditions "whereby subsistence production is possible," for example, by letting the land lie fallow. (3) Self-identification: "The creation and maintenance of local identity is

---

24. The structure at Ramat Beit Hakerem also does not follow the four-room plan, but this could have been the result of later changes and modifications, because the building was used, probably continuously, into the Persian period (Davidovitz et al. 2006). We should note that a few additional small structures in the countryside were reported elsewhere over the last couple of years, but some of those were probably secondary structures of larger farmsteads (perhaps the structure at Har Gillo West; Peleg and Feller 2004).

essentially rooted in economic practice and social reproduction, but is manifested in the manipulation of boundaries both physical and symbolic. Residents of communities thus share a common sense of membership to that organization . . . in addition to whatever other social grouping they belong." Of course, there are different definitions of a community, but Kolb and Snead conclude: "we therefore consider the community to be a minimal, spatially defined locus of human activity that incorporate social reproduction, subsistence production, and self-identification" (Kolb and Snead 1997: 610–11, and discussion and bibliography there).

The villages discussed in this chapter contain all three of the basic conditions mentioned by Kolb and Snead in their definition of a community: they were large enough to entail social reproduction through the interactions of their components; the community enabled a subsistence economy; and the existence of boundary walls shows that the communities maintained a large degree of self-identity and differentiated themselves from the outside world.

The Corporate Group

Belonging to a community is no substitute for belonging to other social groups, especially a "corporate group." This term has received several definitions (Hayden and Cannon 1982: 133–35). According to the *Macmillan Dictionary of Anthropology*, the corporate group is "a social group which owns and controls a significant property or resources" (Seymour-Smith 1994: 55). As Hayden and Cannon say, "according to anthropological definitions corporate groups include a wide range of sizes, extending from the nuclear family to the entire community," but they believe these two extreme groups should be excluded (Hayden and Cannon 1982: 136).

Small villages, where there was a large degree of sharing in the sites' management and organization, were probably identical to kinship units, and the entire village (and entire community) can be seen as a corporate group, despite Hayden and Cannon's reservations. In the larger villages, there were several units of this sort. Corporate groups thrive under a moderate degree of agrarian pressure, while in extreme conditions (abundance of land on the one hand, or land scarcity, on the other), it is more likely that land is used and competed over on an individual basis (Hayden and Cannon 1982: 150–51). In certain cases, these groups develop "not from land scarcity per se, but rather from the need to maintain cohesive land tract sizable enough to make cash crop production profitable, as well as from the additional need to maintain sufficient labor force to work the land" (1982: 150). Indeed, at the end of the Iron Age (in the eighth and seventh centuries B.C.E.), the land of Israel reached one of its settlement peaks (Broshi and Finkelstein 1992) but without exhausting its ability to support the population (compare with the Byzantine period). There is even archaeological evidence for the production of an agricultural surplus (at Beit Aryeh, for instance), and this shows that there were indeed cash crops in the agricultural-rural sector in this period.

The Composition and Structure of the Rural Community

The composition and structure of traditional rural society has been discussed in many sociological and anthropological studies (Schwartz and Falconer 1994, and

additional bibliography there). In one of the most important of them, Robert Redfield expressed his opinion that the agricultural villages were "homogeneous" and
that their population was composed of agricultural food producers who were equal
in socioeconomic status (Redfield 1953). Redfield's opinion was very influential in
research. Thus, for instance, according to Wolf, in rural communities there was community sharing in the redistribution of the land and balancing mechanisms that
maintained relative economic and social equality (E. R. Wolf 1955). According to the
image portrayed in many studies, there was indeed a large degree of communality
and organization in the rural community in ancient times (Diakonoff 1975). While in
recent years a different opinion has become prevalent, that even in villages one can
observe social stratification and economic gaps (Schwartz and Falconer 1994: 3), the
analysis conducted here supports Redfield's conclusions regarding the nature of rural settlements. The analysis of rural settlements during the period of the Monarchy
shows a large degree of commonality and equality, and no real social stratification
can be identified.

While we must take into consideration the criticism of Redfield, Wolf, and other
scholars as having an overly simplistic approach, this criticism does not completely
rule out the picture they presented (also R. G. Fox 1977: 9–11). Indeed, there is probably some truth in Bendor's argument (Bendor 1996) for the presence of internal tensions within the *mishpahah* (that is, the lineage and sometimes even the village), and
we have already seen that absolute equality does not exist. However, the theories of
Wolf and Redfield are at least partially supportable, even if the picture appears to
have been more complex than they believed.[25] The criticism, at least regarding rural
society in the land of Israel in Iron Age II, only clarifies the picture and indicates the
relatively small differences and gaps existing in a relatively egalitarian society.

*Organization of the Rural Community: Archaeological Evidence
versus Written Sources*

In chap. 1, we reviewed many studies about Israelite society based on biblical
descriptions and on comparisons with other societies in the ancient Near East and
other regions. According to the prevailing opinion, traditional Israelite society (during Settlement period) was composed of *batei av* (households), *mishpahot* and tribes.
A similar picture arises from the archaeological finds from Iron Age II villages.

A comparison of the residential houses in the cities and villages in terms of their
size and internal division shows that, during the period of the Monarchy, nuclear
families lived in the cites while extended families, typical of traditional society, lived
and worked in the villages. These families were probably identical to the *batei av* of
the Bible.

A similar picture arises from an analysis of the production facilities, their size,
and distribution. In the city, the facilities were operated by nuclear families, while
in the village, these facilities were operated in larger frameworks. Various signs
show that the organizing framework was larger than the extended family and that

---

25. The conclusions of this study do not support Redfield and his colleagues' conclusions regarding
the status of rural communities on the social scale. This status was higher than they believed.

it should be identified with what the Bible calls the *mishpahah*. This framework was sometimes identical with the entire settlement, and in other cases there were several of these families in the village. Large-scale storage facilities and systems of agricultural terraces around the settlements also show that the organizing body was larger. This framework can be considered a corporate group. In this context, the words of David Hopkins come to mind, although they refer to Iron Age I:

> The small size and the relative instability of the "bet ʾab" does not match the regular agricultural labor demands. . . . The seasonal flow of labor demand as well as the occasional need for larger quanta of labor and the requirement of supra-household planning and cooperation further impel the formation of larger sodalities. Since social relations are the best insurance against subsistence failure for the individual cultivating family, the "mispaha" must be conceived as forming the social context—the risk-spreading context—for the agricultural life if the family. Mutual aid was not reserved for "emergencies" but was a regular function of this group. (Hopkins 1985: 260–61)

As we have seen, the *batei av* (meaning the extended families) were organized within a larger framework, the *mishpahah*. According to most scholars, this kinship unit matches the anthropological term "clan," though other scholars use various terms, such as "lineage,"[26] or "protective associations of families" (e.g., Gottwald 1979: 257). This unit was subtribal, as is apparent both from the Bible (for example, Josh 7:14) and from epigraphic finds (the Samaria ostraca; Aharoni 1979: 356–68).

At the same time, this was probably not the only organization level above the household. According to Halpern, this sort of unit (the clan as the subtribal entity) is impractical and cannot manage affairs of internal politics. In his opinion, there was another intermediate unit, which he terms the "clan section," that mediated between the clan and the household (Halpern 1991: 52–59; Lemche [1985] also referred to two different kinship units at this level). This suggestion solves the problem, and is worth accepting in general outline. The largest subtribal unit was the clan (the *mishpahot* mentioned in the Samaria ostraca included a large number of villages, but their reference to the founding father [or, in this case, also the mother] was mythical and not a real genealogy, so they were clans), while the smaller units, with which this chapter has dealt, were lineages. However, the biblical term *mishpahah* was probably flexible and described both types of groups.

In any case, even if the crops and produce were the responsibility of a *mishpahah* framework that was sometimes smaller than the entire village (lineage), it is clear that the settlement itself had an organizing framework (the village or *mishpahah* elders). Their activity is reflected in the existence of an overall settlement plan, expressed mainly in the existence of a boundary wall. In settlements that had more than one lineage or *mishpahah*, this matter required a larger organizational framework. This indicates the existence of an institution common to all members of the

---

26. Lineage and clan are similar kinship groups. One of the differences between them is that a clan is based on a mythical connection to an ancestor, while a lineage is based on a real connection to an ancestor. In many cases, the clan is larger and sometimes includes several lineages. On these differences, see Seymour-Smith 1994: 38, 169; Howard 1996: 175, 178; R. Fox 1967: 49–50; Parkin 1997: 17–20. Anthropologists are aware of the lack of terminological clarity; see, for instance, Fried 1970.

settlement, the institution of the village elders, who made decisions for the entire community. We learn about the existence of this body from the written sources as well (see Reviv 1989); also indicative is the fact that the construction of a freestanding boundary wall required use of a the settlement's buildings or resources (including work days).

A settlement (*'ir*) and a kinship group were sometimes viewed as identical, as is well known (e.g., Bendor 1996: 98–107; compare Demsky 1986; Galil 1990). This is expressed in various stories in the Bible. Thus, for instance, Gideon's town, "Ophrah of the Abiezrites" (Judg 8:32), belonged to the Abiezer family. The genealogies also assume this identity, for example, in this description: "The sons of Caleb brother of Jerahmeel: Mesha his firstborn, who was the father of Ziph. The sons of Mereshah father of Hebron" (1 Chr 2:42); and in epigraphic finds (the Abiezer and Halak families are mentioned in the Samaria ostraca; Aharoni 1979, and additional bibliography there). This norm is supported by analysis of the finds in the rural sector during the Monarchy. In this settlement sector, the *mishpahah*-community is indeed identical with the settlement in many cases (for a similar reality in other societies, see Freedman 1958; Chun 1996: 430).

Types of Rural Settlement in the Ancient Near East

Based on studies of the texts from the Alalaḫ archives (level VII), ethnographic observations, and archaeological finds (mainly the study of Magness-Gardiner 1994; compare Falconer 1995), three types of village in the ancient Near East have been described: (1) Villages owned by the palace or the urban elite, who functioned as absentee landlords. The standard of living in these villages was low (mere subsistence), because the profits were diverted to the urban center, where the landlords lived. (2) Private villages, whose owners lived there. Ethnographic studies observed villages of this sort, which consisted of one stone building and several mud huts. These finds may attest a wealthy family that controlled the site.[27] (3) Communal villages in which residents enjoyed a higher standard of living, as indicated by the finds showing relative wealth and a higher construction standard. Falconer excavated Tell el-Hayyat in the Beth Shean valley, and in his opinion, this site (from the Middle Bronze Age) is a communal site (Falconer 1995: 401–2; his exemplary analysis, however, suffers from a lack of comparative material; see Faust 2005a).

In light of this typology, the villages discussed in this chapter (apart from fortress villages, which are discussed in the next chapter) belonged to the third group—that is, they were "communal villages." Large stone houses, large facilities, and "luxuries" such as a boundary wall indicate a standard of living that was clearly higher than mere subsistence, and so there is no reason to assume that these villages belonged to the palace (for such villages belonging to the palace, see chap. 8, below). Nor is there any evidence of large, grand buildings that contrast with the rest of the residential houses, which one would expect in a private village, and all the buildings are large and spacious. These data are in complete contrast to the approach prevalent

27. It is possible, of course, that the central building was inhabited by the representative of the landlord (a wealthy individual or the palace itself), but the distinction is irrelevant to the present discussion.

in research on ancient Israel regarding the rural sector. According to this approach, the villages were inhabited by a poor population that was living merely at subsistence level (e.g., Coote and Whitelam 1987: 111). However, this approach was unfamiliar with the archaeological finds and was based solely on an interpretation of the biblical texts (which do not refer directly to the rural sector) and on anthropological and sociological comparisons.

Large Villages and Farms

We have seen that there were two subtypes of rural settlements that were special because of their size:[28] large villages (townships) and farms. Most of the residents of the large villages were apparently organized into extended families and lived in large four-room houses. These extended families were organized into lineages, as manifest by the existence of several industrial areas—one for each lineage. The large villages were probably inhabited by several *mishpahot*, and so there were probably more differences and struggles compared with small villages, inhabited by only one *mishpahah* (on this sector, see the distinctions of Coote and Whitelam 1987: 114). These settlements, however, had an even larger organizing framework, as evidenced by the walls surrounding some of them, the construction of which required cooperation and decisions made jointly by the various lineages.

Some economic gaps can be identified in these settlements, such as the difference between the two buildings at Kh. Banat Barr. The finds are sparse but indicate that processes of social change were already taking place on this site. Presumably, there were also individuals who did not belong to a lineage in the township, because several agricultural facilities were found not in the concentrations but in private homes.[29] These people may have lived as nuclear families. The differences in building size indicate a certain degree of inequality, in contrast to the situation in smaller villages. It is possible that the very size of the larger villages enabled the development of a more complex economy and the accumulation of wealth by individuals, and perhaps they were also influenced by the kingdom, the impact of which was felt here more than in the "regular" villages.

Most of the farms, like the rest of the rural sites, were inhabited by extended families. According to Safrai, residing in an isolated building is more appropriate to an extended family than a nuclear family (Safrai 1998: 38). The farms were isolated residential buildings on the agricultural plots and were considered part of the form. This quality is also expressed in the jubilee laws in Leviticus (Lev 25:29–32): a house in a walled *ʿir* (usually translated 'town' or 'city' but actually meaning a 'settlement', including a 'village') could be redeemed within a year of its sale, and if a year had passed, this house did not return to its original owners during the jubilee. A different law applied to the "houses of the *haserim* that have no wall around them," which "shall be classed as open country: they may be redeemed, and they shall be released

---

28. Other types of villages are discussed separately: on "fortress villages," see chap. 5, and on non-Israelite villages, see chap. 8.

29. It is likely that similar processes were operating also in "regular" villages, but their impact was much weaker and is not easily identified archaeologically (when compared with other types of settlements).

through the jubile" (Lev 25:31). The explanation "classed as open country" was appropriate to farms that were located in the heart of agricultural plots, where the main "property" was indeed the land rather than the house. The land returned to its owner in the jubilee with the farmhouses (the "houses of the *haserim*") it contained, because they were only appended to the land (for a more detailed discussion, see Faust 2003d; 2009a; 2009b).

Israel and Judah

Most of the villages (such as H. Malta, Kh. Jemein, Kh. Umm Kahal, and Beit Aryeh) were discovered in the Kingdom of Israel. In Judah, fewer villages have been discovered, and because they have been less extensively excavated, our knowledge about them is very limited.[30] On the other hand, most of the "unique" villages—all the "fortress villages"—and most of the typical farms (except for the foothill farms, which are a different case) are known from the Kingdom of Judah. The result is that Israel contained villages and townships, while only a few "ordinary" villages were excavated in Judah, along with many fortress villages and farms. However, at this stage of the research, clear conclusions should not be formed regarding the differences in the nature of rural settlements between the kingdoms of Israel and Judah. The difference between the two kingdoms can be interpreted as the difference between the more "developed" system in the Kingdom of Israel (a system including villages of different sizes) and the "simpler" system in Judah (composed mainly of farms and a few villages; on the differences in the sizes of the settlement systems in the two kingdoms, see chap. 6 below). It is even possible that the relatively large number of fortresses in the Kingdom of Judah is related to the fact that this was a sparse rural area, where the security level was low (see below, chap. 5).

We should also mention that there are special reasons for the discovery of so many settlements in western Samaria and so many farms around Jerusalem. Parts of western Samaria are an ecological fringe region that was not intensively settled in later periods, so the settlements under discussion were well preserved. The Jerusalem area has been extensively developed in recent years, and this has led to many salvage excavations in the area, resulting in the discovery of many farms.[31] Notably, at least one of the reasons for the discovery of many settlements in these regions was the massive development in both the western slopes of Samaria and northern Judea (the area of which the northern boundary is the northern neighborhoods of modern Jerusalem and of which the southern boundary is Gush Ezion) in recent years. However, this does not explain the large number of villages in Israel and the large number of farms in Judah, so the difference requires additional discussion.

---

30. Thus, for example, the village discovered at Kh. Jarish in Judah is very similar to a typical Israelite village, but it is worth asking whether all the houses of the site are uniform. Only one complete residential house was discovered, but were the rooms excavated in the other building part of a four-room house? Or was the situation at Kh. Jarish different from the other villages?

31. The large number of farms resulted from the intensive growth of Jerusalem during the Iron Age and should not be surprising. See Faust 1997; 2003d.

The Development of the Rural Settlement

The settlements of the rural sector were founded in the ninth–seventh centuries B.C.E. and usually were not continuations of settlements from Iron Age I. The renewal of rural settlement in Israel was earlier than in Judah. In Israel, there was significant settlement already in the ninth century and a settlement peak in the eighth century. In contrast, in Judah, significant settlement began only later, and its peak was probably not until the seventh century. However, these are only preliminary conclusions (see more in chap. 9, below).

Chapter 5

Fortified Structures in the Countryside: Between the Military and the Administration

Iron Age II fortified structures, located in the countryside, have long been cited in the scholarly literature. In the past, almost all structures of this type were defined as "fortresses," but it appears that there was some exaggeration in the use of the term. Thus, for instance, thorough research has shown that the structures known today as the "foothill farmsteads" are not fortresses but farms (Hasharon Survey 1973; Finkelstein 1978; 1981), and according to most scholars, the "Negev fortresses" are not fortresses either, at least not in the full sense of the word (see Finkelstein 1985; Meshel 1994; Faust 2006c, and additional bibliography there; but see Cohen 1986; Cohen and Cohen-Amin 2004). However, many structures in the territories of both the Kingdom of Israel and the Kingdom of Judah are still interpreted today as "fortresses." The purpose of the following review is not to provide a detailed, exhaustive description of these structures but to present the phenomenon as evidence for the existence of a state and an army (or at least the core of a permanent military organization; see map 3).

"Real Fortresses"

Kingdom of Israel

The definition "fortress" is appropriate for several sites in the area of the Kingdom of Israel (only a few of which will be described below) for several reasons: they are located at strategic points along important roads rising toward Samaria from the east, they have tactical control over their surroundings, and there is a unique, uniform plan common to all of them (Zertal 1989 and additional bibliography there).

- *el-Makhruq*: In the early Bronze Age, a city was erected at this site, located above the junction between the north—south road (along the Jordan Valley) and the west—east road (along Wadi Far'ah toward the Adam Bridge). Several structures from Iron Age II have survived, of which two have been excavated: a circular structure and a rectangular structure. The circular structure is composed of three concentric stone circles, the diameter of the external one being approximately 19 meters. In a nearby structure (described as a tower), two stages were identified: in the first stage the structure's area was 10 × 15 meters, and in the second stage it was enlarged to the dimensions of 18 × 23 meters (Zertal 1989: 83).
- *Kh. esh Shaqq*: A similar site has been found in a small valley on the boundary between the edge of the Manasseh highland and the Jordan Valley. It

178

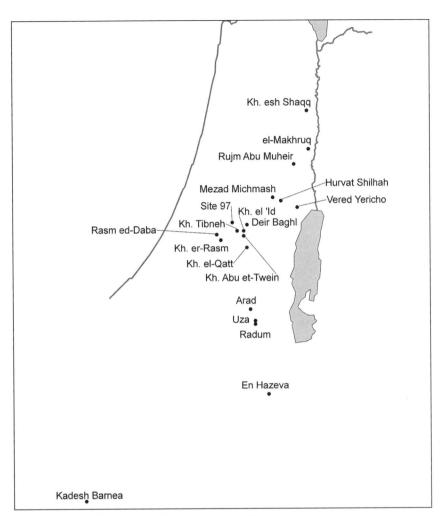

Map 3. Map showing the forts discussed in chap. 5.

also includes a circular structure and a rectangular structure. Their shape and dimensions are similar to those of the structures at the previous site (Zertal 1989: 83–84).

- *Rujm Abu Muheir*: Another similar site was found near the convenient ascent from Phasaelis (Fasayil) to Samaria. The site includes a structure of about 19 meters in diameter, also composed of three concentric circles. It appears that nearby there was a square building completely covered with ancient stoning mounds (Zertal 1989: 84–85).

In this context, we should also mention some fortified sites around the city of Samaria (Zertal 1992: 55; nos. 224, 237–40, 250), known only from a survey. Due to the wall noted around all of them (at least partially), the surveyor assumed that these sites were fortresses that constituted part of the defense system around the city of Samaria (for a more extensive description, see Zertal 1998). However, even without

Photograph 6. The fort at Arad.

ruling out the possibility that some of them were indeed fortresses, we can say that at least some of these sites were villages. As we have seen, many villages had enclosing walls, and the existence of walls does not therefore prove the military nature of a particular site. Despite the paucity of sites that can be considered fortresses with any certainty, their very existence reflects the presence of a state mechanism that constructed them and a permanent army that maintained them. These data indicate the existence of some form of state organization, surplus production, and professional specialization.

Kingdom of Judah

Many more fortresses are known in the Kingdom of Judah. First and foremost, there is a series of sites in the southern part of the kingdom that includes large fortified structures with towers. Several of them existed throughout most of Iron Age II, while some were constructed only in the eighth—seventh centuries B.C.E. Although the ethnic identity of the residents of some of the fortresses is unclear (Naʾaman 1987; Ussishkin 1994: 5), most of them were Judahite, as confirmed by the epigraphic finds in some of them.

- *Arad* (photograph 6): A fort with towers that measures about 50 × 50 meters was built on a salient hill overlooking the Arad valley (Aharoni 1981; Herzog et al. 1984; Herzog 1998). Living quarters, storage rooms, a temple, and a water reservoir have been discovered at the site. It is not only the structure's location, size, and fortifications that indicate its role as a fort but also the ostraca discovered on the site. These letters were sent to the fortress's commander, and they provide a clear picture of the Arad fortress as the military-administrative center of the biblical Negev region during the period under discussion.
- *Kadesh Barnea*: A large fortress (approximately 52 × 34 meters) fortified with towers was unearthed at the southern edge of the Kingdom of Judah (M. Dothan 1963; Cohen 1992; Cohen and Bernick-Greenberg 2007; Ussishkin 1994).
- *En Hazeva*: A sequence of three Iron Age fortresses was discovered on the site, but only two of them are relevant to the present discussion. In the ninth–

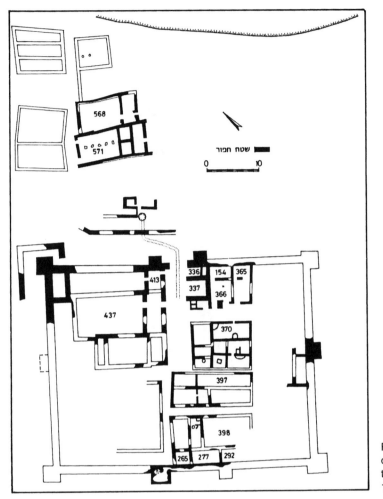

שטח חפור ▬ 0 10

Fig. 34. Kh. Uza: plan of the fortress and the village (Beit-Arieh 1983: 33).

eighth centuries B.C.E. (level 5), a large fortress (approximately 100 × 100 meters) was built that was surrounded by casemate rooms and strengthened by towers. Storerooms, silos, and a massive gatehouse were discovered at the site. Toward the end of the Iron Age (level 4), a smaller, poorly constructed fortress was built, but very few of its remains have been excavated (Cohen and Yisrael 1995; 1996).

- *Hurvat Uza* (fig. 34): A fortress with towers (42 × 51 meters) that probably controlled and guarded the road from the Negev to Edom that passed through the nearby wadi (Beit-Arieh 1986; 1991; 2007).
- *Hurvat Radum* (fig. 35): This fort (perhaps a "subsidiary fort" of Hurvat Uza) probably controlled another section of the road to Edom, which could not be overlooked by the fort at Hurvat Uza (Beit-Arieh 1992; 2007).

All these sites served as fortresses, and in some of them administrative ostraca were found that inform us about the soldiers and military units that were stationed there (e.g., Aharoni 1981; Beit-Arieh 1986).

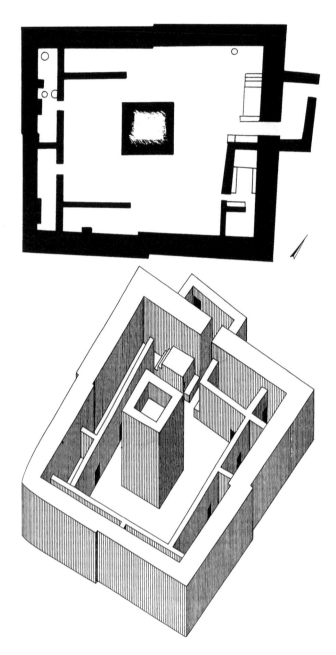

Fig. 35. Kh. Radum: plan and reconstruction (Beit-Arieh 1992: 88).

While the above is sufficient to prove the existence of some sort of state organization in both the Kingdom of Israel and the Kingdom of Judah (see more in chap. 6), I believe there is more that can be learned from an examination of isolated, fortified structures. A number of additional structures that have traditionally been identified as forts were unearthed in the Kingdom of Judah, and it is these structures that I would like to discuss now.

Fortified Structures in the Rural Areas
of the Kingdom of Judah

Description of the Fortified Structures

In addition to the large fortresses (tower fortresses), other sites that have been interpreted as fortresses are known in different parts of Judah: around Jerusalem, on the slopes of Mount Hebron, along the Shephelah, in the Benjamin area and even in the Judean Desert. The partial review below (mainly of sites on the slopes of Mount Hebron, in the Shephelah, and in Benjamin) provides sufficient data for the discussion later.

- *Khirbet Abu et-Twein*: On a hilltop on the slopes of Mount Hebron, a square structure (29.5 × 31 meters) was found that had a central yard surrounded by rooms. In the rooms and in the interior of the structure, parallel to the outer walls, rows of monolithic pillars were unearthed (A. Mazar 1982).
- *Deir Baghl*: A fortified structure, similar to Kh. Abu et-Twein in construction, size (approximately 30 × 30 meters), and plan, including casemate rooms around a square yard (Kochavi [ed.] 1972: 41; A. Mazar 1982).
- *Khirbet Tibnah*: The site is located in the same region. The western half of the fortified structure discovered on the site was well preserved, but its eastern section had been completely eroded. The length of the western wall was about 30 meters, and thus we can surmise that the dimensions of the entire structure were similar to those of the previous fortified building (about 30 × 30 meters). As in Kh. Abu et-Twein, some square monolithic pillars were found (A. Mazar 1982: 105).
- *Khirbet el Qatt*: This structure (30 × 30 meters), discovered in the emergency survey, is similar in plan to the Deir Baghl fort. In its earliest stage, it was a casemate fortress without towers. A few Iron Age II sherds were discovered on the site (Kochavi [ed.] 1972: 50; A. Mazar 1982: 106–7).[1]
- *Khirbet er-Rasm* (in the hill country): This structure was discovered in the emergency survey on the slopes of Mount Hebron (reference point 15021158). The main find is from the Persian period (the survey did not report finds from Iron Age II); however, its dimensions are similar to many Iron Age II fortresses (27 × 29 meters), and its strategic location on a hilltop with a wide view may indicate that it was part of the fortress system during the period of the Monarchy (on the structure, see Kochavi [ed.] 1972: 46; on the fort system, see A. Mazar 1982).
- *Khirbet el ʿId*: At this site, close to Kh. Abu et-Twein, Kh. Tibnah, and Deir Baghl, a large Iron Age II fort was surveyed (55 × 110 meters). The location of the fort between the other three fortified structures and its large dimensions led the surveyor to conclude that this was the area's central fortress (Baruch 1996; 1997).

---

1. According to A. Mazar (1982: 109 n. 17), only Persian period sherds were discovered at this site, but he too assumes that it originated in the Iron Age.

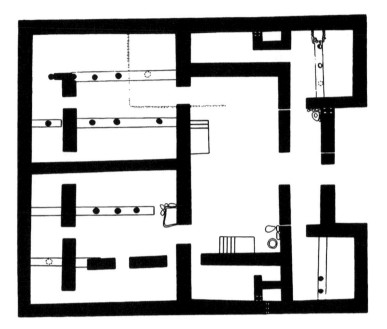

Fig. 36. Vered
Yericho: plan of the
site (Eitan 1983: 43).

- *Site 97*: On this site, an Iron Age II fort was surveyed, measuring about 0.3 hectares (Dagan 1992: 129–30, 247–48).
- *Khirbet Rasm ed-Daba*: At this site, a large Iron Age II fortress was surveyed (Rachmani 1964).
- *Khirbet er-Rasm* (in the Shephelah): A square structure (about 30 × 30 meters) was excavated on a conspicuous hill and appears to have been constructed during Iron Age II as a fort (Faust and Erlich 2011).
- *Hurvat Shilhah*: A large structure was uncovered on a hilltop in the desert fringe of Benjamin. The excavators raised the possibility that it served as a fortress, but they also offered other possible interpretations (Mazar, Amit, and Ilan 1996; see also above).
- *Mezad Michmash*: According to the excavator, the structure that was discovered near an ancient road not far from the previous site is a fortress (Riklin 1995). However, considering the difference between it and the other fortresses, it seems that a different interpretation is more plausible, and it is more likely that it was a farm.
- *Vered Yericho*: The structure uncovered on the site includes two connected four-room houses (10 × 12 meters each), with a yard in front (fig. 36). Although it is clear that the site was planned, it is difficult to evaluate the structure's nature with any certainty (Eitan 1983; for a summary of the sites in the Benjamin and northern Judean Desert region, see Stern 1994).

As we have seen (chap. 4 above), in some of the cases, small settlements, defined as villages, were found at the foot of the fortified structures. These "villages" are different from most of the other villages known from the Iron Age, because they lacked many of the features found in other villages, such as boundary walls, storehouses, communal installations, and other things. The study of these villages is in its infancy, and our knowledge about them is very limited, even compared with our knowledge of the rural sector as a whole. However, it is not groundless to conclude that these villages did not have the communal and organizational systems in place in other villages during the period under discussion. This conclusion should be taken into account in any interpretation of the function of the fortified structures.

The Function of the Fortified Structures
and the Settlements below Them

In contrast to the consensus on the nature of the Judahite tower fortresses, there are other possible interpretations posited for the role of the fortified structures in the rural areas.[2] As we shall see, the first two possibilities (interpreting the structures as farms or as private estates) are not very likely, and the last two options (royal estates or forts) are more likely, and perhaps a combination of both approaches the truth.

Farms. The weakest possibility is that these structures were fortified farmsteads. Many Iron Age farms are known in the land of Israel in general, especially in Judah (for the sites and plans, see above, chap. 4; and also Faust 1997; 2003d), and they are very different from the sites under discussion. These have uniform building plans and, typically, strategic locations (on hilltops) that are also unsuitable for farms. The deciding factor against the interpretation of these structures as farms is that below several of them there were small villages. The location of the villages in relation to the fortified structures and the assessment of their relative areas show that they constituted one system, with the main component being the fortified structure and the secondary or accompanying component being the village; a farm, however, is typically an isolated house in the agricultural area (the biblical *haser*), rather than a large structure with an accompanying village.

Private Estates. Another possible interpretation is that wealthy people lived in the fortified structures and owned the nearby lands; the villages (where they are present) were inhabited by (vassal?) peasants who worked the land for them. In the ancient Near East, villages owned by the palace or by estate owners typically reveal a clear distinction between one of the residences (which was prominent in size and construction quality) and the other buildings. Thus, according to this interpretation, there was a similar distinction between the fortified structure, used as the residence of the landowner or his agent, and the village at its foot. This interpretation has significant implications for the understanding of the agrarian regime and social structure in Judah, because it is based on the assumption of a landless lower class, contrary to the common reality in the rural sector.

However, other data also make this interpretation unlikely. One should note that villages were not found at the foot of all the fortified structures. So where did the landless peasants live who worked the land in fortified structures without villages? Moreover, the uniform construction plan of many of the fortified structures does

---

2. On attempts to interpret the isolated structures in rural areas and on the distinction (in another period) between estates and farms, see Safrai (1998) and additional bibliography there.

not accord with the argument that these were private estates. Were someone to argue that this was mere "fashion" and that the estate owners tended to build similar estates, it should be stressed that, not only is the building style similar, but also the dimensions of the structures are very close.

Royal Estates. The difficulties presented so far in interpreting the structures as private estates do not appear if we interpret them as royal estates, because then the uniformity in building can be understood as resulting from state activity. In this interpretation, the central structures were the residences of the people who cultivated the estate lands, but we are not required to conclude that these workers were landless peasants. They may have been "civilians" brought to the site as corvée laborers (*mas ʿoved*), who lived in the central structure during the fixed duration of their work; the villages developed alongside to provide the people who lived there and the workers with services and family residences (for the officials who resided there), and so forth. This explanation also accords with the fact that villages were not found near all the structures.

Forts. Because there is no doubt about the very existence of forts in the area of Judah (as stated at the beginning of this chapter), we may assume that the Kingdom of Judah operated a military and/or administrative system that built and maintained forts of this sort in locations that needed them. Can the fortified structures also be considered fortresses? This interpretation is most appropriate due to the uniformity of construction and the strategic location on hilltops of the structures under discussion (a location more suitable for forts than for estates). This interpretation also explains the absence of a separate compound for the family residence (if we posit that the structures were farms) or wealthy landowner (if they were private estates) or estate manager (if they were royal estates).[3]

If the fortified structures served as fortresses, perhaps the villages served as residences for the soldiers' families (A. Mazar 1981: 237; Gitert and Amiran 1996: 115; Baruch 1997: 52), for local farmers (A. Mazar 1981: 237), for various service providers and others attracted to the economic potential of the military force and to the security it provided. The heterogeneous nature of this population would explain the lack of evidence for planning and communal organization in these villages. Historical parallels for the formation of villages alongside fortresses are known from many places (Safrai 1994: 346; Crow 1995: 63–73; Birley 1977: 69–79; Faust 1995b: 85–87), and in some cases a market was established (even a tiny one). Because the forts under discussion are quite small, the villages alongside are also of modest proportions.[4] If the villages were a by-product of the activity in the forts, they should not be viewed (socially) as part of the rural sector, although they (like the forts) were located in the countryside.[5]

---

3. The distinction between officer dwellings and soldier barracks is not as necessary as the above distinctions. But perhaps we should also not expect significant differences between the residences of foremen and their workers (compare with the conditions in the slave plantations in the southern United States described by Orser 1988: 737). If such structures are fully excavated, differences may be found in the standard of living within them.

4. In contrast, in many cases, "real" cities developed around Roman military camps.

5. Thus, again, the definition of a village depends on the land usage rather than on the nature of the landscape (chap. 4 above). It is clear that at least some of the villages discussed here belonged to this special

Combination Explanation.   A very likely possibility is that the fortified structures served both as fortresses and as royal estates. This dual responsibility was for cultivating the state-owned lands in the area and for security of the area and its roads. A study of the locations of some of the structures supports this theory. Thus, for instance, Khirbet el ʿId and Deir Baghl are located in sparsely populated areas. This reveals the fact that much of the land in the area was available for cultivation, but it also required a higher level of security. These two sites are located above Wadi Fukin, which contains springs and good soil, and thus it is reasonable to assume that the cultivation of lands in this area was their responsibility. The development of villages below some fortified structures and not below others appears to have resulted from local conditions, the amount of workers, and the amount of land being exploited in each region, and so on.

Discussion

There is no detailed scholarly study of the way that the forts (neither the "real" forts nor the fortified structures) were operated in terms of maintenance and staffing. The only issue discussed in detail is the security aspect, but this is done with exclusive reliance on the Bible, and the nature of the discussion is mainly descriptive and typological.[6] The Bible and the epigraphic finds clearly indicate the existence of a permanent army and of a well-developed administrative system in the eighth—seventh centuries B.C.E. (see also Beit-Arieh 1999a; see also below, chap. 6). The costs involved in maintaining a large regular army were, presumably, too great for small kingdoms,[7] so it is reasonable to assume this was no more than the core of a regular army. However, we presume that, in parallel with the permanent military system (and as backup for it), the kingdoms of Israel and Judah had a wider recruitment system to realize the regime's initiative, such as corvée labor or similar frameworks (Rainey 1968; Artzi 1968; Fritz 1995: 171–74, and references there to biblical and epigraphic sources). These workers and also day laborers were employed in the construction of various public buildings (including the forts) and their maintenance and perhaps also in cultivating fields and orchards that belonged to royal estates.[8] It seems that these workers constituted a pool of human resources for the army (beyond the limited core of permanent officers), and they also staffed the forts in times of peace.

Notably, the main role of the inhabitants of the fortified structures was agricultural work, haulage, and construction.[9] We should remember that, in antiquity,

---

type of settlement, the whole essence of which derived from the fortified structures alongside them. Note, for example, the villages below the forts at Tel Arad and Hurvat Uza, which certainly served as fortresses.

6. Thus, for instance, Yadin 1964. The name of Yadin's article, "The Army Reserves of David and Solomon," largely reflects the time of its writing. The centrality of security issues in modern Israeli society has inevitably influenced scholars (in archaeology, history, and biblical studies) to prefer discussing certain issues rather than others (see Geva 1992).

7. On the organization of the army, compare Reviv 1971.

8. This means that there was not necessarily any need for permanent workers living on site (with the exception of the "managers" or overseers, of course).

9. This was typical of antiquity. Even Roman legionaries, who were certainly professional soldiers, devoted much of their time to construction (Luttwak 1976: 40–41; Tsafrir 1982: 365). Roman legionaries,

training was marginal for most units and did not consume much of their time. Much of the field fighting was conducted by those who were trained for it, that is, the soldiers of the regular army (on battles in open areas, see Yadin 1964: 301–6), but maintenance of the cities and forts did not require much training (on city defense, see Yadin 1964: 311–15; Stern 1964: 404), and the responsibility was borne (certainly during emergencies) by the entire population (see, for instance, the Lachish reliefs; on public life in a besieged city, see Eph'al 1997: 142–50).

The epigraphic finds also hint at the existence of this sort of system. The reaper's letter from Mezad Hashavyahu mentions a serf or worker (as part of corvée labor) who did not fill his quota (Ahituv 1993: 97).[10] Another clue appears on one of the ostraca from Hurvat Uza, which was probably a census list or placement order (Ahituv 1993: 102; Beit-Arieh 1986: 36–37; 1999a; see now also Mendel 2011). The ostracon lists several names with the individuals' places of origin beside their names. Because the settlements mentioned are in the Negev and the Shephelah, these people clearly came to Hurvat Uza from elsewhere. If they were regular soldiers, we would expect the list to include their unit rather than their place of origin (unless the military units were named after settlements, though there is no evidence of this sort of practice). So it is reasonable to assume that these people were not soldiers but civilians who arrived in the context of corvée labor. The fact that people from different places were mentioned on one ostracon (probably intended for the site's officer or superior) reflects an extensive organizational framework, but this was not necessarily an emergency organization (as Beit-Arieh assumed).

Thus it appears that the state system was based on a limited core of regular officers and clerks (Aharoni 1981: 142–48) and on large, changing groups of temporary workers or recruits. These workers performed many roles. Their main occupation was construction and agriculture, but they also, to a limited extent, performed combat duties. Thus, administrative and military roles on all levels were overlapping. The system functioned, of course, not only at the forts but in all the branches of the state system, including in the cities.

Summary

This comparison of Israel and Judah has revealed a clear difference between them with regard to the sites that scholars agree were used as military sites. Sites of this sort uncovered in the Kingdom of Israel are quite small, and it would be more accurate to call them "strongholds" rather than "fortresses." In Judah, larger

---

prepared for field fighting, spent much time in training (probably more than the permanent armies of the Iron Age), while the recruits in the Iron Age did not train at all (or trained very little), so their time was free for other work. This comparison does not ignore the vast differences between the kingdoms of Israel and Judah in the eighth–seventh centuries B.C.E. and the Roman Empire but demonstrates the point: if in the Roman army this was the case, so much more so would it have been in the small armies of the kingdoms of Israel and Judah.

10. For purposes of the sociological discussion, it does not matter if the fortress discovered at this site belonged to the Kingdom of Judah, as most scholars believe (Naveh 1961: 127; Halpern 1991: 63; Ahituv 1993: 96), or not (Na'aman 1987: 12–14).

structures that constituted real "forts" have been found.[11] Moreover, in Judah there is a greater number of these sites compared with Israel. These two differences indicate the differing needs of the two kingdoms. We should remember that more farms are known in Judah compared with Israel, and the absence of central settlements in rural areas, which were settled almost exclusively by farmsteads, may have constituted a security problem that required the construction of forts. While the large "tower forts" are located in the south, facing the desert, there is a concentration of additional fortified structures in Judah on the northwestern slopes of the Hebron hills, an area with only a few villages and farmsteads and no cities (though structures of this sort are known in other regions too).[12] This distribution reveals the importance of security but does not rule out an explanation of a combined function for these structures of both fortress and royal estate.[13]

The state organization of the Kingdom of Judah and probably also the Kingdom of Israel included a military and administrative system that were intertwined. The people recruited for corvée labor were employed in all the tasks that this system was required to complete, from participation in "regular" security to helping with construction projects, the hauling of supplies, and field cultivation. So it appears that, despite the preservation of the traditional structure of society in the rural sector, there were agricultural lands that were also being cultivated in another framework, owned by the monarchy (see further below, chap. 8). The operation of this system required regularly handling a vast surplus of produce, collecting and redistributing it, and performing regular security tasks (it seems unlikely that the fortified structures discussed here were intended to serve in a large-scale war). The fortified structures, located and operated outside the urban centers, were probably similar in nature and function to the public buildings in the cities. Thus it appears that the system discussed here was in fact a branch of the urban sector, located in the countryside.

---

11. In the current state of research, no significant difference can be found between the Judahite fortress systems in the eighth and the seventh centuries B.C.E., but very few of them were built before the eighth century.

12. This region has not been intensively studied by archaeology, and even the survey of the Judean Hills has not reached this area; see Ofer 1998: 41. On the scarcity of settlement in Judah compared with Israel, see Broshi and Finkelstein 1992: 54; and also chaps. 3–4 (above).

13. It is reasonable to assume that this phenomenon occurred in the Kingdom of Israel as well, but it has not been noticed so far by archaeologists due to the scarcity of evidence. An indirect testimony to the existence of royal estates in Israel (at least to a limited degree) may be found in the Samaria ostraca. According to Rainey (1988), the ostraca testify to the parallel existence of two collection systems: the "ordinary" tax system, collecting taxes from "independent" villages; and the king-regent's system, collecting taxes from estates (or at least receiving their produce; see below, chap. 9).

Chapter 6

Political Organization in the Kingdoms
of Israel and Judah

In chaps. 1–5, we have focused on the level of individual settlements. The finds from the various settlements in the kingdoms of Israel and Judah were analyzed in order to assess socioeconomic stratification and to identify elements of social organization in these settlements. On the basis of the accumulated data, various aspects of the overall social structure were discussed. In chap. 6, I intend to expand the discussion of those overall aspects on the basis of the information gathered so far and additional data testifying to the condition of Israelite society; I will concentrate on the eighth century B.C.E., the peak of the development of settlements during the period of the Monarchy.[1]

Archaeological Evidence for the Existence of a State:
General Characteristics

Chiefdom and State

The level of social organization of a given society is usually rated on a scale of complexity ranging from "bands," the simplest, through "tribes" and "chiefdoms" to "states," which are the most complex (see, for example, Service 1962; see also Carniero 1970; H. Wright 1977; Renfrew 1984: 225–45; Renfrew and Bahn 2004: 179–82, 207–20; Earle 1987; Flannery and Marcus 2003; Spencer 2003; Yoffee 2005; Kirch 2010; A. T. Smith 2011; and various essays in Earle [ed.] 1991, and Feinman and Marcus [eds.] 1998; and bibliographical references).[2] For our purposes, it is sufficient to define the difference between the two highest levels, chiefdom and state, and explain how this difference would be expressed in archaeological terms. Renfrew, for example, listed 20 features of a chiefdom that can be identified archaeologically, including evidence for a system for redistributing resources, social ranking, cen-

---

1. In most regions of Judah, the seventh century was the settlement peak of the Iron Age, but discussion of the eighth century allows a comparative examination of the situation in both kingdoms.

2. There are additional subdivisions for different types of state, and there is no consensus among scholars regarding the various definitions or their importance. For our purposes in this chapter, a general reference to the developmental scheme generally accepted by current scholars will suffice. It is also worth noting that, while classification into various development levels is convenient for research, in reality most political entities fail to match the categories precisely but belong to intermediate states between the ideal types. In any case, this is not a unilinear evolutionary scheme that requires, for instance, that every chiefdom will eventually develop into a state. Reality is more complex: many chiefdoms do not become states, and sometimes they even disintegrate. However, despite these reservations regarding the terms *state* and *chiefdom*, they are still accepted in research and will be used in this chapter.

tral settlements, a rise in the status of the priesthood, specialization, special status symbols for senior officials, and more (Renfrew 1984: 225–45; compare Renfrew and Bahn 2004: 214; for an attempt to identify a chiefdom in the land of Israel during the Chalcolithic period from an archaeological point of view, see T. E. Levy 1986). Some of these features are also characteristic of a state, and it seems that the main differences between the two levels relate to the nature of social hierarchy and the level of administration (see also Renfrew and Bahn 2004: 207–20; Finkelstein 1989: 47, and additional bibliography there). Administration in a chiefdom is based on the chief's entourage (often his relatives). The ruling mechanism is simple and is influenced by society's tendency to split. In other words, in a chiefdom, there is no organized framework of ruling and no system to enforce the ruler's decisions.

The administration of a state, in contrast, is based on a complex system of specialized officials who are not necessarily blood relations of the ruler. The ruling mechanism tends toward centrality, in order to enable the regime to support its decisions with force (Renfrew and Bahn 2004: 180–81). Society in a chiefdom is also differentiated, of course, but differences are based mainly on genealogy, whereas society in states is usually stratified, and social classes emerge (compare Renfrew and Bahn 2004: 179). Let us now discuss a few signs that indicate the existence of a state (in the sense of the most complex level of social organization), which to a large extent are phenomena that result from the operation of a complex administrative system and that can be identified materially.

As already noted, many scholars used different definitions for the various "types" of states (such as Classen and Skalnik 1978). While various divisions and definitions of early states are abundant, for our purposes, as we shall see, the typology of Lenski and Lenski (1974: 207–62), which distinguishes different types of agrarian societies, seems most useful. I must stress, however, that the terminology is less significant, and the important thing is to identify and understand the social processes involved, no matter what we call them.

Public Buildings

Public buildings, the construction of which requires a great investment of resources (especially human resources), reflect a phenomenon known as conspicuous consumption. Because human behavior is usually dictated by efforts to save resources and energy, extravagant waste (mainly through employing other people) symbolizes power (see Bunimovitz 1992: 225, and bibliography there; compare Whitelam 1986). Thus, monumental architecture represented the power of the ruler; the employing lower classes in their construction aimed at glorifying him, showing them their place on the social scale, and stressing their inferiority (Trigger 1990). Many studies have shown that societies that constructed monumental buildings were stratified societies, and thus the identification of these buildings testifies to the society's structure (Rathje and McGuire 1982: 709). However, Bunimovitz has presented examples of the existence of public works in societies that were not states but were chiefdoms, or in societies that were not stratified (Bunimovitz 1992: 226; Renfrew and Bahn 2004: 204). It is therefore necessary to examine the public works case by case and to ask whether real experts were required for their construction (compare Bunimovitz 1992). If the answer is negative, it is possible that the society that constructed them was closer to a chiefdom; but if it is positive and there is reason to believe that a complex administrative system was behind their construction, this indicates that the social framework was a state (on Iron Age II, see Finkelstein 1996b: 177; Dever 1995: 423; for a general discussion, see for example Wason 1994: 146–49).

Various types of public work have been discovered in most of the cities in the land of Israel—first and foremost the cities' fortifications and gates. Monumental walls and/or gates were built in Jerusalem, Beth-Shemesh, Beersheba, Dan, Hazor, Megiddo, Mizpah (Tell en-Nasbeh), Gezer, Lachish, Tel ʿEton, and other cities. The massive walls discovered in all the cities are in stark contrast to the poor walls we find in the villages. It transpires that the nature of the construction reflects the social context: defensive city walls were constructed as an initiative of the regime, while village boundary walls were set up as a local enterprise. Most cities also contained impressive water systems (Jerusalem, Beth-Shemesh, Beersheba, Hazor, Megiddo, Gibeon, Gezer, and others) and usually also other public buildings of various types, such as storehouses, "governor's residences," palaces, fortresses, and so on. The public nature of these works, their vast extent, the quality of their construction, and their geographic distribution all clearly reflect a state rather than a chiefdom, as we have already deduced in the previous chapters. These various types of structure were part of the royal construction. Their typical grandeur implies that their planning was not conducted at the level of the local settlement, and the administrative functions they reflect represent a superurban interest. The presence of the public works implies that the cities of the kingdoms of Israel and Judah served as state centers during the period of the Monarchy, and the Monarchy felt responsible for them in military-security terms by establishing fortifications (walls and gates) and planning for supplies (storehouses and water systems). State investment is apparent, in differing degrees, in all the urban settlements (see also Herzog 1997a: 276), and it does not reflect concern for individual citizens but for the system itself: the grand buildings (in Hazor, for example) probably served the senior officials, and the storehouses stored produce belonging to the kingdom. Public works are also indicative of social stratification. At the lower end of the social scale were those who actually built the walls (day laborers, forced workers, and perhaps even slaves), and at the upper end were those who lived in the grand houses and enjoyed the public works (more below).

Fortresses

The existence of military fortresses also implies a developed administrative system, or more precisely, the military aspect of this system. As we have seen, the two kingdoms maintained systems of fortresses, and the state character of these systems is reflected in the uniformity of their construction, in their geographical distribution, and in the administrative documents found inside some of them. The fortresses were not only constructed and maintained, like other public works; they were also staffed with soldiers (and officials) who received their "salaries" from the state. A military system is composed, at least to some extent, of people who are not food producers, and its very existence implies a system of collecting surplus in the form of taxes, meaning extensive personnel and employment stratification. While it is possible that some of the people staffing the fortresses were corvée laborers who produced food, each fortress contained at least a skeleton crew of regular, nonproductive army personnel. In Arad, for instance, the epigraphic finds show that there was even a mercenary army that had its needs met by the state (Aharoni 1981). Nor should we ignore in this context the fact that fortresses (outside the settlements) first appeared throughout the land of Israel in the period under discussion. This phenomenon is not attested before (apart from Egyptian fortresses), and the very appearance of the fortresses with their provision of security for wide areas (not just the cities and their immediate surroundings, as in the past) resulted from the establishment of territorial kingdoms in the land of Israel. In addition, the fortresses imply a system capable of supporting the ruler's decisions with force (which does not happen in a chiefdom).

Administrative Documents and Epigraphic Evidence

The most obvious product of a complex administrative system is bureaucratic paperwork. Administrative documents (or other relevant epigraphic finds) have been discovered in sites that served as administrative centers—cities and fortresses—and are mostly dated to the eighth–seventh centuries B.C.E. The relative prevalence of written documents and their wide distribution in the various sites shows that various scribes were active during this period (for a collection of inscriptions, see Aḥituv 1993; 2005), and from this we may deduce the existence of scribal schools, which were an integral part of any administrative system (see for example Jamison-Drake 1991: 35). According to Jamison-Drake, the very existence of literacy in society, which was common (in parts of the population) at least in the eighth century B.C.E. (Dever 1995: 426; Demsky 1997: 366, and additional bibliography there), also implies a stratified social structure (Jamison-Drake 1991: 37). Here are some examples.

The Samaria ostraca (Israel, ninth–eighth centuries). Most scholars believe that the 63 ostraca found in the royal complex in Samaria are from the second half of the ninth century or the first half of the eighth century B.C.E. The Samaria ostraca were most likely some sort of receipt for agricultural produce, although there is debate regarding their exact nature, such as whether they originated with the officials and tax collectors who collected the produce or with the estate owners who sent it to the palace (or perhaps others). But most scholars agree that the contents of the documents and the location of their finds reflect some sort of taxation system (e.g., Yadin 1960; Aharoni 1979; Rainey 1988; see also chap. 5 and chap. 9).

The lmlk *('To the King') Seal Impressions* (Judah, late eighth century). Stamps with a place-name (Ziph, Socho, Hebron, or *mmšt*), a symbol (probably royal), and the inscription *lmlk* ('to the king') were found on the handles of large storage jars unearthed throughout the Kingdom of Judah (see, e.g., Ussishkin 1976; 1977; Naʾaman 1979; Rainey 1981; Garfinkel 1984; Vaughn 1999).[3] Sometimes names of

---

3. Recently, Lipschits et al. (2010; see also Lipschits et al. 2011) attempted to challenge the late-eighth-century dating of some of the impressions. This is a problematic suggestion and was already rejected by a

individuals, perhaps officials, were also stamped (Garfinkel [1984] discussed various interpretations, all of which are somewhat problematic due to the size and nature of the sample). Presumably the jars were part of preparations made in Judah for the military campaign of Sennacherib in 701 B.C.E. (e.g., Naʾaman 1979). Opinions are divided over the exact nature of the system that produced and used these jars (see, e.g., Rainey 1981; Vaughn 1999), but their distribution and the contents of the inscriptions most likely imply an administrative system that handled the collection of the jars and their contents, concentrated, stored, and distributed them for use.

The Lachish Letters (Judah, seventh century).   The contents of the ostraca discovered in stratum II at Lachish concern administrative and military matters. The documents, for example, refer to officials in the military administration stationed at different sites (Torczyner et al. 1938; Aḥituv 1993: 31–54; 2005: 50–82).

The Arad letters (Judah, seventh century).   These ostraca, the Arad letters, deal with matters of military administration and probably belonged to the commander of the fortress at Arad (Aharoni 1981; Aḥituv 1993: 54–96; 2005: 82–143).

Lists from Hurvat Uza and Tel ʿIra (Judah, seventh century).   According to Aḥituv, the list of names on two ostraca from H. Uza is indicative of administrative-military correspondence (Aḥituv 1993: 102–4; 2005: 156–61). Another ostracon published recently lists individual names under the title "ten," which appears to be a basic military unit (Beit-Arieh 1999a; Aḥituv 2005: 161–63). An ostracon discovered at Tel ʿIra contains a list of names under the title "census" and thus constitutes an administrative document (Beit-Arieh 1983; Aḥituv 2005: 169).

Settlement Hierarchy

Another sign of a state and of social organization is the existence of a developed settlement hierarchy, meaning a sequence of settlements of varying sizes (Renfrew and Bahn 2004: 183, and more below).[4] As we shall see in detail below, in both Israel and Judah there was such a hierarchy, which is manifested by the existence of large capital cities, central administrative cities, provincial towns, townships, villages, and farms.

Socioeconomic Stratification

In previous chapters, we tried to quantify the size and quality of structures in different settlements by using the Lorenz Curve in order to engender conclusions regarding socioeconomic stratification. These data can also serve us in examining the degree of stratification in all of Israelite society (Israel and Judah), while paying attention to the differences between the urban and rural sectors.[5] The basic datum is

number of scholars (see Ussishkin 2011 for a detailed refutation; see also Barkay 2011: 170; note that additional points can be raised against the new theory, but this is beyond the scope of the present monograph).

4. Because most scholars view urbanization as synonymous with a state-level society (e.g., Childe 1950; R. G. Fox 1977: 24; M. E. Smith 2009; and many bibliographical references; for a summary and reference of different views, see also Cowgill 2004), the mere existence of Iron Age cities can indicate that Israel and Judah were states.

5. For details regarding the data, see the appendix to this chapter. For technical reasons, our analysis included all the buildings for which we possessed data up to the time of calculation, which was toward the end of 1997. Since then, more buildings have been added (mainly in the rural sector), but they are similar

the size of the buildings, to which we added the quality of the buildings. The results yield a number that expresses the "inequality index."

The inequality index is an economic value calculated on the basis of family income data. Because we cannot know the income level of Israelite families in Iron Age II, we used the datum of building size during this period as a substitute. This alternative datum slightly skews the inequality level downward, and presumably, if we possessed income data the inequality level would be even higher than the results (which are quite high) obtained in our analysis.

We compared the quality of the buildings with the basic datum of their size. For this purpose, all the buildings were divided into two groups: high-quality buildings (nicely built) and low-quality buildings (crudely built).[6] We discover a gap when the nicely-built buildings are concentrated high up on the graph of building size (meaning that they are large), and the crudely-built buildings are concentrated at the bottom of the graph (meaning that they are small). In order to ascertain the full significance of these comparisons, we must note the degree of overlap between the groups. The smaller the overlap between the two groups, the more significant the status differences are that they reflect, and vice versa: the greater the overlap, the more blurred the status differences become.

In practical terms, a "large overlap" means, for example, that there are high-quality and low-quality buildings of all sizes, while a "small overlap" means that the high-quality buildings are usually (or almost always) also the especially large buildings, while the low quality buildings are small. If the overlap is large, there is no clear pattern regarding dispersal of the variable datum over the fixed datum, and the graph cannot be used to learn about the degree of wealth or poverty. If the overlap is small, there is a clear concentration of the variable datum at one end (or the other) of the basic datum, and the existence of social polarization can be deduced.

According to the results we obtained, the index of inequality for the entire society is 0.246. As a comparison, the inequality index in modern Israeli society is about 0.3 (for the late 1990s; information received from Prof. Silver). This is a rather high value, and it was obtained without including in the calculation the area of the palaces of the royal families and their entourage; had we included the "upper percentile," the gap would have been even larger. It also transpired that there was a noticeable difference between the urban sector and the rural sector: the inequality index in the cities was 0.233, while in the rural areas it was only 0.126.[7] This means that the socioeconomic gaps in the cities were much starker than in the countryside.

---

to the previous buildings, so their exclusion from the calculation did not distort the results. I am grateful to Prof. Jack Silver of the Department of Economics at Bar-Ilan University, who processed the data. Responsibility for errors, either in the data themselves or in their analysis, is mine alone.

6. Of course, this division is somewhat simplistic. It is possible to note an intermediate group of "less-nicely-built" buildings (compare with the distinction of three groups of buildings at Tell en-Nasbeh in chap. 3), but for our purposes here, this was unnecessary, and in any case, our analysis showed clearly that the decisive parameter is the size. On the axis referring to the buildings' size, the group of nicely built buildings is distinct from the rest of the buildings. For the grading of the buildings, see the discussion in chap. 3 above.

7. The inequality in the rural group is slightly larger than expected, because we calculated all the finds from the rural sector, including, for example, the farmhouse from the Hebron hills, the area of which is

In analyzing the degree of inequality in the urban sector, we examined the results of the calculations in the group of high-quality (nicely-built) buildings separately from the low-quality buildings (all the rest). Within each of the two groups, the inequality index was low (0.17 in the nicely built group of structures, compared with 0.152 in the other group), and this datum shows a general correlation between a building's quality and its size. It also transpired that the degree of overlap between the groups was very low, amounting to only 0.003. This means that, according to all the comparisons, the buildings are clearly and sharply distinguished: on the one hand are the largest buildings (average area of 138.7 square meters), which are also the better-built buildings; and on the other hand are the smaller buildings (average area of 65.4 square meters), which are also the crudely built ones.[8] These results indicate a serious degree of inequality and the existence of a distinct social elite.

Israel and Judah

It is clear from the discussion above that the social organization in both Israel and Judah can be considered a "state" and that both kingdoms reveal clear indications of social stratification and economic polarization. However, many data indicate that the two kingdoms were not identical in social character.

Social Stratification

Lenski and Lenski divided agrarian societies into two types: advanced and simple (Lenski and Lenski 1974: 207–62). One of the differences between the two types is that in a simple agrarian society there are only two socioeconomic strata: a very limited wealthy class, and a very widespread poor class (1974: 216–17). In an advanced agrarian society, there are more social strata (1974: 241–48). As we have seen, the architectural data of the buildings in the urban sector indicated economic inequality and social stratification in both Israel and Judah. However, a more detailed analysis, presented below in graph form, shows that the nature of the stratification in the two kingdoms was not identical.[9]

---

about 300 square meters. Although such a datum is enough to affect the results significantly, this building does not represent a very high standard of living, despite its size, and perhaps its inclusion and comparison with the other buildings created a bias.

8. Another comparison was made between building size and the degree of wall-sharing, and here, too, the buildings were divided into two groups: buildings that shared walls with other buildings and buildings with separate walls. The results of this test were less unequivocal. The average area of the buildings with shared walls was 74.43 square meters, and of the buildings with separate walls 106.7 square meters (a much smaller difference than in the previous comparison); the overlap was relatively high: 0.032. But it is likely that the mismatch between the expected result and the actual result stems from problems with the usage of the data. Thus, for instance, the "governor's house" at Beersheba was defined as a building with shared walls; but, if the buildings it was joined to were public buildings, its inclusion in this category was unjustified. So it is possible that the large size of this building (250 square meters) skewed the results and reduced the gap between the different groups.

9. The limitations of these graphs were discussed above, in chap. 3. The inclusion of several settlement systems on the same graph may blur the differences between groups, but it seems permissible to weight the data and present them on graphs that include more than one settlement, due to the great similarity in the area and form of the buildings in the different settlements (and not just within the same settlement) and also due to the fact that they clearly belonged to the same social system.

The Kingdom of Judah. Graph 17 reflects the architectural finds from the cities of the Kingdom of Judah: Tell Beit Mirsim, Mizpah (Tell en-Nasbeh), Beth-Shemesh, and Tel Beersheba. The upper line is a curve calculating the cumulative grade of the buildings, while the second (lower) line reflects only the grade of the buildings. According to the graph, almost all the buildings are more or less identical, but toward the end of the graph there is a sudden jump in the quality and size of the buildings.[10] This is clear evidence that in the Judan cities we can identify severe polarization between two classes: the small, wealthy, upper class; and the poor lower class that was much larger; but there was no middle class. This state of affairs is typical of simple agrarian societies (Lenski and Lenski 1974: 216–17).

The Kingdom of Israel. Graph 18 is the architectural finds from the cities of the Kingdom of Israel: Hazor, Tirzah (Tell el-Farʿah, north), and Shik-

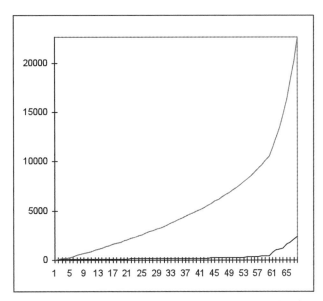

Graph 17. The Kingdom of Judah: differences in the quality of buildings.

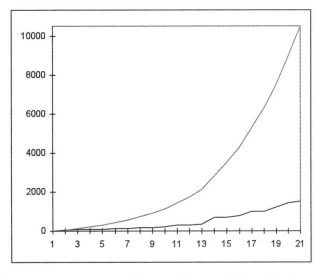

Graph 18. The Kingdom of Israel: differences in the quality of buildings.

mona. The fact that the graph is very concave indicates severe stratification; however, the absence of sharp jumps shows that in the Kingdom of Israel there was more of a

10. Despite the relative similarity within the large group of small buildings, it contains larger differences than the entire rural sector. This issue also indicates that, despite the relative nature of differences observed in the curve (meaning the inability to deduce the "quantity" of stratification based on the various analyses), one can conclude, first, that there was great equality in the rural sector, and second, that stratification in the cities is certainly apparent.

socioeconomic continuum, and it contained a middle class. This situation is typical of advanced agrarian societies (Lenski and Lenski 1974: 241–48).

Settlement Hierarchy

Both kingdoms had a developed settlement hierarchy, from large capital cities (Samaria, Jerusalem), through central administrative cities (Hazor, Megiddo, Gezer, Lachish), to smaller administrative towns (Beersheba), provincial towns (Tell Beit Mirsim, Mizpah [Tell en-Nasbeh], and perhaps also Tirzah [Tell el-Farʿah, north]), down to townships, villages, and farms. The very existence of such a developed settlement hierarchy clearly indicates the highest level of social organization and stratification (Renfrew and Bahn 2004: 183; see further below).

The wealth of data enables us to follow many archaeological studies that borrow theories from the discipline of geography (such as Grant [ed.] 1986; Bunimovitz 1988; 1990). For our purposes, two geographical models that explain various types of urban hierarchy are important (compare Efrat 1995: 68–75). The first model, known as the "Law of the Primate City," refers to the phenomenon whereby the largest city in a polity (the primate city) is often several times larger than the next city after it in the ranking (Jefferson 1939; the term "law" is somewhat misleading, because this is actually a phenomenon observed in many cases, not a law).

The second model, known as "rank-size distribution," examines the entire settlement hierarchy. According to this model, if one arranges the cities in a polity in decreasing order of population, a certain ratio can be found obtained between a city's size and its place in the ranking: the second city will have half the population of the largest city, the third city will have one-third of this population, and so on (e.g., Zipf 1941).

It appears that the "primate city" model provides a suitable description of the urban hierarchy in undeveloped states and/or states in which the level of urban development is low (Gibbon 1984: 294–98; E. Jones 1990: 7–11; a similar phenomenon can occur with the capital of an empire, but the reason for this is similar), while the "rank-size distribution" model characterizes industrial states and those with advanced urban development (Efrat 1995: 73).[11]

The transition from a state fitting the "primate city model" to a ratio appropriate to the "rank-size distribution" depends on several factors, such as the duration of the urbanization process and the complexity of the economic and political systems. In young, simple urban societies, there are fewer forces and factors pulling toward the "rank-size distribution" model, and the urban hierarchy obtained will be similar to the "primate city model," with clear gaps in the settlement continuum. As the process of urbanization continues, and societies become larger and more complex, the number of forces pulling toward the "rank-size distribution" model increases; settlements of all sizes are formed, and the graph is "completed" (Gibbon 1984: 294–98).

---

11. On the possible existence of several settlement ranks in an advanced agrarian state, see Lenski and Lenski 1974: 234; this generalization is not an inflexible law, but because it turns out to be correct in most cases, this is reason enough to "warrant looking for explanations for exceptions to the rule" (E. Jones 1990: 10).

Although the geographical studies that discuss this phenomenon refer to modern states, it appears that the logic behind the generalizations is also true for earlier periods (see Gibbon 1984: 294–98). However, application of the geographical models to the current context requires us to adapt the method to the available archaeological data. The basic datum for geographers is the number of residents, but due to the difficulty of calculating the number of residents in ancient sites (Gibbon 1984: 234), archaeologists prefer settlement size data. Nevertheless, most archaeologists agree that there is a high correlation between area and population, at least within the same culture. The population density in relation to the built-up area can vary greatly from culture to culture, but within one culture we may assume a general similarity in area use and density within settlements of the same magnitude (there are, of course, differences between different settlement sectors, but in examining the settlement ranking here, we only took into account the largest settlements; see more below). This is the premise behind most studies that deal with ancient demography (Broshi and Gophna 1984; 1986; Broshi and Finkelstein 1992, and additional bibliography there; this is not the place to discuss the many problems associated with this premise). From a methodological point of view, it is worth noting that this analysis is based on the assumption that all the settlements existed in the same period (in this case, the eighth century B.C.E.)[12] and constituted part of one regional system (political or economic; Gibbon 1984: 221–25). Including different systems or ignoring part of a system may also lead to significant errors and deviations.[13]

Attempting to calculate the area of a multiperiod settlement at each stage of its existence is very difficult. This problem exists to a great extent in the sites excavated, because in many cases the excavated area is quite limited, but it is critical in sites that were merely surveyed. Many surveyors have debated this problem, but it still has no accepted answer (for example, Ofer 1998: 42–43). However, despite the difficulty in estimating the area of unexcavated sites, clearly one cannot make do only with data from excavations, because only some of the large sites have been excavated, and analyzing them alone would create a serious distortion in the results (in contrast to Jamison-Drake 1991: 9). Therefore, there is no alternative but to use data from surveys (where possible, using data supplied by the surveyors themselves). Fortunately, many of the largest sites have been excavated sufficiently for us to estimate their size during the period under discussion, while the deviation in the smaller sites is not significant for the calculations. The lists below include mainly the urban sites with an area above 2.5 hectares; sites with smaller area are noted only if they are discussed in this book. For purposes of the analysis, the 20 largest sites in each kingdom were chosen from the list (smaller sites are not significant), and the data were processed in graphs to compare them with the "models" described. We should note that we possess more information on the Kingdom of Judah, because

---

12. Mid-eighth century for Israel, and late eighth century for Judah.
13. On the importance of setting boundaries for the various calculations, see Kletter 1995: 31–37. Although one can argue about the exact boundaries of Israel and Judah, there is no disputing the attribution of the large cities considered in the current calculation. The contemporaneous existence of the sites is clear from the results of the surveys and especially the excavations. So it is clear that the study's data meet these methodological requirements.

Table 12. Cities in the Kingdom of Israel [a]

Site	Area (hectares)	Source of Data	Comments
Samaria	60	Barkay 1992: 320; Broshi and Finkelstein 1992: 51	Some believe the area of the city to be about 7.5 hectares (*NEAEHL*), while Herzog (1997a: 229) believes its area was 40–50 hectares.
Dan	20	*NEAEHL*	Compare Broshi and Finkelstein 1992: 50
Gezer	13	*NEAEHL*	According to Shiloh (1981: 279), the site's area is about 10.8 hectares.
Shimron	12	Kempinski 1989: 9	According to Raban (1982: 70), who surveyed the region, the tell's area is 15 hectares.
Hazor	12	*NEAEHL*	Area of the upper tell; compare Broshi and Finkelstein 1992: 50
Dor	10	Broshi and Finkelstein 1992: 53	The excavation report (Stern 1996: 9) says the tell's area is about 500 × 500 meters, which is much larger than 10 hectares. But an examination of the tell's plan indicates that the lower estimate is correct.
Kh. Bel'ameh (Ibleam)	9	Zertal 1992: 114	Compare with the salvage survey data of Gophna and Porat 1972: 210.
Tirzah (Tell el-Far'ah, north)	8	Zertal 1996: 383	According to Stern and Aḥituv (1982: 937), the site's area is about 18 hectares; compare Manor's area calculation (Manor 1992: 574)
Megiddo	6	*NEAEHL*	
Dothan	6	Shiloh 1981: 279	The area of the tell's peak is about 4 hectares, and with the slopes, about 10 hectares. Iron Age II was the time of the settlement's peak, and it was probably entirely settled (*NEAEHL*).
Abel Beth Maacha	6	Broshi and Finkelstein 1992: 50	
Shechem	5	Shiloh 1981: 279	
Tel Qarney Hittin	5	Gal 1990: 61[b]	An area of about 5 hectares was walled in Iron Age II.
Tel Gath Hepher	5	Gal 1992a: 18	
Tel Hannathon	5	Gal 1992a: 23	

Table 12. Cities in the Kingdom of Israel [a]

Site	Area (hectares)	Source of Data	Comments
Tel Ein Hadda	5	Gal 1992a: 33	
Ta'anach	4.5	*NEAEHL*	
Tel Rechesh	4.5	Gal 1992a: 31	
Jericho	4	*NEAEHL* (Hebrew edition)	
Beth Shean	4	*NEAEHL*	
Jokneam	4	*NEAEHL*	
En Gev	3	*NEAEHL*	The tell's area is about 120 × 250 meters.
Kh. Marjameh	3	*NEAEHL*	
Tel Adami-Hanneqeb	2.5–3	Gal 1990: 54; 1992: 35	
Kinrot	0.8	*NEAEHL*	In the ninth–eighth centuries B.C.E., the walled settlement area was only about 0.8 hectares.
Shikmona	0.8	Elgavish 1994: 28	

a. One site, Tell Aphek, has been removed from the list. According to Kochavi (1989a: 15), the area of the tell is around 12 hectares, but the eighth century B.C.E. remains are very sparse (ibid., 90). Broshi and Finkelstein (1992: 53) also excluded the area of this site in their calculations.

b. The size is not indicated in the English version of the book, and this is why I refer here to the Hebrew edition.

most of its area has been surveyed (on Benjamin, see Magen and Finkelstein 1993; on the Shephelah, see Dagan 1992; 2000; and elsewhere; on the Judean Hills, see Ofer 1993 and elsewhere), in contrast to the Northern Kingdom, which has been studied less. Thus, we still do not possess data from comprehensive surveys in the valleys, but because all the large sites in these regions are known, this is not a real problem (the data are taken from reports the of excavators or surveyors; or from the *New Encyclopedia of Archaeological Excavations in the Holy Land* [= *NEAEHL*]; and from appendix 3/a in Ofer 1993). Only the largest sites contributed to the final form of the graphs, while small deviations in the areas of the medium or small sites (from the following list) are not really reflected in the graphs.

The first analysis includes the finds from the Kingdom of Israel. The uniform concave graph (graph 19, dotted line) represents the urban ranking predicted by the "rank-size distribution," when the largest city is 60 hectares large (the presumed size

Table 13. Cities in the Kingdom of Judah

Site	Area	Source of Data	Comments
Jerusalem	60	Faust 2005b, and references	According to Barkay (1988), the city's area at the end of the period reached 90–100 hectares, but it is likely that before the process of growth ended, its area was smaller.
Lachish	7	Herzog 1992b: 258	This was the area only in Iron Age II. The site's area, including slopes, is about 12.4 hectares. Shiloh (1981: 279) mentions a figure of 15 hectares.
Tel ʿEton	6	Broshi and Finkelstein 1992: 52; Dagan 1992: 63, 235; Faust 2011c	
Gibeon	6	Feldstein et al. 1993: 315	
Kh. Rabud	6	NEAEHL	Compare Ofer 1993: appendix.
Tel Socho	6	Dagan 1992: 134	
Tel Livnin	5.5	Dagan 1992: 151	
Keilah	5	Broshi and Finkelstein 1992: 52	According to Dagan (1992: 83), the site's area is about 5.5 hectares.
Azekah	4.5	Dagan 1992: 28, 107	According to Shiloh (1981), the site's area is about 5.6 hectares.
Tel Zorah	4.5	Dagan 1992: 78	
Beth-Shemesh	4	Shiloh 1981: 279	Dagan (1992: 83) states an area of 4.5 hectares, while according to NEAEHL, the site's area is 3.8 hectares.
Ras et-Tawil	3.9	Ofer 1993: appendix	
Hebron	3.6	Ofer 1993: appendix	
Idna	3.5	Dagan 1992: 179	Broshi and Finkelstein (1992: 52) estimate the area at 3–4 hectares.
Tel Tekoa	3.5	Ofer 1993: appendix	
Tel Adullam	3.5	Dagan 1992: 141	
Tel Burna (Burnat)	3.5	Dagan 1992: 154	

Table 13. Cities in the Kingdom of Judah

Site	Area	Source of Data	Comments
Mizpah (Tell en-Nasbeh)	3.2	NEAEHL (Hebrew edition)	This is the walled area; compare Shiloh: 1981.
Tel Goded	3.2	Dagan 1992: 42, 155	Dagan notes that another 1.5 hectares of remains are spread on the slopes; according to NEAEHL, the site's area is about 2.5 hectares.
Tell Beit Mirsim	3.0	NEAEHL	Compare Shiloh 1981: 279; according to Dagan (1992: 238), the site's area is about 6.0 hectares.
Tel Zanoah	2.5	Dagan 1992: 92	
Kh. el-Qom	2.5	Dagan 1992: 190	
Tel Maresha	2.4	NEAEHL	This datum is estimated on the basis of the Hellenistic city (the tell's area is 150 × 150 meters); compare Dagan 1992: 45, 162. The city's eighth-century existence is evidenced by the *lmlk*-stamps found there; see Garfinkel 1984: 35.
Beersheba	1.1	NEAEHL	

of the city of Samaria, the capital of Israel). The lower graph (graph 19, continuous line) represents the actual urban ranking in the Kingdom of Israel on the basis of table 12.

The second analysis includes the finds from the Kingdom of Judah. Here, too, the uniform concave graph (graph 20, dotted line) represents the settlement hierarchy predicted by the "rank-size distribution" model, where the largest city refers to the presumed size of Jerusalem, the capital of Judah, meaning an area of 60 hectares. The second graph (graph 20, continuous line) represents the actual hierarchy in the late eighth century B.C.E.

The difference between the graphs is clearest when they are compared with each other. The upper graph (graph 21, continuous line) represents the settlement hierarchy in the Kingdom of Israel, while the lower graph (graph 21, dotted line) represents the hierarchy in the Kingdom of Judah. The size of the capital cities of Israel and Judah (in the eighth century) is quite similar. On the eve of its destruction, Samaria occupied an area of about 60 hectares, and Jerusalem reached a similar size on the eve of Sennacherib's campaign (in the seventh century B.C.E., the city was probably even larger; Barkay 1988; Faust 2005b, and references).

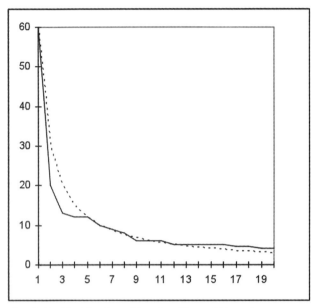

Graph 19. The Kingdom of Israel: settlement hierarchy

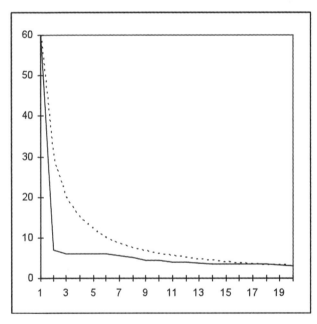

Graph 20. The Kingdom of Judah: settlement hierarchy

The cities at the bottom of the ranking in both kingdoms are quite small. However, there is a significant difference between the two kingdoms regarding the ratio of the capital city to the other cities. The central cities in the Kingdom of Israel are larger than their counterparts in the Kingdom of Judah, and there seems to be a marked difference between the two kingdoms.[14]

Although the general framework of the graphs is identical (the upper range is about 60 hectares), there is a contrast between them regarding the existence of intermediate settlements of 7–20 hectares: settlements of this size are absent in Judah but existed in the Kingdom of Israel (about seven settlements of this size). The graph of the Kingdom of Judah reflects a situation where there is a very large city (Jerusalem) with an immense gap (nearly ten times larger) between it and the largest of the other cities (at the end of the eighth century; as noted, this gap increased further in the seventh century; Barkay [1988] noted this phenomenon and correctly identified it as the "primate city" model). Not only was Judah a smaller and less dense kingdom than Israel (Broshi and Finkelstein 1992: 54; Baron 1952: 60; Oded 1984: 135; Miller and

---

14. This difference continues farther down the scale: the number of farms in Judah is much larger than in Israel, where the villages were dominant. However, as noted, both the farms and the villages are very small and have no impact on the graphs of the hierarchy represented here.

Hayes 1986: 233–34; Finkelstein 1999b), its cities were also smaller compared with the Northern Kingdom.

The graph of the Kingdom of Israel presents a different picture. While Samaria, its capital, is approximately three times the size of the next-largest cities (slightly more than the gap predicted by the "rank-size distribution," which is twice the size), the settlement hierarchy generally matches the "rank-size distribution" model.[15] The fact that the settlement ranking in the Kingdom of Israel behaves according to the "rank-size

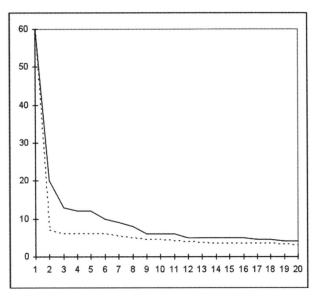

Graph 21. Settlement hierarchy in the Kingdoms of Israel and Judah.

distribution," while the settlement ranking in the Kingdom of Judah reflects the "primate city" model leads to the same conclusion as the one arising from the analysis of the socioeconomic stratification conducted earlier: Israel should be considered an advanced agrarian society, while Judah (at least in the eighth century B.C.E.) should be considered a simple agrarian society.

We must be careful not to draw excessive conclusions. These data do not indicate that the Kingdom of Judah was established later than the Kingdom of Israel (see, for example, Finkelstein 1996b; 1999b). Even though the data do not rule out this chronological conclusion, neither do they require it. Social systems do not necessarily evolve unilinearly and certainly not at a fixed rate. Thus, our conclusions do not rule out the existence of a state during the tenth century B.C.E., and they cannot decide the argument around the existence of the United Monarchy (see for example Finkelstein 1996b; 1998; 1999a; 2003; Finkelstein and Silberman 2001; 2006; A. Mazar 1997a; 1998a; 2006b, and many others).

The methodological danger entailed in applying a typological-sociological conclusion to chronology can be demonstrated by analyzing the finds from seventh-century B.C.E. Judah. In this period, the Judahite settlement hierarchy approached the "primate city" model even more closely, because Jerusalem was greatly enlarged (probably to an area of about 100 hectares), while some other large cities that had

---

15. The graph describing the settlement hierarchy in Israel is very similar to the graph predicted by the "rank-size distribution" mode, but is not identical to it. There may be several explanations for this, but in any case one should not expect full accordance with a model. Moreover, it is not clear what the size of Samaria was. In this graph, the maximal figure of 60 hectares was chosen, but if the researchers who limit Samaria's size to about 40–50 hectares (Herzog 1997a: 229) are correct, then the real graph would be even closer to the model's theoretical graph.

existed during the eighth century were destroyed and abandoned (Beth-Shemesh
and Tel ʿEton, for instance) or did not return to their original size (Lachish, for example; Ussishkin 2004: 90–92). These developments increased the gap between the
capital city and the rest of the kingdom's towns even further. This process, which
was a direct result of historical events that are well-known to us (Sennacherib's campaign, which damaged most of Judah's large cities in the Shephelah and exiled some
of their residents on the one hand and led to the growth of Jerusalem on the other
hand; for a detailed discussion of the impact of Sennacherib's campaign, see Faust
2008, and references), is in contrast to the development expected in theory. As time
passes and the state develops, the settlement hierarchy is expected to move away
from matching the "primate city" model and approach the "rank-size distribution."
In other words, unilinear evolution would have led to a reduction in the gap between
the capital city and the rest of the settlements in the hierarchy, but in reality the gap
actually widened. Thus, it is clear that one should not make simplistic deductions
about the tenth and ninth centuries B.C.E. based on data from the eighth century.

The Nature of Rural Settlement

In an advanced agrarian society, there is a more varied settlement hierarchy than
in a simple agrarian society, meaning a greater range of settlements of different
sizes (Lenski and Lenski 1974: 234). While it is difficult to apply this distinction to
the findings from the rural sector in the two kingdoms, since our knowledge of this
sector is partial, it appears that there are sufficient data to conclude that there was a
basic difference between Israel and Judah. The rural sector in Israel was composed
mainly of villages, even large villages, while the rural sector in Judah was composed mainly of farms, and villages were relatively rare. It appears that settlement
development in Israel was more advanced than in Judah. Most of the rural sites in
Israel matured and reached the development level of a village or even a large village, while the development of the sites in Judah remained more limited. The data
indicate that during the eighth century B.C.E. Israel was an advanced agrarian state
with a relatively large number of social strata and a varied settlement hierarchy,
while Judah was a simple agrarian society with two main social strata and a more
limited settlement hierarchy.

Summary

All the evidence indicates that, no later than the eighth century B.C.E., the kingdoms of Israel and Judah were already "states," with all the implications about social
structure that we associate with the term (on the situation during earlier stages of
the Iron Age, see below, chap. 9). The evidence also shows that each of the kingdoms
had its own unique sociological profile. The Kingdom of Israel was more "advanced"
in terms of its social stratification and settlement hierarchy (in both the urban and
the rural sectors) than with the Kingdom of Judah.

In the seventh century B.C.E., after the destruction of Israel, Judah existed on
its own. Its nature as a state was undoubtedly maintained: public buildings were
still present in the various settlements, and the administrative system (military and

civilian) continued to function. The Shephelah, which was economically and demographically one of the central districts of the kingdom, was destroyed almost completely in Sennacherib's campaign, and parts of it were transferred to Philistine control. Other parts of the kingdom, including fringe areas, flourished in the seventh century and reached their peak at the time (Faust 2008, and references).

An analysis of the archaeological evidence reveals important economic developments that occurred during the seventh century B.C.E. Judah was incorporated, along with Philistia, into the international economic system that flourished in the Mediterranean basin, and was driven by the Phoenicians (Faust and Weiss 2005; 2011).

It is reasonable to assume that the Assyrian campaign of 701 B.C.E. damaged the traditional economic system that functioned in some parts of Judah and that to compensate for this the state administration, centered in Jerusalem, grew stronger. This situation is reflected in the deepening gap in the settlement ranking. On the one hand, settlements spread to new regions (the Negev and the Judean Desert), probably due to the need to develop fringe areas after good, central regions were removed from the kingdom as a consequence of Sennacherib's campaign (Finkelstein 1994), and also because of the above-mentioned economic processes. On the other hand, while a large part of the urban sector disappeared in the Shephelah, and the area of the surviving cities was reduced, Jerusalem's area increased. According to Jones, a primate city is perceived not only as an enlarged concentration of people and as "national influence" but as representing the whole state ("Paris is France") and as being "the embodiment and expression of a society and a culture" (E. Jones 1990: 9, 11). This phenomenon explains why Jerusalem became a city that represented the whole of Judah, at least from the eighth century B.C.E. onward. This process was intensified after the destruction of Israel, especially after Sennacherib's campaign. In this period, Jerusalem's status, and perhaps even the number of its residents, was equal to the rest of the area of Judah. This development is also reflected in the contemporary biblical sources, in which the expression "Judah and Jerusalem" became common (Barkay 1988, and references to relevant texts there).

Appendix:
Residential Buildings in Iron Age II

Tables 14 and 15 present the data of all the buildings that were processed to produce the "inequality index" (the vast majority of the structures are of the four-room type). The data presented below are given in case the reader would like to check the data that were used to reach the above conclusions and is not intended to be a comprehensive list of all the structures known today. A number of buildings that were mentioned in previous chapters do not appear here because they were not included in the database when it was processed. In addition, in at least one case, there is a small difference between the data in chaps. 3–4 (which were updated on the basis of recent publications) and the table below (which served for the analysis of the inequality index). Any of those potential differences have no implications for the analysis however, first of all because most of the data by far were included in

Table 14. Buildings in the Urban Sector

Site	Building	Area	Nicely Built/ Crude	Shared Walls	Comments (Location)
Hazor	10037c	73	1	No	Near economic complex
	2a	160	1	No	Separate neighborhood?
	48	70	0+	Yes	Residential neighborhood
	14a	70	0	Yes	Residential neighborhood
	111	85	0	Yes	Residential neighborhood
	49	49	0	Yes	Residential neighborhood
	28	55	0	Yes	Residential neighborhood
	29	75	0	Yes	Residential neighborhood
	3169	120	1	No	Near fortress
	3148	100	1	No	Near fortress
	Bldg. in area L	45	0+	No	Near waterworks
Kinrot	974	66	0	Yes	Level I
	928	65	0	Yes	Level I
	Area C	90	0	Yes	Level II
	Area A	100	1	No	Level II
Tell es-Saidiyeh	Uniform bldg.	55	0+	Yes	Part of uniform quarter
	Uniform bldg.	55	0+	Yes	Part of uniform quarter
	Uniform bldg.	55	0+	Yes	Part of uniform quarter

the examination, and also because the new data are generally in accordance with the older data that were used in the analysis.

For purposes of calculation, a nicely built building was defined as 1, while a crudely built building was given a value 0. Buildings about which it was difficult to decide (noted with values of 0+ or 1–) were considered crude and calculated as though their value was 0, without subdividing the group of crude buildings.

Table 14. Buildings in the Urban Sector

Site	Building	Area	Nicely Built/ Crude	Shared Walls	Comments (Location)
Tell es-Saidiyeh	Uniform bldg.	55	0+	Yes	Part of uniform quarter
	Uniform bldg.	55	0+	Yes	Part of uniform quarter
	Uniform bldg.	55	0+	Yes	Part of uniform quarter
	Uniform bldg.	55	0+	Yes	Part of uniform quarter
	Uniform bldg.	55	0+	Yes	Part of uniform quarter
Tell el-Far'ah, north (Tirzah)	328	113	1	Partly	
	327	150	1	Partly	
	336	90	0	Yes	
	366	76	1–	Yes	
	148	150	1	No	
	362	65	0	Yes	
Shechem	1727	110	1	No	
Shikmona	North	55	0	Yes	
	Central	55	0	Yes	
	Corner	150	1	No	
Tell en-Nasbeh	125.01	60	0	Yes	
	141.01	90	0	Yes	
	141.02	57	0	Yes	
	141.03	70	0	Yes	
	141.04	60	0	Yes	
	141.05	55	0	Yes	
	141.06	30	0	Yes	
	142.01	120	0	Yes	
	142.02	50	0	Yes	
	142.03	52	0	Yes	
	142.04	47	0	Yes	
	142.05	55	0	Yes	
	142.06	57	0	Yes	
	142.07	43	0	Yes	
	142.08	47	0	Yes	
	142.09	54	0	Yes	
	142.10	49	0	Yes	

Table 14. Buildings in the Urban Sector

Site	Building	Area	Nicely Built/ Crude	Shared Walls	Comments (Location)
Tell en-Nasbeh	142.11	63	0	Yes	
	150.01	56	0	Yes	
	159.02	65	0	Yes	
	159.03	90	0	Yes	
	159.04	42	0	Yes	
	159.05	41	0	Yes	
	379	180	1	No	
	226	125	1	No	
	23	115	1	No	
Lachish	Lower	47	0	Yes	
	Middle	40–	0	Yes	
	Upper	105	0	Yes	
	1002	85	0	Yes	
Tell Beit Mirsim	31:10,11	80	0+	Yes	
	31:7,8,9	60	0	Yes	
	32:5,6,7	65	0	Yes	
	32:9,12	65	0	Yes	
	22:10	100	0	Yes	
	22:9,11	62	0	Yes	
	32:1,3,4,5	95	0	Yes	
	21:11,12	85	0	Yes	
	21:9,10	88	0	Yes	
	22:4,5,13,14	95	0	Yes	
	11:4,5	60	0	No	
	11:2,3,8,9	65	0	Yes	
	11:1	61	0	Yes	
	12:2,3,9,8	90	0	Yes	
	13:1	150	0	Yes	
	13:8,9	63	0	Yes	
	Tower	220	1	No	
	51:5,6	60	0	Yes	
	4:1,2,4	56	0	Yes	
	24:3,4,5	70	0	Yes	
	23:12,13	90	0	Yes	
	33:9,11,12,13	100	0	Yes	

Table 14. Buildings in the Urban Sector

Site	Building	Area	Nicely Built/ Crude	Shared Walls	Comments (Location)
Beersheba	75	60	0	Yes	
	25	60	0	Yes	
	607	50	0	Yes	
	630	50	0	Yes	
	855	110	1	Yes	
	812	105	?	?	
	529	60	0	Yes	
	522	65	0	Yes	
	526	50	0	Yes	
	673	60	0	Yes	
	770	65	0	Yes	
	Basements house	170	1	No	
	Governor's residence	250	1	Yes?	
Jerusalem	Ahiel house	100	1	?	
Tel Batash	743	90	1–	Yes	
	East area F	50	0	Yes	
	West area F	50	0	Yes	

Table 15. Buildings in the rural sector

Site	Building	Area	Att./Unatt.	Shared Walls	Comments (Location)
Rosh Zayit		150	1	No?	
H. Malta		120	1–	No?	
Kh. Jemein	100 S.	125	1	Partly	
	100 N.	117	1	Partly	
	50 S.	117	1	Partly	
	50 N.	122	1	Partly	
	500 E.	121	1	Partly	
	500 W.	134	1	Partly	
	193	121	1	Partly	
Tel Zeror		120	0	?	
Beit Aryeh	340	105	1–	Yes	
	410	120	1–	Yes	
	420	110	1–	Yes	
	450	85	1–	Yes	
	540	105	1–	Yes	
	190	110	0	Yes	
	900	120	1–	Yes	
	890	105	0	Yes	
	497	130	1–	Yes	
Jarish	B	170	0+	Yes	
Nahal Zimri	Farm house	120	1–	–	
French Hill	Farm house	100	0	–	
Kh. er-Ras	Kh. er-Rasm 1	130	1–	–	
	Kh. er-Rasm 2	165	1–	–	
Pisgat Zeev A	Farm house	80/125	0/1–	–	
H. Shilhah	Farm house?	130	1–	–	
Wadi Fukin	Farm house	300	0	–	

Chapter 7

The Four-Room House and Israelite Society

The four-room house is a unique feature of Iron Age settlements in the land of Israel, and many studies have therefore been devoted to various aspects, such as its architectural plan and its presumed origins, its functions, and the ethnic background of its builders and inhabitants.[1] In the present context, we are interested in the four-room house as a central feature of Israelite society. After briefly summarizing our current knowledge regarding this construction type, we will try to formulate a framework for understanding its predominance in Israelite society. From this study, we should be able to ascertain social indicators such as ethnic identity, ideological principles, and world view.

In contrast to the typical "broad" structures common in earlier periods, the four-room house was a long building, composed of four basic spaces on the ground floor (each space can be further subdivided into several rooms; see below). The buildings' entrances were in the narrower side, and one entered a long space, to the left and right of which were two identical, parallel spaces. The spaces were usually separated by walls and, in some cases, by stone pillars (monoliths). At the end of the three long spaces, perpendicular to them, was a broad space.

Although these four spaces, all of them or some of them, were subdivided into rooms in various ways, according to the residents' changing needs, the basic plan of the long building was maintained, with a (changing) number of long spaces at the front, a broad space at the back, and an entrance placed in one of the long spaces (usually the middle one). In most cases, there was also a yard in front of the house (as in Beersheba, Beit Aryeh, and on many farms), and presumably most of the buildings of this type used the space in front of them (see previous chapters; also, on Jerusalem region farms, see Maitlis 1989: 64; on Shikmona, see Elgavish 1994: 59; on Iron Age I buildings, see Meyers 1997: 16), even where no yard has been explicitly identified.[2]

Along with the main type, composed of four spaces, there are other subtypes that included only two long spaces (three spaces total), or an additional space, usually long (amounting to five spaces; see fig. 37, p. 214). These differences are typologically

---

1. See, for example, Shiloh 1970; 1973; Stager 1985; Holladay 1992; Netzer 1992. See also Bunimovitz and Faust 2002; 2003; Faust and Bunimovitz 2003; forthcoming; with references). The origin of this construction type is unclear. Some scholars believe it originated with nomad tents (Kempinski 1978: 36; Finkelstein 1988b: 257; Shiloh 1987b; Herzog 1984: 75–77). Today, some scholars believe that it originated with the Late Bronze Age structures discovered in the Shephelah (Lederman 1986; A. Mazar 1985b; Giveon 1995; 1999). This issue is not relevant to the questions discussed here.

2. On the use of the space in front of a residential house, even if not defined as part of the building, see Hirschon 1981.

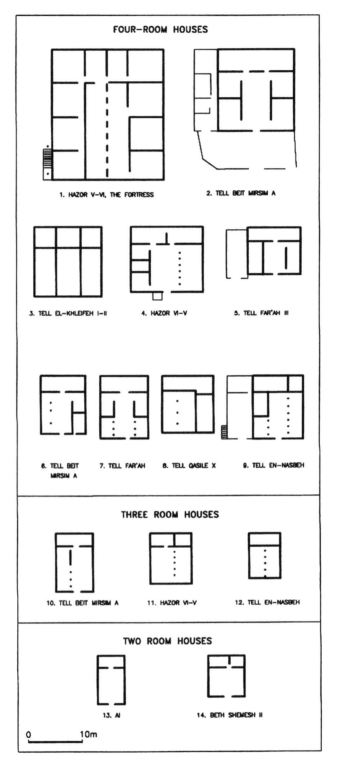

Fig. 37. The four-room house and its subtypes.

negligible and should not be seen as more than subtypes of the main type, although, as we shall see, they might have had some sort of social significance.[3]

Opinions are divided regarding the nature of the central space. In the past, the prevailing opinion was that this was an open courtyard where most of the household's activities took place (see for example, Shiloh 1973: 280; Dar 1986b: 77; Barkay 1992: 332; Fritz 1995: 141). Today, in contrast, it is generally thought that this space was roofed, along with the rest of the rooms of the house (Stager 1985; Netzer 1992: 196–98; Holladay 1992). This argument is linked to the question of the presence of an upper floor in these houses. In the past, it was assumed that there was a second floor only above the back (broad) room, but today it is thought that the upper floor usually covered the house's entire area (Stager 1985: 15–17; C. H. J. de Geus 1986: 226–27; Netzer 1990: 196–98), and it may have served as the main living level (Netzer 1992: 196–98; Stager 1985: 15–17). Stone stairs, which were discovered in many of these buildings, probably led to the second floor; in other cases, a ladder or wooden stairs may have been used for climbing to the second floor.

This construction type first appeared during Iron Age I (the first fully developed buildings of this type are probably from the eleventh century B.C.E.; A. Mazar 1990: 486), but during Iron Age II it became the most common residential house in the land of Israel. The dominance of this type in terms of distribution was nearly absolute: almost all the houses known in Israelite cities and villages were of this type, even on sites in which many Iron Age II buildings (even dozens) were discovered. This was the case in Tell Beit Mirsim, Mizpah (Tell en-Nasbeh), Tirzah (Tell el-Far'ah, north), Tell es-Saidiyeh (level V), and Beersheba, and of course also in sites where fewer buildings have been found, such as Shikmona, Shechem, Jerusalem, and others. The dozens of rural sites discovered in the central hills also contained four-room houses. Fritz (1995: 142), summarized: "(A)part from a small variation in the way in which the building was carried out, this normal Israelite form of house exhibits an astonishing rigidity in concept, as well as wide distribution." Notably, in no other period in the history of the region was there such great uniformity in the architecture of residential houses, and the building types common in other periods were never so uniform.

A quick glance at the plan of a four-room house is sufficient for identifying it (and dating it to the Iron Age), whereas descriptions of common house types from other periods are typically based on the presence of only a few prominent architectural elements in the plan (such as a courtyard), and in most cases a glance at the plan is not sufficient for identification of its type and period.[4] This is even more surprising when one takes into account the four-room plan's architectural complexity. Additionally, this type of house disappeared completely during the sixth century B.C.E., and is not found in the Persian period (e.g., Stern 2001: 470–79; Yezerski 1995:

---

3. In most cases, the term *four-room house* will used here as a generic term that includes all subtypes.

4. Notably, the Arad house of the Early Bronze Age also predominated to some extent, but this was a very simple house form (usually only one room), whereas the four-room house was much more complex, and its prevalence is therefore surprising. The four-room house should therefore be compared with the courtyard house, which is also complex (but its plan is not rigid).

113–14; Wolff 2002: 132, 133, 136; see also Faust 2004b; forthcoming; and many additional references).[5]

The Essence of the Four-Room House

From the Ethnic Explanation to the Functional Explanation

In an attempt to explain the great popularity of the four-room house, Yigal Shiloh suggested that this was an "Israelite" house type, and hence its distribution matches the distribution of this population (Shiloh 1973; 1978). Although some scholars still accept this explanation (see, for example, Holladay 1992), many scholars now reject it (such as Finkelstein 1996a: 204–6; Ahlström 1993: 339–40). Their main criticism is based on the lack of congruence between the distribution of the buildings and the distribution of Israelite settlements. They claim that buildings of this type have been discovered on sites considered not to have been inhabited by Israelites, such as Tel Qasila and sites in the Transjordan. The fact that most of the structures are concentrated in the hills rather than the valleys is attributed by some scholars to reasons such as the nature of the local rocks and is seen as a regional phenomenon (see, e.g., Thompson [1992: 283], though this argument is problematic, as we shall see later).

The alternative explanation, which is prevalent today, arose out of scholarly interest in the high functionality of the four-room house, using ethnoarchaeology, among other things (see, for example, Stager 1985; Holladay 1992). According to this explanation, four-room houses became common because they fulfilled the various needs of agricultural families, providing space for people, livestock, crops, and so on (see, in addition to Stager and Holladay, Ahlström 1993: 340; Meyers 1997: 15; some of these scholars still link the house to the Israelites). There were spaces for sleeping, livestock, storage, cooking, and so on; the plan of the house suited all these needs, and it contained rooms suited to all the activities. In this view, the unique suitability of the house to the needs of highland families was the reason for its dominant position in the architectural landscape of the Iron Age.

The Problems with the Functional Explanation

The functional explanation is not without problems, and there are some counterarguments that significantly reduce its likelihood. First and foremost, one wonders what the limit to the functionality argument is. In the accepted view, the four-room house served the needs of farming families in the rural sector. However, not only were buildings of this type discovered in all settlement types from isolated farms

---

5. The following are apparently the only four-room buildings that existed after the destruction of Judah: (1) the three-room house at Alona, although it is not clear whether this house was actually built during the Persian period or was simply reused at the time; (2) a house at Kerem Ben Zimra in the Galilee (Alon de Groot, personal communication); (3) three large four-room houses from Mizpah (Tell en-Nasbeh) that the excavator dated to the Iron Age (see also Branigan 1966; McClellan 1984; Herzog 1997a: 237–39) but that Zorn believes (on the basis of a reexamination of finds from the site) was built after the destruction (Zorn 1993). It seems likely that the buildings were constructed during the Iron Age (as most scholars believe; and see discussion above, in chap. 3), but even if Zorn is indeed right, the construction of the buildings immediately after the destruction of Judah on a site that probably served as an alternative ruling center does not deviate from the Iron Age's "cultural zone."

to villages and cities, but even public buildings were built in this style, such as the fortress at Hazor, buildings in Jericho, the "ashlar house" in Jerusalem (and perhaps also the western tower at Tell Beit Mirsim, and others). One cannot assume that in all these sites the buildings fulfilled the needs of a typical farming family. Furthermore, private structures of the four-room type housed small, large, nuclear, extended, rich, and poor families and in some cases may even have served as residences for soldiers (see Singer-Avitz 1996). The plan was also used, as we have seen, for public buildings and fortresses and at one stage also for burial caves (Barkay 1994; 1999, Faust and Bunimovitz 2008, and additional bibliography there). This indicates the importance of this form to the population.

Were the functional explanation correct, one would expect similar artifacts to be discovered in equivalent rooms of four-room houses on different sites. This expectation has not been realized. Thus, for instance, regarding the back (broad) room, in certain cases it contained dozens or hundreds of storage jars (H. Eli, Kh. er-Ras, and others; Hizmi 1998; Feig 1995: 5), while in other cases, it contained only a few everyday vessels (Beit Aryeh; Riklin 1993: 39). Similarly, finds from the various spaces in several houses in Beersheba and Hazor did not indicate uniformity in the functions of the buildings (S. Geva 1989; Singer-Avitz 1996; see also the appendix to chap. 3), and this conclusion is now also supported by detailed studies of the finds in a large number of structures (Cassuto 2004: 133–34; Aizner 2011).[6] This means that the use of the spaces varied even though the general plan was similar (compare Rapoport 1990: 13, 18).

Furthermore, several factors show that the four-room type had an importance beyond mere functionality. It is hard to believe that this type of house maintained its vast popularity for 600 years due solely to its functionality. And if it was so functional, why did it disappear completely after the destruction of Judah? Could its functional quality have suddenly vanished during the Persian period? Although the function of the four-room house should not be ignored, it is clear that, even if functionality inspired the plan, it did not lead to its distribution in space and time.[7] Moreover, not only does the "new" functional explanation fail to withstand criticism, but the arguments against the more traditional ethnic explanation were not at all decisive, as we shall see below.

The Distribution of Four-Room Houses outside Israel and Judah

Some of the proponents of the functional explanation argued against the ethnic explanation, noting that four-room houses have also been discovered in non-Israelite settlements, and so they should not be considered typical of Israelite society. This argument is not justified theoretically, and it cannot withstand empirical scrutiny.

From a theoretical point of view, the general argument that the four-room house was typical of Israelite society does not mean that every single four-room house had

---

6. The lack of uniformity should not be attributed to the fact that only the ground floor of two-floor houses has been excavated, because the functionality should have been observable even on the ground floor.

7. Because its distribution included sites outside the highlands, where the four-room house was less "functional" (according to the above "functional" explanations related to the highlands); see more below.

to have been inhabited by an Israelite family. There is no doubt that Israelites usually resided in these houses, because they constitute the majority of buildings in sites that were certainly Israelite, and even if others used them occasionally, this does not contradict the observation that this building type served Israelites. If we discovered a site without any four-room houses, it would be justifiable to ask whether Israelites lived there.

This argument does not mean that non-Israelites could not live in these houses. It is not enough just to find a few buildings of this type on non-Israelite sites to disprove its ethnic uniqueness. Perhaps non-Israelite residents copied it or developed it in parallel times and places. This, for example, would explain the similar remains found at Tel Qasila and perhaps also in the Transjordan. Moreover, we should recall that Israelites did live in part of this region, perhaps even beyond the official boundaries of the Kingdom of Israel (see Ji 1995; 1997a; 1997b; Herr 2000: 178; 2001; and extensive discussion in Faust 2006b: 71–84, 221–26; on Tel Qasila, see Bunimovitz and Faust 2001; Faust 2006b: 191–220).

In empirical terms, it transpires that a significant proportion of the non-Israelite houses that were presented in research as four-room houses are not in fact four-room houses at all. The famous house at Sahab (Transjordan) that has been referred to quite often in scholarly literature can serve as an example. In discussing a building found at Sahab, Ibrahim (1975: 72–73) added:

> There are just a few examples of the "pillared house" [note the terminology and its alternation] excavated in East Jordan. A series of pillared houses from the Iron Age II were excavated at Tell es-Sa'idiyyeh in the Jordan valley, Crystal Bennet excavated a very similar structure at Tawilan near Petra.
>
> However, this type of room has been excavated in a large number of Palestinian sites, especially at Tell Beit Mirsim, Tell el-Far'ah, Tell el-Qadi (Hazor) [sic], Tell en-Nasbeh, Tell el-Mutassallim (Megiddo), Jericho and others. Most of those examples were considered in various discussions, including two articles by Y. Shiloh. I would like to discuss the development of this house-type after completing excavations in this area. At least one point should be mentioned, that the examples found within the Ammonite and Edomite regions do not fit with the conclusion of Shiloh: "The four room plan was thus used as a standard plan for buildings of very different function within the Israelite city."

Not only did the author confuse the pillared house with the four-room house, but the house he excavated at Sahab and that led to this discussion belongs to neither of these two types. The structure discussed was a large building containing one room divided into two by several monoliths (see Ibrahim 1975: 71 for the plan). The reason for the mistake in this case, as in others, is the tendency of scholars to confuse the use of monoliths with the four-room building and to refer to both as representing "Israelite construction."

The same thing can be said with regard to buildings excavated at Medeinet al-Mu'arradjeh (Olavarri 1983: illustrations 3–4). One of the spaces in the building discovered at this site was indeed divided by three pillars, but this does not make it a four-room house. In contrast, it is clear from the reports of a building excavated at

Tell el-Umeiri (Clark 1996; Herr 2000; 2001) that a four-room house was excavated there. But according to the excavator, this site is linked to Israelite settlement (Herr 2000; 2001). Indeed, additional (real) four-room houses were discovered in various sites in Transjordan (see for example, Hart 1988: 92), and it is clear that there are four-room houses in this region. Their number is smaller than is usually assumed, and some of them can be connected with Israelites settlements there.

Some scholars have argued that four-room houses were discovered at Tel Qiri, Tel Keisan, and Afula (on the first site, see Gilboa 1987: 60; on the other two sites, see Ahlström 1993: 339), but this claim does not accord with the plans published and even contradicts the words of the excavators. Portugali stated that the only four-room house found at Tel Qiri was a public building and that the residential buildings were not of this type (Portugali 1987: 138; the definition of the public building as a four-room house is also doubtful, because a study of the plan shows that it lacks the broad space). Humbert commented explicitly regarding the building at Tel Keisan that "it cannot be defined as a 'four-room house'" (Humbert 1993: 865). In Afula as well, no buildings of this type were discovered,[8] nor were the buildings near the gate at Ekron (Tel Miqne) four-room houses, although they were long houses (see Gitin 1989). It is worth stressing that not all buildings with four rooms belong to the four-room house type (and many have made the mistake of confusing a house with four rooms with a four-room house; for instance, Ahlström 1993: 339).

While there are examples of four-room houses in areas outside the main areas of Israelite settlement,[9] they are fewer than commonly believed. Most of them can perhaps be explained as emulation, and a few can be seen as signs of Israelite families living in these settlements or of connections with Israelites (Ji 1997a; Kautz 1981: 33). Most of the examples of this type belong to Iron Age I, prior to the final formation of ethnic groups in this region (e.g., Daviau 1999: 132; Kautz 1981; Faust 2006b and references there). Even if we explain these houses as an independent development, it is still clear that this type is rare in non-Israelite sites, in complete contrast to its frequency in Israelite settlements.

Social and Cognitive Aspects of Four-Room Houses

Thus, we return to Shiloh's suggestion and accept his argument that four-room houses were the typical residences of Israelite society. It is possible that during Iron Age I, when this type had only just appeared and was not yet very common, it was used by various settlers in the hill regions of the land of Israel, by both Israelites and non-Israelites (on the difficulty in identifying the "Israelites" during this period, see for example, Dever 1993b; 1996; 2003; Finkelstein 1996a; Finkelstein and Silberman 2001; for a comprehensive discussion, see Faust 2006b), because they found that, like

---

8. M. Dothan 1978: 35 (cited by Ahlström) describes four broad rooms (one of which was divided by monoliths) surrounded by a yard on three sides, but this description does not match a four-room house. A study of the report (M. Dothan 1955: 29–30, illustration 3) does not reveal four-room houses either, and it appears that the use of monoliths or the number of rooms confused Ahlström.

9. Especially in Transjordan, where boundaries were more blurred; see detailed discussion in Faust 2006b: 221–26.

other buildings, it had various functional advantages (the functional advantages, as we have seen, were noted by Stager 1985; Holladay 1992 and others). However, over time, the four-room house became the type that was characteristic of the Israelites, even if other ethnic groups may have continued living in this type of house on occasion (though rarely).

We may assume that the Israelites adopted this house-type because some of its features corresponded with their cognitive and social world. This is implied by the fact that the four-room house served as an archetype not only for dwellings but also for other purposes, such as public buildings, burial caves, and perhaps even temples (if the Arad temple—the only archaeological example of a temple in Israel and Judah—can be interpreted in this way).[10] The following passages offer possible explanations that complement each other. These suggestions are merely a preliminary outline, but the whole subject requires more detailed study.

Ethnicity

Any ethnic group that is in the process of self-definition negotiates its identity with various groups within and outside itself. In many cases, elements of material culture are used in this ethnic negotiation and in the process of boundary maintenance between groups. These elements may be a product of specific ethnic behavior or may be chosen (for whatever reason) to convey a message regarding ethnic identity (on these terms, see more in chap. 8 below).[11] Even without examining the process of Israelite ethnogenesis in detail, we may state that its main formation took place during Iron Age I (Faust 2006b, and many references there; see also Dever 2003; Killebrew 2005; R. D. Miller 2005). It is thus possible that the four-room house was chosen to serve as this kind of distinguishing element (that is an ethnic marker) and, due to the ethnic identification it embodied, its distribution became almost identical to the distribution of the ethnic group that used it (see further discussion below).

Expression of Ideology

A unique feature of the four-room house becomes evident when we apply a new research method called *access analysis*. Following the work of Hillier and Hanson (1984; compare Foster 1989; Blanton 1994 and others) with regard to the social logic of space, we find that different building plans can be analyzed and compared for their *space syntax*. This term refers to the spatial configuration within a built structure and the hierarchy of accessibility or passage from one room to the other. The social meaning of space syntax is the possible contact between a building's inhabitants and strangers, as well as among the inhabitants themselves. Different syntaxes hint, therefore, at different systems or codes of social and cultural relations.

---

10. Yadin 1982: 167; Herzog 1991: 81; 1997a: 204–5; Fritz 1995: 148–49.

11. This statement should not be confused with the simplistic and mistaken act of identifying a "material culture" with an ethnic group; see, for example, Barth 1969; McGuire 1982; Emberling 1997; Faust 2006b; see also chap. 8 below.

Each architectural plan has a unique access plan with a varying degree of depth.[12] An examination of the graphs that represent the various types of houses may shed light on the society that created and used the examined buildings. If access analysis is applied to the buildings that were common in the land of Israel in the various periods, we find that the diagram characteristic of a four-room house is a flat (shallow) tree (fig. 38), while most of the other buildings have a linear, pathlike diagram, or a diagram that is like a deeper tree (meaning that at least one of the branches spreads into a column; see also chap. 8 below). Buildings of this sort restrict movement possibilities

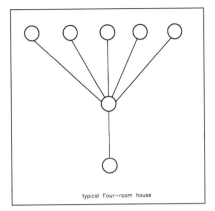

typical Four-room house

Fig. 38. The four-room house: access analysis.

and thus reflect a hierarchical approach (see, e.g., Banning and Byrd 1989: 156; F. E. Brown 1990: 103), in contrast to four-room houses, where one can move from the central room directly into each of the other rooms (even if in practice not everyone was allowed to enter each room, this was not dictated by the architecture and was not prominently expressed in the building's plan).

The hierarchical organization of the living and sleeping areas in a house reflects a complex household typical of settlements (or societies) where there are many families and large households (Blanton 1994: 64). This hierarchy is expressed in restricting or compartmentalizing access to certain spaces based on age and/or gender differences. Thus, for example, there were distinct spaces intended for married family members. This sort of hierarchical organization is in opposition to random arrangements of space (such as shared sleeping areas) that are typical of societies with a simpler structure. In the four-room house we find, on the one hand, a lack of depth, indicating a lack of hierarchy, and on the other hand, we find many rooms, indicating complexity. Four-room houses, particularly rural or wealthy houses, contained five to eight rooms on the ground floor alone (as subdivisions of the four main spaces, not including the front yard), and there was probably a similar number of rooms on the second floor. This complex situation implies the existence of clear arrangements for using the space, and thus the lack of depth should be interpreted as avoiding a hierarchical organization.

This exceptional reality can be explained as expressing an egalitarian ideology. Many scholars have noted that a "democratic" and egalitarian spirit of Israelite society was reflected in the biblical texts,[13] and this argument was given great momentum following Mendenhall and Gottwald (Mendenhall 1962; Gottwald 1979).

---

12. Access analysis is expressed in a graph composed of lines and circles: a line represents an opening where movement is possible, and a circle represents a space. If there is access from space to space, the two circles are linked by a line.

13. See, for example, Lods 1932; C. U. Wolf 1947; Yeivin 1979: 141; Gordis 1971; Speiser 1971: 283–84; Weisman 1984: 94; Cross 1988; Shapira 1998; Berman 2008; see also Faust 2006b: 92–107, and other references there.

It is difficult to accept this view, because real egalitarian societies do not exist, and it is quite clear that a society as complex as the Israelite society was not egalitarian.[14] However, it is clear that the Bible reflects an egalitarian ethos. The openness of the four-room house and the fact that it refrains from imposing a hierarchy on the movement of its residents matches the ruling egalitarian ideology, even if this ideology was not actually applied to all areas of life or even in managing a household itself. Thus, for instance, Lemche recognized a discrepancy between reality and ideology in Scandinavian societies.[15] A similar gap exists in Saudi Arabia, where extremely wealthy kings are buried in a simple burial due to their religious ideology of egalitarianism.[16] Thus, a society's egalitarian ideology may be expressed in its material culture, but only careful research can distinguish between the society's ideal and the actual reality (Trigger 1990). In any case, the existence of an egalitarian ideology in Israel was confirmed in other ways. Thus, for instance, Portugali examined the geographical terms in the Bible and concluded that the Israelite perception of space was based on "a collective mental map of an egalitarian and decentralized (= non-ranked) society" (Portugali 1999: 72; for extended discussion of the egalitarian ideology and its material expression, see Faust 2006b). But even if four-room houses were created against a background of egalitarian ideology during Iron Age I, it is possible that their increased appearance during Iron Age II was due to other reasons as well.

The explanation suggested here is also valid for explaining the appearance during the Iron Age of another similar building type, the public pillared building. Long pillared buildings appear from the end of Iron Age I to the end of Iron Age II. Like the four-room house, the pillared building is a long building (and in this respect they both deviate from the architectural tradition of the land of Israel in the Bronze Age). Both contain three internal, long spaces, and both often use stone pillars (monoliths). In this context, Herzog's description of pillared buildings is remarkably similar to a description of the front three spaces of a four-room house (ignoring the section about troughs):

> Pillared buildings are a well-defined architectural group in the framework of Iron Age construction. They are rectangular and their space is divided longitudinally by pillars into three narrow halls. The flanking halls are generally paved with flagstones, and the floor in the central hall is beaten earth. Shallow troughs, made of single stone with a depression on the top or of unhewn stones, are set in the spaces between the pillars. The entrance to the pillared building was generally in the short side, making its plan that of a longhouse. At several sites complexes of several adjoining pillared

---

14. Price and Feinman 1995: 4–5; Wason 1994: 1. According to Lemche (1985: 223): "Instead of speaking of egalitarian societies it would be more appropriate to speak of societies which are dominated by an egalitarian ideology." Lemche rejected Gottwald's approach and did not accept the existence of an egalitarian ideology in Israelite society (1985: 277), although he admitted that this matter had not been examined in detail (1985: 407).

15. Lemche (1985: 223 n. 99) also states: "this would allow for the fact that a society whose ideology is egalitarian need not in fact be egalitarian." Such a discrepancy is apparent, for example, between the American ethos and the social reality in the U.S.A.

16. Huntington and Metcalf 1979: 122. See also Faust 2004a. Trigger (2006: 453) also stated on the basis of this description that in several societies simple burials reflect a social ideology of egalitarianism that was not reflected in practice in everyday life. Compare Kelsky 1999.

buildings have been uncovered, whereas at others there was only a single structure. (Herzog 1992a: 223)

In chap. 3, I suggested that pillared buildings served, among other things, as a refuge for the society's poor and oppressed and as a place of justice. In this interpretation, public pillared buildings expressed an ideology of "justice and righteousness" to which Israelite society felt committed, just as private four-room houses expressed an ideology (or ethos) of equality. These two ideological principles are, of course, linked to each other. Thus, ideological commitments were manifested both on the individual level and on the public level (we cannot determine whether one of the factors preceded the other or whether both developed parallelly and each influenced the other).

The state's duty to uphold justice and to care for underclasses was similar to duties imposed on family members in traditional society (compare Schloen 2001). Fathers and elders served, to a great extent, as judges in relation to their family members, and the Bible often notes an individual's duty to care for the weaker elements of society. The similarity between four-room houses and the pillared buildings may also be related to the ideological message of mutual responsibility that they both express: the residential houses reflect a concern for the weak members of the family, its poor and unfortunate, just as the public buildings reflect this attitude toward the society's oppressed, poor, and unfortunate in the cities. However, this does not mean that the ideology did not lose validity over time or that it ever dictated public behavior.

Privacy and Contact Regulation

Another feature revealed by access analysis is that four-room houses allowed residents maximum privacy. From the central space, each room had its own separate entrance (on the idea of privacy in a different society, see Nevett 1999: 71–73). The front yard also emphasized privacy (of the house as a whole). If people were concerned with issues of purity (as might be suggested from the biblical laws), the ability to enter each room directly from a central space without needing to move through another intermediate room was a necessity. The purity laws of the Priestly source, for example, do not require a menstruating woman to leave the house (in contrast to the situation in Mesopotamia; Milgrom 1991: 952–53) but are very strict regarding the transmission of impurity from object to object. The four-room house, for example, enables a menstruating woman to reach her room without passing through any other room, and thus avoids the danger of making other people or objects unclean; similarly, no other person is forced to pass through her room on the way to other rooms in the house.[17] This would not be possible in houses with a lineal access diagram, because any attempt to reach a certain room would involve passing through another room, and impurity could be transmitted to the people in the room or contracted by the passing person. This is not to argue that the four-room house

---

17. In discussing the nature of the four-room house, Netzer (1992: 199 n. 24) wrote: "In a general discussion of this subject with Prof. M. Weinfeld of the Hebrew University, one of the subjects tentatively explored was the issue of the separation between purity and impurity—such as the avoidance of women during menstruation." This comment was probably the first scholarly reference to the idea developed here.

was designed in advance to meet religious requirements but that the match between these specific needs and the architectural plan motivated (and perhaps also accelerated) the adoption of this particular building type by Israelite society. It is also possible that the existence of the four-room house enabled the laws to develop this way, which was slightly different from other societies (in which unclean individuals such as menstruating women were supposed to leave the settlement completely; Milgrom 1991: 952–53). There are interrelations between buildings and society: people design the houses, and the houses shape them (compare with Bourdieu 1977; Giddens 1979).

Means of Communication

Buildings are an important element in systems of nonverbal communication in society. Two of these types of communication are *canonical communication* and *indexical communication* (e.g., Blanton 1994: 8–13). *Canonical communication* refers to cosmological messages that may be expressed in the interior of a house. Cosmological principles serve to affirm and strengthen traditional order and justify differences with regard to age and gender. *Indexical communication*, on the other hand, refers mainly to inter-house messages related to social status. These messages are usually expressed on the exterior of a house. Sometimes the canonical and indexable messages are identical, and sometimes a canonical message may become indexical (for instance, when religious piety has social importance; Blanton 1994: 12). If canonical symbols are displayed in public, the buildings speak to their residents' acceptance of society's traditional values and stress the residents' connection to the local community (in these cases, even though the symbols are displayed in public, the messages are not indexical only). In many cases, there is tension between the various messages. The canonical message "I am part of the community" and the indexical message "I am better" contradict each other, but they may exist side by side (compare with Wiessner 1990).

If the interior of a four-room house expressed the egalitarian ethos of Israelite society, this ethos should be seen as a canonical message. The general similarity between the many buildings supports this, manifesting the message "we are part of the same group."[18] However, the uniformity message was just one of the messages that the buildings conveyed. Studied parallel to each other, they also express a message of variance, because there are distinct differences between them. Some of these differences, for example in urban centers during the period of the Monarchy, were connected to differences of status and wealth, as we have seen.

A message of difference is also evident in the use of three-, four-, and five-room houses. Four-room houses were usually larger and better constructed than three-room houses. Size differences can of course be explained functionally: larger buildings require more internal walls and/or pillars to support the ceiling, and thus more

---

18. Buildings that are not of the four-room type were discovered mainly in the big cities. Perhaps they belonged to very poor families, who could not afford investing in this sort of message, or to "foreigners" who did not belong to the group at all and so were not interested in such messages (see further, chap. 8 below).

interior spaces are created. However, this does not explain quality distinctions. For example, small four-room houses were usually more nicely built and of a higher quality of construction (building 10037 at Hazor, for instance). This difference cannot always be explained as an economic gap: four-room houses were inhabited by the wealthy, while three-room structures housed the poor. We also cannot always assume that rich families lived in the smaller four-room houses. Moreover, almost all the rural houses were the four-room type, even though rural areas were not the richest sector. In sum, wealth is only a partial explanation for the differences between the four- and three-room houses and for their distribution.

Perhaps the solution to this problem lies elsewhere. In chap. 4, I analyzed the family structure and presented evidence that in the rural sector there were mainly extended families, while in the urban sector there were mainly nuclear families. We also saw that among the urban rich there were extended families (compare with Yorburg 1975: 8). This evidence matches the distribution of the building types. Perhaps we may conclude that four-room houses represent extended families (and the strategy of multigenerational continuity), while three-room houses represent nuclear families. To be precise: this does not mean that each and every four-room house was inhabited only by extended families or that every three-room house was inhabited by a nuclear family but merely that the number of spaces conveys a social message regarding family structure.

This theory is confirmed by the use of the four-room plan in Judahite tombs (A. Mazar 1977: 123; Barkay 1994: 147–52; 1999; Hopkins 1996; Faust and Bunimovitz 2008). These tombs served a multigenerational family: for many generations, the deceased were placed on benches; after a while, their bones were gathered into a repository, and the newly deceased were placed on the benches. Thus, four-room tombs convey a social message of multigenerationalism similar to houses (on the connection between buildings and tombs in other cultures, see, e.g., Hodder 1994). No tombs have been found carved in a three-room shape, but it appears that the majority of the population was buried in simple inhumations that did not usually survive (Barkay 1994: 148; see also Faust 2004a; Faust and Bunimovitz 2008). Thus it is possible that simple inhumations reflect the section of society that lived in three-room houses as nuclear families, while four-room houses and Judahite tombs represent the section of society that lived as extended families.

The Materialization of a World View

According to Mary Douglas, many biblical laws, particularly laws related to holiness, purity, and impurity, are based on an attempt to protect the principle of order (Douglas 1966, particularly the chapter on the "abominations of Leviticus"). Holiness is identified with order, and its breach constitutes confusion (1966: 53). In this way, she interprets many laws relating to all aspects of life. Thus, for example, animals are classified according to certain definitions into different groups (on land: quadruped, ruminating, and cloven hoofed; at sea: finned and scaled); animals that meet these standards are pure and permitted for eating, while all other animals are automatically forbidden. This interpretation also explains the serious taboo on cross-breeding, because such crossbreeds are a threat to any type of framework or order.[19]

If this interpretation is true, presumably this concern with "order" influenced the Israelites' entire way of life (and not only the issues mentioned in the Bible), and systematic activities of this sort would certainly be expressed in the material culture (see also Faust 2006b: 58–60). The necessity of maintaining a particular order can explain the dominant position and wide distribution of the four-room house. If this building type was perceived by Israelite society as the most "ordered" architectural frame of reference or the "correct" building, then any building that did not match its basic outline would be considered a deviation from the norm. According to this description, the perception of order operated as a powerful mechanism to unify construction styles based on the standard of the four-room house.[20]

Realizing a Perception of Space

The Israelites' perception of space was expressed both in settlements and in residential houses (on the relation between residential houses and the city in terms of the perception of space, see Rapoport 1969: 69–78). In our discussion of perceptions of space in Israelite cities, we divided spaces into three types: private space, meaning the home; communal space, encompassing the public areas of the city; and public space, meaning the areas outside the city where everyone could move freely. A similar perception of space existed regarding residential houses: private spaces for residents were their rooms and intimate activity spaces, such as the rooms of the nuclear families within the extended family; the central space, and perhaps also the front yard, was perceived as a space that was shared by all the house's inhabitants; while the spaces beyond the house were considered public (or outside the family unit; fig. 39).

The perception of the house using the same concepts that served for the perception of space in the settlement is related to certain preferences with cosmological reasons, such as the prominent tendency to orient the entrances of both buildings and settlements to the east, and in any case, to avoid entrances facing west (Faust

---

19. Today Douglas interprets the allowing and banning of animals differently: predators, mutilated animals, and animals that "lack something that they need" are banned (Douglas 1993: 18). This change is connected to other changes in her approach (see Fardon 1999: 185–205), which are beyond the scope of this discussion. It seems that her original ideas are more suited to the reality of Israelite society. In any case, even in her new approach (though this is not stressed), Israelite society sanctifies order, and the bans are linked to cosmic order (Douglas 1993: 21), which is "righteousness," and this supports the connection I am making with the buildings.

20. One possible theoretical argument is that the appearance of the four-room plan in residential houses, tombs, public buildings, and so on was the result of a royal effort to enforce an egalitarian ideology, covering up the gaps existing in society, while the population was at the same time being exploited by the elite (compare with Greenberg 1999 regarding the Early Bronze Age). However, the fact that the various types of four-room houses were widespread in both kingdoms (Israel and Judah) shows that this construction type was not necessarily linked to a state. Since Israel and Judah were different states, any forced attempt to create a uniform reality could have harmed their various interests more than helping them. Each state had an interest in promoting its uniqueness and justifying its existence, especially given that their ethnic sentiments were probably shared (see, for instance, 1 Kgs 12:28–33; the historical reliability of this story is a separate issue; for Israelite identity, see Faust 2006b; and more below).

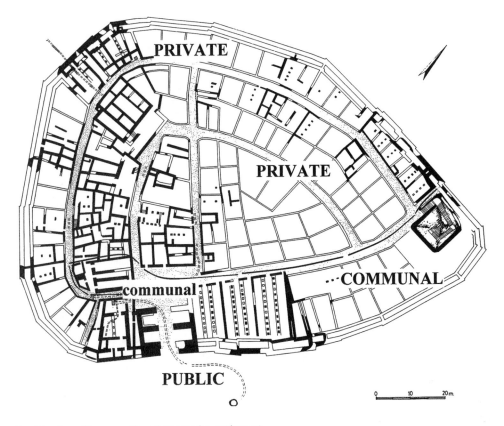

PRIVATE

PRIVATE

COMMUNAL

communal

PUBLIC

0   10   20 m.

Fig. 39a. Israelite perception of space: the settlement.

1999a; 2001; the avoidance of entrances facing west expresses an attempt to protect weak points); this issue is also related to nonverbal communication, which was discussed above.

Summary

During Iron Age I, a new, unfamiliar construction type appeared in the hilly regions of the land of Israel on both sides of the Jordan River. At this early stage, it was not yet fully formed and certainly did not predominate. Its use was probably originally motivated by functional agricultural needs (as many scholars have suggested),[21] and it was probably for these same reasons that it was also used by different populations in various places. But in the eleventh century B.C.E., the four-room house crystallized into a unique architectural type. Because it suited the "mind set" of the developing Israelite society, the house was adopted and became the dominant

21. These studies referred to hill-country farmhouses, meaning rural Iron Age I buildings excavated in the highlands (e.g., Stager 1985), but this definition is not suitable for all the buildings of this type in Iron Age II.

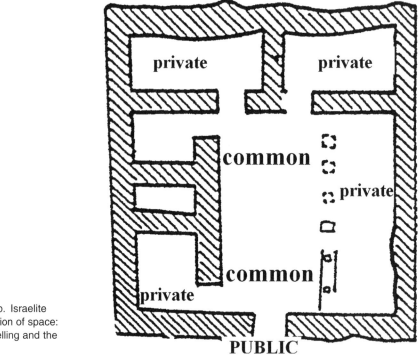

Fig. 39b. Israelite
perception of space:
the dwelling and the
world.

building type in the period of the Monarchy (and as such, we should view the adoption of the house by the Israelites as expressing an ethnically specific behavior).[22] Other ethnic groups ceased using it almost completely (and thus, the house may also have been an ethnic marker). At this stage, its agricultural function ceased to be the motivation for choosing this building type, because we find it also in urban and even fortified buildings (although its functionality may have remained relevant to small hill farmers). The main reason for its exclusive use was that it was perceived as the standard and therefore legitimate building style. As its usage became established, a complex system of social messages formed around its various subtypes. An individual's choice of a certain building type expressed intersocial differences such as "I am wealthier," "I am part of an extended family," and so on.

The four-room house ceased to be used during the sixth century as a result of historical events. The destruction of the Kingdom of Judah, the death of many people, and the various exiles led to the disintegration of communities and of Judahite society as a whole. This collapse created far-reaching changes in the social structure and ethnic composition of the region, and the traditional building model disappeared along with the social world that was identified with it.[23]

---

22. On ethnically specific behaviors and ethnic markers, see chap. 8 below.

23. Similar processes took place after the destruction of the Kingdom of Israel in the eighth century B.C.E. and the succeeding disintegration of Israelite society there.

This description has implications for understanding several aspects of Israelite society in the Iron Age and necessitates taking a polemical stand against the minimalist school. Scholars belonging to this school of thought treated Israelite society as a society typical of the region in the ancient era and try to place it on a long-term historical continuum with the society that existed in the land of Israel during the Late Bronze Age (see, for example, Lemche 1996). These studies analyzed the Late Bronze Age society well. Scholars saw it as a society divided between a small elite and the masses and noted the lack of a common denominator between the two groups and the absence of a "national identity."

But these scholars also applied this description to the Iron Age Israelite society, despite the many clear differences between the Canaanite society of the late Bronze Age and the society of Iron Age II.[24] One difference, which I have clarified in the present chapter, is that in complete contrast to the heterogeneity typical of the Bronze Age population Israelite society was far more homogeneous. Even though there were undoubtedly differences in wealth, property and status, the archaeological findings reflect an unprecedented architectural uniformity in all strata of society and in both kingdoms (evidence for a degree of shared ethnic identity). This uniformity is also reflected in the Bible[25] and accepted by many historical studies of Israelite society (e.g., Pedersen 1926: 54, 57; Gordis 1971; Perdue 1997: 167; and see above, chaps. 1–2; and see more below).

Recognizing the homogeneity of Israelite society should not be interpreted as arguing that this society was isolated from its environment. Many studies have noted the links connecting Israel to the cultures of the ancient Near East and making it an inseparable part of the region.[26] However, within this general context, and like each of these cultures, Israelite society had its own unique characteristics. Presumably, the transition to the organizational level of a territorial kingdom created equivalent changes in other ethnic groups as well (and this deserves further study). Regardless of what we think about the ethnogenesis of Israel—tribes arriving from the transjordan or from Egypt, local nomads, rebel Canaanite farmers, or other theories (see Faust 2006b: 170–87, and references there)—during the period of the Monarchy, Israelite society was cohesive and differed from Canaanite society in many ways (see further below, chap. 8). This difference was expressed in all realms of life and also manifested itself in the material remains.[27]

---

24. The comparison is also problematic because during Iron Age II there were territorial states, not just city-states as in the Late Bronze Age. This argument is true not only for Israel but also for Moab, Ammon, and other polities and groups.

25. Although minimalists see the picture arising from the Bible as a deliberate forgery of course.

26. Mutual responsibility and concern for the poor and similar ideas existed in the ancient Near East and were not exclusive to Israel, but this does not negate the characteristics and perceptions that were unique to Israel and Judah.

27. Other elements that indicate a shared ethos (between Israel and Judah, in contrast to other groups) can be seen in the comparative lack of royal inscriptions, as well as in the lack of decoration on local pottery, the use of simple inhumations (until the 8th century), and more (for the ethos that underlined many of these patterns, see Faust 2006b: 92–107, and references. See also Rendsburg 2007).

Chapter 8

Pots and Peoples:
Ethnic Groups in the Kingdom of Israel

In previous chapters, we have noted the differences between various groups within Israelite society. We have mainly discussed the differences between the rural and urban sectors and the socioeconomic gaps between various groups within the urban sector. In this chapter, I will present a social group of a different type: on the one hand, it constitutes a class of its own, and on the other hand, it spans some of the distinctions described above, because its traces are found both in the country and in the city. This group is the non-Israelite population, which can be termed *Canaanite-Phoenician* (on the connections between these two terms, see Millard 1973: 36; Ap-Thomas 1973: 262–64; see also Röllig 1983). This double term points up its link to the local population of the northern valleys, meaning the descendants of the original residents, who were called *Canaanites* by the authors of the biblical sources. At the same time, the dominant ethnic group of the northern coast of Syria–Palestine in the Iron Age is more acceptably considered to have been the *Phoenicians*.[1]

The attribution of material findings to ethnic groups raises a series of problems, both in theory and in practice. Hence, the first part of this chapter is devoted to a theoretical and methodological clarification of this issue, and only afterwards shall we turn to analyzing the findings.

Archaeology and Ethnicity

Research Development

As Colin Renfrew wrote, "The most problematic of all the concepts which we have tended to use is that of 'a people'" (Renfrew 1993: 20). The attempt to identify ethnic groups in the archaeological record raises many complex problems. In the past, archaeologists tended to classify the various finds as "archaeological cultures," which were considered the material reflections of ethnic groups or "peoples" (for a summary of research, see S. Jones 1997). Childe (1929: v–vi) summarized this view: "We find certain types of remains—pots, implements, ornaments, burial rites and house forms—constantly recurring together. Such a complex of associated traits we shall term 'cultural group' or just a 'culture.' We assume that such a complex is the material expression of what today would be called a 'people.'"

In the archaeology of the land of Israel, for example, many scholars attempted to identify the Israelites, Philistines, and other groups and "their" archaeological

---

1. We do not know how these people saw themselves; however, it is reasonable to assume that they were considered non-Israelites by themselves and "others" by the Israelite population.

cultures (see Faust 2006b: 20–29 for a summary of research and interpretation; on the various groups, see also B. Mazar 1981; Aharoni 1979). However, it is quite clear today that this approach was simplistic and incorrect. Many factors shape and influence material cultures, and ethnicity is only one of them, along with social status, wealth, gender, occupations, ecology, and more. Following the anthropologists and sociologists, archaeologists began to understand that ethnic groups are not uniform. Ethnic identity (or "ethnicity") is subjective and flexible and is in a constant process of change (see for instance, Barth 1969; Shennan 1989; 1991; Emberling 1997; S. Jones 1997; Faust 2006b; and additional bibliography there). In light of this realization, some scholars have doubted the ability of archaeology to identify ethnic groups (concerning our region, see Herzog 1997b). However, it appears that in most cases, complex as they may have been, some relation did exist between ethnicity and the material culture (McGuire 1982; Kamp and Yoffee 1980; Emberling 1997; and others; see also Howard 1996: 239–40), and if we relinquish in advance any chance of identifying ethnic groups through archaeological finds, we will be "throwing out the baby with the bathwater."

Methodological Assumptions and Problems

McGuire noted that "the nature and persistence of ethnic groups depend on the existence of an ethnic boundary which ethnic groups maintain through the manipulation and display of symbols" (McGuire 1982: 160, and bibliography there). In his opinion, "What is important to the maintenance of such boundaries is not the totality of the cultural traits contained by them but those traits that the groups utilize as symbols of their identity separate from other groups. These symbols may be behavioral or material in form" (see also Kamp and Yoffee 1980: 96; Emberling 1997: 299; Barth 1969: 14, 15). According to McGuire (for a full discussion, see McGuire 1982: 163):

> Material symbols of ethnic identity provide the most direct archaeological reflections of boundary maintenance [between groups], but, for a number of reasons, these are most likely to be scarce in the archaeological record. . . . The material correlates of ethnically specific behaviors are more likely to be represented in the archaeological record than the material symbols of ethnic identification. . . . Material correlates of such behavioral differences may include variations in rubbish disposal patterns . . . or differences in floor plans of dwellings.

It is clear, therefore, that identity markers or symbols (for example, a yarmulke) are the best avenue to recognizing ethnic groups; however, they are as difficult to identify as they are arbitrary, and we may even see them without identifying them as markers. Ethnically specific behavior (the avoidance of pork, for example, which gave rise to a great deal of scholarly discussion; see, e.g., Hesse 1990; Faust 2006b: 35–40, and many references; see also below), on the other hand, is much easier to identify.

These observations can be exemplified by the results of excavations at "Parting Ways," a site in Massachusetts in the United States (Deetz 1996: 187–211). The archaeologist James Deetz analyzed the finds from an eighteenth-century building. The items found there were similar to items found at other sites in the region, but there were also differences. A detailed study showed that the site was inhabited by freed African slaves who did indeed use material items identical to their "European" neighbors' items, but whose life-styles and usage methods were very different from those of their neighbors: "(T)he occupants of the site constructed their houses differently, disposed of their trash differently, arranged their community differently. But because the artifacts themselves were so familiar to us, the essential differences were disguised behind them, and only when more basic consideration of different perceptions of the world was made did the picture come into focus" (Deetz 1996: 210).

This example demonstrates the unique problems we face and also provides a possible solution. We should not rule out the possibility that various objects can indeed serve as ethnic markers, but it is worthwhile to examine archaeological finds while assuming that not only the form of the vessels but also the way they were used is important, because the way they were used may indicate the ethnic identity of the residents of the site being excavated.

McGuire analyzed the archaeological evidence for the existence of ethnic groups in Arizona during the second half of the nineteenth century, using historical evidence and anthropological and sociological research. His conclusion was that three main factors influence the formation and transformation of ethnic groups.

1. A sense of **competition** plays a central role in the maintenance of boundaries between ethnic groups. Ethnic boundaries function in the competition between groups and individuals for material, social, and psychological reward. However, competition does not explain why group formation is channeled along ethnic lines (McGuire 1982: 169–70).

2. A sense of **ethnocentrism** is what channels competition along ethnic lines: "Ethnocentrism is the tendency for members of an ethnic group to regard their physical appearance, behavior pattern, and ideals as superior," and their respect for other groups depends on the similarities of these phenomena to their own (McGuire 1982: 170). If ethnocentrism does not separate the groups, then competition will not be channeled along ethnic lines. "Ethnocentrism, however, can only be regarded as an independent variable in an initial contact situation" (1982: 170). After that, ethnocentrism will be shaped by the action of other forces.

3. **Differential distribution of power**: this is the key variable in explaining changes in ethnic boundary maintenance, "The relationships of power are fundamental to the competition for resources within a society. . . . The way in which the relationships of power in a society structure competition will shape ethnocentrism and determine the degree of ethnic boundary maintenance" (McGuire 1982: 171). Power determines the distribution of at least a large part of the wealth possessed by a society, and its importance can be viewed from the perspective of the individual as a strategy for gaining access to material, social, and psychological rewards. If the disparity between two ethnic groups is great, then strong boundary maintenance can be expected, because members of the weaker group cannot hope to gain high prestige or wealth on a societal level. The weaker group, however, will create a

smaller stage upon which individuals can compete for power. The dominant ethnic group reinforces its position by encouraging extensive boundary maintenance both between inferior ethnic groups and between itself and others (McGuire 1982: 171).

Emberling (1997: 303) also believes that "ethnic groups often exist in hierarchical relationships—whether dominant or subordinate—to other groups or to a state, although stratification is not an essential feature of relations between ethnic groups." It should be noted that in some cases "the ascription of ethnic identity to a particular group of people . . . has, in itself, been a major mechanism of political control" used by the state (Ucko 1988: xi; see also Small 1997: 279–81; Patterson 1991: 79; Emberling 1997: 304).

McGuire summarized the relationship between the three components thus: "Competition provides the motivation for group formation, ethnocentrism channels it along ethnic lines, and the differential distribution of power determines the nature of the relationship" (McGuire 1982: 173). In order to test his theory, McGuire (1982: 174) suggested that two variables should be measured: the degree of ethnic boundary maintenance (through examination of food, refuse, ceramics, and architecture, which he believes have proved to be more ethnically sensitive) and the disparity of power between the ethnic groups (through their size, control over resources such as wealth and military strength, etc.).

Although McGuire's study deals with a period that is well documented historically (and despite other differences between the case studies), it is very important to our context, because it discusses different ethnic groups existing within one political unit. We should be aware that ethnicity is not the only social aspect reflected by material items. Economic status, prestige, religion, profession, location (urban versus rural, etc.), and other characteristics should also be taken into account (McGuire 1982: 164; see also Kamp and Yoffee 1980: 97; London 1989; Skjeggestand 1992: 1790–80; Orser and Fagan 1995: 215–16; Emberling 1997: 305–6, 310–11). In most cases, the "symbolic content" of material culture is not unambiguous but is mixed. Contradictions between different symbols may be discovered, for instance, if a member of one ethnic group whose economic status was low acquired a higher status over time.

The difficult task is, therefore, to identify the aspects of material culture that are connected with ethnicity and are not a result of ecology, wealth, status, setting (urban versus rural), and so on. In order to differentiate between the various "groups," we must examine a society fully to identify other factors as well (for example, see Kamp and Yoffee 1980). Only after the other elements have been identified can we attribute "ethnic" labels to some traits of material culture—whether as symbols or as material results of ethnic behavior.

The second step, of course, should be to find the actual connection between these material traits and the ethnic group under discussion. However, due to the difficulties facing any attempt to identify symbolic traits in the archaeological record, special attention should be given to other sources, especially written. These sometimes very problematic sources should be examined carefully in order to extract the most out of them, as they can give some important insights into any society (see also J. M. Hall 1997: 142).

Implementation of the Methodology in Analyzing Sites from Northern Israel

The sites discussed below are all located in the northern valleys. The Kingdom of Israel governed most of the territory in this area. However, other political entities existed nearby: the northern coastal plains were probably controlled by Phoenician cities (Stern 1997: 10), while large areas of the northern Transjordan, including the Golan or parts of it, belonged to the Aramean kingdoms (at least during certain periods). The boundaries between these kingdoms and the Kingdom of Israel changed during the course of Iron Age II, but this is irrelevant to the discussion that follows below (for a general discussion, see Aharoni 1979). The polities active in the region during this period had various types of relationships and many shared elements and even mutual influences can be clearly identified (see, for example, Burney 1977: 188–89; Holladay 1995: 380–81; Gal 1995). The northern valleys were among the main settlement regions of the Kingdom of Israel and hence contained many cities. The region has good agricultural land and served as an important crossroads on the regional, transregional, and international routes (map 4).

Thus in the main cities of this region, we should expect to discover a reflection of many cultural influences. Though one would expect the mutual influences and connections between groups to increase ethnic awareness (e.g., Olsen and Kobylinski 1991: 7; Barth 1969: 9–10; Kamp and Yoffee 1980: 93; see also below), it is much more difficult for archaeologists, given the limited extent of area exposed and the random selection of excavated areas, to identify the various groups present in a single excavation. Furthermore, even if the remains of different groups were found, they might well be defined by archaeologists as belonging to one "culture" due to their concentration in one site.

It is therefore difficult to rely on finds (only) from the major cities in this region in identifying and isolating ethnic groups. The key to isolating material remains in a manner that reveals the ethnicity of their original owners is found primarily in villages. Unfortunately, archaeological knowledge of rural settlement is very limited (as we have seen in previous chapters). As Ahlström noted, Syro-Palestinian archaeology is "tell-minded" (see Ahlström 1982a: 25; London 1989). It appears, however, that it is in this rural sector that there is a reasonable chance of isolating and identifying ethnic groups with less external influence, or to be more precise, less mixed archaeologically (on the mixed nature of some of the levels at Megiddo, see Kempinski 1989; 1993; Holladay 1995: 383; Faust 2006b: 215–18). After comparing these remains with their parallels from rural sites in other regions (see also London 1989: 42, 50, 52; of course, ecological and other considerations must be taken into account), we can reevaluate the findings from the urban sites.

The Rural Sites in the Northern Valleys

Tel Qiri

The site known as Tel Qiri is located at the foot of the Carmel range and borders on the Jezreel Valley (Ben-Tor and Portugali 1997; Ben-Tor 1993). It is not really a tell but a long terrace descending eastward from the Carmel that is reached by a road from the direction of Kibbutz Ein Hashofet. The remains of an unwalled rural

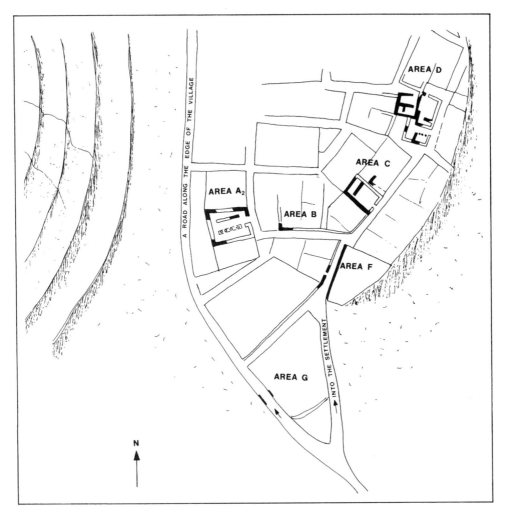

Fig. 40. Tel Qiri: general plan of the village (Portugali 1987: 136).

site were discovered on the terrace (fig. 40). According to the excavators, its layout indicates that this was an unplanned site. No destruction levels were discerned between the five Iron Age strata, and it appears that each level was connected to the previous one. Many buildings were found on the various levels. Most of the residential buildings were small, and their areas (including unroofed yards) averaged 20–80 square meters (fig. 41). According to the excavators, these buildings represent ordinary rural houses based on one to three rooms in a row, each room leading to the next. Some of the entrances were through an open yard. Several agricultural installations were also found on the site: silos and an industrial oil-producing installation.

In one of the buildings (level VIII from the eleventh century B.C.E.), unique pottery was found, which along with the animal bones also discovered led the excavators to believe that this building had a ritual function. In addition, in two

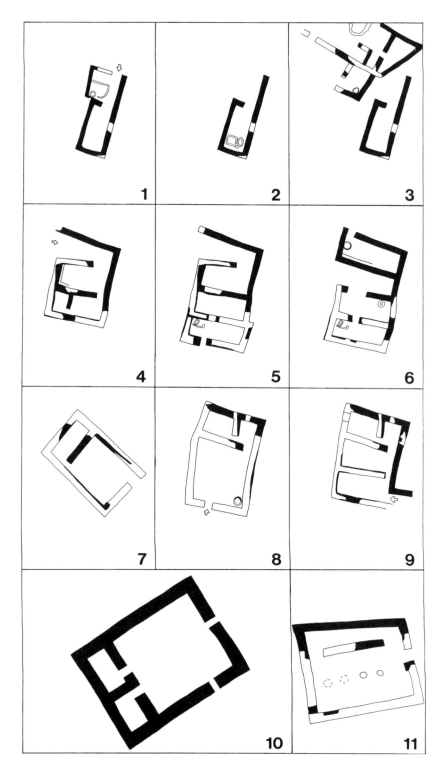

Fig. 41. Tel Qiri: excavated buildings (Portugali 1987: 135).

different strata of the site, two public buildings were found. Because there were only two of these buildings, the excavators found it difficult to reach general conclusions, but they considered one of them to be a four-room house (this conclusion appears to be mistaken: while the typical four-room house has many subtypes, all subtypes include a broad space at the back; however, this sort of room does not exist in the building under discussion). The lack of information on the rural sector in the rest of the country led the excavators to suggest that the four-room house was an essentially urban building, and so they assumed that on a rural site such as Tel Qiri it could only have served public purposes (Portugali 1987: 133–34).

The excavators believed that it was not possible to ascertain the residents' ethnic background—Israelite or not (Ben-Tor and Portugali 1987: 84)—on the basis of the material culture discovered on the site, but they assumed "based on historical considerations" that the residents were "non-Israelites." In contrast, other scholars have compared Iron Age I Tel Qiri to Israelite sites from the hill region (Thompson 1997: 170).

Tel Amal (Nir David)

Tel Amal is a site occupying 0.2 hectares and located in the Beth Shean valley, near Kibbutz Nir David, where four Iron Age II levels have been discovered (Edelstein 1969; 1972; Levy and Edelstein 1972). The upper levels were damaged by later activity.

On level III, two large buildings were discovered. The area of one of them is about 225 square meters, and in one room objects were discovered that indicate, in the excavator's opinion, that the room was used for ritual purposes. In a building from level IV, a series of weights was found along with wooden remains that were probably part of a loom, indicating that the building served as a textile mill. Many cooking pots with the remains of paint were also discovered, as were many heating ovens. These findings raise the possibility that the site was also used for dyeing textiles. The plans of the buildings that have been published are unlike the buildings known from most of the rural sites in this period.

Tel Hadar

Tel Hadar is located on the eastern shore of the Sea of Galilee, about seven kilometers north of En Gev (Kochavi 1993a: 291). According to the excavator, during this period the site served as an agricultural satellite village of the town located at En Gev (Kochavi 1994: 140).

In level III (ninth century B.C.E.), several four-room houses were discovered that contained monoliths. The excavator identified streets and plazas on the site plan. The defensive wall, constructed prior to this level, continued to serve a defense capacity. Clear changes to the site plan occurred in levels I–II (eighth century B.C.E.), which are the subject of current discussion (fig. 42). The wall that was present in the previous levels had ceased to be used. Private houses were found outside it that were similar in shape to "broad buildings," and no more of the four-room houses that had been characteristic of the previous level were found. Most of the

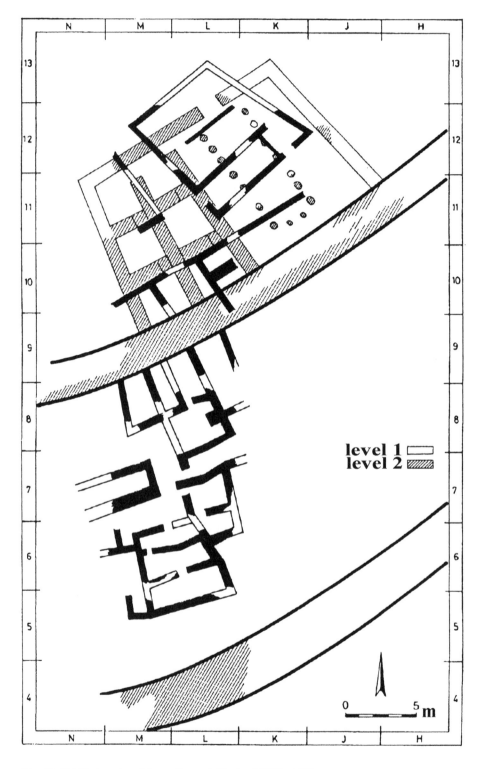

Fig. 42. Tel Hadar: plan of the settlement (Kochavi 1993c: 733).

buildings contained one room, and in some cases a small square room was added on the narrow side. Larger buildings contained two or three broad rooms that were arranged one after the other. The excavator remarked that the village plan differed from all the settlements known from this period. An Aramaic inscription was also found that was similar to inscriptions found in nearby En Gev and Bethsaida. The differences in the material culture and the language of the inscriptions indicate in the excavator's opinion that the Aramean Kingdom of Geshur took control of this region (Kochavi 1994) and that the site's residents were not Israelites (Kochavi 1993c: 734). It should be noted that the plan of the residential houses is similar in many respects to the buildings excavated at Tel Qiri and also to buildings found in Syria (Kochavi et al. 1992: 84 n. 16).

Analysis:
The Unique Features of the Sites

If we compare the three rural sites described above with the other Iron Age II rural sites (discussed in chaps. 4–5 above), it is immediately apparent that they are different in several key ways: the typical plan of the residential houses, the general plan of the sites, the existence or absence of public buildings, and the average size of the residential houses. To these we should add some additional data that can help determine the uniqueness of these sites, such as the findings of animal bones and the pottery discovered. We shall discuss these features and offer possible explanations for the differences between the sites in the northern valleys and their equivalents in the rest of the country.

The Plan of the Residential Houses

The most prominent feature of the three sites is the absence of the four-room type of residential house. The residential houses discovered were broad buildings, in clear contrast to the common construction method of the Iron Age. The absence of four-room houses at Tel Qiri led Portugali to conclude that four-room houses were essentially urban buildings (Portugali 1987: 133–34), while their absence at Tel Hadar led Kochavi to argue that the eighth-century settlement there differed from the rest of the sites known in Israel (Kochavi 1993a: 293).

However, as we saw in chap. 7, the four-room house was an Israelite construction type, and its absence from a site only raises the suspicion that the site was not inhabited by Israelites. It is unlikely that this reflected a regional difference, because four-room houses have been discovered in other settlements in the north, including in the valleys: for example, in urban centers such as Megiddo (Kempinski 1989: 125–27, see also figs. 40.13, 40.15, and 40.18), Hazor (see, e.g., Yadin 1972: figs. 46, 48, 49, 52), Jokneam (Ben-Tor et al. 1987: 8), Kinrot (Fritz 1993: 200; see also illustrations 7–8), Beth Shean (A. Mazar 1998b; 2006a), and probably also in Tel Gath Hepher (Gal 1994); and in rural sites in the Galilee, such as H. Malta (Covello-Paran 1998; see also fig. 21 above) and H. Rosh Zayit (Gal and Alexandre 2000).

In fact, most of the residents of cities and villages in the central hills and the Galilee as well as many of the residents of cities in the northern valleys lived in four-room houses. The distribution of this building type only emphasizes the difference between the residential houses in the three rural sites discussed here and the rest of the sites in the northern valleys and in the rest of the country during the period of the Monarchy.

Despite the relative rarity of the broad-room building type discussed here, it is not without parallels. Similar residential buildings have been found in stratum 9 (Iron Age I) at Tel Keisan in the coastal plain near Akko, and the excavator noted the similarity of these buildings to Bronze Age houses (Humbert 1993: 864–67; the Iron Age II settlement was small and poor, but there was clear continuity between it and the previous stage). The fact that the site is located in the northern coastal plain is one indication that its population was not Israelite; according to the excavator of Tel Keisan, the site's residents were the ancestors of the Jeturites (Humbert 1993: 866), but it is more likely that this was a Phoenician settlement (A. Mazar 1990: 357). In this regard, it is worth noting the coastal influences and the connections with Cyprus that were identified in the site. Similar buildings were discovered in Bronze Age villages from the Beth Shean valley, such as Tell el-Hayyat (Falconer 1995) and a site near Kfar Rupin (Gophna 1979). Similar buildings from closer periods are also known from Megiddo (the "treasure house"; see, e.g., T. Dothan 1982: 70–76, fig. 12) and Akko (M. Dothan 1985: plan 1), as well as during Iron Age II at Kinrot (e.g., Fassbeck 2008: 17) and Tel Rehov (A. Mazar 1999; 2008; see also 2009: 333).[2] The residents of the villages being discussed in this section shared a similar background.

Kempinski's analysis of the finds from Megiddo also accords with this description. Kempinski identified two contrasting trends in the plans of the Iron Age buildings at Megiddo: continued use of the Bronze Age courtyard buildings on the one hand, and the appearance of new architectural elements such as the four-room house on the other hand. He explained this combination as reflecting the mixed population of the city and attributed the traditional architecture to the fact that, "in Megiddo, where the local Canaanites segment of the population was probably stronger, the traditional house form of the Bronze Age absorbed the new form" (Kempinski 1989: 127; and see below).

The difference between the broad buildings found at the three sites under discussion and the more common construction type of the four-room house is not just a matter of architectural form but also of different functionality, implying a difference in the social structure. As we have seen above, access analysis of the buildings shows that the four-room house presents a very "flat tree" diagram, while in these villages the houses show a linear pattern (fig. 43).

The linear pattern implies that there were hierarchical restrictions imposed on movement into the various spaces (see, for example, Banning and Byrd 1989: 156; F. E. Brown 1990: 103), and we find this pattern not only in the buildings of the three sites discussed here but also in Bronze Age buildings (as can be seen, for instance,

---

2. Amihai Mazar, Tel Rehov's excavator, accepts the connection between the four-room house and the Israelites but, because no such houses were unearthed at Tel Rehov (which was located within the Kingdom of Israel), he (2008: 333) regards the site as an exception. However, because the inhabitants were not Israelites, the situation in Rehov fits the overall pattern in the northern valleys very nicely. See also chap. 7 above.

in the plans published by Ben-Dov 1997) and even in some other urban Iron Age buildings in the north (see more below). The courtyard buildings also tended to have a "deep" pattern; even though their access pattern is a "tree," some of the "branches" form quite a deep line (path), meaning a line that extends beyond more than one room. This tendency contrasts with the maximal freedom of movement enabled by the flat "tree" pattern of four-room houses, the lines of which do not typically exceed one room. This characteristic may also reflect a different ethnic background of the residents of the three sites. As we saw above, the four-room houses are indicative of ethnicity, and it appears that this is also true in the northern valleys.

The Settlement Plan

The settlements excavated at Tel Qiri and Tel Amal (Nir David) were completely unwalled. One of the walls erected in an earlier stratum at Tel Hadar no longer existed in the eighth century, although another wall might still have been standing. These unwalled settlements are in contrast to most of the villages of this period, which were surrounded by boundary walls (chap. 4 above). In this respect as well, there is a clear similarity between the villages in the northern valleys and the Bronze Age Canaanite villages in the same region, which were also mostly unwalled (Faust 2005a, and references).

The Israelite preference for constructing walls around villages may have stemmed from several factors. Perhaps, for example, it reflects the form of social organization that was typical of the Israelites: in most of the villages, there was a social organization (the biblical *mishpahah*) that was able to raise the resources for joint projects such as the building of boundary walls. It may also have resulted from cultural differences. We have already mentioned the study of the Bronze Age in Britain by Thomas, concluding that walled settlements reflect a kinship structure that was based on endogamic marriages (within the group). Boundary walls in these settlements served as symbols of the barrier between "us," as members of the group (kinship group and settlement), and "them," the outsiders (Thomas 1997). Thus, boundary walls were used to demarcate spaces and could be an important factor in maintaining community identity (compare with Parker-Pearson and Richards 1994). This may have corresponded to the reality of Israelite society (for example, see de Vaux 1965: 30–31; McAfee 1993: 690) but apparently not of Canaanite-Phoenician society, or at least not in the villages discussed here, which were not organized along the same lines and probably did not function as a community in the same way.

Surrounding villages with walls may be reflected in the biblical laws. The biblical jubilee law states that during the jubilee year the agricultural lands reverted to their owners, and this applied to "the houses of the *haṣerim* that have no walls around them" (Lev 25:31), because these buildings were to "be counted as the fields of the country: they may be redeemed, and they shall be released through the jubilee." This is different from settlements (including villages) that were surrounded by a wall and the houses of which were sold permanently. For our purposes, it does not matter whether this law was actually applied during the period of the Monarchy

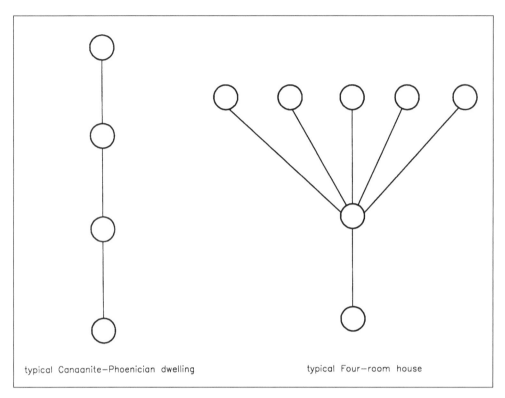

typical Canaanite—Phoenician dwelling   typical Four—room house

Fig. 43. Access analysis: the four-room house and a simple Canaanite house compared.

(if the passage is early) or whether it only reflects the memory of a time in which villages were surrounded by walls (if the law is late). The law reflects the situation in highland villages, and the villages in the northern valleys do not fit into this picture.

Public Buildings

In most of the Iron Age villages of ancient Israel, as we have seen, there were no public buildings, apart from buildings that were probably used for storage (compare Faust 1995b: 55–57, 60; 2000d; Finkelstein 1988b). This fact may imply that the Israelite villages were autonomous to some extent and did not require public buildings constructed by the authorities (from outside the village). In contrast, at Tel Qiri there were probably public buildings, and this was also the case at Tel Amal (Nir David; this explains the large building of 225 square meters). Regarding Tel Hadar, there is limited information, but it appears that it too had public buildings (Kochavi et al. 1992: 41–42; Kochavi 1993a; note the large building on the site plan). Perhaps the villages in the northern valleys served as outposts of the city or palace, and the public buildings belonged to it (see below). Particularly noteworthy are the cultic rooms discovered at Tel Amal (Nir David) and Tel Qiri,[3] which is in complete

───────────────

3. At Tel Qiri, this is an Iron Age I building, but due to the similarity and continuity between all the Iron Age levels of the site, it seems that if such a building was required during Iron Age I a similar build-

contrast to the situation in all the other Iron Age II villages; in the other villages, no cultic buildings (or rooms) have been discovered, even though some of them have been almost completely excavated. In this respect, the three northern villages are similar to the few Bronze Age villages excavated, all of which contained cultic rooms or even temples. This was the case in the nearby sites of Tell el-Hayyat (Falconer 1995) and Kfar Rupin (Gophna 1979: 28–29) and also in the villages of Givat Sharett (Bahat 1972: 66–67), Nahal Rephaim (Eisenberg 1994: 91–92; see Faust 2005a), and Manahat (Edelstein 1994: 101). The similarity between the Bronze Age sites and the Iron Age villages in the northern valleys indicates similar religious practices and is in contrast to the vast majority of the Iron Age II villages, which are detached from any connection to Bronze Age practice. Interestingly, evidence for cult is also relatively common in Iron Age cities in the valleys (when compared with its absence in the highlands, for example)—for example, at several areas of Tel Rehov (A. Mazar 1999: 23–28; 2008: 2016–18) and Kinrot (Fassbeck 2008).

The Size of the Residential Buildings

Most of the residential houses in the three northern villages are very small. The roofed area of some of the buildings at Tel Qiri does not exceed 20 square meters (Portugali 1987: 133–34). The complete plan of Tel Hadar has not yet been published, but the excavator's descriptions indicate small houses with one room (sometimes with an additional small room at the side) and larger houses with two or three rooms in a row. The area of the largest buildings in the published plan is only about 50 square meters, and the area of the small buildings is around 20 square meters (see Kochavi 1993a: 292).

In the plan of Tel Amal (Nir David) one can also identify buildings with one room, the average size of which is 25–30 square meters (according to the excavator, some of the buildings were part of a larger building, but this suggestion is not supported by the plan; the similarity between these buildings and the others discussed here also hints that these were independent buildings). The limited area of these buildings is particularly noticeable in comparison with the typical area of rural houses in other regions (120 square meters or more, on average). Furthermore, the buildings discussed here are small even in comparison with urban buildings of this same period.

It is worth considering a sociological explanation: the size of the buildings in the three villages reflects a nonegalitarian society with a large percentage of poor people.[4] In the villages discussed here, there is indeed a wider range of building

---

ing would have been required during Iron Age II (but due to the limited amount of area that has been excavated, this building has not yet been discovered).

4. Other theoretical explanations may also be considered. for instance, that many residents of these villages were unmarried young people who lived alone or that some family members did not reside in the main house during most of the year (for example, if they were herding livestock for a living). However, it is unlikely that herding was very important in this area in particular, because the northern valleys are highly suited to cultivating crops. Nor is the pattern of children's leaving their parents' homes before marriage known from this part of the world in any period until the Modern Age. The fact that explanations of this sort should be raised indicates how different the society in the northern valleys villages was from the society known from other villages.

sizes compared with other villages from this period, where, as we have seen, the buildings were quite uniform in size. However, the small houses could not contain more than a few residents. Even if one prefers a higher density per area than the number usually accepted (6–10 roofed square meters per person; see, e.g., Naroll 1962; Kramer 1979; Stager 1985: 17–18; Ember and Ember 1995: 98–99), the question should still be asked: how many people could crowd into a one-room building of 20 square meters?

Apparently, the small buildings were inhabited by nuclear families, while the other villages of this period were inhabited by extended families.[5] Our knowledge about Canaanite society is somewhat limited, but existing data enable us to cautiously suggest that the common family type in Canaanite society was indeed the nuclear family. The texts from Ugarit show that small families were the common family type in the rural sector (which is the sector discussed here). Although this culture is not identical to the Canaanite-Phoenician culture in terms of time and place, the comparison might be illuminating (compare Rainey 1966: 109–11; Heltzer 1976: 103; but see Lemche 1985: 206–7; Martin 1989: 101), especially in light of the fact that other societies in the ancient Near East were characterized by large, extended families (see, e.g., Heltzer 1976: 103, and additional bibliography there; Diakonoff 1975).

A similar picture arises from the Bible. According to Lemche, there is very little information in the Bible about nuclear families: hence it is interesting that two of the few examples he presents for such families refer to non-Israelite families: (1) The story of the rape of Dinah (Genesis 34) is, in his opinion "the clearest example of the existence of nuclear family" in the Bible (Lemche 1985: 253): Even though Hamor, father of Shechem, negotiated the marriage, after the marriage Shechem has his own "house" (Gen 34:26), as transpires from the fact that Dinah is taken from there (Shechem's house) at the end of the story (for the place of this story in biblical editing, see Lemche 1985: 253 n. 25). (2) Lemche believes that Esau's family was also a nuclear family, because in Gen 36:6 only Esau, his wives, sons, and daughters are mentioned, while the wives of his sons are not mentioned (Lemche 1985: 252). This verse can be compared with the description of Jacob's family (Gen 46:8–28), where we read of an extended family of three generations (see also Weisman 1985: 7–11).

The weight of the biblical evidence depends largely on its interpretation, and admittedly these passages can be understood differently. Thus, for instance, the fact that all Shechem's men are circumcised might indicate closeness to Jacob's family, while the description of Esau's family may reflect anti-Edomite propaganda. On the other hand, if a nuclear family such as Esau's family is described in negative terms, this negative description still testifies to a different norm in Judah. This is further recognition of the distinctive character of Canaanite society. Despite the scarcity of biblical evidence, when added to the data presented above, the biblical

---

5. This is not the place to examine the entire archaeological record for the Bronze Age sites. However, an examination of the rural sites from this period shows that some of them, such as the site near Kfar Rupin (Gophna 1979), and Givat Sharett (Bahat 1972: 65) contained very small buildings (for a similar situation, at least regarding some of the buildings, see Edelstein 1994). Other sites, such as Nahal Rephaim, probably contained larger buildings (Eisenberg 1994: 86–91). See also Faust 2005a.

evidence strengthens the suggestion that the families living in non-Israelite villages in the northern valleys were indeed nuclear. Another, more general consideration can be added to these arguments: in agricultural societies, "the extended family is most prevalent among the rich and the land-owning peasants" (Yorburg 1975: 9). However, although the definition "land-owning peasants" is appropriate for most of the villages of the period, it does not fit the three villages discussed here (see below),[6] where the social structure was different from the structure prevailing in the other villages.

In any case, even scholars who prefer a different explanation and do not accept the premise that these houses were inhabited by nuclear families must admit that a society characterized by such great density in its residential houses is different in character from the society in other parts of the country. This datum is also affirmed by the fact that the many buildings typical of the three villages contained only one room, while in the rest of the villages in the country the buildings had many rooms (and were mainly of the four-room type).

Faunal Remains

An analysis of the faunal remains seems to enrich the discussion. The report on Tel Qiri, the only site for which a complete final report has been published, shows that a relatively large quantity of pig bones were discovered at the site (S. Davis 1987: 249). Pig bones constitute about 1.5% of all the animal bones discovered in Iron Age levels, and in terms of occurrence, they are the third group after sheep/ goat, and cattle bones. One of the prominent features of Israelite settlement in the hills is the almost complete absence of pig bones. The frequency of pig bones in Israelite sites is usually 0%–0.1%; in certain cases it is larger (0.4%), but it is always less than 1.0% (Hellwing 1984: 112; Hesse 1990; Bunimovitz and Lederman 2009: 123–24; Finkelstein 1996a: 206; 1997; Faust 2006b: 35–40, and references). Some scholars believe that the absence of pig bones is the best indication of the presence of Israelites in Iron Age I sites (e.g., Finkelstein 1996a: 206). So, it must be inferred that the bones at Tel Qiri imply that the taboo against eating pork was not known to its residents. Hesse and Wapnish have recently stressed that avoiding eating pork was also known in other parts of the ancient Near East, and thus not every site that lacks pig bones should necessarily be defined as Israelite (Hesse and Wapnish 1997; but see also Faust 2006b). However, what is relevant to our discussion is that the Israelites avoided eating pork; it does not matter whether they were the only ones to do so, because the presence of pig bones on the site implies that we can at the very least define its residents as "non-Israelites."

Examining Middle and Late Bronze Age sites does not provide sufficient evidence regarding the Canaanites' eating habits (following Finkelstein 1997: 227–28, fig. 1; for possible explanations, see Hesse and Wapnish 1997). In some sites, a

---

6. In Canaanite society, it is likely that all family types (including extended) existed, but presumably in the villages discussed here the social spectrum was not represented in its entirety, and they were composed mainly of nuclear families (as in Ugarit). Perhaps the author of the biblical texts discussed above applied his knowledge of contemporary (Iron Age II) "Canaanites-Phoenicians" to his description (and understanding) of the ancient Canaanites.

high percentage of pig bones was found, for instance at Nahal Rephaim (Middle Bronze Age): 8%; Shiloh (Middle Bronze Age): 3.5%; and Tel Michal (Middle Bronze Age): 6.3%; while at other sites a relatively low percentage was found, for example, at Shiloh (Late Bronze Age): 0.17%; and at Ekron (Tel Miqne): 0% (Lev-Tov 2006: 210–11). The percentage of pig bones at Tel Qasila (a non-Israelite site) was similar to that at Tel Qiri, around 1% (S. Davis 1985: 148). The eating habits of the Canaanites have yet to be studied in detail (see also Faust and Katz forthcoming), but these partial results hint that the residents of Tel Qiri may have been Canaanites.

Pottery

There is no doubt that pottery may have great importance to the study of ethnic identity, but attempts to see ethnic indicators in Iron Age pottery have not been simple or straightforward so far (but see Faust 2006b). Sometimes distinctions among various pottery types are insufficient to reveal the ethnic identity of the residents (London 1989; Finkelstein 1996a: 203–4; even comparisons between entire assemblages raise problems; see Bunimovitz and Yasur-Landau 1996: 96); however, there may be greater potential in analyzing the *usage* of pottery by different ethnic groups—that is, ethnic behavior (McGuire 1982: 163; see also Faust 2006b). This sort of analysis requires detailed study of all the finds in each architectural unit. Unfortunately, the state of research in the rural sector does not permit this sort of analysis, because the finds of most of the rural sites have not been fully published (apart from the results of the excavations at Tel Qiri). From the limited data about the pottery unearthed in the rural sector, we can currently draw only partial and tentative conclusions.

The finds from Tel Qiri contain a wide range of pottery types, including imported vessels (see Hunt 1987: 200–203). The data on the excavations at Tel Amal (Nir David) are much less detailed, but the situation there appears to be similar (Gal 1995: 89–90; Edelstein 1969: 25–35). A completely different situation can be seen at Kh. Jemein and Beit Aryeh, the only two sites in the highlands for which pottery finds have been published, even partially. According to the excavator of Kh. Jemein, the pottery assemblage at the site was very limited, and no imported vessels at all were found (Dar 1986a: 38), as was the case at Beit Aryeh (Riklin 1997: 12; for a comprehensive discussion, see also Faust 2006b: 49–64).

These differences may attest to regional differences in patterns of trade and economy. Another study of pottery assemblages discusses both the urban and the rural sector in the northern valleys (the Jezreel Valley, the Beth Shean Valley, and the eastern Jordan Valley) and reveals close connections between these residents and the Phoenician world (Gal 1995). However, examination of the pottery assemblages at many sites in Israel and Judah shows that they contained very few imported vessels, if at all. This was the case not only in the rural highlands sites at Kh. Jemein and Beit Aryeh but also in H. Malta in Galilee (Covello-Paran 2008: 33, 46)[7] and probably

---

7. In most rural sites, not a single imported sherd was found. At H. Malta (Covello-Paran 2008: 33, 46) only two fragments were identified (and both were not rim fragments, so statistically, they should not even be counted).

also in the village excavated at Rosh Zayit.[8] This is also the case in many urban sites such as Jerusalem (I. Eshel 1995: 62; Franken and Steiner 1985: 5, 125, 128), Beersheba (Bachi 1973: 42; Singer-Avitz 1999), and others. The rarity of imported vessels does not indicate limited trade, because other findings from the same sites reflect extensive trade and importing (on Jerusalem, see Auld and Steiner 1996: 63–65; Franken and Steiner 1985: 123–25; on Beersheba, see Liphshitz and Biger 1991: 171–72; Singer-Avitz 1999; for a comprehensive discussion, see Faust 2006b: 49–64). Thus it appears that the rarity of imported vessels in Israelite sites contrasts with their relative frequency in the Canaanite-Phoenician (and Philistine) sites, and that this contrast is related to cultural preferences.[9]

There is additional evidence to support this interpretation. As far as the archaeological record is concerned, the local pottery in the kingdoms of Israel and Judah is characterized by having almost no painted decoration (see, e.g., Barkay 1992: 354; Aharoni 1982: 177; Franken and Steiner 1985: 91; Dever 1997b: 465; Lapp 1992: 442), particularly in comparison with the pottery produced in the neighboring regions during this period, such as in Ammon (Barkay 1990: 181–82), Edom (Barkay 1992: 358; E. Mazar 1985), Phoenicia (Barkay 1992: 325–26, 336–38), and Philistia (Barkay 1992: 335; Ben-Shlomo, Shai, and Maeir 2004). This contrast certainly reflects a cultural preference (see Wood 1990: 88; for a general discussion, see Faust 2006b: 41–48).

As far as the textual evidence is concerned, it is interesting to note the negative attitude that the Bible expressed toward traders (see, for example, the entry "trade" in *Encyclopedia Miqrait*; and also Elat 1977: 203), and it is no coincidence that the Bible uses the loaded (and pejorative) term *Canaanite* to refer to traders (Hos 12:8 and more). Against this background, a statement by Bunimovitz and Yasur-Landau regarding the Iron Age I is interesting. They refer to the "poorness and isolation reflected in the Israelite assemblage," suggesting that those "reflect more than just functional and/or social constraints" and may "hint at *ideological* behavior of the kind that created the pig taboo among the proto-Israelites" (Bunimovitz and Yasur-Landau 1996: 96). Some of the differences to which Bunimovitz and Yasur-Landau refer continued into Iron Age II, and if they are correct in their interpretation, we

---

8. Gal 1992b; 2001: 137. The final report has since been published (Gal and Alexandre 2000), which contain statistics about the pottery unearthed in the various strata and areas, but it should be noted that, for the purposes of this study, the statistics are unusable because, in contrast with the local pottery, the calculations included each and every fragment of imported pottery (including body fragments). Thus, the data used in the tables cannot be used to learn the percentage of imported vessels in the different levels of the site, and the situation must be examined by scrutinizing the plates; these indicate that in the village (as opposed to the fortress) there was a remarkably low percentage of imported vessels (see also Faust 2006b: 55).

9. The relative frequency of imported vessels in Israelite sites such as Samaria may result from foreign influences originating in the close ties that the capital city had with Phoenicia (including royal marriages), as described in the book of Kings. In light of the difference in the ceramic repertoire between Samaria (and similar sites) and most of the sites in the kingdoms of Israel and Judah, the criticism of the prophets regarding these connections and their influence is clear; the differences in the finds reflect the fact that foreign influences led to social changes, including changes to culturally laden habits of vessel consumption and usage.

should not ignore the possibility that the differences in the pottery assemblages described above reflect differences in the ethnic identity of their users.

Burial

We have no knowledge of the burial customs in the rural sector (or in the Kingdom of Israel as a whole). However, Bloch-Smith, who studied Iron Age burial customs, identified substantial links between the northern valleys and the Phoenician world (Bloch-Smith 1992: 143). In her opinion, "Israel encompassed the Jezreel and Beth Shean Valleys, whose population employed coastal and northern forms of interment throughout the Iron Age."

While not all the evidence linking the northern valleys to the Phoenician world cited in the studies of Gal (above, regarding pottery) and Bloch-Smith is related to ethnic identity, it nevertheless manifests mixed cultural patterns in this part of the Kingdom of Israel.[10]

Ethnic Groups in the Northern Valleys

Historical Background

Most scholars believe that there were no Israelite Iron I settlement sites in the northern valleys and that even in the urban sites there are no signs of Israelite presence.[11] Several collared rim pithoi have been discovered at Megiddo; however, some have suggested that they may have originated in trade and should not be seen as signs of Israelite settlement. Furthermore, although these pithoi have been discovered mainly in the central hills, it is usually accepted by scholars that their presence cannot prove Israelite presence.[12] In any case, it seems that significant Israelite settlement in this area did not precede the beginning of Iron Age II (see, e.g., Finkelstein 1988b; Kochavi 1984: 60, 62–63, 66; for a different opinion, see Gilboa 1987: 57–63). There is general agreement that the region became part of the Israelite state in early Iron II (B. Mazar 1982: 64–65; A. Mazar 1990: 374; Ahlström 1993: 469, 476; compare Yeivin 1962: 52; and many others). Iron II Megiddo, with its palaces, public buildings, waterworks, and impressive fortifications, was an important urban center of the Kingdom of Israel. The same applies (though perhaps on a smaller scale) to the nearby urban center at Jokneam (Ben-Tor et al. 1987) and

---

10. Another difference between the northern valley villages and their counterparts in other regions is that two out of the three villages discussed here existed during the tenth century B.C.E., in clear contrast to the rest of the country; see below, chap. 9.

11. See, for example, Gal 1982: 80–81; 1992a: 87; Kochavi 1984: 66; Finkelstein 1988b: 92; A. Mazar 1990: 355. Several Iron I sites (which ceased to exist during the twelfth or eleventh centuries B.C.E.) have been discovered in the northern valleys, such as Tell el-Wawiyat (Alpert-Nakhai et al. 1993), Afula (M. Dothan 1955) and a site near Tel Menorah (Gal 1979). However, the ethnic identity of their residents is uncertain, and they were probably Canaanites (Gal 1979). In any case, these sites did not exist during Iron Age II, and so they are not discussed here. See also Faust 2006b.

12. Finkelstein 1996a: 204; the connection between these pithoi and ethnic identity is debated. For a summary of the distribution of these pithoi, see Esse 1991; 1992; Wengrow 1996: 312–16; Small 1997. I believe that there is some connection between these pithoi and the Israelites, although in a different manner, but the issue exceeds the scope of this chapter and does not have implications for the present study (see extended discussion in Faust 2006b: 191–220).

to other urban centers in the northern valleys, such as Hazor (Yadin 1972; Geva 1989), Kinrot (Fritz 1993), and others. Indeed, along with the impressive public construction in these cities connected to the Kingdom of Israel, one can also identify connections in the private sector with the material culture of the hill region—the Israelite "core." Thus, for example, four-room-type houses have been discovered in these Iron II urban settlements (Kempinski 1989; 1993; Ben-Tor et al. 1987; Yadin 1972; and others).

It appears that the urban centers were also inhabited by Israelite people who settled there as part of the administrative system (or parallel to it). This fact is manifest by the written sources, which view these settlements as important centers for the Kingdom of Israel, and is supported by the archaeological finds. In the urban centers, there are indications of Israelites and Canaanites-Phoenicians living side by side. Israelite officials, merchants, soldiers, and officers probably settled in the main cities alongside the local population, which probably continued to live in these cities without their lives being drastically changed.[13]

In contrast, the rural sector probably remained less ethnically mixed, because the rural settlements did not attract the new functionaries. The urban centers were the main source of Israelite influence on the villagers, who visited them now and then.[14] This reconstruction explains why the villages under discussion differ from all the other villages in the rest of the country. The villages in the northern valleys did not change when control of the region passed over to the Kingdom of Israel. It seems that the farmers of this region had previously been vassals on estates owned by the Canaanite elite, and after the region became part of the Israelite state, "the estates of the lowland simply received new overlords" (Chaney 1986: 60–61).[15] The local residents continued to live their lives as before, in the same sort of houses and without changing their family structure or community and settlement organization. The public buildings probably served the needs of the local government or the "landowners" in the nearby cities.[16]

---

13. See, for instance, Ahlström 1993: 479–80; compare Bright 1972: 197; Noth 1960: 193. It should be noted that many scholars assumed, relying on the Bible, that part of the Canaanite elite was incorporated into the administration of the United Monarchy (see, for example, Yeivin 1962: 53; 1979: 150–51; see also Reviv 1993: 96). Some of these studies are now considered outdated, but they correctly noted the inevitable process of the assimilation of part of the local elite within the new elite, a process the influences of which were probably mutual; see Noth 1960: 217–18.

14. Ahlström stressed that, during this period, when large regions with "foreign" populations were conquered, the kingdom established urban centers (not necessarily at new sites) in order for them to serve as cultural agents to introduce the Israelite culture to the different populations (see Ahlström 1982b). Whitelam saw the construction of the urban centers as royal propaganda aimed at portraying power and receiving legitimacy (see Whitelam 1986).

15. See also Yeivin 1962: 52. Na'aman (1981) showed that parts of this region were royal lands during the Late Bronze Age. Because this was also the case during the Second Temple period, Na'aman hypothesized that there was continuity that also lasted through the Iron Age. He noted (1981: 44) that, in the absence of evidence from the First Temple period, there is no proof of this continuity but hoped that archaeology would be able to help verify this. The analysis above supports Na'aman's hypothesis and even his expectation that archaeology could help solve the problem.

16. According to Yeivin (1962: 52), large portions of the northern valleys became royal estates after they were conquered by the Kingdom of Israel, but their residents continued to cultivate the land as vassals. It is possible, however, that some or all of these regions had become royal land even earlier.

If Chaney is correct in assuming that the villagers were vassals, presumably they had no social frameworks to enable the organization of community projects (such as building boundary walls), and in any case nobody was interested in investing in projects of this sort, because all the profits and surpluses would reach the nearby cities anyway; the landowners had no interest in investing in the villages, and the local population had no surpluses to use for this purpose (when surplus was required). Villages whose lands were owned by the urban elite (or the palace/king) are familiar from the ancient Near East (Magness-Gardiner 1994: 45; see also above, chap. 4). According to Magness-Gardiner, the residents of these sites "would have been kept at subsistence level," and in her opinion, they can often be identified archaeologically and distinguished from other villages. It seems that the villages discussed here belong to this category.

Hazor During Iron Age II: Different Ethnic Groups in an Urban Environment

Although ethnic groups lived and even flourished in urban environments (Olsen and Kobylinski 1991: 7; Kamp and Yoffee 1980: 93, and additional bibliography there), the discussion so far has concentrated on the rural sector. Attempts to deal with the potentially mixed finds from the cities pose difficulties for archaeologists who wish to distinguish the objects, buildings, and symbols that belonged to the different groups. However, now that we have identified some of the traits of the ethnic groups discussed here (Israelites and Canaanites-Phoenicians), we can reexamine the complex finds from the urban sector. The site most suited to this purpose is Hazor (we shall discuss stratum VI), the only urban site in northern Israel where a sufficient number of residential houses has been excavated and published (see Yadin et al. 1958–61; 1989). Moreover, the buildings in the site have been extensively analyzed (e.g., S. Geva 1989), with particular attention being given to the socioeconomic stratification (1989: 52–62; Faust 1999c; and see above, chap. 3).

As we have seen above, several groups of buildings have been identified in Hazor: (1) large, impressive buildings, usually of the four-room type, probably representing the wealthy and upper class; (2) a small group of average-to-small-size buildings, with evidence of some planning, representing the middle–low class; (3) a large group of relatively small buildings, not built to any plan. The different building types were even concentrated in different neighborhoods. In the third group, Hazor differs from most of the other cities in the land of Israel. Even though socioeconomic differences have been identified in all the cities, in Hazor the lower class lived in small buildings that lacked any plan; in other cities, such as Tell Beit Mirsim, Beersheba, Mizpah (Tell en-Nasbeh), Tirzah (Tell el-Farʿah, north), Shikmona, and others, most of the lower class lived in three-room houses (and sometimes even in four-room houses). As noted above, this type of building existed on all Israelite sites. The complexity of the situation at Hazor results from its being an urban center that was probably inhabited by more than one ethnic group. Thus, it is not sufficient to identify the symbols or characteristics of one group, and one cannot draw conclusions from one group regarding the ethnic identity of all the city's residents.

The finds from Hazor represent two different groups: on the one hand, the upper and middle class (including all the officials), composed of Israelites; and on the other hand, the lower class (and perhaps some of the middle class), composed mainly of Canaanite-Phoenician population. In this context, it is worth noting the similarity between buildings such as 14a and 28 and the rural buildings described above (building 111 was composed of two architectural units of this sort). Indeed, Holladay (1987: 290 n. 99, 291 n. 109) believed that the resident of building 14 on stratum V was Phoenician (but see chap. 3 above, where we rejected the interpretation of this building as a wealthy house).

The urban location of the different groups did not weaken the ethnic identity and more likely even strengthened it. The daily contacts between the groups only sharpened the natural friction points between the groups: struggles, competition, and power differences (Olsen and Kobylinski 1991: 7; Barth 1969: 9–10; and so on). If members of the socially inferior group obtained power and influence, they probably adopted the symbols of the wealthy and dominant group (the Israelites), even though they maintained their ethnic identity at the first stage (McGuire 1982: 164, 171–72). If Hazor changed hands during the period under discussion (see Finkelstein 1999a), even if this had no immediate impact on the composition of the local population, it only worsened the struggles between the groups.

It is not only the historical background of the northern valleys that explains the special situation at Hazor compared with other urban sites. Its uniqueness also stemmed from the site's geographical location in the Hula Valley, near the northern and eastern borders (and even the western border) of the Kingdom of Israel. It is possible, therefore, that a similar reality obtained in similar sites in the north of Israel, such as Dan, Kinrot, and perhaps even Shikmona and others.

Identifying the Ethnic Groups: Arameans or Canaanites-Phoenicians?

Presumably, it is inaccurate to include all the sites discussed above in the category "Canaanite-Phoenician," and the non-Israelite population included more than one ethnic group.[17] Thus, for example, the excavator of Tel Hadar suggested, based on the site's material culture that during the relevant period the site was under Aramean control. The new finds from nearby Bethsaida also indicate Aramean presence in the area, and perhaps Bethsaida was an important city in the Aramean Kingdom of Geshur (Arav and Barnett 1997: 202; but see Arav 1995; Brandel 1995: 151; on the importance of the site, see also Arav 2000).

On the other hand, despite the geographical proximity of the two sites, they are different in character. Bethsaida is a city, while Tel Hadar is a village. Based on the considerations raised in this chapter, presumably the population composition at Tel Hadar remained unaltered, and the local population did not undergo the changes that were taking place in the nearby city. The situation in the two sites, however, is unclear,[18] and the reality in the Kingdom of Geshur, its state formation processes, and a range of ethnic characteristics are also insufficiently clear, so it is

17. This is not the place to discuss the problematic nature of the term *Canaanite*.
18. Incidentally, the excavator believes that there were population changes at Tel Hadar.

difficult to evaluate the findings in relation to them (Kochavi et al. 1992). For now, it is reasonable to posit that the rural population of this region underwent processes similar to the rural population of the northern valleys that were controlled by the Kingdom of Israel, although this was a region that was included (at least for part of the time) within another political entity, and that the population can be considered (in an inaccurate generalization) Canaanite-Phoenician.

Israel and Judah

The ethnic complexity discussed here is only attested with regard to the Kingdom of Israel and has no equivalent in Judah. It is possible, of course, that different ethnic groups lived side by side in the Kingdom of Judah as well, but the relevant research method (which is still in its infancy) has yet to expose any traces of this.[19] It is more likely, however, that these results (partially, at least) were due to an essential difference between the two kingdoms. The Kingdom of Israel was larger and richer, occupied more extensive territories, and had contacts with more states and cultures, and so the Canaanites-Phoenicians, who in any case were a considerable component of its population, managed to maintain their distinct ethnic character; while in small Judah, the non-Israelite segment of the population (which was smaller to begin with) was (almost?) completely assimilated into the dominant ethnic group.

Summary

Given the current state of research, it appears that the key to identifying ethnic groups during Iron Age II lies in the rural sector. Searching for these groups in the urban sector, about which there is a plethora of data, is like searching under the street lamp on the main road for a coin that had been lost in a dark alley. Only after a careful examination of the rural sector and identification of the traits of the different ethnic groups can (or should) we examine the situation in the urban sector.

A comparison of the finds from the villages in the northern valleys and the villages in the rest of the country, and even between the villages in the valleys and the urban settlements in the same region, shows that their populations came from different social and ethnic systems. It appears that the residents of the valley villages were Canaanites-Phoenicians. This conclusion is supported by the great similarity between the villages discussed here and the Bronze Age villages.

Special attention has been devoted to studying the household, about which Emberling wrote: "In particular, we suggest that the household structure might be methodologically valuable [for purposes of analyzing ethnicity] because of its close, meaningful and significant relationship with daily life" (Emberling 1997:

---

19. Lachish is the only settlement in Judah where exceptional architectural finds have been discerned. For instance, no four-room-type building was found there. Despite the importance of this observation, however, the areas exposed are too limited, and we must wait for additional data before any ethnic explanation can be evaluated. At any event, even if it transpires that a significant non-Israelite population did indeed inhabit Lachish, this would not be surprising, considering Lachish's location far from the population centers of the Kingdom of Judah and on the border of the coastal plain, and also because it was a central royal city. The situation in the south also constituted an exception (see Thareani 2011).

325). We should also consider important the religious differences (the existence or absence of temples and cultic structures) and differences in food consumption (the percentage of pig bones) between the villages discussed here and their counterparts in the hills. The region's special settlement history supports this conclusion that the valley villages were Canaanites-Phoenicians and reduces the likelihood of other explanations that focus on factors such as ecology, wealth, status, location, and so on.

McGuire's terms ("competition," "ethnocentrism," and "differential power") accord with the situation in the northern valleys during Iron Age II. The finds enable us to reconstruct a competition between the new elite and the local population in the northern valleys (mainly in Hazor). Because in the period under discussion the Israelite ethnic identity had already been formed (e.g., Dever 1995: 420–21; this process is in many cases equivalent to state formation; see Shennan 1989: 16; see in detail Faust 2006b), the competition was channeled along ethnic lines. The differences in the distribution of power that existed between the groups maintained the ethnic differences (because preserving the differences was to the advantage of the stronger group [see McGuire 1982: 170] and perhaps also to the advantage of the state [see Ucko 1988: xi; Small 1997: 270–81]).

In the villages discussed above, the distinction between the groups was more static (and most or all of the inhabitants belonged to the lower class), whereas in the cities, a more complex process was in effect: members of the former elite and sometimes members of lower classes gained power or status and became assimilated into the stronger group, or at least adopted some of its material characteristics.[20] These processes demonstrate the fluid nature of ethnic identity.

They are also a reminder that the Canaanites-Phoenicians of Iron Age II are not identical to the Canaanites of earlier periods, despite the similarities between the groups. One of the prominent differences stems from the fact that the Canaanites-Phoenicians discussed here constituted the lower status or social group, while the earlier Canaanites were a complete society. In the transition from the Bronze Age and Iron Age I to Iron Age II, the lower class in Canaanite society apparently became what is termed here "Canaanite-Phoenician," meaning the "other" of the more dominant group (the Israelites), while members of the upper class in Canaanite society (at least some of them) were assimilated into the Israelites. Against this background, we can assume that in the northern valleys the "symbols of power" functioned mainly (in relation to the local population) to provide legitimacy to the new regime and social order.[21]

The discussion above reveals the complex reality that obtained in the ethnically diverse society in the Kingdom of Israel (compare with Finkelstein 1999b) and the various processes that influenced relations between the groups in the urban and rural sectors, with special attention paid to the differences between the different

---

20. McGuire 1982: 171–72; Howard 1996: 239; on processes that enabled the local elite to join the new administration, see Yeivin 1979: 150–51. These complex processes are well demonstrated in Hazor, where there was a socio-ethnic hierarchy.

21. Compare Whitelam 1986; it is less likely that the purpose of the authorities was to "educate" ["Israelize"] the local population (see Ahlström 1982b); though this purpose might have been relevant to the local elite.

regions of the kingdom. If this reconstruction is correct, it reveals a dialectical relationship between the social and ethnic aspects of society—a system in which the different social status of the population of the northern valleys both influenced and was influenced by its ethnic identity.

Chapter 9

From Hamlets to Monarchy:
Israelite Society from the Settlement Period
to the End of the Period of the Monarchy

In this chapter, we summarize the historical and social processes that created changes in the structure of Israelite society and turned it from a relatively simple society (as summarized in chap. 1) into a complex, stratified society (described in chaps. 3–8). In the following pages, we use historical information and interpretation (mainly from the summary in chap. 1) to illustrate the social processes discussed. Since this information and the data on which it relies are problematic and hotly debated, I must stress that the discussion below is not based on this historical information, and the data are only used to accompany and illustrate the social reconstructions presented below.

The Settlement Period

Traditional Society at the End of Iron Age I

Traditional society was extensively discussed in chap. 1, and there is no point in repeating the discussion here. It is sufficient to note that, in general, during Iron Age I, Israelite settlement was concentrated in the central hill country. Most of the settlements were very small, and it appears that each was inhabited by a kinship group, or a *hamulah*, composed of several extended families (see, for example, Stager 1985; Finkelstein 1988b; 1989; see also Lehmann 2004). Society was relatively egalitarian, and although in this period there were already certain gaps in wealth (see, e.g., Lemche 1985), there were probably no real class differences. These conclusions are derived from an analysis of the archaeological evidence and seem to be, generally speaking, in agreement with the common historical interpretation of the biblical sources.

Settlement in the Central Hill Country during the Transition to Iron Age II

Rural settlements characteristic of Iron Age I underwent extreme changes during the transition to Iron Age II. It transpires that almost all of these small settlements, which were the prominent characteristic of the Settlement period, disappeared during the end of Iron I or the beginning of Iron Age II (eleventh–tenth centuries B.C.E. according to the traditional or modified traditional chronology). The trend itself was already observed by A. Mazar (1990: 301), Dever (1994: 218; 1997a: 182), and

Gal (1992a: 94–96), but its full scope was not addressed (probably because most archaeological studies tended to concentrate on the excavation of major sites—usually
tells—with historical or biblical importance) until recently (see Faust 2000b; 2003a;
2007b; and below).

Most of the settlements were destroyed or abandoned, although a few of them
grew into urban settlements. The first group of Iron I sites that were abandoned or
destroyed and did not continue into Iron Age II includes, for example, Kh. Raddana,
Ai, Izbet Sartah, Shiloh, Giloh, Karmiel, Kh. Zaʿakuka, Jebel el-Habun, the Bull site,
Mt. Ebal, Kh. Avot, Sasa, Nahal Yatir, and more. The second group, which included
sites that were transformed into cities in Iron Age II, is composed, for example, of
Mizpah (Tell en-Nasbeh), Dan, Hazor, and probably also Bethel and others. However, the process of decline in the countryside is not manifested only by abandonment of the existing Iron I villages but can also be seen in the fact that almost all the
rural settlements of Iron Age II, founded mainly from the ninth century onward,
were new sites that did not continue from Iron Age I (see practically all the sites discussed in chap. 4 above as well as many other sites).[1] Hence it is clear that these facts
reveal a new settlement phenomenon that was distinct from the earlier settlements.

It appears that during most of the early phase of Iron Age IIA (tenth century
B.C.E.) there were hardly any rural settlements in the land of Israel, especially in the
highlands. A full analysis of this issue would exceed the scope of this book (see Faust
2000b; 2003a; 2007b), but this phenomenon seems have been very extensive, and the
data we possess indicate this clearly.[2] Graph 22 reflects the period of occupation of

---

1. The phenomenon is also supported by a detailed study of all the (published) salvage excavations
(see Faust and Safrai, forthcoming).

2. Finkelstein (2005) had recently attempted to challenge the idea of large-scale abandonment of rural
sites during the transition from Iron Age I to Iron Age II. His claims do not stand up under scrutiny and,
since the issue is not essential for the main theme of this book, I do not wish to develop this issue here
at length (see Faust 2007b for a more detailed response and many more bibliographical references; see
now also Dever 2008). Nevertheless, because his arguments were printed, a few brief words are in order.
Finkelstein criticized my argumentation and, more importantly, suggested that the surveys prove that
the overall pattern is of settlement continuity from Iron Age I to Iron Age II. He also claimed that such a
large-scale abandonment of the countryside is not logical ("bizarre"). Regarding his recourse to survey
results—not only are surveys much less reliable than excavations (especially for a period such as Iron Age
IIA; see now also Garfinkel and Ganor 2010; for additional examples, see Kh. el-Burj 1973: 26; Bienkowski
1998: 164; Dessel 1999: 12–14; Cresson 1999: 97; see also Wolff 1998: 449; Dagan 2011: 7*, 15*, 16*; and the list
is long), but a close examination of the results of the surveys shows that, when small sites are examined, a
significant decline during Iron Age IIA is evident in this set of data as well (Faust 2007b). More important,
however, is the archaeological evidence from nearly 100 excavated Iron Age rural sites, which clearly
shows a major decline in the rural sector during the time discussed here (the decline is also identified in a
qualitative and systematic study of settlement patterns in the region throughout history; Faust and Safrai
2005: 143–45; forthcoming). Notably, in his rejoinder Finkelstein did not mention the many excavated rural
sites that were supposed to have existed at the time, and one can only wonder why he avoided mentioning
any of these. Furthermore, three of Finkelstein's stoutest supporters (Herzog, Grabbe, and Silberman; see
their comments in Faust 2007b) were invited by an *NEA* editor to contribute to the discussion that followed, but they also neglected to mention sites that were supposedly in existence at the time (because most
of them were not archaeologists, it is perhaps understandable that they chose to concentrate on arguments
concerning the historicity of the Bible, etc., and not on the actual archaeological debate between Finkelstein and me). It seems to me that the available archaeological database is quite large (about 100 excavated
sites), and the pattern is clear and straightforward, exhibiting a major disruption in the rural sector at the
beginning of Iron Age II (mainly in the highlands, but not only there; see also B. Routledge 2008; Gal 1992a:

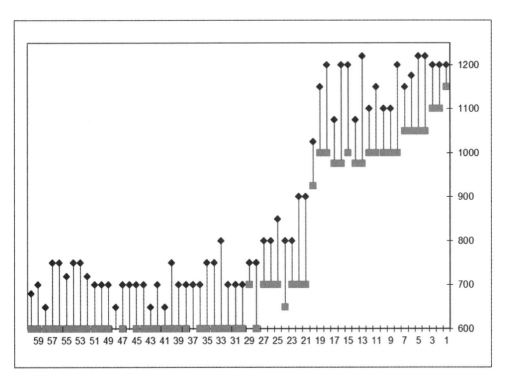

Graph 22. Rural settlement in the hill country and the Beersheba Valley in the Iron Age—schematic chronological chart of select (excavated) sites.

Site list: 1. the Bull site; 2. Mt. Ebal; 3. Giloh; 4. Kh. Raddana; 5. Ai; 6. Shiloh; 7. Tell el-Ful; 8. Kh. Avot; 9. Sasa; 10. Karmiel; 11. Kh. Za'akuka; 12. Jebel el-Habun; 13. Tel Masos; 14. Nahal Yatir; 15. Kh. Umm et-Tala; 16. Izbet Sartah; 17. Tel Esdar; 18. Kh. el-Maqatir; 19. Beth-Zur; 20. Kh. ed-Dawwara; 21. Beit Aryeh (Kh. Hadash); 22. H. Malta; 23. H. Eli; 24. Kh. Jemein; 25. H. Rosh Zayit; 26. Noqdim; 27. Beitar Ilit (west); 28. Site 49 (Beersheba); 29. Kh. el Qatt; 30. farmstead southeast of Wadi Fukin; 31. farmstead at R.P. 1618/1239; 32. Har Gillo (west); 33. Mevasseret Yerushalayim; 34. Kh. er-Ras 1; 35. French Hill; 36. Nahal Zimri; 37. Malhah; 38. East Talpiot; 39. Beit Hakerem farmstead; 40. Mamilla; 41. Kh. Anim; 42. Pisgat Zeev A; 43. Kh. er-Ras 2; 44. Pisgat Zeev D; 45. Givat Homa; 46. H. Alona; 47. Ramot Farmstead (5 farms); 48. Beit Hakerem; 49. Sansanna; 50. Shim'a; 51. Kh. Jarish; 52. Kh. Abu Shawan; 53. Kh. Abu et-Twein village; 54. The village below the fortress at Arad; 55. the village at H. Uza; 56. Kh. Abu Tabaq; 57. Kh. es-Samaria; 58. Kh. el-Maqari; 59. Farm east of Anatot; 60. H. Shilhah.

94–96; Gophna 1966; Gazit 2008; and many others). As for Finkelstein's claim that large-scale abandonment of the rural sector is "bizarre," I must first note that this is not really a claim. If this is the pattern that is identified, it needs to be addressed; denying the finds will not change them. Furthermore, abandonments of this sort are evident in many periods and throughout the world (see Faust 2003a; 2007b for many of these examples, and there are many others that I do not present there), and Finkelstein himself identified such episodes during Iron Age I in the land of Israel, referring (regarding the coastal plain) to "an almost complete abandonment of the countryside" (Finkelstein 1995: 232) or "an annihilation of the countryside" (Finkelstein 2000: 169). At any event, this is not the place for a detailed discussion of these and other arguments, and readers are referred to the entire exchange (Faust 2003a; Finkelstein 2005; Faust 2007b [and the discussion here that includes comments by some of Finkelstein's supporters]); I only ask readers to examine the exchange in its entirety and to differentiate between data and rhetoric.

selected rural settlements in the highlands throughout the Iron Age. Two distinct chronological groups can easily be discerned, with a gap around the beginning of Iron Age II (Kh. ed-Dawwara [18] is the only settlement bridging this gap).[3]

The process reflected in the graph is linked to the processes of the formation of the Israelite state, the preceding security problems, and additional factors that cannot be listed here (for an extensive discussion, see Faust 2000b; 2003a; 2006b; 2006c; 2007b; one possible additional factor is the Monarchy's aim to control the means of production; see Sherratt and Sherratt 1991). Suffice it to note that the abandonment process of rural sites probably began in the hill country as a result of the security threat posed by the Philistines and gradually spread to other regions such as the Beersheba basin, the Samaria foothills and parts of Galilee. This second stage was also probably the result of a process of forced settlement by the new state (see also Halpern 2001: 465; Cohen-Amin 2004: 134; Cohen and Cohen-Amin 2004: 156; Faust 2006c). For our purposes, it is important to note that, during the initial phases of Iron Age II, in parallel with the establishment of the Monarchy, there were almost no rural settlements in the kingdom's heartlands.[4] The movement of the population to the central sites, which later became towns, is thus one of the processes that accompanied the formation of the Israelite state in the central hill country and led to it. The abandonment of villages and the move to central settlements was the origin of the reurbanization process of Iron Age II (on the reurbanization, see, e.g., A. Mazar 1990; C. H. J. de Geus 1988; Dever 1994; 1997a).

The Period of the Monarchy

It is reasonable to infer that the concentration of the population in central settlements created an environment in which intellectual life flourished (compare Demand 1990: 3; Marcus and Flannery 1996: 158). A process of this sort is intertwined with the formation of a leadership and the concentration of authority in its hands, and the beginning of Iron Age II is probably when the Monarchy in Israel was created. This becomes clear from analyzing the settlement dynamic in the rural sector. An examination of finds from some of the cities founded indicate monumental construction, which also implies the existence of a state.

Some scholars date the formation of the state in Israel and Judah later, in the ninth–eighth centuries B.C.E., thus denying the existence of the United Monarchy. This issue is currently a subject of intense debate in the field, and this is not the

---

3. This generalization also applies to other sites not included in this graph. As noted, during Iron Age I, there were rural sites that grew during Iron Age II and became urban settlements. These settlements are not included in this graph, but they fit into the general picture presented here.

It appears that Kh. ed-Dawwara is the only small site that excavations have shown to have existed during the period under discussion; see, e.g., Finkelstein 1988a; 1990. However, it is very unlikely that this site was rural in nature, and it was probably a relatively central settlement (Finkelstein 1988b: 262–63; 1990: 202; see also Faust 2003a: 156)

4. Most of the inhabitants of the larger settlements (the settlements in which the population was concentrated and which by the end of the process became towns) were farmers, of course, and they continued to practice agriculture, but some of the fields were now relatively distant (see more below).

place to expand on it.[5] However, most scholars still hold the traditional view (this issue also arises out of other aspects of the material culture; compare Faust 2002b). Although we accept the historicity of the United Monarchy (which seems to be manifested in settlement patterns in various parts of the country and in contemporary changes in material culture; e.g., Faust 2002b; 2004c; 2006c; 2007b; Stager 2003; Master 2001; and more), for our purposes, suffice it to use a generalization accepted by all: at some stage during the first centuries of the first millennium B.C.E., a kingdom (or kingdoms) was established in the central hill country, and hence, we will discuss the social processes that took place following its establishment.

The Urbanization Process

Although the process that led to the concentration of a large population in the central settlements started at the end of Iron Age I, real cities were probably only founded in the highlands following the establishment of the Monarchy (on this process, see Fritz 1996; C. H. J. de Geus 1988; see also Master 2001).

The urbanization process that the region underwent in Iron Age II is reflected first and foremost in the urban centers discovered at sites such as Dan, Hazor, Megiddo, Jokneam, Shikmona, Dor, Samaria, Shechem, Tirzah (Tell el-Far‘ah, north), Jerusalem, Gezer, Beth-Shemesh, Lachish, and Beersheba. This intensive process probably reached its peak during the eighth century B.C.E. (and in parts of Judah in the seventh century), but it is already evident in the beginning of Iron Age II and thus constitutes evidence for the existence of a state during this period. It appears that among the urban settlements founded or rebuilt at the time we should include the central settlements that developed in the hills during the end of Iron Age I and also many central settlements in the valleys and the plains. These sites became regime centers of the new Monarchy.

Differences in the Urbanization Process in the Hills and the Lowlands

The early days of the Monarchy were accompanied by expansion, especially in the lower regions, though not only there (according to biblical reports, for example, Jerusalem itself was also conquered). The excavations and surveys show that most of the urban centers and impressive construction projects were set up in regions recently incorporated into the state. The written sources also describe urban settlements and important centers in these regions from the beginning of the period of the Monarchy (for example, 1 Kgs 9:15–18).

The vast investment in these regions could stem from several reasons. First, these were the key regions through which important roads passed and had economic and military importance. Second, the lower regions were largely inhabited by a foreign population, and so it was necessary to establish stronger rule there. This interest is revealed by the monumental construction projects and conspicuous consumption

---

5. For the existence of the United Monarchy (and also on the debate over Iron Age chronology in Israel), see, for instance, Whitelam 1996; Dever 1996; Na²aman 1996a; 1996b; 1997; Finkelstein 1996b; 1999b; 2001; 2010; Finkelstein, Fantalkin, and Piasetsky 2008; Finkelstein and Piasetsky 2011; Finkelstein and Silberman 2001; 2006; A. Mazar 1997a; 1998a; 2006b; 2010; 2011; Mazar and Bronk Ramsey 2008; Stager 2003; Master 2001. See also Faust 2000b; 2004c; 2006c; 2007b.

typical of fortified settlements and public buildings used for various needs (administration, military or propaganda; compare Whitelam 1986; Ahlström 1982b; see above, chap. 8).[6] Furthermore, the high degree of urbanization in the lower regions of the country was certainly influenced by the long urban tradition of these regions.

It is also possible that the process of urbanization in the lowlands contributed to a population migration from the hill regions. During this period, some of the Israelites in the hill country joined the administrative and military systems (Stager 1985; Holladay 1995; according to B. Mazar 1974, for example, the priesthood was also an administrative system). The presence of these systems was dominant in the lower regions of the country, partly due to their military and commercial importance. At the end of Iron Age I, much of the good land in the hills was probably already cultivated, and the available land was relatively more difficult to use.[7] In contrast, many of the lands in the valleys belonged to the young state rather than to a traditional social system of kinship groups (see above, chap. 8). Some of these lands were "opened up" to the people who staffed the administrative and military systems. Thus, the lower regions had great appeal.

During the urbanization process, many people moved to new, central settlements. Some of them probably had positions in the state system being formed (Stager 1985), but it is likely that many of them became day laborers (especially in the larger settlements in the lowlands), thus forming part of the lower class in the new urban system. In regions inhabited by the Canaanites-Phoenicians, the latter probably formed (at least in part) the basis for the lower class. At this stage, the urban centers (and the settlements in which the rural population concentrated) in the hills were still small and relatively weak,[8] and the urbanization developed mainly in the lower regions of the country. Thus the kingdom was a "tribal kingdom," still maintaining (at this stage) its kinship structure and relationships in the highlands (compare Master 2001), while in the lowlands a different process had already begun.

---

6. It is also possible that similar monumental construction in the hill regions would not have been culturally accepted by the Israelite population; see Faust 2006b: 92–107.

7. Stager 1985. However, it appears that we should not accept the view that during this period the central hills were filled with settlements and completely "closed" to new settlements. This view is problematic because the central hills were even more populated by settlements during the eighth century (without any significant technological advance to cause a population increase), and this view does not match the available evidence; in addition, many settlements in the central hills were abandoned during the period under discussion, and their residents probably moved to the urban centers. Living in urban centers does not intensify cultivation of land, since urban centers are distant from some of the agricultural lands, and therefore not *all* of the land in the hills was cultivated during this period. Thus, there were uncultivated lands left, but clearly they were more difficult to cultivate than land in the valleys.

8. Part of the current debate among scholars regarding the tenth century B.C.E. and the reliability of historical information about the United Monarchy revolves around the time that Jerusalem began to be an important city. According to some of those who date the Monarchy later, Jerusalem only became an important city during the seventh century B.C.E. (on this opinion, held by some of the minimalists, see Lemche and Thompson 1994: 20; for a detailed response, see Naʾaman 1997, and additional bibliography there), or the ninth–eighth centuries B.C.E. (Finkelstein 2001; 2003). For further discussion, see Ussishkin 1998; Cahill 2002; de Groot 2002; A. Mazar 2006b. In any case, it is not essential for the capital of a kingdom to be particularly large; see Faust 2004c.

Land Ownership in the Hills and Lowlands

So, from early Iron II onward, there were two parallel settlement systems: one in the hills and the other in the lowlands. This reconstruction is similar to that presented by Chaney, who wondered what lands David could have granted his followers (Chaney 1986: 67–68).[9] According to his analysis, David could not have given lands in the hills, because most of them were privately owned by farmers who were his supporters, but he was able to grant the "new" fertile lands in the valleys. According to Chaney, the land in the valley regions was not owned by the peasants who cultivated them but by other landlords (compare chap. 8). As a result, there was no special difficulty in transferring them to new owners, and it appears that such a process was almost inevitable. So, according to Chaney, henceforth there were two systems of land ownership: in the central hills, most of the lands were privately owned, while in the lowlands, especially in the northern valleys, a large portion of the land was owned by the monarchy or its representatives or agents. The changes that occurred in the lowlands and the penetration of the Israelite population took place mainly in the urban centers, while the population in the rural settlements remained relatively unchanged, and many of the residents were vassals of the new regime and its representatives.

An analysis of the limited archaeological evidence from early Iron Age II (tenth century B.C.E.) indeed indicates differences in the social structure of the hills and the lowlands. It appears that in the hills, society remained largely traditional and kinship based (despite other changes, such as population movement to more central settlements). Thus, for instance, in Tirzah, an urban settlement in Samaria, there is a great deal of similarity among all the residential buildings of the time—evidence of quite an egalitarian society (see, e.g., de Vaux 1965: 72–73). However, in Shikmona on the Carmel coast, already in this period there are signs of social stratification. At both Tell Beit Mirsim and Mizpah (Tell en-Nasbeh), severe social stratification developed only at a later stage. The social conservatism typical of the hill regions is also reflected in the Samaria ostraca, indicating that even at a relatively late stage the kinship inheritance was still significant and important.[10] A similar picture also arises from several biblical descriptions, such as the purchase of Samaria's lands by Omri (1 Kgs 16:23–24) and the story of Naboth's vineyard (1 Kings 21; compare Reviv 1993: 66–69).

Renewal of Rural Settlement in the Hill Regions

Presumably, after the rural settlements of Iron Age I were abandoned, cultivation of agricultural lands was conducted from the central settlements. But at some stage

9. On the nature of the plots granted, see Chaney 1986: 60–61; for our purposes, it does not matter whether the leader was David, Ahab, or any other leader.

10. The Samaria ostraca are composed of two main groups of ostraca. According to Rainey 1988, the two groups were written in the same year and belonged to two systems of collection: one system collected ordinary taxes for the king (ostraca from year 15), while the second system collected produce for the king-regent (ostraca from years 9–10). In the ostraca of the first group, the settlement name usually appears along with the name of the clan/*mishpahah*, which indicates the continued existence of the traditional land-ownership system.

after the establishment of the Monarchy, many farmers who have been forced by circumstances to live in central settlements in the central hills left their towns (such as Tirzah/Tell el-Far'ah (N), or Mizpah/Tell en-Nasbeh) and set up new villages and farms near the agricultural lands. At first, they may have established temporary dwellings (*izbets*) and later, permanent settlements (compare Grossman 1976). This migration probably occurred at a relatively early stage of the urbanization process (already in the ninth century in Israel), when the social changes in Israelite society had yet to occur. The farmers maintained the traditional structure, which had not yet been damaged even in the central settlements in the highlands at this point, built new rural settlements, and continued their traditional, kinship-based life-style there.[11]

Israel and Judah

After the division of the Monarchy, Israel and Judah developed along two separate paths. In the opinion of most scholars, the Northern Kingdom was wealthier in resources and manpower and had definite geographical advantages. Thus, Israel became the more dominant and developed of the two, while Judah remained a small, isolated mountain kingdom (see above, chap. 6). Although most scholars believe the social situation in the two kingdoms was very similar (for example, Reviv 1989: 102; see also chaps. 1–2 above), it appears that, due to its size and external connections, Israel was more heterogeneous than Judah, and its population was more ethnically diverse and stratified. The Kingdom of Judah, in contrast, was less "developed" than Israel in the eighth century B.C.E.[12]

In addition to the archaeological finds from the eighth century B.C.E., there is earlier evidence indicating the relative strength of the Kingdom of Israel, particularly regarding monumental construction. Almost all the early urban settlements, reflecting the period when the urbanization process commenced, were in the Kingdom of Israel (Hazor, Gezer, Shikmona, Megiddo, and others).[13] Furthermore, many of the famous construction projects of the United Monarchy, as described in the Bible

---

11. Interestingly, the early Iron II buildings at Tirzah are relatively large, and in this respect resemble the buildings in the (later) Iron II villages. Perhaps many of the characteristics of rural settlements during Iron Age II resulted from the concentration of population in the central settlements that was followed by partial movement of some of the people to new rural (re)settlements. This may explain the possible differences between the Iron Age I villages and their Iron Age II successors—for example, in regard to the architecture of the extended family (compounds in Iron I villages versus large houses in Iron II villages). This issue, however, is beyond the scope of the present discussion.

12. According to Finkelstein (e.g., 1996b), this stems from Judah's being a younger kingdom, but as we have already seen in chap. 6, the less "developed" status of Judah does not clearly indicate the kingdom's age.

13. The evidence regarding urban settlements in Judah during the tenth century B.C.E. is very limited, and what we know about settlements dated to this period is not always unambiguous. Thus, for example, most accept that the planned city at Beersheba originated already in the beginning of Iron II, even though only a very limited area has been excavated (Herzog 1993: 171). Similarly, only a small area of level V at Lachish has been excavated, and it was probably not fortified (Ussishkin 2004: 77). Regarding Jerusalem, too, there are various problems (Ussishkin 1998; Na'aman 1996b). But see Faust 2004c; A. Mazar 2006b; see now also the new discoveries at Kh. Qeiyafa; Garfinkel and Ganor 2008; 2010.

(1 Kgs 9:15), are located in the north: Hazor, Megiddo, and Gezer (of course, Jerusalem is an exception to this rule).

Many scholars have learned of the superior position of the Northern Kingdom from the Bible. This is indicated by descriptions of the relations between the two kingdoms (e.g., Yeivin 1968) and from the early prophets; large parts of the books of Kings are derived from story cycles related to Elijah and Elisha, who were both Northerners, but there are no parallel stories originating in the Kingdom of Judah. The first two prophets in the book, Amos and Hosea, also operated in the Kingdom of Israel. So it transpires that the Kingdom of Israel was already more important and "developed" before the eighth century B.C.E.[14]

Changes in the Power Centers

The concentration of power in the hands of the Monarchy and the urbanization process had an impact on the social situation. There are some clues indicating that the Monarchy gradually assumed the power and authority that were traditionally held by the elders (see chap. 1). This, according to some scholars, arises out of the biblical descriptions referring to the mid-ninth century B.C.E. Reviv, for example, believes that the story of Naboth the Jezreelite contains evidence that, alongside the elders, there already were 'nobles' (חרים), who were state officials (1 Kgs 21:8, "to the elders and the nobles who were in his city"; compare v. 11).[15] In the story of Jehu's rebellion, we read: "Jehu wrote letters and sent them to Samaria, to the rulers of Jezreel (שרי יזרעאל 'the city officials'), to the elders, and to the guardians of Ahab's children, saying [...]" (2 Kgs 10:1). According to Reviv, Jehu wrote to three different bodies: the rulers ('the officials' שרים), the elders, and the guardians of Ahab's children (Reviv 1989: 126–27). His argument is supported by the verse listing those who replied to Jehu: "The steward of the palace and the governor of the city and the elders and the guardians" (2 Kgs 10:5). This shows that the "rulers of Jezreel" were the senior officials "over the palace" and "over the city."

These terms are hints that, in the central settlements, the rule had mainly been transferred to the "rulers" (even if at this stage the institution of the elders still existed in parallel), and perhaps the official "over the city" was responsible for the urban sector ("over the palace" probably denotes a more senior position). An analogous picture arises from the epigraphic evidence. A similar administrative term ('ruler of the city' שר העיר) appears in an inscription from Kuntillet Ajrud (the site is usually dated to the end of the ninth century B.C.E.). Several seals with "the ruler of the city" on them (from the eighth–seventh centuries B.C.E.) indicate that, at the end of the

---

14. We have seen that various considerations enable us to define Israel as a more "mature" state than Judah. In the urban sector in Israel, the settlements were larger than in Judah, and a similar difference also obtained in the rural sector. But it should be stressed once more that it does not necessarily follow that the Kingdom of Judah was chronologically "younger."

15. Reviv 1989: 124–26. The fact that these two bodies served in parallel led him to conclude that the elders (זקנים) at this period still had relatively great power. While he remarks (1989: 43) that in the Bible the terms 'elders' and 'rulers' ('officials' שרים) are sometimes interchanged, this is not the case here, because the terms reflect two systems existing in parallel. As we shall see later, the officials gradually gained superiority during the second half of the ninth century B.C.E.

process, control of urban settlements was transferred to the administrative system (Avigad 1977; Barkay 1977; Aḥituv 1993: 132; Heltzer 1998). The lack of evidence for community organization in the cities during the period under discussion (see chap. 3 above) also reflects the decline in the power of the traditional leadership during the eighth century B.C.E.

Changes in Israelite Society

The rise in the power of the central regime and the population migration to the urban centers led to changes in the family structure and social organization in these settlements. The continuation and strengthening of the urbanization process entailed a decline in the importance of agriculture and a rise in professional specialization. Some of the residents of the cities were employed in providing services, in various crafts, in public construction, and so on. The growing towns were probably a magnet for some of the rural population, who sought their luck in the city because they were expelled from the new rural systems, or who left the new villages for various other reasons. Presumably, a large proportion of this new population, like some of the older population, did not achieve economic success. These people belonged to the lowest social class and barely earned their living as day laborers or something similar. Thus, the processes of urbanization and specialization gradually caused major social stratification.

Another outcome, no less important, was the collapse of the extended family typical of traditional society and the rise of the nuclear family in urban settlements (mainly due to the transition to hired labor rather than the urbanization process per se; see further above, chaps. 3–4);[16] most of the lower classes could not support an extended family. Evidence for changes in the kinship structure is perhaps found in a comparison of the formulation of the law regarding the rape of a virgin girl in the Covenant Code (Exod 22:15–16) and the equivalent formulation in Deuteronomy (Deut 22:28–29).[17] The Covenant Code requires the rapist to pay a dowry, while Deuteronomy requires him to pay a specific sum ("fifty shekels of silver") as a fine.[18] Societies in which a dowry is customary are usually composed of large kinship frameworks, and a dowry is usually interpreted as a payment to the bride's father in exchange for the labor he is losing (Safrai 1983: 129–30, following Rubin 1972). But this concept was no longer relevant in Deuteronomy, which required the payment of a fine. It appears that this terminological and the practical difference implied the decline in status of the extended family.

---

16. There is, in most cases, a high correlation between hired labor and urbanization, but it is the former (rather than the latter) that is actually responsible for the disintegration of the extended family (see, e.g., Greenfield 1961). Hired labor enabled members of the family to leave the household—something that would have been very difficult if they were still working "for" the family because they would have had no direct access to resources that allowed them to live on their own.

17. Some see the Covenant Code as the earliest collection of laws in the Bible (see, e.g., Weinfeld 1993: 124; Jackson and Achtemeier 1996: 596), while Deuteronomy was probably written in the seventh century B.C.E. (see, e.g., Rofé 1994: 53–74; Clements 1993: 165).

18. Some believe that there is no contradiction between the two versions and bridge them by arguing that Deuteronomy details the sum of the dowry (a datum missing in Exodus); see Malul 1994: 174. However, in my opinion, the idea presented here is more likely than this suggestion.

These processes took place initially in the lowlands. Their impact on the traditional frameworks in the hill country increased during the period of the Monarchy, but in this region they applied mainly to the central settlements (as noted, before these processes affected the hill country settlements, many families had left the central settlements in this region and established new villages and farmsteads, maintaining a traditional structure). The changes were probably apparent among most of the cities' residents—not only the day laborers who could not afford to support an extended family but also some of the administrative officials, soldiers, and so on.[19] As we have seen, the change in the family structure and the transition to nuclear families have been recognized by Bible scholars and are also reflected in archaeological finds. But this process was not pervasive: according to the archaeological record, this process did not apply in the rural sector, and even in the urban sector, the extended family was still considered important among the wealthy and the elite.

Socioeconomic Stratification during the Eighth Century B.C.E.

Most scholars dealing with Israelite society have stated that it became a very stratified society. One of the main pieces of evidence for this situation is the prophets' references to social stratification: they strongly denounce oppression of the poor (on a similar phenomenon in agricultural societies in general and the mechanism behind it, see Lenski and Lenski 1974: 228). This trend is apparent, to various degrees, in the prophecies of Amos, Isaiah, Micah, and Jeremiah (Hosea is probably the only one whose prophecies do not reflect this trend; see Weisman 1994: 20; Uffenheimer 1973). We have seen these differences clearly expressed in the archaeological record, and the scholars who believed that there were socioeconomic gaps in this period were correct (see also Houston 2004). However, we have also learned that these gaps did not exist in all the settlements, and that reality was different in the rural sector.

In the urban sector as well, reality was not homogeneous. Although socioeconomic gaps probably existed in all cities, it seems that the gap was not as wide in some places as in others. Thus, for example, we noted the social difference between society in the hills and in the valleys, as reflected in building size. The extensive use of four-room houses in the hill country towns compared with its use in the central cities in the valleys and plains also indicates the existence of a more traditional ("Israelite") society in the hill country (see chap. 7).

The Traditional System in the Rural Sector

Apparently, the greatest change in social organization occurred in large urban centers, such as Samaria, the capital of Israel, and of course in the lowlands, which had a different social reality from the beginning. Both the archaeological record and epigraphic evidence show that in the renewed rural sector in the highlands the traditional structure of society, based on extended families and lineages, was preserved (or "reinvented"). Presumably, a similar process took place in the Kingdom of Judah, and there a difference also emerged between the hill and the lower regions (mainly the Shephelah).

---

19. For the stress on extended families and lineages at this time, see also Faust and Bunimovitz 2008.

This picture is supported by Uffenheimer's proposed analysis of the prophecy of Jeremiah. While Jeremiah resided at Anathoth, he did not mention social problems in his prophecies at all. Only when he moved to Jerusalem did such issues begin to appear in his prophecies.[20] If Uffenheimer is correct, this change shows that at least in Judah in the seventh century B.C.E. these problems existed mainly in the cities and not in the countryside, and we may extend this conclusion to the reality of the late Iron Age in general.

The Kingdom of Israel's Final Days

As mentioned in chap. 1, several scholars believe that the Kingdom of Israel was greatly weakened toward the end, and as a result, the social gaps were not as wide. This assumed drop in social tension is supposed to explain why Hosea does not refer to social gaps and injustices (in contrast to the rest of the prophets; Uffenheimer 1973; Weisman 1994: 20). But all this is unlikely. In cases of a decline in a state's power, the elite are likely to make an effort to maintain their power, thus increasing the socioeconomic gap. In these circumstances, a continued decline leads to more exploitation (positive feedback) and eventually to collapse, as indeed has happened in many instances (compare the process reconstructed by Dever [1989] regarding the collapse of the Early Bronze Age culture).

In many cases, archaeologists are unable to distinguish levels with enough precision to differentiate single decades, and hence it is difficult to identify archaeologically the processes that took place in the final years of the Kingdom of Israel. However, at Hazor, one of the central sites of the Kingdom of Israel, there is a sufficiently detailed stratigraphic sequence to show us both the last years of the kingdom and the period of prosperity that preceded them. As we have seen above (chap. 3), the finds from level V at Hazor (documenting the final days of the Kingdom of Israel) show that socioeconomic stratification continued up to the end of the kingdom. During this period, the large, fine buildings near the fortress were built, and it appears that the gap was not reduced and may even have widened.

Between the Eighth Century and the Seventh Century B.C.E.

The opening chapters of this book presented various opinions regarding the differences between the two centuries. Both the archaeological finds and the Bible (for instance, Jer 50:17) were usually interpreted as indicating that Judah was poorer in the seventh century than in the eighth century B.C.E. Although a significant number of eighth-century cities no longer existed in the seventh century (such as Tel ʿEton, Beth-Shemesh), and others were reduced in area and importance (such as Lachish), this view seems highly exaggerated. The Shephelah was indeed devastated, and

---

20. Uffenheimer 1968. According to Uffenheimer, Jeremiah was not interested in social issues (even when he prophesied in Jerusalem), and he was criticizing society as a whole. But there is no doubt that his urban prophecies contain extensive references to oppression of the poor and distortion of justice (for example, Jer 5:27; 22:3, and elsewhere). So it appears that, after Jeremiah arrived in the big city, he became acquainted with this issue and mentioned it in his prophecies (although of course he condemned other issues as well).

large sections of this region were transferred to Philistine rule, but the kingdom spread into other regions (the Negev and the Judean Desert), where new economic branches were developed, and most regions prospered at the time (see, e.g., Finkelstein 1994; Faust and Weiss 2005; Faust 2008; this issue requires a discussion that exceeds the scope of this book).

However, despite these changes, examination of the evidence does not indicate sharp social differences between the two centuries. Some of the settlements in the central hills continued to exist without observable changes during the seventh century B.C.E. (such as Mizpah/Tell en-Nasbeh and Gibeon). The clear social gap that can be identified in Jerusalem during this period is no different from the gap in the eighth century B.C.E. In the rural sites known from the seventh century B.C.E., the framework of extended families was maintained, and so far they do not show any social differences developing in the transition between the centuries (for possible exceptions, see the discussion over the Ramot farmsteads in chap. 4). The social differences between the two centuries, however, require a more systematic study.

Shaping Israelite Society

The various processes that took place in the land of Israel in Iron Age I led to the formation of an independent group, known as "Israel." Even if we avoid discussing the question of when it became a distinct ethnicity (see extensive discussion and references in Dever 2003; Killebrew 2005; Faust 2006b), it is clear that its existence during Iron Age II cannot be denied.

Many factors unified Israelite society into one ethnicity during Iron Age II, despite the political division between Israel and Judah, and this is evident in the archaeological record (and, as most Bible scholars believe, in the textual evidence; for example, Perdue 1997: 167; in contrast to Hopkins 1996). This unity is manifested archaeologically, for example, in the new, complex building style that rapidly took over the previous local architectural style—the four-room house (see extensive discussion in chap. 7). Despite the differences between the various buildings, which imply differences in wealth and class, there is great similarity in their basic plans. Because this similarity is not explainable functionally, clearly its roots should be sought in the symbolism. As we have seen, this similarity indicates a society with a "world view" (or "ethos" or "ideology") shared by all classes despite their differences. Furthermore, the similarity between the private building style and the monumental construction style (the pillared buildings) indicates a connection between the two building types. A new understanding of public buildings as serving certain social purposes (see chap. 3 above) may strengthen the argument for the existence of social solidarity in Israelite society, especially if one examines the different social reality that obtains in sites that were probably not Israelite. This "ideology" was not imposed and should not be seen as a message transmitted to the entire population by the central regime as propaganda (on this sort of ideology in a different period, see Greenberg 1999), because the unifying elements were shared by the populations of two different political units (Israel and Judah), whose relations were sometimes hostile.

In a similar vein, there are additional traits that indicate that the Israelite population, in both kingdoms, had in common their ideology, world views, and even their identity. These traits include an absence (or rarity) of decoration on pottery, an aversion to imports and trade, an absence (or extreme rarity) of royal inscriptions, a rarity of temples, and more (some of these traits were briefly noted in chap. 8; for a detailed discussion with many bibliographical references, see Faust 2006b). All these data clearly show that the affinity between the kingdoms of Israel and Judah was real and was not invented by the biblical authors.

Summary

The urbanization process that took place in the land of Israel during the period of the Monarchy is clearly reflected in the archaeological finds. It was preceded by a migration of the rural population into the central settlements (most likely part of the formation process of the United Monarchy), and it is possible that this population movement continued (perhaps with some changes) after the Monarchy was established, possibly by force (see Faust 2000b; 2003a; 2006a; 2006c; 2007b). This urbanization (the formation of real cities) is expressed first and foremost in the lower regions of the country, and the process in the highlands was weaker, due to social factors (even though the process of settlement nucleation there had already begun in Iron I). After awhile, the rural sector recovered, and new agricultural settlements were established, first in Israel and later in Judah as well. During the period of the Monarchy, Israel was a "state," which at least during the eighth century could be defined as an "advanced agrarian society." The Kingdom of Judah at this time could be defined as a "simple agrarian society."

The following conclusions may be reached from the various data. First, both the written and the archaeological sources show that throughout its existence the Kingdom of Israel was more developed than the Kingdom of Judah. Second, in the valleys and plains the process of urbanization was more extensive and wider, as was social stratification (this may have resulted partly from the presence of non-Israelite residents, who constituted a lower class of the population), while in the hill country, the urbanization process and its social implications came into being only at a later stage. Third, most of the processes of social change took place in the urban sector, while the rural sector in the hill country maintained a more traditional and a relatively egalitarian nature. Fourth, Israelite society was homogeneous with a clear ethnic consciousness of itself alongside other ethnic groups.

Epilogue

This book made a first comprehensive attempt to examine Israelite society during the period of the Monarchy on the basis of the archaeological evidence. In contrast to previous studies of Israelite society, the many finds discovered in excavations attributed to this period served as the primary source, while the written sources were employed to complement the picture or to illustrate it. Although the nature of these latter sources raises many complex problems, it appears they should not be ignored and, as we've seen in the various chapters, they contain information that is irreplaceable in an attempt to reconstruct ancient societies.

In this study, we examined society as a whole, with its different strata, classes, regions and sectors. Each aspect of the social reality (particular classes, settlement sectors, regions and so on) was examined both in itself and in light of the other aspects. The comparative dimension lends a wide perspective and sometimes enables a solution to problems that had seemed insoluble. Thus, for example, the question of whether the archaeological finds in the cities imply sharp socioeconomic stratification might have remained unsolved due to the absence of clear criteria for evaluating degrees of stratification, but comparing it with the socioeconomic stratification in the rural sector emphasized the severity of the stratification in the cities.

Another example is the differences between the kingdoms of Israel and Judah, differences that only become apparent when the two kingdoms are compared with each other. Most of the issues, such as questions about social stratification in each settlement, community organization, and the rural sector in Israel and Judah received their first extensive archaeological coverage here. We also attempted to discuss certain cognitive aspects of the society under discussion, and to use them to explain the enigma of the four-room house, although naturally the conclusions in this field still require further study. Many factors related to the small finds did not receive extensive attention here either, and complementary studies are required.

The Status of the Kingdoms of Israel and Judah

An analysis of the archaeological finds shows that during the transition from Iron Age I to Iron Age II (traditionally dated to the end of the eleventh century and the beginning of the tenth century B.C.E.) a state formation process took place in the land of Israel, leading to the establishment of the Monarchy. This arises from an analysis of the settlement patterns during this period and also from an analysis of the finds in some of the period's cities (e.g., see chap. 9; see also Halpern 2000: 559; 2001: 219). However, most of the archaeological information available derives from the eighth–seventh centuries B.C.E., and the discussion in this book focuses on this period. During this time, the kingdoms of Israel and Judah were clearly "states" (Israel, of course, only until its destruction, toward the end of the eighth century B.C.E.). Both of them manifested social and settlement stratification, had a complex administrative system, and even had impressive public works that were constructed as a result of royal initiative. This conclusion accords with the picture arising from the historical sources, both biblical and extrabiblical.

However, the two kingdoms were not equal in all aspects. Israel was much larger and more developed than Judah. The social stratification in this kingdom was more complex and comprised an entire spectrum, while in Judah there were only two main social strata: a minority class of wealthy people and a majority of lower-class people. A similar picture arises out of an analysis of the settlement hierarchy. In the Kingdom of Israel, the distribution is to a very large extent like a rank-size model, while the Kingdom of Judah is similar to a "primate-city" model. The explanation for the difference between the two kingdoms is probably their different developmental levels. The "primate city law" characterizes societies with a level of urbanization that is relatively low, while the "rank-size distribution" usually characterizes societies with a more developed urbanization level. Accordingly, two-class social stratification is typical of "simple agrarian societies," while multiclass stratification describes the situation known in "advanced agrarian societies." In this case as well, the sociological conclusion matches our knowledge from the historical sources, according to which Israel was more developed than Judah.

The Question of Social Stratification

As we have seen in chaps. 1–2, most Bible scholars, historians, and even some archaeologists believe that Israelite society during the period of the Monarchy, especially in the eighth–seventh centuries B.C.E., was characterized by major social stratification. According to most scholars, the traditional system was destroyed, the kinship units (the *mishpahah* and perhaps also the *bet av*) ceased to function, and most of the land was concentrated in a few hands. This opinion is based primarily on analyzing the biblical evidence, particularly the admonishments of the prophets. Only a few scholars believe that the social structure remained unharmed, the land continued to be owned by the farmers, and the prophets' criticism referred mainly to power struggles within the traditional social system. There are also some intermediate opinions of scholars who assume that the traditional system was indeed damaged, but not completely destroyed, while others have noted the difficulty in attributing complete reliability to the angry prophecies.

Chapters 3–4 were devoted to a careful examination of the question of social stratification, using various research methods, some of which were developed in this book. An analysis of the findings showed that there were indeed wide social gaps in both kingdoms, but mainly in the urban sector. The processes of the strengthening of the wealthy and the weakening of the poor usually took place in the cities, while in the rural sector there were independent agricultural settlements that probably cultivated their own land, lived above a subsistence level, and accumulated a surplus. The picture arising in this book is between the two extreme positions proposed in previous studies: there was undoubtedly social stratification (sometimes even severe), but this stratification did not occur in the entire social system but was limited mainly to the urban sector. Regarding the rural sector, those who argued that this was a traditional, family-oriented, autonomous society were probably right. This complex reality is also reflected in the epigraphic evidence, indicating exploited classes on the one hand (the reaper's letter from Mezad Hashavyahu), and the preservation of a traditional system on the other hand (the Samaria ostraca).[1] It should also be noted that comparative studies of agrarian societies show that in their urban settlements there were indeed wide social gaps (Lenski and Lenski 1974: 242), and at least half the income (or produce) of these societies belonged to the upper class (1974: 230).

City and Country

In all the settlements that can be defined as "urban," there are traces of state activity to varying degrees, and it is clear that the kingdom's involvement was a central factor in the processes that changed the social structure. It accelerated the urbanization process itself and probably also caused a significant increase in economic specialization, trade, and hired labor. Hired work was one of the main reasons for the dissolution of the traditional kinship framework and the change in the traditional social structure based on this framework. Settlements where there was no direct state involvement, even large settlements (such as Kh. Banat Barr and Deir el-Mir, which were larger, though less dense, than most cities), did not turn into urban settlements.

The archaeological finds show that the socioeconomic gaps identified in urban settlements were not found in villages during the period under discussion, and the socioeconomic situation in these settlements was more or less uniform. So it appears that the rural-sector settlements that were mainly in the hill country, maintained a traditional way of life, and many of the affects of "progress" did not reach them. They were affected to a certain degree by these processes, but this influence was much weaker in the rural sector than in the cities.

Social Identity

Many scholars dealing with ancient Israel believe that this society had a clear social identity and that there was great deal of similarity between the kingdoms of Israel and Judah. This view has been subjected to strong criticism in recent years, and many consider it to be a product of the fictional picture drawn in later editing layers in the Bible, while in reality there was no one Israelite identity. However, this study has shown that there was indeed a great deal of similarity between the kingdoms of Israel and Judah. An analysis of the four-room house also shows that this was a society almost all of whose members participated in nonverbal forms of communication that conveyed, among other things, unifying messages of shared identity. And the same can be seen in many other facets of material culture (see

---

1. The development apparent in the prophecies of Jeremiah over time, if identified correctly, also indicates that the social problems were concentrated in the city.

brief discussion in chap. 9; see also Faust 2006b). It seems that the shared messages did not contradict the gaps existing within this society (between city and village and between rich and poor); unifying and distinguishing messages were conveyed parallelly and were directed at different levels within Israelite society. In light of this, it seems that the Israelite identity that is reflected in the Bible was not just a later fiction created by an editor but a real message that is also reflected—at least to some extent—in the material findings.

Directions for Continuing a Socioarchaeological Study of the Period of the Monarchy

This book constitutes only a first step along the way to studying the society in the period under discussion. In order to reconstruct the society, many more studies must be undertaken, especially excavations with a suitable orientation. Social and cognitive questions should be stressed and given greater attention as we analyze the archaeological data that we currently possess. These questions have so far not received sufficient attention in the archaeological study of the southern Levant. Turning them into a desirable, or at least worthy direction of study is the first step to providing answers. This methodological step can be taken by means of a new analysis of old excavations (as has been done here). At the second stage, new excavations will be required, with a strategy that enables the gathering of the relevant information:

Selecting sites and excavation areas: Continuation of this research requires excavating rural sites and urban residential quarters and requires devoting less attention to fortifications, palaces, and so on than is currently normal. The former have so far received little archaeological attention, and a significant number of data about the sites has only been obtained in salvage excavations.

Publication: The painful topic of publishing is relevant to almost all archaeological studies. And, although planned excavations relatively often reach final publication, salvage excavations are usually doomed to be forgotten. Even when the finds of a planned urban settlement excavation are published, in many cases the authors prefer to publish the impressive and the the monumental finds (particularly before the final report is prepared). Residential neighborhoods and rural settlements seem less important and thus receive less attention in publications than is essential for research. Obviously, this situation must be remedied.

The form of publication: When scholars attempt to study society, their ability to reconstruct the original location of objects within a house is particularly important. This matter, mainly related to the nature of documentation, requires a detailed and separate publication of the various findings. It is not sufficient to publish general statistics regarding the various types of pottery, as is done in some publications. A discussion of ethnic differences (see chap. 8) clarifies this issue. If members of different ethnic groups lived in one settlement, publication of the finds in a general way blurs the differences between the groups. If the assemblages of each household are not investigated individually, including the faunal and botanical remains unearthed inside the building, an all-inclusive publication disguises the features of all the groups, not just one of them.

Excavation tactics: Many today believe that excavating limited areas is more "scientific," but this is not the case. According to Renfrew, for example, if we wish to learn about social organization, individual sites must be analyzed carefully, using a more creative approach to sampling problems and giving greater emphasis to horizontal excavation than is sometimes done (Renfrew 1974: 91; Barker 1993). It is insufficient to reveal partial complexes,[2] which leave too many questions unanswered, if we want to learn about the society, the nature of the buildings, and so on. We need wide exposure.

The problem of ethnicity once more provides a suitable illustration. Whole buildings must be uncovered in order to analyze them and note the ethnic differences in the behavior of their residents. Fortresses constitute another example (see chap. 5). Complete excavation of such a site and discovering the exact functions of the various spaces might determine whether this was an agricultural site, a fortress, or some combination of the two. It is also difficult to determine degrees of social stratification on the basis of the excavation of just a few buildings. If the buildings are similar or identical, a conclusion could be formed that this was a relatively egalitarian society. However, perhaps in a nearby neighborhood (not excavated), there were larger and grander buildings, the excavation of which would reveal the opposite conclusion regarding the findings (see Tod 1974: 86–87).

The conclusion should not be that it is essential to excavate entire sites. Such a step would be very costly, and in the case of tells, even impossible. We also know that excavating completely allows no time for criticizing the excavation and correcting possible mistakes in the future. However, it does appear that it is worth the effort to excavate almost the entire area of several representative sites.[3]

In any case, we must hope that in the future greater attention will be paid to the archaeological analysis of social and cognitive issues related to Israelite society.

---

2. Paradoxically, this form of excavation raises problems in the stratigraphic analysis as well, because when an excavated element's function is uncertain (whether it is a yard, a house floor, etc.), it is difficult to understand the context of associated finds.

3. For severe methodological criticism with regard to partial excavations, see for example Barker 1993: 79–88; Bunimovitz 1995: 65. V. J. K. de Geus (1982) also calls for more extensive excavations for the purpose of learning about Israelite society.

Bibliography

Abells, Z., and Arbit, A.
  1995   *The City of David Water Systems.* Jerusalem: Faculty of Printing Techniques, Hadassah College of Technology.
Aharoni, Y.
  1962   The Districts of Israel and Judah. Pp. 110–15 in *The Kingdoms of Israel and Judah*, ed. A. Malamat. Jerusalem: Israel Exploration Society. [Hebrew]
  1973   The Israelite City. Pp. 13–18 in *Beer-Sheba I*, ed. Y. Aharoni. Tel Aviv: Tel Aviv University Press.
  1975   *Investigations at Lachish: The Sanctuary and the Residency.* Lachish 5. Tel Aviv: Gateway.
  1979   *The Land of the Bible: Historical Geography.* Philadelphia: Westminster.
  1981   *The Arad Inscriptions.* Jerusalem: Bialik.
  1982   *The Archaeology of the Land of Israel.* Philadelphia: Westminster.
  1993   Ramat Rachel. Pp. 1261–67 in vol. 4 of *NEAEHL*.
Aharoni, Y., and Lowenstam, S. A.
  1963   Geographical Concepts in the Bible. Cols. 742–54 in vol. 4 of *EncMiq*. [Hebrew]
Aḥituv, S.
  1982   Shaphan. Cols. 252–53 in vol. 8 of *EncMiq*. [Hebrew]
  1993   *Handbook of Ancient Hebrew Inscriptions.* Jerusalem: Bialik. [Hebrew]
  2005   *HaKetav VeHaMiktav: Handbook of Ancient Inscriptions from the Land of Israel and the Kingdoms beyond the Jordan from the Period of the First Commonwealth.* Jerusalem: Bialik. [Hebrew]
Ahlström, G. W.
  1982a   *Royal Administration and National Religion in Ancient Palestine.* Leiden: Brill.
  1982b   Where Did the Israelites Live? *JNES* 41: 133–38.
  1993   *The History of Ancient Palestine from the Paleolithic Period to Alexander's Conquest.* JSOTSup 146. Sheffield: Sheffield Academic Press.
Aizner, A.
  2011   *The Finds in Iron Age II Dwellings as a Reflection of Society.* M.A. thesis. Bar-Ilan University.
Albright, W. F.
  1943   *The Excavation of Tell Beit Mirsim*, vol. 3: *The Iron Age.* AASOR 21–22. New Haven, CT: American Schools of Oriental Research.
  1993   Beit Mirsim, Tell. Pp. 177–80 in vol. 1 of *NEAEHL*.
Alpert-Nakhai, B., et al.
  1993   Wawiyat, Tell El-. Pp. 1500–1501 in vol. 4 of *NEAEHL*.
Amit, D.
  1989–90a Elʿazar. *Excavations and Surveys in Israel* 9: 158–60.
  1989–90b Khirbet Jarish. *Excavations and Surveys in Israel* 9: 157–58.
  1992   Farmsteads in Northern Judea (Betar Region) Survey. *Excavations and Surveys in Israel* 10: 147–48.
Amit, D., and Cohen-Amin, R.
  forthcoming   Iron Age Rural Settlements in the Northern Hebron Hill Country. *ʿAtiqot*. [Hebrew]

Ap-Thomas, D. R.
  1973   The Phoenicians. Pp. 259–86 in *Peoples of Old Testament Times*, ed. D. J. Wiseman. Oxford: Clarendon.
Arav, R.
  1995   Bethsaida, Tzer and the Fortified Cities of Naphtali. Pp. 193–201 in *Bethsaida: A City by the North Shore of the Sea of Galilee*, ed. R. Arav and R. A. Freund. Kirksville, MO: Thomas Jefferson University Press.
  2000   The Excavations and Study of Bethsaida. *Ariel* 139: 115–24. [Hebrew]
Arav, R., and Barnett, M.
  1997   An Egyptian Figurine of Pataikos at Bethsaida. *IEJ* 37: 198–213.
Artzi, P.
  1968   *Sevel.* Cols. 995–96 in vol. 5 of *EncMiq.* [Hebrew]
Auld, G., and Steiner, M.
  1996   *Jerusalem*, vol. 1: *From the Bronze Age to the Maccabees.* Cambridge: Lutterworth.
Avigad, N.
  1977   The Governor (Sar Ha-ʿIr). *Qadmoniot* 10 (38–39): 68–69. [Hebrew]
  1982   Samaria: Story of the Excavations. Cols. 148–62 in vol. 8 of *EncMiq.* [Hebrew]
  1983   *Discovering Jerusalem.* Nashville: Thomas Nelson.
Avishur, Y.
  1996   [Various entries] in *Scrolls: The Song of Songs*, ed. M. Fuchs and J. Klein. The World of the Bible Series. Tel Aviv: Davidson Ati. [Hebrew]
Avishur, Y., and Heltzer, M.
  1996   *Studies on the Royal Administration in Ancient Israel in the Light of Epigraphic Sources.* Jerusalem: Acadamon. [Hebrew]
Avraham, N.
  2000   *Marginal People in Israelite Society in the Biblical Period.* Ph.D. Dissertation. Haifa University. [Hebrew]
Bachi, G.
  1973   Several Kraters from Stratum II. Pp. 38–42 in *Beer-Sheba*, vol. 1, ed. Y. Aharoni. Tel Aviv: Tel Aviv University Press.
Bahat, D.
  1972   Excavations at Givat Sharet near Beit Shemesh. *Qadmoniot* 8 (30–31): 64–67. [Hebrew]
Banning, E. B., and Byrd, B. F.
  1989   Alternative Approaches for Exploring Levantine Neolithic Architecture. *Paleorient* 15/1: 154–60.
Barkay, G.
  1977   A Second Bulla of a Sar Ha-ʿIr. *Qadmoniot* 10 (38–39): 69–71. [Hebrew]
  1988   Jerusalem as a Primate City. Pp. 124–25 in *Settlements, Population and Economy in Ancient Eretz Israel*, ed. S. Bunimovitz, A. Kasher, and M. Kochavi. Tel Aviv: Tel Aviv University Press. [Hebrew]
  1989   The Priestly Benediction on the Ketef Hinnom Plaques. *Cathedra* 52: 37–76. [Hebrew]
  1990   The Iron Age II. Pp. 83–233 in vol. 9 of *The Archaeology of Ancient Israel in the Biblical Period*, ed. A. Ben-Tor. Tel Aviv: The Open University of Israel. [Hebrew]
  1991a   Jerusalem's Cemeteries in the First Temple Period. Pp. 102–23 in *Jerusalem in the First Temple Period*, ed. D. Amit and R. Gonen. Jerusalem: Yad Ben-Zvi. [Hebrew]
  1991b   'Your Poor Brother': A Note on an Inscribed Bowl from Beth Shemesh. *IEJ* 41: 239–41.

1992   The Iron Age II–III. Pp. 302–73 in *The Archaeology of Ancient Israel*, ed. A. Ben-Tor. New Haven, CT: Yale University Press.

1993   A Group of Stamped Handles from Judah. *ErIsr* 23 (Biran Volume): 113–28. [Hebrew]

1994   Burial Caves and Burial Practices in Judah in the Iron Age. Pp. 96–164 in *Graves and Burial Practices in Israel in the Ancient Period*, ed. I. Singer. Tel Aviv: Yad Ben-Zvi. [Hebrew]

1999   Burial Caves and Dwellings in Judah during Iron Age II: Sociological Aspects. Pp. 96–102 in *Material Culture, Society and Ideology: New Directions in the Archaeology of the Land of Israel*, ed. A. Faust and A. Maeir. Ramat Gan: Bar-Ilan University Press. [Hebrew]

2000   The Necropoli of Jerusalem in the First Temple Period. Pp. 233–70 in *The History of Jerusalem: The Biblical Period*, ed. S. Aḥituv and A. Mazar. Jerusalem: Yad Ben-Zvi. [Hebrew]

2011   A Fiscal Bulla from the Slopes of the Temple Mount: Evidence for the Taxation System of the Judean Kingdom. Pp. 151–78 in vol. 17 of *New Studies on Jerusalem*, ed. E. Baruch, A. Levy-Reifer, and A. Faust. Ramat Gan: Ingeborg Rennert Center for Jerusalem Studies, Bar-Ilan University. [Hebrew]

Barker, P.
1993   *Techniques of Archaeological Excavation*. London: Batsford.

Baron, S.
1952   *A Social and Religious History of the Jews*, vol. 1. Philadelphia: Jewish Publication Society.

Barth, F.
1969   Introduction. Pp. 9–38 in *Ethnic Groups and Boundaries*, ed. F. Barth. Bergen: Universitets Forlaget.

Baruch, Y.
1996   Khirbet el-ʿId: An Additional Example of an Iron Age II Casemate Fortress in the North Part of Mount Hebron. P. 4 in *Judea and Samaria Research Studies: Proceedings of the Sixth Annual Meeting*, ed. Y. Eshel. Lecture Abstracts. Ariel: Judea and Samaria College. [Hebrew]

1997   Khirbet el-ʿId: An Iron Age Fortress on Northwest Mount Hebron. Pp. 49–55 in *Judea and Samaria Research Studies: Proceedings of the Sixth Annual Meeting*, ed. Y. Eshel. Ariel and Qedumim: Eretz. [Hebrew]

2001   Khirbet Abu Shawan. *Hadashot Arkheologiyot: Excavations and Surveys in Israel* 113: 95*–97*, 141–43.

2007   A Farmstead from the End of the Iron Age and Installations at the Foot of Khirbat Abu Shawan. *ʿAtiqot* 56: 25–44, 71*–74*.

Basset, C., et al.
1992   Introduction. Pp. 1–7 in *Death in Towns: Urban Responses to Dying and the Dead, 100–1600*, ed. S. Bassett. Leicester: Leicester University Press.

Beit-Arieh, I.
1973   The Western Quarter. Pp. 31–37 in *Beer-Sheba*, vol. 1, ed. Y. Aharoni. Tel Aviv: Tel Aviv University Press.

1983   A First Temple Period Census Document. *PEQ* 115: 105–8.

1985   Tel ʿIra: A Fortified City of the Kingdom of Judah. *Qadmoniot* 18 (69–70): 17–25. [Hebrew]

1986   Horvat ʿUzza: A Border Fortress in the Eastern Negev. *Qadmoniot* 19 (73–74): 31–40. [Hebrew]

1991   Hurvat Uza: A Fortified Outpost on the Eastern Negev. *BA* 54: 126–35.

1992   A Small Border Frontier Citadel at Horvat Radum in the Judean Negev. *Qad-moniot* 24 (95–96): 86–88. [Hebrew]

1999a   Ostracon from Horvat ʿUza. *ErIsr* 26 (Cross Volume): 34–40. [Hebrew]

1999b   *Tel ʿIra: A Stronghold in the Biblical Negev.* Tel Aviv: Tel Aviv University Press.

2007   *Horvat Uza and Horvat Radum: Two Fortresses in the Biblical Negev.* Tel Aviv: Tel Aviv University Press.

Bendor, S.

1996   *The Social Structure of Ancient Israel: The Institution of the Family* (beit ʾab) *from the Settlement to the End of the Monarchy.* Jerusalem: Simor.

Ben-Dov, M.

1992   Middle and Late Bronze Age Dwellings. Pp. 99–104 in *The Architecture of Ancient Israel, from the Prehistoric to the Persian Periods*, ed. A. Kempinski and R. Reich. Jerusalem: Israel Exploration Society.

Ben-Shlomo, D.; Shai, I.; and Maeir, A. M.

2004   Late Philistine Decorated Ware ("Ashdod Ware"): Typology, Chronology, and Production Centers. *BASOR* 335: 1–35.

Ben-Tor, A.

1992   Notes and News: Tel Hazor, 1992. *IEJ* 42: 254–60.

1993   Qiri, Tel. Pp. 1228–29 in vol. 4 of *NEAEHL*.

1996   The Yigael Yadin Memorial Excavations at Hazor: Aims and Preliminary Results of 1990–1992 Seasons. *ErIsr* 25 (Aviram Volume): 67–81. [Hebrew]

1999   Solomon's City Rises from the Ashes. *BAR* 25/2: 26–37, 60.

2008   Hazor. Pp. 1769–75 in vol. 5 of *NEAEHL*.

Ben-Tor, A., et al.

1987   A Regional Study of Tel Yoqneʾam and Its Vicinity. *Qadmoniot* 20 (77–78): 2–17. [Hebrew]

Ben-Tor, A., and Portugali, Y.

1987   *Tel Qiri.* Qedem 24. Jerusalem: Hebrew University.

Berman, J.

2008   *Created Equal: How the Bible Broke with Ancient Political Thought.* New York: Oxford University Press.

Bertholet, A.

1926   *A History of Hebrew Civilization.* London: Harrap.

Bevan, B.

1997   Bounding the Landscape: Place and Identity during the Yorkshire Wolds Iron Age. Pp. 181–91 in *Reconstructing Iron Age Societies: New Approaches to the British Iron Age*, ed. A. Gwilt and C. Haselgrove. Oxford: Oxbow.

Bienkowski, P.

1998   Comments on the essays by Kitchen, Whitelam, and Finkelstein on pp. 65–163 in *The Origin of Early Israel—Current Debate: Biblical, Historical and Archaeological Perspectives*, ed. S. Aḥituv and E. D. Oren. Beersheba: Ben-Gurion University of the Negev.

Biran, A.

1992   *Dan: 25 Years of Excavations at Tel Dan.* Jerusalem: Israel Exploration Society. [Hebrew]

1996   The *huzot* in Dan. P. 17 in *The Twenty-Second Archaeological Congress in Israel.* Lecture Abstracts. Tel Aviv: Israel Exploration Society. [Hebrew]

Birley, R.

1977   *Vindolanda: A Roman Frontier Post on Hadrian's Wall.* London: Thames & Hudson.

Blakely, J. A.
2002   Reconciling Two Maps: Archaeological Evidence for the Kingdom of David and
        Solomon. *BASOR* 327: 49–54.
Blanton, R. E.
1994   *Houses and Households: A Comparative Study.* New York: Plenum.
Blenkinsopp, J.
1997   The Family in First Temple Israel. Pp. 48–103 in *Families in Ancient Israel,* ed.
        L. G. Perdue et al. Louisville: Westminster John Knox.
Bloch-Smith, E.
1992   *Judahite Burial Practices and Beliefs about the Dead.* JSOTSup 123. Sheffield: Shef-
        field Academic Press.
Blomquist, T. H.
1999   *Gates and Gods.* Stockholm: Almqvist & Wiksell.
Borowski, O.
1987   *Agriculture in Iron Age Israel.* Winona Lake, IN: Eisenbrauns.
Bourdieu, P.
1977   *An Outline of a Theory of Practice.* Cambridge: Cambridge University Press.
Braemer, F.
1982   *L'architecture domestique du Levant á l'âge du fer.* Paris: Éditions Recherche sur les
        civilisations.
Brandel, B.
1995   An Israelite Bulla in Phoenician Style from Bethsaida (el-Tell). Pp. 141–64 in
        Bethsaida: A City by the North Shore of the Sea of Galilee, ed. R. Arav and R. A.
        Freund. Kirksville, MO: Truman State University Press.
Branigan, K.
1966   The Four Room Buildings of Tell en-Nasbeh. *IEJ* 16: 206–9.
Bright, J.
1972   *A History of Israel.* London: SCM.
Brody, A. J.
2009   "Those Who Add House to House": Household Archaeology and the Use of
        Domestic Space in an Iron II Residential Compound at Tell en-Naṣbeh. Pp. 45–
        56 in *Exploring the Longue Durée: Essays in Honor of Lawrence E. Stager,* ed. J. D.
        Schloen. Winona Lake, IN: Eisenbrauns.
2011   The Archaeology of the Extended Family: A Household Compound from
        Iron II Tell en Nasbeh. Pp. 237–54 in *Household Archaeology in Ancient Israel and
        Beyond,* ed. A. Yasur-Landau, J. R. Ebeling, and L. B. Mazow. Leiden: Brill.
Broshi, M.
1973   Excavations in the House of Caiaphas, Mount Zion. *Qadmoniot* 5: 104–7.
        [Hebrew]
1988   Book Review of Y. Hirschfeld, *Dwelling Houses in Roman and Byzantine Palestine.*
        Qadmoniot 20 (79–80): 126–27. [Hebrew]
1992   Nasbeh, Tell en-. Pp. 1080–84 in vol. 3 of *NEAEHL.* [Hebrew]
1996   Fire, Soil, and Water: The Three Elements That Enabled the Settlement of the
        Hilly Regions of Palestine in Early Iron Age I. *ErIsr* 25 (Aviram Volume): 94–98.
        [Hebrew]
2001   *Bread, Wine, Walls and Scrolls.* Journal for the Study of the Pseudepigrapha
        Supplement 36. Sheffield: Sheffield Academic Press.
Broshi, M., and Finkelstein, I.
1992   The Population of Palestine in Iron Age II. *BASOR* 287: 47–60.

Broshi, M., and Gophna, R.
1984   The Settlement and Population of Palestine during the Early Bronze Age II–III. *BASOR* 253: 41–52.
1986   Middle Bronze Age II Palestine: Its Settlement and Population. *BASOR* 261: 73–90.

Brown, B. M.
1987   Population Estimation from Floor Area: A Restudy of 'Naroll's Constant.' *Behavior Science Research* 21: 1–49.

Brown, F. E.
1990   Comment on Chapman: Some Cautionary Notes on the Application of Spatial Measures to Prehistoric Settlements. Pp. 93–109 in *The Social Archaeology of Houses*, ed. R. Samson. Edinburgh: Edinburgh University Press.

Bunimovitz, S.
1988   Reconstructing Political Systems Using Spatial Analysis. Pp. 39–56 in *Settlements, Population, and Economy in Ancient Eretz Israel*, ed. S. Bunimovitz, M. Kochavi, and A. Kasher. Tel Aviv: Tel Aviv University Press. [Hebrew]
1990   *The Land of Israel in the Late Bronze Age: A Case Study of Socio-Cultural Change in a Complex Society*. Ph.D. dissertation. Tel Aviv University. [Hebrew]
1992   Middle Bronze Age 'Fortifications': A Reflection of Social Organization and Political Formation. *Tel Aviv* 19: 221–34.
1995   How Mute Stones Speak: Interpreting What We Dig Up. *BAR* 21/2: 58–67, 96–100.
2001   Cultural Interpretation and the Bible: Biblical Archaeology in the Postmodern Era. *Cathedra* 100: 27–46. [Hebrew]

Bunimovitz, S., and Faust, A.
2001   Chronological Separation, Geographical Segregation or Ethnic Demarcation: Ethnography and the Iron Age Low Chronology. *BASOR* 322: 1–10.
2002   Ideology in Stone: Understanding the Four Room House. *BAR* 28/4: 32–41, 59–60.
2003   Building Identity: The Four-Room House and the Israelite Mind. Pp. 411–23 in *Symbiosis, Symbolism, and the Power of the Past: Canaan, Ancient Israel, and Their Neighbors from the Late Bronze Age through Roman Palaestina*, ed. W. G. Dever and S. Gitin. Winona Lake, IN: Eisenbrauns.
2010   Re-constructing Biblical Archaeology: Toward an Integration of Archaeology and the Bible. Pp. 43–54 in *Historical Biblical Archaeology and the Future: The New Pragmatism*, ed. T. E. Levy. London: Equinox.

Bunimovitz, S., and Lederman, Z.
1997   Beth-Shemesh: Culture Conflict in Judah's Frontier. *BAR* 23/1: 42–49, 75–77.
2004   Jerusalem and Beth-Shemesh: A Capital and Its Borders. Pp. 37–50 in *New Studies on Jerusalem*, vol. 10, ed. E. Baruch and A. Faust. Ramat Gan: Rennert Center for Jerusalem Studies. [Hebrew]
2008   Beth-Shemesh. Pp. 1644–48 in vol. 5 of *NEAEHL*.
2009   The Archaeology of Border Communities: Renewed Excavations at Tel Beth-Shemesh, part 1: The Iron Age. *NEA* 72: 114–42.

Bunimovitz, S., and Yasur-Landau, A.
1996   Philistine and Israelite Pottery: A Comparative Approach to the Question of Pots and People. *Tel Aviv* 23: 88–102.

Burckhardt, J.
1998   *The Greeks and Greek Civilization*. New York: St. Martin's Press.

Burney, C.
  1977   *From Village to Empire: An Introduction to Near Eastern Archaeology*. Oxford: Phaidon.
Cahill, J.
  2002   Jerusalem at the Time of the United Monarchy: The Archaeological Evidence. Pp. 21–27 in *New Studies on Jerusalem*, vol. 7, ed. A. Faust and E. Baruch. Ramat Gan: Bar-Ilan University Press. [Hebrew]
  2003   Jerusalem at the Time of the United Monarchy: The Archaeological Evidence. Pp. 13–80 in *Jerusalem in Bible and Archaeology*, ed. A. Vaughn and A. Killebrew. Atlanta: Society of Biblical Literature.
Callaway, J. A.
  1983   A Visit with Ahilud. *BAR* 9/5: 42–53.
Cameron, C. M.
  1999   Room Size, Organization of Construction, and Archaeological Interpretation in the Puebloan Southwest. *JAA* 18: 201–39.
Campbell, E. F.
  1994   Archaeological Reflections on Amos's Targets. Pp. 32–52 in *Scripture and Other Artifacts*, ed. M. D. Coogan et al. Louisville: Westminster John Knox.
  2002   *Shechem*, vol. 3: *The Stratigraphy and Architecture of Shechem/Balatah I: Text*. Boston: American Schools of Oriental Research.
Carniero, R.
  1970   A Theory of the Origin of the State. *Science* 169: 733–39.
Cassuto, D. R.
  2004   *The Social Context of Weaving in the Land of Israel in Iron Age II*. M.A. thesis. Bar-Ilan University.
Chambon, A.
  1984   *Tell El-Farʿah*, vol. 1. Paris: Éditions Recherche sur les civilisations.
Chaney, M. L.
  1986   Systematic Study of the Israelite Monarchy. Pp. 53–76 in *Social Scientific Criticism of the Hebrew Bible and Its Social World: The Israelite Monarchy*, ed. N. K. Gottwald. Semeia 37. Decatur, GA: Society of Biblical Literature.
Childe, V. G.
  1929   *The Danube in Prehistory*. Oxford: Oxford University Press.
  1950   The Urban Revolution. *Town Planning Review* 21: 3–17.
Chun, A.
  1996   The Lineage-Village Complex in Southeastern China: A Long Footnote in Anthropology of Kinship. *Current Anthropology* 37: 429–50.
Clark, D. R.
  1996   Early Iron Age Pillared Buildings at Tell al-Umaryi. *BA* 59/4: 241.
Clarke, D. L.
  1977   Spatial Information in Archaeology. Pp. 1–32 in *Spatial Archaeology*, ed. D. L. Clarke. London: Academic Press.
Classen, H. J. M., and Skalnik, P.
  1978   The Early State: Models and Reality. Pp. 637–50 in *The Early State*, ed. H. J. M. Classen and P. Skalnik. The Hague: Mouton.
Clements, R. E.
  1993   Deuteronomy, the Book of. Pp. 164–68 in *The Oxford Companion to the Bible*, ed. B. M. Metzger and M. D. Coogan. Oxford: Oxford University Press.

Clines, D. J. A.
   1993   Pentateuch. Pp. 579–82 in *The Oxford Companion to the Bible*, ed. B. M. Metzger
             and M. D. Coogan. Oxford: Oxford University Press.
Cohen, R.
   1986   *The Settlements of the Central Negev in the Light of Archaeology and Literary Sources
             during the 4th–1st Millennia* B.C.E. Ph.D. Dissertation. Hebrew University.
             [Hebrew]
   1992   Kadesh-Barnea. Pp. 841–47 in vol. 3 of *NEAEHL*.
Cohen, R., and Bernick-Greenberg, H.
   2007   *Excavations at Kadesh Barnea (Tell el-Qudeirat) 1976–1982*. Jerusalem: Israel An-
             tiquities Authority.
Cohen, R., and Cohen-Amin, R.
   2004   *Ancient Settlement of the Negev Highlands II*. Jerusalem: Israel Antiquities Au-
             thority. [Hebrew]
Cohen, R., and Yisrael, Y.
   1995   The Iron Age Fortresses at En Haseva. *BA* 54: 223–35.
   1996   The Excavations at En Haseva: Israelite and Roman Tamar. *Qadmoniot* 112:
             78–92. [Hebrew]
Cohen-Amin, R.
   2004   The Finds (Iron Age IIA). Pp. 121–42 in *Ancient Settlement of the Negev Highlands
             II*, ed. R. Cohen, and R. Cohen-Amin. Jerusalem: Israel Antiquities Authority.
Coogan, M.
   1982   Gate. Cols. 231–36 in vol. 8 of *EncMiq*. [Hebrew]
Coote, R. B., and Whitelam, K. W.
   1987   *The Emergence of Early Israel in Historical Perspective*. The Social World of Biblical
             Antiquity 5. Sheffield: Sheffield Academic Press.
Coulter, P. B.
   1989   *Measuring Inequality*, Boulder, CO: Westview.
Coupland, G., and Banning, E. G. (eds.)
   1996   *People Who Lived in Big Houses: Archaeological Perspectives on Large Domestic
             Structures*. Madison, WI: Prehistory Press.
Covello-Paran, K.
   1998   Horbat Malta. *Excavations and Surveys in Israel* 18: 27–28.
   2008   Excavations at Horbat Malta, Lower Galilee. *ʿAtiqot* 59: 5–86.
Cowgill, G. L.
   2004   Origins and Development of Urbanism: Archaeological Perspectives. *Annual
             Review of Anthropology* 33: 525–49.
Cowling, G.
   1988   The Biblical Household. Pp. 179–92 in *Wunschet Jerusalem Frieden*, ed. M. Au-
             gustin and K. D. Schunck. Frankfurt: Peter Lang.
Cresson, B. C.
   1999   Area F. Pp. 97–102 in *Tel ʿIra: A Stronghold in the Biblical Negev*, ed. I. Beit-Arieh.
             Tel Aviv: Tel Aviv University Press.
Crocker, P. T.
   1985   Status Symbols in the Architecture of El-ʿAmarna. *JEA* 71: 52–65.
Cross, F. M.
   1988   Reuben, First-Born of Jacob. *ZAW* 100 Supplement: 46–65.
Cross, F. M., and Milik, J. T.
   1956   Exploration in the Judean Buqeah. *BASOR* 142: 5–17.

Crow, J.
1995   *Housesteads*. London: National Heritage.
Crowfoot, J. W.; Kenyon, K. M.; and Sukenik, E. L.
1942   *Samaria-Sebaste*, vol. 1: *The Buildings at Samaria*. London: Palestine Exploration Fund.
Currid, J. D.
1992   Puzzling Public Buildings. *BAR* 18/1: 52–61.
Dagan, Y.
1992   *The Shephelah during the Period of the Monarchy in Light of Archaeological Excavations and Survey*. M.A. Thesis. Tel Aviv University. [Hebrew]
1993   A Map Survey of Beth Shemesh and Nes Harim. *Excavations and Surveys in Israel* 13: 94–95.
2000   *The Settlement in the Judean Shephelah in the Second and First Millennium* B.C.: *A Test Case of Settlement Processes in a Geographic Region*. Ph.D. dissertation, Tel Aviv University. [Hebrew]
2011   Archaeological Surveys and Excavations along the Cross-Israel Highway: A Case Study for the Collection of Data from the Field. *ʿAtiqot* 64: 3*–61*. [Hebrew]
Dalhamiya
1970   Dalhamiya. *Hadashot Arkheologiyot* 33: 14–15. [Hebrew]
Dar, S.
1982   Ancient Agricultural Farms near Wadi Beit-ʿArif. *Nofim* 16: 47–60. [Hebrew]
1986a   Khirbet Jemein: A First-Temple Period Village in Western Samaria. Pp. 13–73 in *Shomron Studies*, ed. S. Dar and Z. Safrai. Tel Aviv: Hakibbutz Hameuchad. [Hebrew]
1986b   *Landscape and Pattern: An Archaeological Survey of Western Samaria, 800* BCE–*636* CE. British Archaeological Report 308. Oxford: British Archaeological Report.
1993   The Survey of Western Samaria. Pp. 1314–16 in vol. 4 of *NEAEHL*. [in: Samaria, Region]
Dar, S.; Safrai, Z.; and Tepper, Y.
1986   *Um Rihan: A Village of the Mishnah*. Tel Aviv: Hakibbutz Hameuchad. [Hebrew]
Dark, K.
1995   *Theoretical Archaeology*. London: Duckworth.
Daviau, P. M. M.
1993   *Houses and Their Furnishings in Bronze Age Palestine: Domestic Activity Areas and Artifacts Distribution in the Middle and Late Bronze Ages*. JSOT/ASOR Monograph Series 8. Sheffield: Sheffield Academic Press.
1996   The Fifth Season of Excavation at Tell Jawa (1994): A Preliminary Report. *ADAJ* 40: 83–100.
1999   Domestic Architecture in Iron Age Ammon: Building Materials, Construction Techniques, and Room Arrangement. Pp. 113–36 in *Ancient Ammon*, ed. B. MacDonald and R. W. Younker. Leiden: Brill.
Davidovitz, U., et al.
2006   Salvage Excavations at Ramot Forest and Ramat Bet-Hakerem: New Data regarding Jerusalem's Periphery during the First and Second Temple Periods. Pp. 35–111 in *New Studies on Jerusalem: The 11th Volume*, ed. E. Baruch, Z. Greenhut, and A. Faust. Ramat Gan: Bar-Ilan University Press.

Davis, S.
1985   The Large Mammal Bones. Pp. 148–50 in *Excavations at Tell Qasile*, vol. 2, ed. A. Mazar. Qedem 20. Jerusalem: Hebrew University.
1987   The Faunal Remains of Tell-Qiri. Pp. 249–51 in *Tell Qiri*, ed. A. Ben-Tor and Y. Portugali. Jerusalem: Hebrew University.
Davis, T. W.
1993   Faith and Archaeology: A Brief History to the Present. *BAR* 19/2: 54–59.
2004   *Shifting Sands: The Rise and Fall of Biblical Archaeology*. New York: Oxford University Press.
Deetz, J.
1996   *In Small Things Forgotten: An Archaeology of Early American Life*. New York: Doubleday.
Demand, N. H.
1990   *Urban Relocation in Archaic and Classical Greece*. Bristol: Bristol Classical.
Demsky, A.
1966   The Houses of Achziv. *IEJ* 16: 211–15.
1986   The Clans of Ephrath: Their Territory and History. *Tel Aviv* 13: 46–59.
1987   The Family of Saul and the el-Jib Handles. *Samaria and Benjamin* 1: 22–30. [Hebrew]
1997   Literacy. Pp. 362–69 in *The Oxford Encyclopedia of Archaeology in the Near East*, ed. E. M. Meyers. New York: Oxford University Press.
Dessel, J. P.
1999   Tell ʿEin Zippori and the Lower Galilee in the Late Bronze and Iron Ages: A Village Perspective. Pp. 1–32 in *Galilee through the Centuries*, ed. E. M. Meyers. Winona Lake, IN: Eisenbrauns.
Dever, W. G.
1989   The Collapse of the Urban Early Bronze Age in Palestine: Toward a Systematic Analysis. Pp. 225–46 in *L'Urbanisation de la Palestine á l'âge du bronze ancien*, ed. P. de Miroschedji. British Archaeological Report 527. Oxford: British Archaeological Reports.
1993a   Biblical Archaeology: Death and Rebirth. Pp. 706–22 in *Biblical Archaeology Today, 1990: Proceedings of the Second International Congress on Biblical Archaeology*, ed. A. Biran. Jerusalem: Israel Exploration Society.
1993b   Cultural Continuity, Ethnicity in the Archaeological Record, and the Question of the Israelite Origins. *ErIsr* 24 (Malamat Volume): 22*–33*.
1993c   Gezer. Pp. 496–506 in vol. 2 of *NEAEHL*.
1994   From Tribe to Nation: State Formation Processes in Ancient Israel. Pp. 213–29 in *Nuove fondazioni nel Vicino Oriente Antico: Realtˆe ideologia*, ed. S. Mazzoni. Pisa: Giardini.
1995   Social Structure in Palestine in the Iron Age II Period on the Eve of Destruction. Pp. 416–31 in *The Archaeology of Society in the Holy Land*, ed. T. E. Levy. London: Leicester University Press.
1996   The Identity of Early Israel: A Rejoinder to Keith W. Whitelam. *JSOT* 76: 3–24.
1997a   Archaeology, Urbanism and the Rise of the Israelite State. Pp. 172–93 in *Urbanism in Antiquity: From Mesopotamia to Crete*, ed. W. E. Aufrecht, N. A. Mirau, and S. W. Gauley. JSOTSup 244. Sheffield: Sheffield Academic Press.
1997b   Ceramics: Syro-Palestinian Ceramics of the Neolithic, Bronze and Iron Ages. Pp. 459–65 in vol. 1 of *The Oxford Encyclopedia of Archaeology in the Near East*, ed. E. Meyers. New York: Oxford University Press.

1997c   Qom, Khirbet el-. Pp. 391–92 in vol. 4 of *Oxford Encyclopedia of Archaeology in the Near East*, ed. E. Meyers. New York: Oxford University Press.

1998a   Archaeology and Political Development in Ancient Judah: Why the 'Revisionists' Are Wrong. Pp. 84–96 in *New Studies on Jerusalem*, vol. 3, ed. A. Faust and E. Baruch. Ramat Gan: Bar-Ilan University Press. [Hebrew]

1998b   *Gezer: A Crossroad in Ancient Israel.* Jerusalem: Israel Exploration Society. [Hebrew]

1998c   Archaeology, Ideology, and the Quest for an "Ancient," or "Biblical" Israel. *NEA* 61/1: 39–52.

2000   Save Us from the Postmodern Malarkey. *BAR* 26/2: 28–35, 68–69.

2001   *What Did the Biblical Writers Know, and When Did They Know It?* Grand Rapids, MI: Eerdmans.

2003   *Who Were the Israelites and Where Did They Come From?* Grand Rapids, MI: Eerdmans.

2008   Archaeological Anthropology. Review of *Israel's Ethnogenesis, Settlement, Interaction, Expansion and Resistance*, by Avraham Faust. *BAR* 34/6: 74–75.

Diakonoff, I. M.
1975   The Rural Community in the Ancient Near East. *Journal of the Economic and Social History of the Orient* 18: 121–33.

Dinur, U.
1987   Sites from the Period of the Monarchy between Geva and Jerusalem. *Samaria and Benjamin* 1: 67–70. [Hebrew]

Dothan, M.
1955   The Excavations at 'Afula.' *ʿAtiqot* 1: 19–70.

1963   The Fortress of Kadesh-Barnea. Pp. 100–117 in *Elath: The Eighteenth Archaeological Convention.* Jerusalem: Israel Exploration Society. [Hebrew]

1978   Afula. Pp. 32–37 in vol. 1 of *Encyclopedia of Archaeological Excavations in the Holy Land*, ed. M. Avi-Yonah. Jerusalem: Israel Exploration Society.

1985   A Phoenician Inscription from Akko. *IEJ* 35: 81–94.

Dothan, T.
1982   *The Philistines and Their Material Culture.* Jerusalem: Israel Exploration Society.

Douglas, M.
1966   *Purity and Danger: An Analysis of the Concept of Pollution and Taboo.* Harmondsworth: Penguin.

1993   The Forbidden Animals in Leviticus. *JSOT* 59: 3–23.

Dybdahl, J. L.
1981   *Israelite Village Land Tenure: Settlement to Exile.* Ph.D. Dissertation. Pasadena: Fuller Theological Seminary.

Earle, T.
1987   Chiefdoms in Archaeological and Ethnohistorical Perspective. *Annual Review of Anthropology* 16: 279–308.

Earle, T. (ed.)
1991   *Chiefdoms: Power, Economy and Ideology.* Cambridge: Cambridge University Press.

Edelstein, G.
1969   *Weavers' Settlement form the Unified Kingdom Period.* Nir David: Museum for Mediterranean Archaeology. [Hebrew]

1972   Weavers' Settlement at Tel Amal. *Qadmoniot* 4 (15): 84–85. [Hebrew]

1994   Manahat: A Bronze Age Village in Southwestern Jerusalem. *Qadmoniot* 26 (103–4): 96–102 [Hebrew]

2000   A Terraced Farm at Er-Ras. *'Atiqot* 40: 39–63.
Edelstein, G., and Kislev, M.
   1981   Mevasseret Yerushalayim: The Ancient Settlement and Its Agricultural Ter-
            races. *BA* 44: 52–56.
Efrat, E.
   1995   *Urban Geography*. Tel Aviv: Achiasaf. [Hebrew]
Eisenberg, E.
   1994   Nahal Rephaim: A Bronze Age Village in Southwestern Jerusalem. *Qadmoniot*
            26 (103–4): 82–95. [Hebrew]
Eitam, D.
   1979   Olive Presses of the Israelite Period. *Tel Aviv* 6: 146–55.
   1980   *The Production of Oil and Wine on Mt. Ephraim in the Iron Age*. Ph.D. Dissertation.
            Tel Aviv University. [Hebrew]
   1987   Olive Oil Production during the Biblical Period. Pp. 16–35 in *Olive Oil in Antiq-
            uity*, ed. D. Eitam and M. Heltzer. Haifa: University of Haifa.
   1992a   Khaddash: A Royal Iron Age II Settlement in Southwestern Samaria. Pp. 21–22
            in *The Eighteenth Archaeological Congress in Israel*. Lecture Abstracts. Tel Aviv:
            Israel Exploration Society. [Hebrew]
   1992b   Khaddash: Royal Industry Village in Ancient Israel. Pp. 161–82 in *Judea and
            Samaria Research Studies: Proceedings of the First Annual Meeting*, ed. Z. H. Ehrlich
            and Y. Eshel. Jerusalem: Reuben Mass. [Hebrew]
Eitan, A.
   1983   Vered Yericho. *Hadashot Arkheologiyot* 73: 43. [Hebrew]
Eitan-Katz, H.
   1994   *Specialized Economy in Judah in the Eighth–Seventh Centuries* BCE. M.A. thesis. Tel
            Aviv University. [Hebrew]
Elat, M.
   1977   *Economic Relations in the Land of the Bible c. 1000–539 B.C.* Jerusalem: Bialik.
            [Hebrew]
   1982   Trade. Pp. 121–30, 234–38 in *The Age of the Monarchies: Culture and Society*. World
            History of the Jewish People 5. Jerusalem: Am Oved. [Hebrew]
Elgavish, Y.
   1994   *Shikmona*. Jerusalem: Israel Exploration Society. [Hebrew]
Elizur, Y.
   1996   Gibeah: A District—Representative Case. Pp. 47–58 in *Judah and Samaria Re-
            search Studies: Proceedings of the Fifth Annual Meeting*, ed. Y. Eshel. Ariel: Eretz.
            [Hebrew]
Ember, M., and Ember, C. R.
   1995   Worldwide Cross-Cultural Studies and Their Relevance for Archaeology. *JAR*
            3: 37–111.
Emberling, G.
   1997   Ethnicity in Complex Societies: Archaeological Perspectives. *JAR* 5: 295–344.
Emerton, J. A.
   1994   'The High Places of the Gates' in II Kings xxiii 8. *VT* 44: 455–67.
Enoch, Y.
   1985   The Community and Its Patterns. In *Man in Society: Introduction to Sociology*.
            Open University 8. Tel Aviv: Open University. [Hebrew]
Eph'al, I.
   1997   *The Siege and Its Ancient Near Eastern Manifestations*. Jerusalem: Magnes. [He-
            brew]

2000   'You Are Defecting to the Chaldeans.' *ErIsr* 24 (Malamat Volume): 18–22. [Hebrew]

Eph'al, I., and Naveh, J.
1993   The Jar of the Gate. *BASOR* 289: 59–65.

Eshel, H.
1991   Sennacherib's Campaign to Jerusalem. Pp. 143–56 in *Jerusalem in the First Temple Period*, ed. D. Amit and R. Gonen. Idan 15. Jerusalem: Yad Ben-Zvi. [Hebrew]

Eshel, I.
1995   Two Pottery Groups from Kenyon's Excavations on the Eastern Slope of Ancient Jerusalem. Pp. 1–157 in *Excavations by K. M. Kenyon in Jerusalem, 1961–1967*, vol. 4: *The Iron Age Deposits on the South-east Hill and Isolated Burials and Cemeteries Elsewhere*, ed. I. Eshel and K. Prag. Oxford: Oxford University Press.

Eshel, I., and Prag, K. (eds.)
1995   *Excavations by K. M. Kenyon in Jerusalem, 1961–1967*, vol. 4: *The Iron Age Deposits on the South-east Hill and Isolated Burials and Cemeteries Elsewhere*. Oxford: Oxford University Press.

Esse, D. L.
1991   The Collared Store Jar: Scholarly Ideology and Ceramic Typology. *SJOT* 2: 99–116.
1992   The Collared Pithos at Megiddo: Ceramic Distribution and Ethnicity. *JNES* 51: 81–103.

Fager, J. A.
1993   *Land Tenure and the Biblical Jubilee*. JSOTSup 155. Sheffield: JSOT Press.

Falconer, S. E.
1995   Rural Responses to Early Urbanism: Bronze Age Household and Village Economy at Tell el-Hayyat, Jordan. *JFA* 22: 399–419.

Fardon, R.
1999   *Mary Douglas: An Intellectual Biography*. London: Routledge.

Fassbeck, G.
2008   A Decorated Chalice from Tell el-ʾOreme/Kinneret. *ZDPV* 124: 15–37.

Faust, A.
1995a   Settlement on the Western Slopes of Samaria at the End of the Iron Age. Pp. 23–29 in *Judea and Samaria Research Studies: Proceedings of the Fourth Annual Meeting*, ed. Z. H. Ehrlich and Y. Eshel. Tel Aviv: Eretz. [Hebrew]
1995b   *The Rural Settlement in the Land of Israel during the Period of the Monarchy*. M.A. thesis. Ramat Gan: Bar-Ilan University. [Hebrew]
1996   The Biblical "Migraš" and the Archaeological Evidence. *Beit-Mikra* 148: 20–27. [Hebrew]
1997   The Impact of the Expansion of Jerusalem in the Form of Rural Settlement in Its Vicinity. *Cathedra* 84: 53–62. [Hebrew]
1998   Family Structure in Iron Age II Villages. Pp. 131–46 in *The Village in Ancient Israel*, ed. Z. Safrai and S. Dar. Tel Aviv: Eretz. [Hebrew]
1999a   An Entrance to the Past: Architecture, Language and Cosmology in the Iron Age. Pp. 78–95 in *Material Culture, Society, and Ideology*, ed. A. Faust and A. Maeir. Ramat Gan: Bar-Ilan University Press. [Hebrew]
1999b   Differences in Family Structure between Cities and Villages in the Iron Age II. *Tel Aviv* 26: 233–52.
1999c   Socioeconomic Stratification in an Israelite City: Hazor VI as a Test-Case. *Levant* 31: 179–90.
2000a   A Note on Hezekiah's Tunnel and the Siloam Inscription. *JSOT* 90: 3–11.

2000b   From Hamlets to Monarchy: A View from the Countryside on the Formation of the Israelite Monarchy. *Cathedra* 94: 7–32. [Hebrew]

2000c   Social Organization of Iron Age II Villages in Ancient Israel. *Shnaton* 12: 91–104. [Hebrew]

2000d   The Rural Community in Ancient Israel during the Iron Age II. *BASOR* 317: 17–39.

2001   Doorway Orientation, Settlement Planning and Cosmology in Ancient Israel during Iron Age II. *Oxford Journal of Archaeology* 202: 129–55.

2002a   Accessibility, Defense, and Town Planning in Iron Age Israel. *Tel Aviv* 29: 297–317.

2002b   Burnished Pottery and Gender Hierarchy in Iron Age Israelite Society. *Journal of Mediterranean Archaeology.* 15/1: 53–73.

2003a   Abandonment, Urbanization, Resettlement and the Formation of the Israelite State. *NEA* 60: 147–61.

2003b   Judah in the Sixth Century BCE: A Rural Perspective. *PEQ* 135: 37–53.

2003c   Residential Patterns in the Ancient Israelite City. *Levant* 35: 123–28.

2003d   The Farmstead in the Highlands of Iron II Israel. Pp. 91–104 in *The Rural Landscape of Ancient Israel*, ed. S. Dar, A. Maeir, and Z. Safrai. Oxford: Archaeopress.

2003e   Warren Shaft: Yes It Was Used to Draw Water. *BAR* 29/5: 70–76.

2004a   Mortuary Practices, Society and Ideology: The Lack of Iron Age I Burials in Highlands in Context. *IEJ* 54: 174–90.

2004b   Social and Cultural Changes in Judah during the 6th Century BCE and Their Implications for Our Understanding of the Nature of the Neo-Babylonian Period. *Ugarit Forschungen* 36: 157–76.

2004c   The United Monarchy and Anthropology: A Note on the Debate over Jerusalem's Status as a Capital. Pp. 23–36 in *New Studies on Jerusalem*, vol. 10, ed. E. Baruch and A. Faust. Ramat Gan: Bar-Ilan University Press. [Hebrew]

2004d   The Warren Shaft System in Light of New Discoveries. Pp. 7–19 in *New Studies on Jerusalem*, vol. 9, ed. E. Baruch, U. Leibner, and A. Faust. Ramat Gan: Bar-Ilan University Press. [Hebrew]

2004e   Town Planning in Iron Age Israel: Fortifications, Roads, Public Structures, and Cosmology. Pp. 9–26 in *Judea and Samaria Research Studies: Proceeding of the 1st Annual Meeting*, ed. Y. Eshel. Tel Aviv and Ariel: Eretz. [Hebrew]

2005a   The Canaanite Village: Social Structure of Middle Bronze Age Rural Communities. *Levant* 37: 105–25.

2005b   The Settlement on Jerusalem's Western Hill and the City's Status in the Iron Age II Revisited. *ZDPV* 121: 97–118.

2006a   Farmsteads in the Foothills of Western Samaria: A Reexamination. Pp. 477–504 in *"I Will Speak the Riddles of Ancient Times": Archaeological and Historical Studies in Honor of Amihai Mazar on the Occasion of His Sixtieth Birthday*, ed. A. M. Maeir and P. de Miroschedji. Winona Lake, IN: Eisenbrauns.

2006b   *Israel's Ethnogenesis: Settlement, Interaction, Expansion and Resistance.* London: Equinox.

2006c   The Negev Fortresses in Context: Reexamining the Fortresses Phenomenon in Light of General Settlement Processes of the 11th–10th Centuries BCE. *JAOS* 126: 135–60.

2007a   Did Ancient Jerusalem Draw Water through Warren's Shaft?" *BAR* 33/2: 66–67, 69, 77. [contribution to a debate]

2007b   Forum: Rural Settlements, State Formation, and "Bible and Archaeology." *NEA*
         70: 4–25. [with responses by Neil Asher Silberman, Lester L. Grabbe, Alex Joffe,
         and Ze'ev Herzog]

2007c   Private, Communal, and Royal Economy in Iron Age II (the Period of the Mon-
         archy). *Jerusalem and Eretz-Israel* 4–5: 41–58. [Hebrew]

2008   Settlement and Demography in Seventh Century Judah and the Extent and
         Intensity of Sennacherib's Campaign. *PEQ* 140: 168–94.

2009a   "But the Houses of the Villages That Have No Wall Around Them Shall Be
         Counted as the Fields of the Country": Biblical Settlement Terminology in
         Light of the Archaeological Findings. *Iyyunei Mikra Upashanut* 8: 357–67. [He-
         brew]

2009b   Cities, Villages, and Farmsteads: The Landscape of Leviticus 25:29–31. Pp. 103–
         12 in *Exploring the* Longue Durée: *Essays in Honor of Lawrence E. Stager*, ed. J. D.
         Schloen. Winona Lake, IN: Eisenbrauns.

2010a   The Archaeology of the Israelite Cult: Questioning the Consensus. *BASOR* 360:
         23–35.

2010b   The Large Stone Structure in the City of David: A Reexamination. *ZDPV* 126:
         116–30.

2011a   The Interests of the Assyrian Empire in the West: Olive Oil Production as a
         Test-Case. *Journal of the Economic and Social History of the Orient* 54: 62–86.

2011b   Household Economies in the Kingdoms of Israel and Judah. Pp. 255–73 in
         Household Archaeology in the Bronze and Iron Age Levant, ed. A. Yasur-Landau,
         J. Ebeling, and L. Mazow. Leiden: Brill.

2011c   Tel 'Eton Excavations (2006–2009): A Preliminary Report. *PEQ* 143: 198–224.

forthcoming   *Judah in the Neo-Babylonian Period: The Archaeology of Desolation*. Atlanta:
         Society of Biblical Literature.

Faust, A., and Bunimovitz, S.

2003   The Four Room House: Embodying Iron Age Israelite Society. *NEA* 66: 22–33.

2008   The Judahite Rock-Cut Tomb: Family Response at a Time of Change. *IEJ* 58:
         150–70.

forthcoming   The House and the World: The Israelite House as a Micro-Cosmos. In
         *Family and Household Religion: Toward a Synthesis of Old Testament Studies, Ar-
         chaeology, Epigraphy, and Cultural Studies*, ed. R. Albertz, B. Alpert Nakhai, S. M.
         Olyan, and R. Schmitt. Winona Lake, IN: Eisenbrauns.

Faust, A., and Erlich, A.

2011   *The Excavations at Khirbet er-Rasm: The Changing Faces of the Countryside.* Oxford:
         Archaeopress.

Faust, A., and Katz, H.

forthcoming   Philistines, Israelites and Canaanites in the Southern Trough Valley dur-
         ing the Iron Age I. *Egypt and the Levant*.

Faust, A., and Maeir, A.

1999   Material Culture, Society, and Ideology in the Archaeology of the Land of Is-
         rael. Pp. 5–10 in *Material Culture, Society and Ideology: New Directions in the Ar-
         chaeology of the Land of Israel*, ed. A. Faust and A. Maeir. Ramat Gan: Bar-Ilan
         University Press. [Hebrew]

Faust, A., and Safrai, Z.

2005   Salvage Excavations as a Source for Reconstructing Settlement History in An-
         cient Israel. *PEQ* 137: 139–58.

2008   Changes in Burial Practices in the Land of Israel in Light of the Analysis of
         Salvage Excavations. Pp 105–21 in *In the Hill-Country, in the Shephelah, and in the*

Arabah (Joshua 12:8): Studies and Research Presented to Adam Zertal on the Thirtieth Anniversary of the Manasseh Hill Country Survey, ed. S. Bar. Jerusalem: Ariel. [Hebrew]

forthcoming   *The Settlement History of Ancient Israel: A Quantitative Analysis* (working title). [Hebrew]

Faust, A., and Weiss, E.
2005   Judah, Philistia, and the Mediterranean World: Reconstructing the Economic System of the Seventh Century B.C.E. *BASOR* 338: 71–92.
2011   Between Assyria and the Mediterranean World: The Prosperity of Judah and Philistia in the Seventh Century BCE in Context. Pp. 189–204 in *Interweaving Worlds — Systemic Interaction in Eurasia: 7th to 1st millennia BC*, ed. T. Wilkinson, S. Sherratt, and J. Bennet. Oxford: Oxbow.

Feder, O., and Negev, N.
2008   Beʿer Shevaʿ, Ramot Neighborhood, Site 49. *ʿAtiqot* 58: 1–14. [Hebrew]

Feig, N.
1994   Beit Safafa: The Agricultural Hinterland of Ramat Rachel. *Twentieth Archaeological Congress in Israel. Lecture Abstracts* 19. Jerusalem: Israel Exploration Society. [Hebrew]
1995   The Agricultural Settlement in the Jerusalm Area in Iron Age II. Pp. 3–7 in *New Studies on Jerusalem*, vol. 1, ed. Z. Safrai and A. Faust. Ramat Gan: Bar-Ilan University Press. [Hebrew]
1996   New Discoveries in the Rephaim Valley, Jerusalem. *PEQ* 128: 3–7.
2000   The Environs of Jerusalem in Iron Age II. Pp. 387–409 in *The Jerusalem Book: The Biblical Period*, ed. S. Aḥituv and A. Mazar. Jerusalem: Yad Ben-Zvi. [Hebrew]

Feinman, G. M., and Marcus, J. (eds.)
1998   *Archaic States*. School of American Research Advanced Seminar Series. Santa Fe, NM: School of American Research Press.

Feldstein, A., et al.
1993   Southern Part of the Maps of Ramallah and el-Bireh and the Northern Part of the Map of ʿEin Kerem. Pp. 133–264, 28*–47* in *Archaeological Survey of the Hill Country of Benjamin*, ed. Y. Magen and I. Finkelstein. Jerusalem: Israel Antiquities Authority.

Finkelstein, I.
1978   *Rural Settlement in the Foothills and the Yarkon Basin*. M.A. Thesis. Tel Aviv University. [Hebrew]
1981   Israelite and Hellenistic Farms in the Foothills and in the Yarkon Basin. *ErIsr* 15 (Aharoni Volume): 331–48. [Hebrew]
1983   *The ʿIzbet Sartah Excavations and the Israelite Settlement in the Hill Country*. Ph.D. Dissertation. Tel Aviv University. [Hebrew]
1985   Fortresses of the Negev Hills in the Iron Age: Settlement Sites of Desert Nomads. *ErIsr* 18 (Avigad Volume): 366–79. [Hebrew]
1988a   Khirbet ed-Dawwara: A Fortified Settlement of the Early Israelite Kingdom in the Desert of Benjamin. *Qadmoniot* 21 (81–82): 6–10. [Hebrew]
1988b   *The Archaeology of the Israelite Settlement*. Jerusalem: Israel Exploration Society.
1989   The Emergence of the Monarchy in Israel: The Environmental and Socio-economic Aspects. *JSOT* 44: 43–74.
1990   Excavations at Khirbet ed-Dawwara: An Iron Age Site Northeast of Jerusalem. *Tel Aviv* 17: 163–208.
1994   The Archaeology of the Days of Manasseh. Pp. 169–87 in *Scripture and Other Artifacts*, ed. M. D. Coogan et al. Louisville: Westminster John Knox.

1995   The Philistine Countryside. *IEJ* 46: 225–42.

1996a   Ethnicity and Origin of the Iron I Settlers in the Highlands of Canaan: Can the Real Israel Stand Up? *BA* 59/4: 198–212.

1996b   The Archaeology of the United Monarchy: An Alternative View. *Levant* 28: 177–87.

1997   Pots and People Revisited: Ethnic Boundaries in the Iron Age I. Pp. 216–37 in *The Archaeology of Israel: Constructing the Past, Interpreting the Present*, ed. N. Silberman and D. B. Small. JSOTSup 237. Sheffield: Sheffield Academic Press.

1998   Bible Archaeology or the Archaeology of Palestine in the Iron Age? A Rejoinder. *Levant* 30: 167–74.

1999a   Hazor and the North in the Iron Age: A Low Chronology Perspective. *BASOR* 314: 55–70.

1999b   State Formation in Israel and Judah: A Contrast in Context, A Constrast in Trajectory. *NEA* 62: 35–52.

2000   The Philistine Settlements: When, Where and How Many? Pp. 159–80 in *The Sea Peoples and Their World: A Reassessment*, ed. E. D. Oren. University Museum Symposium Series 11. Philadelphia: University Museum Press.

2001   The Rise of Jerusalem and Judah: The Missing Link. *Levant* 33: 105–15.

2003   The Rise of Jerusalem and Judah: The Missing Link. Pp. 81–101 in *Jerusalem in Bible and Archaeology: The First Temple Period*, ed. A. G. Vaughn and A. E. Killebrew. Society of Biblical Literature Symposium Studies 18. Atlanta: Society of Biblical Literature.

2005   [De]formation of the Israelite State: A Rejoinder on Methodology. *NEA* 68: 202–8.

2010   A Great United Monarchy? Archaeological and Historical Perspectives. Pp. 3–28 in *One God – One Cult – One Nation: Archaeological and Biblical Perspectives*, ed. R. G. Kratz and H. Spickermann. Berlin: de Gruyter.

2011   The "Large Stone Structure" in Jerusalem: Reality versus Yearning. *ZDPV* 127: 1–10.

Finkelstein, I., et al.
2007   Has King David's Palace in Jerusalem Been Found? *Tel Aviv* 34: 142–64.

Finkelstein, I.; Fantalkin, A.; and Piasetsky, E.
2008   Three Snapshots of the Iron IIA: The Northern Valleys, the Southern Steppe, and Jerusalem. Pp. 32–44 in *Israel in Transition: From the Late Bronze II to Iron IIa (c. 1250–850 B.C.E.)*, ed. L. L. Grabbe. New York: T. & T. Clark.

Finkelstein, I.; Lederman, Z.; and Bunimovitz, S.
1997   *Highlands of Many Cultures: The Southern Samaria Survey*. Tel Aviv: Tel Aviv University Press.

Finkelstein, I., and Piasetski, E.
2011   The Iron Age Chronology Debate: Is the Gap Narrowing? *NEA* 74: 50–53.

Finkelstein, I., and Silberman, N. A.
2001   *The Bible Unearthed: Archaeology's New Vision of Ancient Israel and Its Sacred Texts*. New York: Touchstone.

2006   *David and Solomon: In Search of the Bible's Sacred Kings and the Roots of the Western Tradition*. New York: Free Press.

Finkelstein, I., and Ussishkin, D.
2000   Archaeological and Historical Conclusions. Pp. 576–605 in *Megiddo*, vol. 3: *The 1992–1996 Seasons*, ed. I. Finkelstein, D. Ussishkin, and B. Halpern. Tel Aviv: Tel Aviv University Press.

Fixler, Y.
  1991   *Computer Processing of Panchromatic Aerial Photographs for Archaeological Mapping in the Lod Plain during the Mishnaic and Talmudic Period.* Ph.D. Dissertation. Ramat Gan: Bar-Ilan University. [Hebrew]
  1992   Aerial Photographs for Locating Ancient Fields in the Shephelah of Lod. Pp. 60–76 in *Studies in the Ancient Agriculture and Economy of the Land of Israel,* ed. S. Dar. Ramat Gan: Bar-Ilan University Press. [Hebrew]
Flannery, K. V., and Marcus, J.
  1994   On the Perils of 'Politically Correct' Archaeology. *Current Anthropology* 35: 441–45.
  2003   The Origin of War: New 14C Dates from Ancient Mexico. *Proceedings of the National Academy of Sciences* 100: 11801–5.
Foster, S. M.
  1989   Analysis of Spatial Patterns in Buildings (Access Analysis) as an Insight into Social Structure: Examples from the Scottish Atlantic Iron Age. *Antiquity* 63: 40–50.
Fox, M. (ed.)
  1996   *Scrolls: Song of Songs.* The World of the Bible. Tel Aviv: Davidson Ati. [Hebrew]
Fox, R.
  1967   *Kinship and Marriage.* Harmondsworth: Penguin.
Fox, R. G.
  1977   *Urban Anthropology: Cities in Their Cultural Settings.* Englewood Cliffs, NJ: Prentice-Hall.
Franken, H. J., and Steiner, M. L.
  1985   *Excavations in Jerusalem, 1961–1967,* vol. 2: *The Iron Age Extramural Quarter on the South-East Hill.* Toronto: Royal Ontario Museum.
Frazer, J. G.
  1918   *Folk-Lore in the Old Testament: Studies in Comparative Religion, Legend and Law,* vol. 3. London: Macmillan.
Freedman, M.
  1958   *Lineage Organization in Southeastern China.* London: Athlone.
Frick, F. S.
  1970   *The City in the Old Testament.* Ph.D. Dissertation. Princeton University.
  1985   *The Formation of the State in Ancient Israel.* The Social World of Biblical Antiquity 4. Sheffield: Almond.
Fried, M. H.
  1967   *The Evolution of Political Society.* New York: Random.
  1970   Clan and Lineages: How to Tell Them Apart and Why, With a Special Reference to Chinese Society. *Bulletin of the Institute of Ethnology: Academia Sinica* 29: 11–36.
Friedman, R. E.
  1987   *Who Wrote the Bible?* New York: Summit.
Fritz, V.
  1990   *Kinneret.* Wiesbaden: Harrassowitz.
  1993   Kinneret: Excavation at Tell el-Oreimeh (Tel Kinrot), 1982–1985 Seasons. *Tel Aviv* 20: 187–215.
  1995   *The City in Ancient Israel.* Sheffield: Sheffield Academic Press.
  1996   Monarchy and Re-Urbanization: A New Look at Solomon's Kingdoms. Pp. 187–99 in *The Origin of the Ancient Israelite States,* ed. V. Fritz and P. R. Davies. JSOTSup 228. Sheffield: Sheffield Academic Press.

Frumkin, A.
2005   Underground Wine Cellars in Western Samaria. Pp. 53–56 in *Judea and Samaria Research Studies: Proceeding of the 14th Annual Meeting*, ed. Y. Eshel. Ariel: Eretz. [Hebrew]

Gadot, Y.
2011   The Rural Settlement along Nahal Rephaim from the Middle Bronze Age to the Hellenistic Period: A Fresh Look from Kh. Er-Ras. In vol. 17 of *New Studies on Jerusalem*, ed. E. Baruch, A. Levy-Reifer and A. Faust. Ramat Gan: Ingeborg Rennert Center for Jerusalem Studies, Bar-Ilan University. [Hebrew]

Gal, Z.
1979   An Early Iron Age Site near Tel Menorah in the Beth Shan Valley. *Tel Aviv* 6: 138–45.
1982   The Settlement of Issachar: Some New Observations. *Tel Aviv* 9: 79–86.
1990   *The Lower Galilee: Historical Geography in the Biblical Period.* Tel Aviv: Israel Exploration Society.
1992a   *Lower Galilee during the Iron Age.* ASOR Dissertation Series 8. Winona Lake, IN: American Schools of Oriental Research.
1992b   Phoenicians and Israelites at Kh. Rosh Zayit. Pp. 12–13 in *The Eighteenth Archaeology Congress in Israel.* Lecture Abstracts. Tel Aviv: Israel Exploration Society. [Hebrew]
1993a   Horvat Rosh Zayit: 1991. *Excavations and Surveys in Israel* 13: 18.
1993b   Rosh Zayit, Horbat. Pp. 1289–91 in vol. 4 of *NEAEHL.*
1994   Tel Gat-Hefer. *Excavations and Surveys in Israel* 14: 54.
1995   The Diffusion of Phoenician Cultural Influence in the Light of the Excavations at Horbat Rosh-Zayit. *Tel Aviv* 22: 89–93.
2001   Regional Aspects of the Iron Age Pottery in the Akko Plain and Its Vicinity. Pp. 135–42 in *Studies in the Archaeology of Israel and Neighboring Lands in Memory of Douglas L. Esse*, ed. S. R. Wolff. Chicago: Oriental Institute / Atlanta: American Schools of Oriental Research.

Gal, Z., and Alexandre, Y.
2000   *Horbat Rosh Zayit: An Iron Age Storage Fort and Village.* Jerusalem: Israel Antiquities Authority.

Gal, Z., and Frankel, R.
1992   An Olive Oil Complex at Hurvat Rosh Zayit. *ZDPV* 109: 128–40.

Galil, G.
1990   The Formation of Judah. Pp. 1–8 in *Proceedings of the Tenth World Conference of Jewish Studies*, division A: *The Bible and Its World.* Jerusalem: World Union of Jewish Studies. [Hebrew]
1996   [Various entries] in *Chronicles I*, ed. G. Galil, M. Garsiel, and M. Kuchman. The World of the Bible. Tel Aviv: Davidson Ati. [Hebrew]

Garfinkel, Y.
1984   The Distribution of Identical Seal Impressions and the Settlement Pattern in Judea before Sennacherib's Campaign. *Cathedra* 32: 35–52. [Hebrew]
1985   A Hierarchic Pattern in Private Seal Impressions on "LMLK" Jar-Handles. *ErIsr* 18 (Avigad Volume): 108–15. [Hebrew]

Garfinkel, Y., et al.
2010   The Contribution of Khirbet Qeiyafa to Our Understanding of the Iron Age Period. *Strata: Bulletin of the Anglo-Israel Archaeological Society* 28: 39–54.

Garfinkel, Y., and Ganor, S.
2008   Khirbet Qeiyafa: Sha'arayim. *Journal of Hebrew Scriptures* 8, article 22.

2010   Khirbet Qeiyafa in Survey and Excavations: A Response to Y. Dagan. *Tel Aviv* 37: 67–78.

Gazit, D.
2008   Permanent and Temporary Settlements in the South of the Lower Besor Region: Two Case Studies. Pp. 75–85 in *Bene Israel: Studies in the Archaeology of Israel and the Levant during the Bronze and Iron Ages in Honour of Israel Finkelstein*, ed. A. Fantalkin and A. Yasur-Landau. Leiden: Brill.

Gelb, I. J.
1967   Approaches to the Study of Ancient Society. *JAOS* 87: 1–8.

Geus, C. H. J. de
1976   *The Tribes of Israel.* Studia Semitica Neerlandica 18. Assen: Van Gorcum.
1986   The Profile of an Israelite City. *BA* 49: 224–27.
1988   The New City in Ancient Israel: Two Questions concerning the Re-Urbanization of ʾEres Yisraʾel in the Tenth Century B.C.E. Pp. 105–13 in *Wunschet Jerusalem Frieden*, ed. M. Augustin and K. D. Schunck. Frankfurt: Peter Lang.
1989   Of Tribes and Towns: The Historical Development of the Israelite City. *ErIsr* 24 (Malamat Volume): 70*–76*.

Geus, V. J. K. de
1982   Die Gesellschaftskritik der Propheten und die Archéologie. *ZDPV* 98: 50–57.

Geva, H.
1999   Was There or Wasn't There? The Problem of Identifying Buildings in Jerusalem. Pp. 17–21 in *New Studies on Jerusalem*, vol. 4, ed. E. Baruch. Ramat Gan: Bar-Ilan University Press. [Hebrew]

Geva, S.
1989   *Hazor, Israel: An Urban Community of the 8th Century B.C.E.* British Archaeological Report 543. Oxford: British Archaeological Reports.
1992   Israeli Biblical Archaeology: The First Years. *Zemanim* 42: 92–102. [Hebrew]

Gibbon, G.
1984   *Anthropological Archaeology.* New York: Columbia University Press.

Giddens, A.
1979   *Central Problems in Social Theory: Action, Structure and Contradiction in Social Analysis.* Berkeley: Macmillan.

Gilbert, J.
1982   Rural Theory: The Grounding of Rural Sociology. *Rural Sociology* 47: 609–33.

Gilboa, E.
1987   *Dwellings in the Land of Israel in the Iron Age I.* M.A. Thesis. Tel Aviv University. [Hebrew]

Girouard, M.
1980   *Life in the English Country House.* Aylesbury: Penguin.

Gitert, R., and Amiran, R.
1996   A Salvage Excavation on the Slope of Tel Arad. *ErIsr* 25 (Aviram Volume): 112–15. [Hebrew]

Gitin, S.
1989   Tel Miqne–Ekron: A Type Site for the Inner Coastal Plain in the Iron Age II Period. Pp. 23–58 in *Recent Excavations in Israel: Studies in Iron Age Archaeology*, ed. S. Gitin and W. G. Dever. Winona Lake, IN: Eisenbrauns for the American Schools of Oriental Research.

Giveon, S.
1995   The Three-Roomed House from Tel Harassim. *Archaeologya* 4: 65–68. [Hebrew]
1999   The Three-Roomed House from Tel Harassim, Israel. *Levant* 31: 173–77.

Gophna, R.
    1966   The "Hazerim" in Southern Pleshet during the Iron Age I. *'Atiqot* 3: 44–51.
    1979   A Middle Bronze Age II Village in the Jordan Valley. *Tel Aviv* 6: 28–33.
Gophna, R., and Porat, Y.
    1972   The Land of Ephraim and Manasseh. Pp. 192–242 in *Judaea, Samaria and the Golan: Archaeological Survey, 1967–1968*, ed. M. Kochavi. Jerusalem: Israel Antiquities Authority. [Hebrew]
Gordis, R.
    1971   Primitive Democracy in Ancient Israel. Pp. 45–60 in *Poets, Prophets and Sages: Essays in Biblical Interpretation.* Bloomington, IN: Indiana University Press.
Gossai, H.
    1993   *Justice, Righteousness and the Social Critique of the Eighth-Century Prophets.* New York: Peter Lang.
Gottwald, N. K.
    1979   *The Tribes of Yahweh.* New York: Peter Lang.
Goulder, M. D.
    1986   *The Song of Fourteen Songs.* JSOTSup 36. Sheffield: JSOT Press.
Grant, Elihu
    1934   *Rumeileh: Being Ain Shems Excavations (Palestine)*, part 3. Haverford, PA: Haverford College.
Grant, Eric (ed.)
    1986   *Central Places: Archaeology and History.* Sheffield: Dept. of Archaeology and Prehistory, University of Sheffield.
Grant, Elihu, and Wright, G. E.
    1939   *Ain Shems Excavations*, vol. 5: *Text.* Haverford, PA: Haverford College.
Greenberg, R.
    1999   Uniformity as Ideology in the Early Bronze Age II. Pp. 15–30 in *Material Culture, Society and Ideology: New Directions in Archaeology of the Land of Israel*, ed. A. Faust and A. Maeir. Ramat Gan: Bar-Ilan University Press. [Hebrew]
Greenfield, S. M.
    1961   Industrialization and the Family in Sociological Theory. *AJOS* 67: 312–22.
Greenhot, Z.
    1990   Ein El-Ghuweir. *'Atiqot* 9: 33–40. [Hebrew]
Groot, A. de
    1991a   Excavations in the City of David. Pp. 40–50 in *Jerusalem in the First Temple Period*, ed. D. Amit and R. Gonen. Idan 15. Jerusalem: Yad Ben-Zvi. [Hebrew]
    1991b   Jerusalem's Water Systems during the First Temple Period. Pp. 124–34 in *Jerusalem in the First Temple Period*, ed. D. Amit and R. Gonen. Idan 15. Jerusalem: Yad Ben-Zvi. [Hebrew]
    2002   "The Hidden City" of the Tenth Century B.C.E. Pp. 29–34 in *New Studies on Jerusalem*, vol. 7, ed. A. Faust and E. Baruch. Ramat Gan: Bar-Ilan University Press. [Hebrew]
Grossman, D.
    1976   The Formation of Subsidiary Settlements and Their Relation to Agricultural Resources. *Karka* 13: 26–30. [Hebrew]
    1994   *Chapters on Rural Geography.* Ramat Gan: Dionon. [Hebrew]
Haiman, M.
    1988   *The Iron Age Sites of the Negev Highlands.* Ph.D. Dissertation. Hebrew University. [Hebrew]

Hall, J. M.
  1997   *Ethnic Identity in Greek Antiquity.* Cambridge: Cambridge University Press.
Hall, M.
  1992   Small Things and the Mobile: Conflictual Fusion of Power, Fear and Desire.
         Pp. 373–99 in *The Art and Mystery of Historical Archaeology: Essays in Honor of
         James Deetz,* ed. A. E. Yentsch and M. C. Beaudry. Boca Raton, FL: CRC Press.
Halpern, B.
  1991   Jerusalem and the Lineage in the Seventh Century BCE: Kinship and the Rise
         of Individual Moral Liability. Pp. 11–107 in *Law and Ideology in Monarchic Israel,*
         ed. B. Halpern and D. W. Hobson. JSOTSup 124. Sheffield: JSOT Press.
  2000   Centre and Sentry: Megiddo's Role in Transit, Administration and Trade.
         Pp. 535–75 in *Megiddo III: The 1992–1996 Seasons,* ed. I. Finkelstein, D. Ussish-
         kin, and B. Halpern. Tel Aviv: Tel Aviv University Press.
  2001   *David's Secret Demons: Messiah, Murderer, Traitor, King.* Grand Rapids, MI: Eerd-
         mans.
Hardin, J. W.
  2001   *An Archaeology of Destruction: Households and the Use of Domestic Space at Iron II
         Tel Halif.* Ph.D. Dissertation. University of Arizona.
  2010   *Lahav II: Households and the Use of Domestic Space at Iron II Tell Halif—An Archae-
         ology of Destruction.* Lahav: Reports of the Lahav Research Project/Excavations
         at Tell Halif, Israel 2. Winona Lake, IN: Eisenbrauns.
Har-Even, B.
  2009   An Iron Age IIB Agricultural Unit at Beitar ʿIlit (West). Pp. 65–72 in *Excavations
         and Discoveries in Benjamin and Judea,* ed. I. Yezerski. Judea and Samaria Publi-
         cation 10. Jerusalem: Israel Antiquities Authority. [Hebrew]
  2011   Khirbet Deir Daqla: A Fortified Settlement from the First Temple Period and a
         Byzantine Monastery on the Western Slopes of Samaria. P. 18 in (Eng. abstracts
         of) *In the Highland's Depth: The Second Western Benjamin Conference in Memory of
         the Late Prof. Hanan Eshel.* Hashmonaim: Midreshet Harei Gophna. [Hebrew]
Harmon, G. E.
  1983   *Floor Area and Population Determination: A Method for Estimating Village Popula-
         tion in the Central Hill Country during the Period of the Judges (Iron Age II).* Ph.D.
         Dissertation. Southern Baptist Theological Seminary.
Hart, S.
  1988   Excavations at Ghrareh 1986: Preleminary Report. *Levant* 20: 89–99.
Hasharon Survey
  1973   Hasharon Survey. *Hadashot Arkheologiyot* 47: 26–28. [Hebrew]
Hatt, P. K., and Reiss, A. J. (eds.)
  1965   *Cities and Society.* New York: Free Press.
Hayden, B., and Cannon, A.
  1982   The Corporate Group as an Archaeological Unit. *JAA* 1: 132–58.
Hayden, B., et al.
  1996   Space per Capita and the Optimal Size of Housepits. Pp. 151–64 in *People Who
         Lived in Big Houses: Archaeological Perspectives on Large Domestic Structures,* ed.
         G. Coupland and E. G. Banning. Madison, WI: Prehistory Press.
Healan, D. M.
  1977   Architectural Implications of Daily Life in Ancient Tollan, Hidalgo, Mexico.
         World Archaeology 9: 140–56.

Hellwing, S.
  1984   Human Exploitation of Animal Resources in the Early Iron Age Strata at Tel
          Beer-Sheba. Pp. 105–15 in *Beer-Sheba*, vol. 2, ed. Z. Herzog. Tel Aviv: Tel Aviv
          University Press.
Heltzer, M.
  1976   *The Rural Community in Ancient Ugarit*. Wiesbaden: Reichert.
  1998   The Head (Commandant) of the City (*sar haʿir*) in Ancient Israel and Judah
          Compared with Neo-Assyrian Functionaries. *Acta Sumerologica* 20: 17–22.
Herr, L. G.
  1988   Tripartite Pillared Buildings and the Market Place in Iron Age Palestine. *BASOR*
          272: 47–67.
  1997   The Iron Age Period: Emerging Nations. *BA* 60: 114–83.
  2000   The Settlement and Fortification of Tell al-Umairi in Jordan during the LB/Iron
          I Transition. Pp. 167–79 in *The Archaeology of Jordan and Beyond: Essays in Honor
          of James A. Sauer*, ed. L. E. Stager, J. A. Greene, and M. D. Coogan. Studies in the
          Archaeology and History of the Levant 1. Winona Lake, IN: Eisenbrauns.
  2001   Excavating the Tribe of Reuben. *BAR* 27/2: 36–47, 64–65.
Herzog, Z.
  1973   The Storehouses. Pp. 23–30 in *Beer-Sheba*, vol. 1, ed. Y. Aharoni. Tel Aviv: Tel
          Aviv University Press.
  1976   *The City Gate of Eretz-Israel and Its Neighbors*. Tel Aviv: Tel Aviv University Press.
          [Hebrew]
  1984   *Beer-Sheba*, vol. 2: *The Early Iron Age Settlements*. Institute of Archaeology, Tel
          Aviv University Press.
  1991   Solomon's Temple. Pp. 68–81 in *Jerusalem in the First Temple Period*, ed. D. Amit
          and R. Gonen. Idan 15. Jerusalem: Yad Ben-Zvi. [Hebrew]
  1992a   Administrative Structures in the Iron Age. Pp. 195–230 in *The Architecture of
          Ancient Israel from the Prehistoric to the Persian Period*, ed. A. Kempinski and
          R. Reich. Jerusalem: Israel Exploration Society.
  1992b   Settlement and Fortification Planning in the Iron Age. Pp. 231–74 in *The Archi-
          tecture of Ancient Israel from the Prehistoric to the Persian Period*, ed. A. Kempinski
          and R. Reich. Jerusalem: Israel Exploration Society.
  1993   Beersheba: Tel Beersheba. Pp. 167–73 in vol. 1 of *NEAEHL*.
  1997a   *Archaeology of the City: Urban Planning in Ancient Israel and Its Social Implications*.
          Tel Aviv: Tel Aviv University Press.
  1997b   Phoenician Occupation at Tel Michal: the Problem of Identifying Ethnic
          National Groups from Archaeological Assemblages. *Michmanim* 11: 31–44. [He-
          brew]
  1998   The Arad Fortress. Pp. 111–292 in *Arad*, ed. R. Amiran et al. Jerusalem: Israel
          Exploration Society. [Hebrew]
Herzog, Z., et al.
  1984   The Israelite Fortress at Arad. *BASOR* 254: 1–34.
Herzog, Z.; Rainey, A. F.; and Moshkovitz, S.
  1977   The Stratigraphy at Beer-Sheba and the Location of the Sanctuary. *BASOR* 225:
          49–58.
Hesse, B.
  1990   Pig Lovers and Pig Haters: Patterns of Palestinian Pork Production. *Journal of
          Ethnobiology* 10: 195–225.

Hesse, B., and Wapnish, P.
1997   Can Pig Remains Be Used for Ethnic Diagnosis in the Ancient Near-East?
        Pp. 238–70 in *The Archaeology of Israel: Constructing the Past, Interpreting the Pres-
        ent*, ed. N. Silberman and D. B. Small. JSOTSup 237. Sheffield: Sheffield Aca-
        demic Press.
Hillier, B., and Hanson, J.
1984   *The Social Logic of Space.* Cambridge: Cambridge University Press.
Hingley, R.
1990   Boundaries Surrounding Iron Age and Romano-British Settlements. *Scottish
        Archaeological Review* 7: 96–103.
Hirschon, R.
1981   Essential Objects and the Sacred: Interior and Exterior Space in an Urban
        Greek Locality. Pp. 72–88 in *Women and Space: Ground Rules and Social Maps*, ed.
        S. Ardener. London: Helm.
Hizmi, H.
1998   Horbat Eli. *Excavations and Surveys in Israel* 18: 51–52.
Hodder, I.
1994   Architecture and Meaning: The Example of Neolithic Houses and Tombs.
        Pp. 73–86 in *Architecture and Order*, ed. M. Parker Pearson and C. Richards.
        London: Routledge.
Holladay, J. S.
1986   The Stables of Ancient Israel: Functional Determinants of Stable Construction
        and the Interpretation of Pillared Building Remains of the Palestinian Iron Age.
        Pp. 65–103 in *The Archaeology of Jordan and Other Studies Presented to Siegfried H.
        Horn*, ed. L. T. Geraty and L. G. Herr. Berrien Springs, MI: Andrews University
        Press.
1987   Religion in Israel and Judah under the Monarchy: An Explicitly Archaeological
        Approach. Pp. 249–99 in *Ancient Israelite Religion*, ed. P. D. Miller et al. Philadel-
        phia: Fortress.
1992   House, Israelite. Pp. 308–18 in vol. 3 of *ABD*. New York: Doubleday.
1995   The Kingdoms of Israel and Judah: Political and Economic Centralization in the
        Iron Age II A–B (ca. 1000–750 B.C.E.). Pp. 368–98 in *The Archaeology of Society in
        the Holy Land*, ed. T. E. Levy. London: Leicester University Press.
1997   Four Room House. Pp. 337–41 in vol. 2 of *Oxford Encyclopedia of Archaeology in
        the Near East*, ed. E. M. Meyers. New York: Oxford University Press.
Hopkins, D.
1985   *The Highlands of Canaan.* The Social World of Biblical Antiquity 3. Sheffield:
        Almond.
1996   Bare Bones: Putting Flesh on the Economics of Ancient Israel. Pp. 121–39 in
        The Origin of the Israelite States, ed. V. Fritz and P. R. Davies. Sheffield: Sheffield
        Academic Press.
Houston, W.
2004   Was There a Social Crisis in the Eighth Century? Pp 130–49 in *In Search of Pre-
        Exilic Israel*, ed. J. Day. London: T. & T. Clark.
Howard, M. C.
1996   *Contemporary Cultural Anthropology.* New York: HarperCollins.
Humbert, J.-B.
1993   Keisan, Tell. Pp. 862–67 in vol. 3 of *NEAEHL*.

Hunt, M.
  1987   The Pottery. Pp. 139–223 in *Tell Qiri*. Qedem 24. Jerusalem: Institute of Archae-
          ology of Hebrew University.
Huntington, R., and Metcalf, P.
  1979   *Celebrations of Death: The Anthropology of Mortuary Ritual*. Cambridge: Cam-
          bridge University Press.
Hurvitz, A.
  1974   The Evidence of Language in Dating the Priestly Code. *RB* 81: 24–56.
  1996   [Various entries]. *Song of Songs, Scrolls*. The World of the Bible. Tel Aviv: David-
          son Ati. [Hebrew]
Ibrahim, M. M.
  1975   Third Season of Excavation at Sahab: 1975 (Preliminary Report). *ADAJ* 20:
          69–82.
Isserlin, B. S. J.
  1998   *The Israelites*. London: Thames & Hudson.
Jackson, S. J., and Achtemeier, P. J.
  1996   Law. Pp. 592–96 in *The HarperCollins Bible Dictionary*, ed. P. J. Achtemeier. San
          Francisco: HarperCollins.
Jamison-Drake, D. W.
  1991   *Scribes and Schools in Monarchic Judah: A Socio-Archaeological Approach*. The So-
          cial World of Biblical Antiquity 9. Sheffield: Almond.
Jefferson, M.
  1939   The Law of the Primate City. *Geographical Review* 29: 226–32.
Ji, C. H. C.
  1995   The Iron I in Central and Northern Transjordan: An Interim Summary of Ar-
          chaeological Data. *PEQ* 127: 122–40.
  1997a   A Note on the Iron Age Four-Room House in Palestine. *Orientalia* 66: 387–413.
  1997b   The East Jordan Valley during Iron Age I. *PEQ* 129: 19–37.
Jones, E.
  1990   *Metropolis: The World's Greatest Cities*. Oxford: Oxford University Press.
Jones, S.
  1997   *The Archaeology of Ethnicity*. London: Routledge.
Kaminsky, J. S.
  1995   *Corporate Responsibility in the Hebrew Bible*. JSOTSup 196. Sheffield: Sheffield
          Academic Press.
Kamp, K., and Yoffee, N.
  1980   Ethnicity in Western Asia during the Early Second Millennium BC: Archaeo-
          logical Assemblages and Ethnoarchaeological Prospectives. *BASOR* 237: 85–104.
Katz, H.
  2008   *'A Land of Grain and Wine . . . a Land of Oil and Honey': The Economy of the King-
          dom of Judah*. Jerusalem: Yad Ben-Zvi. [Hebrew]
Kaufmann, Y.
  1960   *The Religion of Israel, from Its Beginnings to the Babylonian Exile*. Chicago: Univer-
          sity of Chicago Press.
Kautz, J. R.
  1981   Tracking the Ancient Moabites. *BA* 44: 27–35.
Kelm, G. L., and Mazar, A.
  1995   *Timnah: A Biblical City in the Sorek Valley*. Winona Lake, IN: Eisenbrauns.

Kelsky, K. L.
1999   Egalitarian Ideology and Hierarchy in Japanese Unions. *Current Anthropology* 40: 250–52.

Kemp, B. J.
1977   The City of El-Amarna as a Source for the Study of Urban Society in Ancient Egypt. *World Archaeology* 9/2: 123–39.

Kempinski, A.
1978   Tel Masos. *Expedition* 20/4: 29–37.
1989   *Megiddo: A City State and Royal Centre in North Israel.* Munich: Beck.
1993   *Megiddo: A City-State and Royal Centre in North Israel.* Jerusalem: Israel Exploration Society. [Hebrew]

Kh. el-Burj
1973   Kh. el-Burj. *Ḥadashot Arkheologiyot* 45: 26. [Hebrew]

Kh. er-Ras
1982   Kh. er-Ras. *Ḥadashot Arkheologiyot* 77: 28–29. [Hebrew]

Killebrew, A. E.
2005   *Biblical Peoples and Ethnicity: An Archaeological Study of Egyptians, Canaanites, Philistines, and Early Israel 1300–1100* b.c.e. Atlanta: Society of Biblical Literature.

King, P. J., and Stager, L. E.
2001   *Daily Life in Ancient Israel.* Louisville: Westminster John Knox.

Kirch, P. V.
2010   *How Chiefs Became Kings: Divine Kingship and the Rise of Archaic States in Ancient Hawai'i.* Berkeley: University of California Press.

Kletter, R.
1995   *Selected Material Remains of Judah at the End of the Iron Age in Relation to Its Political Borders.* Ph.D. Dissertation. Tel Aviv University. [Hebrew]

Kochavi, M.
1984   The Period of Settlement. Pp. 21–84 in *Israel and Judah in Biblical Times*, ed. Y. Eph'al. The History of the Land of Israel 2. Jerusalem: Keter. [Hebrew]
1989a   *Aphek-Antipatris: 5000 Years of History.* Tel Aviv: Hakibbutz Hameuchad. [Hebrew]
1989b   The Identification of Zeredah, Home of Jeroboam Son of Nebat, King of Israel. *ErIsr* 20 (Yadin Volume): 198–201. [Hebrew]
1992   'Pillared Buildings' on the Main Road: The Ancient Trade Centers of Iron Age Eretz Israel. P. 34 in *The Eighteenth Archaeological Conference in Israel.* Tel Aviv: Israel Exploration Society. [Hebrew]
1993a   The Golan during the Biblical Period. Pp. 285–98 in *Golan Heights and Mount Hermon*, ed. A. Degani and M. Inbar. Tel Aviv: Ministry of Defense. [Hebrew]
1993b   The Land of Geshur: 1991–1992. *Excavations and Surveys in Israel* 13: 24–28.
1993c   The Land of Geshur Regional Project: Attempting a New Approach in Biblical Archaeology. Pp. 725–37 in *Biblical Archaeology Today: Proceedings of the Second International Congress on Biblical Archaeology.* Jerusalem: Israel Exploration Society.
1993d   Zeror, Tel. Pp. 1524–26 in vol. 4 of *NEAEHL*.
1994   The Land of Geshur Project: 1993. *IEJ* 44: 136–41.
1998   The Eleventh Century bce Tripartite Pillar Building at Tel Hadar. Pp. 468–78 in *Mediterranean Peoples in Transition: Thirteenth to Early Tenth Centuries bce*, ed. S. Gitin, A. Mazar, and E. Stern. Jerusalem: Israel Exploration Society.

Kochavi, M. (ed.)
  1972   *Judah, Samaria and the Golan: Archaeological Survey in 1968.* Jerusalem: Israel Antiquities Department. [Hebrew]
Kochavi, M., et al.
  1992   Rediscovered: The Land of Geshur. *BAR* 18/4: 30–44, 84–85.
Kolb, M. J., and Snead, J. E.
  1997   It's a Small World after All: Comparative Analysis of Community Organization. *American Antiquity* 62: 609–28.
Kramer, C.
  1979   An Archaeological View of a Contemporary Kurdish Village: Domestic Architecture, Household Size and Wealth. Pp. 139–63 in *Ethnoarchaeology: Implications of Ethnography for Archaeology*, ed. C. Kramer. New York: New York University Press.

Lang, B.
  1985   The Social Organization of Peasant Poverty in Biblical Israel. Pp. 83–99 in *Anthropological Approaches to the Old Testament*, ed. B. Lang. Philadelphia: Fortress.
Lapp, N. L.
  1992   Pottery, Pottery Chronology of Palestine. Pp. 433–44 in vol. 5 of *ABD*.
Lederman, Z.
  1986   Tel Masos: A Site of 'Canaanite Settlement'? Pp. 27–28 in *The Twelfth Archaeological Congress in Israel. Lecture Abstracts.* Tel Aviv: Israel Exploration Society. [Hebrew]
Lees, S. H.
  1979   Ethnoarchaeology and the Interpretation of Community Organization. Pp. 265–76 in *Ethnoarchaeology: Implications of Ethnography for Archaeology*, ed. C. Kramer. New York: New York University Press.
Lehmann, G.
  2004   Reconstructing the Social Landscape of Ancient Israel: Rural Marriage Alliances in the Central Hill Country. *Tel Aviv* 31: 141–93.
Lemche, N. P.
  1985   *Early Israel.* Leiden: Brill.
  1996   From Patronage Society to Patronage Society. Pp. 106–20 in *The Origin of the Israelite States*, ed. V. Fritz and P. R. Davies. JSOTSup 228. Sheffield: Sheffield Academic Press.
  1998   The Origin of the Israelite State: A Copenhagen Perspective. Pp. 73–83 in *New Studies on Jerusalem*, vol. 3, ed. A. Faust and E. Baruch. Ramat Gan: Bar-Ilan University Press. [Hebrew]
Lemche, N. P., and Thompson, T. L.
  1994   Did Biran Kill David? The Bible in the Light of Archaeology. *JSOT* 64: 3–22.
Lenski, G., and Lenski, J.
  1974   *Human Societies: An Introduction to Macrosociology.* New York: McGraw-Hill.
Lev-Tov, J.
  2006   The Faunal Remains: Animal Economy in the Iron Age I. Pp. 207–33 in *Tel Miqne-Ekron Excavations 1995–1996: Field INE East Slope, Iron Age I (Early Philistine Period)*, ed. M. W. Meehl, T. Dothan, and S. Gitin. Jerusalem: W. F. Albright Institute of Archaeological Research and Institute of Archaeology, Hebrew University.
Levy, S., and Edelstein, G.
  1972   Cinq années de fouilles ʾTell ʿAmal (Nir David). *RB* 79: 325–67.

Levy, T. E.
  1986   Social Archaeology and the Chalcolithic Period: Explaining Social Organiza-
           tional Change during the 4th Millennium in Israel. *Michmanim* 3: 5–20.
  1995   Preface. Pp. x–xvi in *The Archaeology of Society in the Holy Land*, ed. T. E. Levy.
           London: Leicester University Press.
Levy, T. E. (ed.)
  1995   *The Archaeology of Society in the Holy Land.* London: Leicester University Press.
Lieber, Y.
  1968   Family. Cols. 582–88 in vol. 5 of *EncMiq.* [Hebrew]
Lipschits, O., et al.
  2010   Royal Judahite Jar Handles: Reconsidering the Chronology of the *lmlk* Stamp
           Impression. *Tel Aviv* 37: 3–32.
  2011   Judahite Jar Stamped and Incised Jar Handles: A Tool for Studying the History
           of Late Monarchic Judah. *Tel Aviv* 38: 5–41.
Liphshitz, N., and Biger, G.
  1991   Cedar of Lebanon (*Cedrus Libani*) in Israel during Antiquity. *IEJ* 41: 167–74.
Lods, A.
  1932   *Israel, from Its Beginnings to the Middle of the Eighth Century.* London: Kegan Paul,
           Trench, Trubner.
London, G. A.
  1989   A Comparison of Two Life Styles of the Late Second Millennium BC. *BASOR*
           273: 37–55.
  1992   Tells: City Center of Home? *ErIsr* 23 (Biran Volume): 71*–79*.
Luttwak, E. D.
  1976   *The Grand Strategy of the Roman Empire: From the First Century A.D. to the Third.*
           Baltimore: Johns Hopkins University Press.
Magen, Y., and Finkelstein, I.
  1993   *Archaeological Survey of the Hill Country of Benjamin.* Jerusalem: Israel Antiqui-
           ties Authority.
Magness-Gardiner, B.
  1994   Urban-Rural Relations in Bronze Age Syria: Evidence from Alalah Level VII
           Palace Archive. Pp. 37–47 in *Archaeological Views from the Countryside*, ed. G. M.
           Schwartz and S. E. Falconer. Washington, DC: Smithsonian Institution Press.
Mai, N.
  1999   Giv'at Homa. *Excavations and Surveys in Israel* 19: 65*–66*, 93–94.
Maitlis Y.
  1989   *Agricultural Settlement in the Vicinity of Jerusalem in the Late Iron Age.* M.A. thesis,
           Hebrew University. [Hebrew]
  1991   Jerusalem: Wadi Zimra. *Excavations and Surveys in Israel* 10: 125–27.
Malchow, B. V.
  1996   *Social Justice in the Hebrew Bible.* Collegeville, MN: Liturgical Press.
Malul, M.
  1994   [Various entries]. *Deuteronomy*, ed. M. Weinfeld. World of the Bible. Tel Aviv:
           Davidson Ati. [Hebrew]
Manor, D. W.
  1992   Tirzah (Place). Pp. 573–77 in vol. 6 of *ABD.*
Marcus, J., and Flannery, K. V.
  1996   *Zapotec Civilization: How Urban Society Evolved in Mexico's Oaxaca Valley.* Lon-
           don: Thames & Hudson.

Martin, J. D.
  1989   Israel as a Tribal Society. Pp. 95–118 in *The World of Ancient Israel*, ed. R. E. Clements. Cambridge: Cambridge University Press.
Master, D. M.
  2001   State Formation Theory and the Kingdom of Ancient Israel. *JNES* 60: 117–31.
Mazar, A.
  1977   Burial Caves from the First Temple Period North of Damascus Gate. Pp. 114–24 in *Between Hermon and Sinai: Memorial to Amnon*, ed. M. Broshi. Jerusalem: Bialik. [Hebrew]
  1981   The Excavations at Khirbet Abu et-Twein and the System of Iron Age Fortresses in Judah. *ErIsr* 15 (Aharoni Volume): 229–49. [Hebrew]
  1982   Iron Age Fortresses in the Judean Hills. *PEQ* 114: 87–109.
  1985a   Between Judah and Philistia: Timnah (Tel Batash) in the Iron Age II. *ErIsr* 18 (Avigad Volume): 300–324. [Hebrew]
  1985b   Israelite Settlement in Canaan in the Light of Archaeological Excavations. Pp. 61–71 in *Biblical Archaeology Today—1984: Proceedings of the International Congress on Biblical Archaeology, Jerusalem, April 1984*, ed. J. Amitai. Jerusalem: Israel Exploration Society.
  1990   *Archaeology of the Land of the Bible 10,000–586 BCE*. New York: Doubleday.
  1992   Iron Age I. Pp. 258–301 in *The Archaeology of Ancient Israel*, ed. A. Ben-Tor. New Haven, CT: Yale University Press.
  1993   Batash, Tel (Timnah). Pp. 152–57 in vol. 1 of *NEAEHL*.
  1997a   Iron Age Chronology: A Reply to I. Finkelstein. *Levant* 19: 157–67.
  1997b   *Tel Batash I*. Qedem 37. Jerusalem: Institute of Archaeology, Hebrew University.
  1998a   An Evaluation of the United Kingdom in Light of the Archaeological Evidence. Pp. 60–68 in *New Studies on Jerusalem*, vol. 3, ed. A. Faust and E. Baruch. Ramat Gan: Bar-Ilan University Press. [Hebrew]
  1998b   Tel Beth Shean. *Excavations and Surveys in Israel* 18: 43–46.
  1999   The 1997–1998 Excavations at Tel Rehov: Preliminary Report. *IEJ* 49: 1–42.
  2006a   Analysis of Stratum P-7 Building 28636. Pp. 269–78 in *Excavations at Tel Beth-Shean 1989–1996*, vol. 1: *From the Late Bronze Age IIB to the Medieval Period*, ed. A. Mazar. Jerusalem: Israel Exploration Society and Hebrew University.
  2006b   Jerusalem in the 10th Century BCE: The Glass Half Full. Pp. 255–72 in *Essays on Ancient Israel in Its Near Eastern Context: A Tribute to Nadav Na'aman*, ed. Y. Amit et al. Winona Lake, IN: Eisenbrauns.
  2008   Rehov, Tel. Pp. 2013–18 in vol. 5 of *NEAEHL*.
  2009   The Iron Age Dwellings at Tell Qasile. Pp. 319–36 in *Exploring the Longue Durée: Essays in Honor of Prof. Lawrence E. Stager*, ed. D. Schloen. Winona Lake, IN: Eisenbrauns.
  2010   Archaeology and the Biblical Narrative: The Case of the United Monarchy. Pp. 29–58 in *One God – One Cult – One Nation: Archaeological and Biblical Perspectives*, ed. R. G. Kratz and H. Spickermann. Berlin: de Gruyter.
  2011   The Iron Age Chronology Debate: Is the Gap Narrowing? Another Viewpoint. *NEA* 74: 105–11.
Mazar, A.; Amit, D.; and Ilan, Z.
  1989   The "Border Road" between Michmash and Jericho and the Excavations at Horvat Shilhah. *ErIsr* 17 (Brawer Volume): 236–50. [Hebrew]
  1996   Hurvat Shilhah: An Iron Age Site in the Judean Desert. Pp. 193–211 in *Retrieving the Past: Essays on Archaeological Research and Methodology in Honor of Gus W. Van Beek*, ed. J. D. Seger. Winona Lake, IN: Eisenbrauns.

Mazar, A., and Bronk Ramsey, C.
2008   14C Dates and the Iron Age Chronology of Israel: A Response. *Radiocarbon* 50/2: 159–80.
Mazar, A., and Panitz-Cohen, N.
2001   *Timnah (Tel Batash) II: The Finds from the First Millennium* BCE *(Text).* Jerusalem: Hebrew University.
Mazar, B.
1974   *Canaan and Israel: Historical Essays.* Jerusalem: Bialik. [Hebrew]
1981   The Early Israelite Settlement in the Hill Country. *BASOR* 241: 75–85.
1982   The Period of David and Solomon. Pp. 62–81 in *The Monarchy Period: Political History,* ed. A. Malamat. World History of the Jewish People 4. Jerusalem: Am Oved. [Hebrew]
1992a   ʿEn Gedi. Pp. 399–409 in vol. 2 of *NEAEHL.*
1992b   ʿEn Gev. Pp. 409–12 in vol. 2 of *NEAEHL.*
Mazar, E.
1985   Edomite Pottery at the End of the Iron Age. *IEJ* 35: 253–69.
1991   The Ophel of Jerusalem in the First Temple Period. Pp. 135–42 in *Jerusalem in the First Temple Period,* ed. D. Amit and R. Gonen. Idan 15. Jerusalem: Yad Ben-Zvi. [Hebrew]
1997   The Undiscovered Palace of King David in Jerusalem: A Study in Biblical Archaeology. Pp. 9–20 in *New Studies on Jerusalem,* vol. 2, ed. A. Faust. Ramat Gan: Bar-Ilan University Press. [Hebrew]
2007a   Excavations at the City of David (2006–2007). Pp. 7–26 in *New Studies on Jerusalem,* vol. 13, ed. E. Baruch, A. Levy-Reifer, and A. Faust. Ramat Gan: Bar-Ilan University Press.
2007b   *Preliminary Report on the City of David Excavations 2005 at the Visitor Center Area.* Jerusalem: Shoham.
2011   *Discovering the Solomonic Wall in Jerusalem: A Remarkable Archaeological Adventure.* Jerusalem: Shoham.
Mazar, E., and Mazar, B.
1989   *Excavations in the South of the Temple Mount: The Ophel of Biblical Jerusalem.* Qedem 29. Jerusalem: Hebrew University.
Mazor, G.
2006   A Farmhouse from the Late Iron Age and the Second Temple Period in ʿFrench Hillʾ North Jerusalem. *ʿAtiqot* 54: 1*–14*.
McAfee, G.
1993   Sex. Pp. 690–92 in *The Oxford Companion to the Bible,* ed. B. M. Metzger and M. D. Coogan. Oxford: Oxford University Press.
McClellan, T.
1978   Towns to Fortresses: The Transformation of Urban Life in Judah from 8th to 7th Century. Pp. 277–86 in *Society of Biblical Literature Seminar Papers.* SBLSP 13/1. Missoula, MT: Scholars Press.
1984   Town Planning at Tell en-Nasbeh. *ZDPV* 100: 52–69.
McCown, C. C.
1947   *Tell en-Nasbeh, I: Archaeological and Historical Results.* Berkeley: Palestine Institute of Pacific School of Religion and American Schools of Oriental Research.
McGuire, R. H.
1982   The Study of Ethnicity in Historical Archaeology. *Journal of Anthropological Archaeology* 1: 159–78.

McNutt, P. M.
    1999   *Reconstructing the Society of Ancient Israel.* Louisville: Westminster John Knox.
Mendel, A.
    2011   Who Wrote the Ahiqam Ostracon from Horvat ʿUza? *IEJ* 61: 54–67.
Mendelson, Y., and Aḥituv, S.
    1971   Slave, Slavery. Cols. 1–13 in vol. 6 of *EncMiq.* [Hebrew]
Mendenhall, G.
    1962   The Hebrew Conquest of Palestine. *BA* 25: 66–87.
Meshel, Z.
    1994   'Aharoni Fortress' near Quseima and the Israelite Fortresses in the Negev. *BASOR* 294: 39–67.
Mevasseret Yerushalayim
    1979   Mevaseret Yerushalayim. *Hadashot Arkheologiyot* 69–71: 55–56. [Hebrew]
Meyers, C.
    1988   *Discovering Eve: Ancient Israelite Women in Context.* Oxford: Oxford University Press.
    1997   The Family in Early Israel. Pp. 1–47 in *Families in Ancient Israel,* ed. L. G. Perdue et al. Louisville: Westminster John Knox.
    2003   Material Remains and Social Relations: Women's Culture in Agrarian Households of the Iron Age. Pp. 425–44 in *Symbiosis, Symbolism, and the Power of the Past: Canaan, Ancient Israel, and Their Neighbors from the Late Bronze Age through Roman Palaestina,* ed. W. G. Dever and S. Gitin. Winona Lake, IN: Eisenbrauns.
Milgrom, J.
    1991   *Leviticus 1–16.* AB 3. New York: Doubleday.
Millard, A. R.
    1973   The Canaanites. Pp. 29–52 in *Peoples of Old Testament Times,* ed. D. J. Weisman. Oxford: Clarendon.
Miller, J. M., and Hayes, J. H.
    1986   *A History of Ancient Israel and Judah.* Philadelphia: Westminster.
Miller, R. D.
    2005   *Chieftains of the Highland Clans: A History of Israel in the 12th and 11th Centuries B.C.* Grand Rapids, MI: Eerdmans.
Moody, J., and Grove, A. T.
    1990   Terraces and Enclosure Walls in the Cretan Landscape. Pp. 183–91 in *Man's Role in the Shaping of the Eastern Mediterranean Landscape,* ed. S. Bottema, G. Entjes-Niebor, and W. van Zeist. Rotterdam: Balkema.
Morley, M.
    2007   *Trade in Classical Antiquity.* Cambridge: Cambridge University Press.
Mumford, L.
    1962   *The City in History.* London: Secker & Warburg.
Naʾaman, N.
    1979   Sennacherib's Campaign to Judah and the Date of the *lmlk* Stamps. *VT* 29: 61–86.
    1980   The Inheritance of the Sons of Simeon. *ZDPV* 96: 136–52.
    1981   Royal Estates in the Jezreel Valley in the Late Bronze Age and under the Israelite Monarchy. *ErIsr* 15 (Aharoni Volume): 140–44. [Hebrew]
    1986   Migdal-Shechem and the "House of El-Berith." *Zion* 51: 260–80. [Hebrew]
    1987   The Negev in the Last Century of the Kingdom of Judah. *Cathedra* 42: 3–15. [Hebrew]

1993   Population Changes in Palestine following Assyrian Deportations. *Tel Aviv* 20: 104–24.

1994   Hezekiah and the Kings of Assyria. *Tel Aviv* 21: 235–54.

1996a   Sources and Composition in the History of David. Pp. 170–86 in *The Origins of the Israelite States*. JSOTSup 228. Sheffield: Sheffield Academic Press.

1996b   The Contribution of the Amarna Letters to the Debate on Jerusalem's Political Position in the Tenth Century BCE. *BASOR* 304: 17–27.

1997   Cow Town or Royal Capital: Iron Age Jerusalem. *BAR* 23/4: 43–47.

Na'aman, N., and Zadok, R.
2000   Assyrian Deportations to the Province of Samerina in Light of Two Cuneiform Tablets from Tel Hadid. *Tel Aviv* 27: 159–88.

Naroll, R.
1962   Floor Area and Settlement Population. *American Antiquity* 27: 587–89.

Naveh, Y.
1961   A Hebrew Letter from Mezad Hashavyahu. *Yediot* 25: 119–28. [Hebrew]

1981   "Belonging to Makbiram" or "Belonging to the Food-Servers"? *ErIsr* 15 (Aharoni Volume): 301–2. [Hebrew]

Netting, R. M.
1982   Some Home Truths on Household Size and Wealth. *ABS* 25: 641–62.

Netzer, E.
1992   Architecture in the Iron Age. Pp. 193–201 in *The Architecture of Ancient Israel from the Prehistoric to the Persian Period*, ed. A. Kempinski and R. Reich. Jerusalem: Israel Exploration Society.

Neufeld, E.
1960   The Emergence of a Royal Urban Society in Ancient Israel. *HUCA* 31: 31–53.

Nevett, L. C.
1999   *House and Society in the Ancient Greek World*. Cambridge: Cambridge University Press.

Niditch, S.
1997   *Ancient Israelite Religion*. New York: New York University Press.

Noth, M.
1960   *The History of Israel*. New York: Black.

Oded, B.
1984   The Kingdoms of Israel and Judah. Pp. 101–201 in *Israel and Judah in Biblical Times*, ed. I. Eph'al. The History of the Land of Israel 2. Jerusalem: Keter. [Hebrew]

Ofer, A.
1993   *The Highlands of Judah during the Biblical Period*. Ph.D. dissertation. Tel Aviv University. [Hebrew]

1998   The Judean Hills in the Biblical Period. *Qadmoniot* 31 (115): 40–52. [Hebrew]

Ohata, K., and Kochavi, M.
1966–70 *Tel Zeror*, vols. 1–3. Tokyo: Society for Near Eastern Studies in Japan.

Olavarri, E.
1983   La campagne de fouilles 1982: A Khirbet 'Medeinet Al-Mu' arradjeh pres de Smakieh (Kerak). *ADAJ* 27: 165–78.

Olsen, B., and Kobylinski, Z.
1991   Ethnicity in Anthropological and Archaeological Research: A Norwegian-Polish Perspective. *Archaeologia Polona* 29: 5–27.

Orser, C. E.
  1988   The Archaeological Analysis of Plantation Society: Replacing Status and Caste
           with Economics and Power. *American Antiquity* 53: 735–51.
Orser, C. E., and Fagan, B. M.
  1995   *Historical Archaeology.* New York: HarperCollins.
Ortiz, S.; Wolff, S.; and Arbino, G.
  2011   Tel Gezer: Preliminary Report. *Excavations and Surveys in Israel* 123. http://www
           .hadashot-esi.org.il/index_eng.asp.
Orton, C., et al.
  1993   *Pottery in Archaeology.* Cambridge: Cambridge University Press.
Osborne, R.
  2005   Urban Sprawl: What Is Urbanization and Why Does It Matter? Pp. 1–16 in
           Mediterranean Urbanization 800–600 BCE, ed. R. Osborne and B. Cunliffe. Ox-
           ford: British Academy and Oxford University Press.
Parker-Pearson, M., and Richards, C.
  1994   Ordering the World: Perceptions of Architecture, Space and Time. Pp. 1–37
           in *Architecture and Order*, ed. M. Parker-Pearson and C. Richards. London:
           Routledge.
Parkin, R.
  1997   *Kinship: An Introduction to Basic Concepts.* Oxford: Blackwell.
Pasto, J.
  1998   When the End Is the Beginning? Or When the Biblical Past Is the Political Pres-
           ent: Some Thought on Ancient Israel, "Post Exilic Judaism," and the Politics of
           Biblical Scholarship. *SJOT* 12: 157–202.
Patinkin, D.
  1966   *Introduction to Economy.* Jerusalem. [Hebrew]
Patterson, T. C.
  1991   *The Inca Empire: The Formation and Disintegration of a Pre-Capitalist State.* Worces-
           ter: Berg.
Pedersen, J.
  1926   *Israel: Its Life and Culture*, vols. 1–2. Copenhagen: Branner & Korch.
Peleg, Y.
  2004   An Iron Age Site at Noqdim. Pp. 189–205 in *Burial Caves and Sites in Judea and
           Samaria from the Bronze and Iron Ages*, ed. H. Hizmi and A. de Groot. Jerusalem:
           Israel Antiquities Authority.
Peleg, Y., and Feller, Y.
  2004   Har Gillo (West). *Hadashot Arkheologiyot: Excavations and Surveys in Israel* 116:
           74*, 100–101.
Perdue, L. G.
  1997   The Israelite and Early Jewish Family: Summary and Conclusions. Pp. 163–222
           in *Families in Ancient Israel*, ed. L. G. Perdue et al. Louisville: Westminster John
           Knox.
Pope, M. H.
  1977   *Song of Songs.* AB 7C. New York: Doubleday.
Porter, J. R.
  1967   *The Extended Family in the Old Testament.* Holborn: Edutext.
Portugali, Y.
  1984   *Arim, Banot, Migrashim,* and *Haserim*: The Spatial Organization of Eretz-Israel
           in the 12th–10th Centuries BCE according to the Bible. *ErIsr* 17 (Brawer Vol-
           ume): 282–90. [Hebrew]

1987 Construction Methods, Architectural Features, and Environment. Pp. 132–38 in *Tel Qiri*, ed. A. Ben-Tor and Y. Portugali. Qedem 24. Jerusalem: Hebrew University.

1999 *Space, Time, and Society in Ancient Eretz Israel*, part 1: *Social Morphology*. Tel Aviv: Open University of Israel. [Hebrew]

Price, T. D., and Feinman, G. M.
1995 Foundations of Prehistoric Social Inequality. Pp. 3–14 in *Foundations of Social Inequality*, ed. T. D. Price and G. M. Feinman. New York: Plenum.

Pritchard, J. B.
1970 The Megiddo Stables: A Reassessment. Pp. 268–76 in *Near Eastern Archaeology in the Twentieth Century*, ed. J. A. Sanders. New York: Doubleday.

1985 *Tell es-Sa'idiye: Excavations on the Tell, 1964–1969.* Philadelphia: University Museum, University of Pennsylvania.

1993 Saidiyeh, Tell es-. Pp. 1295–96 in vol. 4 of *NEAEHL*.

Raban, A.
1982 *Archaeological Survey of Israel: Nahalal Map (28).* Jerusalem: Israel Antiquities Authority.

Rahmani, L. I.
1964 A Partial Survey of the Adolam Area. *Yediot* 28: 209–14. [Hebrew]

Rainey, A. F.
1966 *A Social Structure of Ugarit.* Jerusalem: Bialik. [Hebrew]

1968 Corvée Labor. Cols. 55–56 in vol. 5 of *EncMiq*. [Hebrew]

1981 Wine from the Royal Vineyards. *ErIsr* 16 (Orlinsky Volume): 177–81. [Hebrew]

1988 a Precise Date for the Samaria Ostraca. *BASOR* 272: 69–74.

1994 The "House of David" and the House of the Deconstructionists. *BAR* 20/6: 47.

Rapoport, A.
1969 *House Form and Culture.* Englewood Cliffs, NJ: Prentice-Hall.

1990 Systems of Activities and Systems of Settings. Pp. 9–20 in *Domestic Architecture and the Use of Space*, ed. S. Kent. Cambridge: Cambridge University Press.

Rathje, W. L., and McGuire, R. H.
1982 Rich Men Poor Men. *ABS* 25: 705–16.

Redfield, R.
1953 *The Primitive World and Its Transformation.* Ithaca, NY: Cornell University Press.

Reich, R.
1992 Palaces and Residences in the Iron Age. Pp. 202–22 in *The Architecture of Ancient Israel*, ed. A. Kempinski and R. Reich. Jerusalem: Israel Exploration Society.

1994 The Cemetery in the Mamilla Area of Jerusalem. *Qadmoniot* 26 (103–4): 103–8. [Hebrew]

Reich, R., and Shukrun, E.
1999 The Tunnel System and Excavations Adjacent to the Gihon Spring. Pp. 5–13 in *New Studies on Jerusalem*, vol. 4, ed. A. Faust and E. Baruch. Ramat Gan: Bar-Ilan University Press. [Hebrew]

2008 The Date of City-Wall 501 in Jerusalem. *Tel Aviv* 35: 114–22.

Rendsburg, G. A.
2007 No Stelae, No Queens: Two Issues concerning the Kings of Israel and Judah. Pp. 95–107 in *The Archaeology of Difference: Gender, Ethnicity, Class and the "Other" in Antiquity—Studies in Honor of Eric M. Meyers*, ed. D. R. Edwards and C. T. McCullough. Boston: American Schools of Oriental Research.

Renfrew, C.
1974   Reply. Pp. 91–94 in *Reconstructing Complex Societies*, ed. C. B. Moore. Cambridge, MA: American Schools of Oriental Research.
1984   *Approaches to Social Archaeology*. Edinburgh: Edinburgh University Press.
1993   *The Roots of Ethnicity: Archaeology, Genetics and the Origins of Europe*. Rome: Internazionale degli istituti di archeologia, storia e storia dell'arte in Roma.
1994   Toward a Cognitive Archaeology. Pp. 3–12 in *The Ancient Mind: Elements of Cognitive Archaeology*, ed. C. Renfrew and B. W. Zubrow. Cambridge: Cambridge University Press.
Renfrew, C., and Bahn, P.
2004   *Archaeology: Theories, Methods and Practice*. London: Thames & Hudson.
Reuben, A., and Peleg, Y.
2009   Caves, Winepresses, and a Three-Room Structure to the East of Anʿata. Pp. 57–64 in *Excavations and Discoveries in Benjamin and Judea*, ed. I. Yezerski. Judea and Samaria Publication 10. Jerusalem: Israel Antiquities Authority. [Hebrew]
Reviv, H.
1971   Army. Pp. 650–59 in vol. 6 of *EncMiq*. [Hebrew]
1982   Social Structure. Pp. 90–104 in *The Days of the Monarchy: Culture and Society*, ed. A. Malamat. The World History of the Jewish People 5. Jerusalem: Am Oved. [Hebrew]
1989   *The Elders in Ancient Israel: A Study of a Biblical Institution*. Jerusalem: Magnes.
1993   *Society in the Kingdoms of Israel and Judah*. Jerusalem: Bialik. [Hebrew]
Reviv, H., and Kuchman, M.
1986   Society and Economy. Pp. **000–00** in *The History of the Jewish People in the First Temple Period*, ed. B. Oded. Open University 8. Tel Aviv: The Open University. [Hebrew]
Riklin, S.
1993   Beit Aryeh. *Excavations and Surveys in Israel* 12: 39.
1994   Ofarim. *Excavations and Surveys in Israel* 13: 53–54.
1995   A Fortress at Michmas on the Northeastern Border of the Judean Desert. Pp. 69–73 in *Judea and Samaria Research Studies: Proceedings of the Fourth Annual Meeting*, ed. Z. H. Ehrlich and Y. Eshel. Kedumim and Ariel: Eretz. [Hebrew]
1997   Bet Aryeʾ. *ʿAtiqot* 32: 7–20. [Hebrew]
Roberts, B. K.
1996   *Landscapes of Settlement: Prehistory to the Present*. London: Routledge.
Rofé, A.
1994   *Introduction to the Composition of the Pentateuch*. Jerusalem: Academon. [Hebrew]
Rogerson, J. W.
1985   The Hebrew Conception of Corporate Personality: A Re-Examination. Pp. 43–49 in *Anthropological Approaches to the Old Testament*, ed. B. Lang. Philadelphia: Fortress.
1986   Was Early Israel a Segmentary Society? *JSOT* 36: 17–26.
1989   Anthropology and the Old Testament. Pp. 17–38 in *The World of Ancient Israel*, ed. R. E. Clements. Cambridge: Cambridge University Press.
Röllig, W.
1983   On the Origin of the Phoenicians. *Berytus* 31: 79–93.
Roseberg, W.
1989   Peasants and the World. Pp. 108–26 in *Economic Anthropology*, ed. S. Plattner. Stanford: Stanford University Press.

Routledge, B.
   2008   Thinking "Globally" and Analyzing "Locally": South-Central Jordan in Tran-
           sition. Pp. 144–76 in *Israel in Transition: From LB II–Iron Age IIB*, ed. L. Grabbe.
           London: T. & T. Clark.
   2009   Average Families? House Size Variability in the Southern Levantine Iron Age.
           Pp. 45–63 in *The Family in Life and Death: The Family in Ancient Israel—Archaeo-
           logical and Sociological Perspectives on Biblical Families*, ed. P. Dutcher-Walls. Lon-
           don: T. & T. Clark.
Routledge, C.
   1995   Pillared Buildings in Iron Age Moab. *BA* 58: 236.
Rowlands, M. J.
   1975   Defence: A Factor in Organization of Settlements. Pp. 298–311 in *Readings in
           Rural Settlements Geography*, ed. R. L. Singh and K. N. Singh. Varansi: National
           Geographical Society of India.
Rubin, N.
   1972   Mourning for Him, Mourning with Him. *Bar Ilan* 10: 117–22. [Hebrew]
Safrai, Z.
   1980   Urbanization in Israel in the Greco-Roman Period. *Studies in the History of the
           Jewish People and the Land of Israel* 5: 105–29. [Hebrew]
   1983   Family Structure during the Period of the Mishna and the Talmud. *Milet* 1:
           129–56. [Hebrew]
   1994   *The Economy of Roman Palestine*. London: Routledge.
   1998   Ancient Field Structures: The Village in Eretz Israel during the Roman Period.
           Cathedra 89: 7–40. [Hebrew]
Sand, E.
   1994   *Common Wall in Old Babylonian Documents*. Ph.D. Dissertation. Bar-Ilan Univer-
           sity. [Hebrew]
Sarna, N. M.
   1982a   Psalms: The Book of Psalms. Cols. 437–62 in vol. 8 of *EncMiq*. [Hebrew]
   1982b   Sun. Cols. 182–89 in vol. 8 of *EncMiq*. [Hebrew]
Sarna, N. M. (ed.)
   1996   *Psalms*. The World of the Bible 1. Tel Aviv: Davidson Ati. [Hebrew]
Scheftelowitz, N., and Oren, R.
   1996   *Trial Excavations in Kh. el-Bira Region*. Tel Aviv: Ramot. [Hebrew]
Schloen, J. D.
   2001   *The House of the Father as Fact and Symbol: Patrimonialism in Ugarit and the Ancient
           Near East*. Studies in the Archaeology and History of the Levant 2. Winona
           Lake, IN: Eisenbrauns.
Schwartz, G. M., and Falconer, S. E.
   1994   Rural Approaches to Social Complexity. Pp. 1–9 in *Archaeological Views from the
           Countryside*, ed. G. M. Schwartz and S. E. Falconer. Washington, DC: Smithson-
           ian Institution Press.
Seligman, J.
   1994   A Late Iron Age Farmhouse at Ras Abu Maᵓaruf, Pisgat Zeᵓev A. *ʿAtiqot* 25:
           63–75.
Service, E. R.
   1962   *Primitive Social Organization*. New York: Random.
Seymour-Smith, C.
   1994   *Macmillan Dictionary of Anthropology*. London: Macmillan.

Shapira, A.
1998 "... He Appointed Judges in the Land in All the Fortified Towns of Judah" (2 Chronicles 19:4–5): An Expression of the Separation of Powers in Israel. Pp. 233–44 in *Judea and Samaria Research Studies: Proceedings of the Seventh Annual Meeting*, ed. Y. Eshel. Ariel: Eretz. [Hebrew]

Shennan, J. S.
1989 Introduction: Archaeological Approaches to Cultural Identity. Pp. 1–32 in *Archaeological Approaches to Cultural Identity*, ed. J. S. Shennan. London: Hyman.
1991 Some Current Issues in the Archaeological Identification of Past People. *Archaeologia Polona* 29: 29–37.

Sherratt, A., and Sherratt, S.
1991 From Luxuries to Commodities: The Nature of Mediterranean Bronze Age Trading Systems. Pp. 351–86 in *Bronze Age Trade in the Mediterranean*, ed. N. H. Gale. Jonsered, Sweden: Åström.

Shiloh, Y.
1970 The Four Room House: Its Situation and Function in the Israelite City. *IEJ* 20: 180–90.
1973 Four-Room House: The Israelite Type-House? *ErIsr* 11 (Dunayevsky Volume): 277–85. [Hebrew]
1978 Elements in the Development of Town Planning in the Israelite City. *IEJ* 28: 37–51.
1981 The Population of Iron Age Palestine in the Light of Urban Plans, Areas, and Population Density. *ErIsr* 15 (Aharoni Volume): 274–82. [Hebrew]
1984 *Excavations of the City of David*, vol. 1. Qedem 19. Jerusalem: Hebrew University.
1987a South Arabian Inscriptions from the City of David, Jerusalem. *PEQ* 119: 9–18.
1987b The Casemate Wall, the Four Room House and the Early Planning in the Israelite City. *BASOR* 268: 3–15.
1993a Jerusalem: The Results of the Excavation. Pp. 701–12 in vol. 1 of *NEAEHL*.
1993b Megiddo. Pp. 1016–23 in vol. 3 of *NEAEHL*.

Shimron, A. E.
2004 Warren's Shaft: No, It Really Was Not Used to Draw Water. *BAR* 30/4: 14–15.

Shukrun, E., and Reich, R.
1999 A Wall from the End of the First Temple Period in the Eastern Part of the City of David. Pp. 14–16 in *New Studies on Jerusalem*, vol. 4, ed. A. Faust and E. Baruch. Ramat Gan: Bar-Ilan University Press. [Hebrew]

Shupak, N.
1996 *Proverbs*. The World of the Bible. Tel Aviv: Davidson Ati. [Hebrew]

Silver, M.
1983 *Prophets and Markets: The Political Economy of Ancient Israel*. Boston: Kluwer-Nijhoff.

Singer-Avitz, L.
1996 Household Activities at Beersheba. *ErIsr* 26 (Cross Volume): 166–74. [Hebrew]
1999 Beersheba: A Gateway Community in Southern Arabian—Long-Distance Trade in the Eighth Century BCE. *Tel Aviv* 26: 3–74.
2011 Household Activities at Tel Beersheba. Pp. 275-301 in *Household Archaeology in Ancient Israel and Beyond*, ed. A. Yasur-Landau, J. R. Ebeling, and L. B. Mazow. Leiden: Brill.

Sjoberg, G.
1960 *The Preindustrial City: Past and Present*. Glencoe, IL: Free Press.

1965   The Preindustrial City. Pp. 179–88 in *Cities and Society*, ed. P. K. Hatt and A. J. Reiss. New York: Free Press.

Skjeggestand, M.
1992   Ethnic Groups in Early Iron Age Palestine: Some Remarks on the Use of the Term Israelite in Recent Research. *SJOT* 6: 159–86.

Small, D. B.
1997   Group Identification and Ethnicity in the Construction of the Early State of Israel: From the Outside Looking In. Pp. 271–88 in *The Archaeology of Israel: Constructing the Past, Interpreting the Present*, ed. N. Silberman and D. B. Small. JSOTSup 237. Sheffield: Sheffield Academic Press.

Smith, A. T.
2011   Archaeologies of Sovereignty. *Annual Review of Anthropology* 40: 415-32.

Smith, M. E.
1987   Household Possessions and Wealth in Agrarian States: Implications for Archaeology. *Journal of Anthropological Archaeology* 6: 297–335.
1994   Social Complexity in the Aztec Countryside. Pp. 143–59 in *Archaeological Views from the Countryside: Village Communities in Early Complex Societies*, ed. G. M. Schwartz and S. E. Falconer. Washington, DC: Smithsonian Institution Press.
2002   The Earliest Cities. Pp. 3–19 in *Urban Life: Readings in the Anthropology of the City*, ed. G. Gmelch and W. P. Zenner. 4th ed. Prospect Heights, IL: Waveland.
2009   V. Gordon Childe and the Urban Revolution: A Historical Perspective on a Revolution in Urban Studies. *Town Planning Review* 80: 3–29.

Smith, M. E., et al.
1989   Architectural Patterns at Three Aztec-Period Sites in Morelos, Mexico. *JFA* 16: 185–203.

Speiser, E. A.
1971   The Manner of the Kings. Pp. 280–87 in *The World History of the Jewish People*, vol. 3: *Judges*, ed. B. Mazar. Jerusalem: Masada.
1982   The Manner of the King. Pp. 153–56 in *The Judges*, ed. B. Mazar. The World History of the Jewish People 3. Jerusalem: Masada. [Hebrew]

Spencer, C. S.
2003   War and Early State Formation in Oaxaca, Mexico. *Proceedings of the National Academy of Sciences* 100: 11185–87.

Stager, L. E.
1976   Farming in the Judean Desert during the Iron Age. *BASOR* 221: 145–58.
1985   The Archaeology of the Family in Ancient Israel. *BASOR* 260: 1–35.
2003   The Patrimonial Kingdom of Solomon. Pp. 63–74 in *Symbiosis, Symbolism, and the Power of the Past: Canaan, Ancient Israel, and Their Neighbors from the Late Bronze Age through Roman Palaestina*, ed. W. G. Dever and S. Gitin. Winona Lake, IN: Eisenbrauns.

Steiner, M. L.
2001   *Excavations by Kathleen M. Kenyon in Jerusalem 1961–1967*, vol. 3: *The Settlement in the Bronze and Iron Ages*. London: Sheffield Academic Press.

Stern, E.
1964   The Fortified City Gate and the Struggle for It under the Monarchy. Pp. 400–409 in *The Military History of the Land of Israel in Biblical Times*, ed. J. Lever. Jerusalem: Maarachot. [Hebrew]
1994   The Eastern Border of the Kingdom of Judah. Pp. 399–409 in *Scriptures and Other Artifacts: Essays on the Bible and Archaeology in Honor of Philip J. King*, ed. M. D. Coogan, J. C. Exum, and L. E. Stager. Louisville: Westminster John Knox.

1996   *Excavations at Dor: Final Report*, vol. 1A: *Areas A and C: Introduction and Stratig-raphy*. Jerusalem: Hebrew University.

1997   The Beginning of Phoenician Settlement along the Northern Coast of Palestine. *Michmanim* 11: 5–15. [Hebrew]

2001   *Archaeology of the Land of the Bible: The Assyrian, Babylonian and Persian Periods (732–332 B.C.E.)*. New York: Doubleday.

2007   *En-Gedi Excavations I: Final Report (1961–1965)*. Jerusalem: Israel Exploration Society.

Stern, E., and Aḥituv, S.

1982   Tirzah. Cols. 937–41 in vol. 8 of *EncMiq*. [Hebrew]

Stirling, P.

1971   A Turkish Village. Pp. 37–48 in *Peasants and Peasant Societies*, ed. T. Shanin. Harmondsworth: Penguin.

Stissi, V.

1999   Production, Circulation and Consumption of Archaic Greek Pottery (Sixth and Early Fifth Centuries BC). Pp. 83–113 in *The Complex Past of Pottery: Production, Circulation and Consumption of Mycenaean and Greek Pottery*, ed. J. H. P. Crielaard, V. Stissi, and G. J. Wijngaarden. Amsterdam: Gieben.

Stone, E. C.

1987   *Nippur Neighborhoods*. Chicago: Oriental Institute of the University of Chicago.

Thareani, Y.

2011   *Tel ʿAroer: The Iron Age II Caravan Town and the Hellenistic–Early Roman Settlement*. Jerusalem: Nelson Glueck School of Biblical Archaeology, Hebrew Union College – Jewish Institute of Religion.

Thomas, R.

1997   Land, Kinship Relations and the Rise of Enclosed Settlement in the First Millennium BC Britain. *Oxford Journal of Archaeology* 16: 211–18.

Thompson, T. L.

1992   *Early History of the Israelite People: From the Written and Archaeological Sources*. Leiden: Brill.

1997   Defining History and Ethnicity in the Southern Levant. Pp. 166–87 in *Can a History of Israel Be Written?* ed. L. L. Grabbe. JSOTSup 245. Sheffield: Sheffield Academic Press.

Tod, I.

1974   Comments on Prof. Renfrew's Paper. Pp. 85–88 in *Reconstructing Complex Societies*, ed. C. B. Moore. Cambridge: American Schools of Oriental Research.

Torczyner, N. H., et al.

1938   *Lachish I: The Lachish Letters*. London: Oxford University Press.

Trigger, B.

1990   Monumental Architecture: A Thermodynamic Explanation of Symbolic Behavior. *World Archaeology* 22: 119–31.

2006   *A History of Archaeological Thought*. Cambridge: Cambridge University Press.

Tsafrir, Y.

1982   The Provinces in Eretz Israel: Names, Boundaries and Administrative Regions. Pp. 350–86 in *Eretz Israel from the Destruction of the Second Temple to the Moslem Conquest: Political, Social, and Cultural History*, ed. Z. Baras et al. Jerusalem: Yad Ben-Zvi. [Hebrew]

Tubb, J. N.

1988   Tell es-Saʾidiyeh: Preliminary Report on the First Three Seasons of Renewed Excavations. *Levant* 20: 23–88.

Tufnell, O.
  1953   *Lachish,* vol. 3: *The Iron Age.* London: Oxford University Press.
Ucko, P. J.
  1988   Preface. Pp. vii–xii in *State and Society: The Emergence and Development of So-
           cial Hierarchy and Political Centralization,* ed. J. Glendhill, B. Bender, and M. T.
           Larsen. London: Hyman.
Uffenheimer, B.
  1968   Urbanization as a Religious and Social Problem for the Prophets. Pp. 207–26 in
           *Town and Community: Proceedings of the Twelfth Conference of the Israeli Historical
           Society.* Jerusalem: Israeli Historical Society. [Hebrew]
  1973   Amos and Hosea: Two Approaches in Israelite Prophecy. Pp. 284–319 in *Zer
           Ligevurot: The Zalman Shazar Festschrift,* ed. B. Z. Luria. Jerusalem: Kiryat Sefer.
           [Hebrew]
Ussishkin, D.
  1976   Royal Judean Storage Jars and Private Seal Impressions. *BASOR* 223: 1–13.
  1977   The Destruction of Lachish by Sennacherib and the Dating of the Royal Judean
           Storage Jars. *Tel Aviv* 4: 28–60.
  1978   Excavations at Tel Lachish 1973–1978: Preliminary Report. *Tel Aviv* 5: 1–97.
  1993a   Lachish. Pp. 897–911 in vol. 3 of *NEAEHL.*
  1993b   The Village of Silwan: The Necropolis from the Period of the Judean Kingdom.
           Jerusalem: Yad Ben-Zvi.
  1994   The Rectangular Fortress at Kadesh-Barnea. *ErIsr* 24 (Malamat Volume): 1–6.
           [Hebrew]
  1998   Jerusalem in the Period of David and Solomon: The Archaeological Evidence.
           Pp. 57–58 in *New Studies on Jerusalem,* vol. 4, ed. A. Faust and E. Baruch. Ramat
           Gan: Bar-Ilan University Press. [Hebrew]
  2004   A Synopsis of the Stratigraphical, Chronological and Historical Issues. Pp. 50–
           119 in *The Renewed Archaeological Excavations at Lachish (1973–1994),* ed. D. Us-
           sishkin. Tel Aviv: Tel Aviv University Press.
  2011   The Dating of the *lmlk* Storage Jars and Its Implications: Rejoinder to Lipschits,
           Sergi, and Koch. *Tel Aviv* 38: 220–40.
Vanderhooft, D. S.
  2009   The Israelite *mišpāḥâ,* the Priestly Writings, and Changing Valences in Israel's
           Kinship Terminology. Pp. 485–96 in *Exploring the* Longue Durée: *Essays in Honor
           of Lawrence E. Stager,* ed. D. Schloen. Winona Lake, IN: Eisenbrauns.
Vaughn, A. G.
  1999   *Theology, History and Archaeology in the Chronicler's Account of Hezekiah.* Archae-
           ology and Biblical Studies 4. Atlanta: Scholars Press.
Vaux, R. de
  1965   *Ancient Israel: Its Life and Institutions.* New York: McGraw Hill.
  1992   Farah, Tell el- (North). Pp. 1297–1302 in vol. 4 of *NEAEHL.* [Hebrew]
Vickers, M., and Gill, D.
  1994   *Artful Crafts: Ancient Greek Silverware and Pottery.* Oxford: Clarendon.
Warren, P. M.
  1983   The Settlement at Fournou Korifi Myrtos (Crete) and Its Place within the Evo-
           lution of the Rural Community of Bronze Age Crete—Les Communates Ru-
           rales: Rural Communities, Second Part. *Recueils de la Société Jean Bodin pour
           l'Histoire Comparative des Institutions* 41: 239–71.
Wason, P. K.
  1994   *The Archaeology of Rank.* Cambridge: Cambridge University Press.

Weinfeld, M.
1973 The Royal and Sacred Aspects of the Tithe in the Old Testament. *Beer-Sheva* 1: 122–31. [Hebrew]
1982 The Literary Work. Pp. 22–53 in *The Monarchy Period: Culture and Society*, ed. A. Malamat. The World History of the Jewish People 5. Jerusalem: Masada. [Hebrew]
1993 [Various entries] in *Exodus*, ed. S. Talmon and J. Avishor. The World of the Bible. Tel Aviv: Davidson Ati. [Hebrew]
2000 *Social Justice in Ancient Israel and in the Ancient Near East.* Jerusalem: Magnes.
Weinfeld, M. (ed.)
1994 *Deuteronomy.* The World of the Bible. Tel Aviv: Davidson Ati. [Hebrew]
Weisman, Z.
1984 The Period of the Judges in Biblical Historiography. Pp. 85–98 in *Israel and Judah in the Biblical Period*, ed. I. Eph'al. History of Eretz-Israel 2. Jerusalem: Keter. [Hebrew]
1985 Diverse Historical and Social Reflections in the Shaping of Patriarchal History. *Zion* 50: 1–12. [Hebrew]
1994 *The Book of Hosea: Twelve*, vol. 1. World of the Bible. Tel Aviv: Davidson Ati. [Hebrew]
Weksler-Bdolah, S.
1999 Alona. *Excavations and Surveys in Israel* 19: 68*–70*.
Wellhausen, J.
1957 *Prolegomena to the History of Ancient Israel.* New York: Meridian.
Wengrow, D.
1996 Egyptian Taskmasters and Heavy Burdens: Highland Exploitation and the Collared-Rim Pithos of Bronze/Iron Age Levant. *Oxford Journal of Archaeology* 15: 307–26.
Wenham, G. J.
1997 The Gap between Law and Ethics in the Bible. *JJS* 48: 17–29.
Wette, W. M. L. de
1805 *Dissertatio Critico-Exegetica: Qua Deuteronomium a Prioribus Pentateuchi Libris Diversum.* Alius Cuiusdam Recentioris Auctoris Opus Esse Monstatuer. Jena.
Whitelam, K. W.
1979 *The Just King.* JSOTSup 12. Sheffield: Sheffield Academic Press.
1986 The Symbols of Power: Aspects of Royal Propaganda in the United Monarchy. *BA* 49: 166–73.
1996 Prophetic Conflicts in Israelite History: Taking Sides with William G. Dever. *JSOT* 72: 25–44.
Whybray, R. N.
1990 *Wealth and Poverty in the Book of Proverbs.* JSOTSup 99. Sheffield: Sheffield Academic Press.
1995 *The Book of Proverbs: A Survey of Modern Study.* Leiden: Brill.
Wiessner, P.
1990 Is There a Unity to Style? Pp. 105–12 in *The Uses of Style in Archaeology*, ed. M. W. Conkey and C. A. Hastorf. Cambridge: Cambridge University Press.
Wilk, R. R.
1983 Little House in the Jungle: The Causes of Variation in House Size among Modern Kekchi Maya. *JAA* 2: 99–116.
Wilk, R. R., and Rathje, W. L.
1982 Household Archaeology. *ABS* 25: 617–40.

Wilson, R. R.
    1977   *Genealogy and History in the Biblical World*. New Haven, CT: Yale University Press.
    1993   The Role of Law in Early Israelite Society. Pp. 90–99 in *Law, Politics and Society in the Ancient Mediterranean World*, ed. B. Halpern and D. W. Hobson. Sheffield: Sheffield Academic Press.
Wilson, T.
    1993   Urbanism and Kinship Bonds. *Social Forces* 71: 703–12.
Wirth, L.
    1965   Urbanism as a Way of Life. Pp. 46–63 in *Cities and Society*, ed. P. K. Hatt and A. J. Reis. New York: Free Press.
Wolf, C. U.
    1947   Traces of Primitive Democracy in Ancient Israel. *JNES* 6: 98–108.
Wolf, E. R.
    1955   Types of Latin American Peasantry: A Preliminary Discussion. *American Anthropologist* 57: 452–70.
Wolff, S. R.
    1998   An Iron Age I Site at ʿEn Hagit (Northern Ramat Menashe). Pp. 449–54 in *Mediterranean Peoples in Transition*, ed. S. Gitin, A. Mazar, and E. Stern. Jerusalem: Israel Exploration Society.
    2002   Mortuary Practices in the Persian Period of the Levant. *NEA* 65: 131–37.
Wood, G. B.
    1990   *The Sociology of Pottery in Ancient Palestine*. JSOTSup 103. Sheffield: Sheffield Academic Press.
Wright, C. J. H.
    1990   *God's People in God's Land*. Grand Rapids, MI: Eerdmans.
    1992   Family. Pp. 761–69 in vol. 2 of *ABD*.
Wright, G. E.
    1965   *Shechem: The Biography of a Biblical City*. New York: Duckworth.
    1970   Beth Shemesh. Pp. 249–53 in vol. 1 of *NEAEHL*.
    1992   Shechem: Tell Balâtah. Pp. 1520–26 in vol. 4 of *NEAEHL*. [Hebrew]
Wright, G. R. H.
    2002   *Shechem, vol. 3: The Stratigraphy and Architecture of Shechem/Tell Batalah, vol. 2: The Illustrations*. Boston: American Schools of Oriental Research.
Wright, H.
    1977   Recent Research on the Origin of the State. *Annual Review of Anthropology* 6: 379–97.
Yadin, Y.
    1960   Pax Payers or Tax Collectors: On the Problem of the l in the Samaria Ostraca. *Yediot* 24: 17–21. [Hebrew]
    1962   Hazor, Gezer, and Megiddo in Solomon's Times. Pp. 66–109 in *The Kingdoms of Israel and Judah*, ed. A. Malamat. Jerusalem: Israel Exploration Society. [Hebrew]
    1963   *The Art of Warfare in Biblical Lands in the Light of Archaeological Study*. New York: McGraw-Hill.
    1964   The Army Reserves of David and Solomon. Pp. 350–61 in *The Military History of the Land of Israel in Biblical Times*, ed. J. Lever. Jerusalem: Maarachot. [Hebrew]
    1972   *Hazor: The Head of All Those Kingdoms*. London: Oxford University Press.
    1975   The Megiddo Stables. *ErIsr* 12 (Glueck Volume): 57–62. [Hebrew]
    1978   Beer-Sheba: The High Place Destroyed by King Josiah. *ErIsr* 14 (Ginsberg Volume): 78–85. [Hebrew]

1982   The Archaeological Sources for the Period of the Monarchy. Pp. 131–68 in *The Monarchic Period: Culture and Society*, ed. A. Malamat. The World History of the Jewish People 5. Jerusalem: Masada. [Hebrew]

Yadin, Y., et al.
1958–61   *Hazor*, vols. 1–2 and 3–4: Part 1. Jerusalem: Magnes.

Yadin, Y., et al. (eds.)
1989   *Hazor*, vols. 3–4: Text. Jerusalem: Israel Exploration Society and Magnes.

Yeivin, S.
1962   The Administration in Ancient Israel. Pp. 47–65 in *The Kingdoms of Israel and Judah*, ed. A. Malamat. Jerusalem: Israel Exploration Society. [Hebrew]
1968   Relations between Israel and Judah in the Time of the House of Jehu. Pp. 37–61 in *Zer Kavod Festschrift*, ed. H. Gevaryahu. Jerusalem: Kiryat-Sefer. [Hebrew]
1979   Administration. Pp. 141–71 in *The World History of the Jewish People—The Age of the Monarchies: Culture and Society*, ed. A. Malamat. Jerusalem: Masada. [Hebrew]

Yeivin, S., and Edelstein, G.
1970   Excavations at Tirat Yehuda. *'Atiqot* 6: 56–67. [Hebrew]

Yezerski, I.
1995   *Burial Caves in the Land of Judah in the Iron Age: Archaeological and Architectural Aspects*. M.A. Thesis. Tel Aviv University. [Hebrew]
1999   Burial-Cave Distribution and the Borders of the Kingdom of Judah toward the End of the Iron Age. *Tel Aviv* 26: 253–70.

Yoffee, N.
2004   *Myths of the Archaic State: Evolution of the Earliest Cities, States and Civilizations*. New York: Cambridge University Press.

Yorburg, B.
1975   The Nuclear and the Extended Family: An Area of Conceptual Confusion. *Journal of Comparative Family Studies* 6: 5–14.

Zakovitch, Y.
1992   *The Song of Songs*. Bible for Israel. Jerusalem: Magnes. [Hebrew]

Zarzeki-Peleg, A.
1997   Hazor, Jokneam and Meggido in the 10th Century BCE. *Tel Aviv* 24: 258–88.

Zertal, A.
1984   *Arubboth, Hepher and the Third Solomonic District*. Tel Aviv: Hakibbutz Hameuchad. [Hebrew]
1989   "From Watchtower to Fortified Cities": On the History of Highway Forts in the Israelite Kingdom. *Qadmoniot* 83–84: 82–86. [Hebrew]
1992   *The Manasseh Hill Country Survey: The Shechem Syncline*. Tel Aviv: Ministry of Defense. [Hebrew]
1998   An Iron Age Fortress Surrounding the City of Samaria. Pp. 9–26 in *Judea and Samaria Research Studies: Proceedings of the Seventh Annual Conference*, ed. Y. Eshel. Kedumim-Ariel: Eretz. [Hebrew]

Zipf, G. K.
1941   *National Unity and Disunity*. Bloomington, IN: Prinicipia.

Zorn, J. R.
1993   *Tell en-Nasbeh: A Re-Evaluation of the Architecture and Stratigraphy of the Early Bronze Age, Iron Age and Later Periods*. Ph.D. Dissertation. University of California, Berkeley.
1994   Estimating the Population Size of Ancient Settlements: Methods, Problems, Solutions and a Case Study. *BASOR* 295: 31–48.

1997   An Inner and Outer Gate Complex at Tell en-Nasbeh. *BASOR* 307: 36–53.
1999   A Note on the Date of the "Great Wall" of Tell en-Nasbeh: A Rejoinder. *Tel Aviv* 26: 146–50.

Index of Authors

Index of Scripture

Index of Sites